International Financial Cooperation

Two volumes from the Centre for Research on the
New International Economic Order, Oxford:

Volume 1
International Financial Cooperation — A Framework
Frances Stewart and Arjun Sengupta
Edited by Salah Al-Shaikhly

Volume 2
**Development Financing — A Framework for
International Financial Cooperation**
Edited by Salah Al-Shaikhly

International Financial Cooperation

A Framework for Change

Frances Stewart

Arjun Sengupta

Editor
Salah Al-Shaikhly

Frances Pinter (Publishers), London
Westview Press, Boulder, Colorado

© The Centre for Research on the New International
   Economic Order, Oxford, 1982

First published in Great Britain in 1982 by
Frances Pinter (Publishers) Limited
5 Dryden Street, London WC2E 9NW

ISBN 0 86187 231 3 (Hardback)
ISBN 0 96187 232 0 (Paperback)

Published in 1982 in the United States of America by
Westview Press, 5500 Central Ave.
Boulder, Colorado, 80301
Frederick A. Praeger, Publisher

ISBN 0-86531-415-2 (Hardback)
ISBN 0-86531-416-0 (Paperback)

Library of Congress No. 82-80428

British Library Cataloguing in Publication Data

Stewart, Frances
        International financial cooperation:
        a framework for change.
        1.   International finance
        I.   Title   II.   Sengupta, Arjun
        332'.042   HG3881

        ISBN 0-86187-231-2
        ISBN 0-86187-232-0   Pbk

Typeset by Anne Joshua Associates, Oxford
Printed by SRP, Exeter, Great Britain

TABLE OF CONTENTS

FOREWORD: THE BACKGROUND TO THE PROJECT

In May of 1978 the North–South Round Table held its first meeting in Rome. Among the topics for discussion was the structure and functioning of the International Financial Institutions. In that meeting I recall an intervention by Dragslov Avormovic on the working of the two main institutions, i.e. the World Bank and the IMF. What he had to say about these two institutions was most impressive.

The idea of a research project into the state of the global economy after the 1974 increase of oil prices has, since that date, been a challenging proposition. The intervention by Mr Avormovic added clarity and substance to the outline of this research.

In 1979 interest was generated in the objectives of the Centre, which was already active in rendering research and technical support to Third World Countries in their efforts to promote a New International Economic Order. A proposal was drawn up by the Centre and submitted to the Regional Bureau for Arab States in UNDP who circulated it to the countries in the Arab Region. The idea was enthusiastically received especially with regard to UNDP's interest in better understanding of the North–South dialogue and issues emanating from it. UNDP, after a useful dialogue with the Centre, had agreed to fund a research topic which bears the title of this book: *A Framework for International Financial Cooperation*. A number of important topics were included in the research programme, some of which were covered in the report that appears in the book, others are still the subject of continuing research at the Centre. These topics were the recycling of funds from surplus to deficit countries; stabilizing the existing International Financial System; securing an adequate level of investment return for surplus countries; the role of the special drawing rights;

commodity stabilization; debt reorganization; and mineral and energy financing.

Over twenty high-level experts and scholars were commissioned to contribute research papers on the subject.* Over forty other specialists participated in the discussion of these papers and contributed in one way or another to their publication. The first Seminar discussed the format of the research work and was held in Oxford in March 1980; the second was to review the papers that were being submitted to the Centre and was held in New York in October 1980; and the last one was to revise the final version of the papers and was held in Oxford in February 1981. Francis Stewart and Arjun Sengupta have very kindly agreed to act as joint co-ordinators of this research project and have prepared the final text of this book.

UNDP involvement in the Centre's activities has not only contributed to the dialogue necessary amongst and within Third World countries to seek conclusions to overwhelming issues facing them, but also strengthened the Centre's capabilities in being a catalyst in North–South issues. Initial reaction to the original report has been extremely positive and a number of the suggestions that appear in this book were put as items for discussion on the agenda of the Committee of Development Planning which was held in New York during the first week of October 1981. It is our hope that the proposals contained in this book may encourage debate and the formulation of a possible strategy policy, and hopefully provide some solutions in any future global negotiations between developing and developed countries.

Salah Al-Shaikhly

Director
Centre for Research on the
New International Economic Order
Oxford, U.K.
October 1981

---

* A number of these papers are appearing in a separate volume entitled *Development Financing; A Framework for International Financial Cooperation.* Selected papers edited by Salah Al-Shaikhly.

ACKNOWLEDGEMENTS

The Director of the Centre for Research on the New International Economic Order gratefully acknowledges the vision and initiative taken by the previous Director of the Centre, Dr Kamal Hossain, who was the main force, not only behind this project, but also of the whole idea and concept of the Centre.

Acknowledgement is also due to Arthur Hazelwood, the Warden of Queen Elizabeth House, for supervising and bringing to a successful conclusion this study and so competently organizing the seminars that were part of the process of preparing this study. The support of the UNDP and the competent officers of the Regional Programming Division of the Bureau for Arab States, namely Fuad Mohammed, Akram Qursha and Dede Davies, is much appreciated.

The contributions of the various authors to this process is obviously self-evident, and the Centre is grateful to all those personnel of the IMF, IBRD and the Institute of Commonwealth Studies, who gave advice and discussed the draft of this study at various stages.

INTRODUCTION: ISSUES IN INTERNATIONAL FINANCIAL COOPERATION

Salah Al-Shaikhly

A historical perspective

Many economic historians would agree that the economic crisis of the late 1970s and early 1980s is not too dissimilar to that of the late 1920s and early 1930s. Although, perhaps, the difference between the two crises is in the magnitude of the resulting damage to the global economy. The present experience of unemployment, trade and payments restrictions, currency uncertainty and the collapse of the international credit system is definitely analogous to that of 1929–31. No one factor can be singled out as the cause of the present recession. It is the accumulation over the past 20 years of many short-sighted policies and an overall mismanagement of the global economy that led to the present-day situation. Raul Prebish calls it 'the second crisis of capitalism'.[1] The events of the past decade proves, if anything, the interrelated character of the present global economic system.

After the Second World War the international community (primarily the USA and Western Europe) was intent on encouraging world economic expansion. This was to be accomplished by several courses of action; for example, the dismantling of trade barriers and payments restrictions; the maintenance of orderly exchange rates and the prevention of disruptive capital movements; the provision of credit facilities for payments adjustments and the resumption of investment flows into developing countries. From the Bretton Woods Conference emerged the institutions, whose rules and procedures governed the post-war international economic system (that is until its collapse in 1971). These institutions are the International Monetary Fund, the International Bank for Reconstruction and Development (IBRD), and the Generalized Agreement on Trade and Tariff (GATT). Although the 'System' achieved some results, in that it revived the world economy, especially that of the USA and Western Europe, it also had a number of important limitations. The universality of membership originally envisaged for the Bretton Woods institutions has never materialized.

The absence of the socialist countries of Eastern Europe and China was one such limitation. Another and more important limitation was that the system was not geared to tackle the special trade and financial problems of developing countries. Furthermore, the developing countries were always left at the periphery of any decision-making process. Hence the call for a North–South dialogue and the aspiration of the developing countries for a New International Economic Order can be seen as a reaction to the imbalance the early institutions lead to. Furthermore, the developing countries always maintained that the development issue should be treated as an integral part of the management of the world economy and that the rules governing international economic relations should be changed in such a way as to take into account the problems of the developing countries.

However, any proposal for change in international economic relations cannot be advanced without an understanding and even an appreciation of how the present system has evolved. The USA, being the initiator of many of the present-day international economic institutions, was also in the position of the single major supplier of capital and technology to Western Europe and Japan. The foreign economic policy of the USA encouraged the technological and economic growth of the aid receiving countries. During the two decades that followed the establishment of these institutions (1950–70) there were changes in the economic balance between the USA and Europe and Japan specially in gross domestic product and foreign trade. In 1950 the two major reserve currency countries (USA/UK) accounted for 50 per cent of the exports of the industrial countries of Western Europe. In 1979, however, this ratio had fallen to 30 per cent with countries like Germany and Japan taking the new lead. A better indication of this change can be seen in the different rates of growth of gross domestic product during the same period. In the USA the average annual growth rate was 3.4 per cent while the ratios for Europe and Japan were 4.4 and 8.4 per cent respectively. In historical perspective the World inflation of the 1970s and the other economic growth and development problems of developed and developing countries alike, can be traced as far back as 1950. For example, the world monetary reserves, measured in dollars at current exchange rates and market gold prices, have increased ten times as much in 10 years as in all previous years since the turn of the century. In 1979 this was still increasing at an annual rate of 62 per cent, which is ten to fifteen times faster than the maximum conceivable growth of world trade and production in real inflationary terms.[2]

The shift in economic balances can be further demonstrated by the analysis of the gross gold and convertible currency reserves. The following table shows the decline in the importance of the USA in favour of the European Economic Community (EEC).

Table (i)   Gross reserves of gold and convertible currencies

Period	Group			
	EEC %	UK %	USA %	Total %
December 1958	33.48	8.63	57.89	100
December 1966	53.35	8.19	38.46	100
May 1967	55.17	8.01	38.82	100

Two important interrelated features distinguished the 1960s, the first was the change from a dollar shortage of the 1950s to a glut in the 1960s and the second was the collapse of the pound sterling as an active reserve currency. This last phenomena should have given the USA ample warning of the shape of things to come since the pound sterling was always regarded as a first line of defence for the dollar.

In 1962 the Federal Reserve System in New York must have got the notion of the difficulties that lay ahead for the dollar. A swap arrangement was therefore concluded with the Central Banks[3] and with the BIS for just over $1 billion. This sum was gradually raised to almost $11 billion. Even these measures in themselves do not seem to have prevented the 'market' speculating against the dollar and in favour of gold. The crisis of the pound sterling in 1967 was also brought about by yet another misjudgement of events and doing too little too late. Britain continued to use the pound sterling as a reserve currency. Its official expenditure overseas had increased manyfold until the mid 1960s. In addition to this external investment programme, Britain was also going through a period of internal economic expansion. Many economists attribute the large balance of payments deficit that Britain had accumulated in this period to the above reasons put together. Of the two classic solutions (i.e. to borrow or to devalue), Britain seems to have been persuaded by the USA to accept a sizeable international loan. This did not help much, since the pound sterling had to be devalued in 1967. Two years later the French franc was also devalued leading to increased speculation in favour of the Deutsche Mark. The DM was allowed to float from March up to 26 October 1969 before it was given a new parity. The see-saw continued, and by the end of the decade of the 1960s the European currencies were strong again, while the American position was considerably weakened.

The 1970s had a different tone about them. The dollar had surfaced as the major reserve currency. At the end of 1971 international liquidity was estimated at about $268 billion. Most of this was in the Euro-dollar market and probably held mainly by the multinational enterprises.

During 1971 the debate continued within the EEC and between the EEC and the USA. For example, the French were proposing the adoption of common controls, whilst the West Germans were advancing the idea of common floating of the currencies. The result of this disarray of policy was that in the end each country took its own uni-lateral course of action.

Such a trend was obviously not conducive to any serious step towards the European monetary union, neither did it prevent continuing pressure on the US dollar. The balance of payments situation of the USA was deteriorating, and dollar holders were massively converting into other currencies. The American decision to remedy the situation not only affected the US internal position, but it had far-reaching effects on the whole international monetary system. Among the decisions taken was the suspension of convertibility for the dollar, thus ending the gold exchange standard system. This in effect marked the collapse of the Bretton Woods System.

During 1972 other European currencies, namely the pound sterling and the lira, came under pressure. The whole classic cycle of selling, intervening and buying, plus Central Bank support, was put into action. In the second half of 1972 speculation against the dollar started once again, and the West German Federal Bank had to buy $600 million. Other steps were also taken to contain the use of Euro-Deutsch Marks in West Germany

In July of the same year, speculation continued in favour of some of the European currencies. The Central Banks of France, Belgium, the Netherlands, Switzerland and West Germany had to intervene repeatedly to buy huge amounts of dollars. A number of meetings took place among the EEC finance ministers and later the heads of state in an attempt to unify their monetary policies, especially in relationship with the dollar. In early January 1973 the dollar was near collapse after the Swiss announced that they had allowed the Swiss franc to float. The European Central Banks intervened once again to support the dollar and bought, between 1 February 1973 and 2 March 1973, $13,000 million; over 70 per cent of which went to West Germany. As a result of this chaos the Ministers of Finance of the EEC met to decide on a unified policy towards the USA. Their meetings achieved very little and to most economic analysts it must have looked as a dialogue of the deaf. Basically the EEC wanted each country to defend its own currency, while the Americans were not able to explain how they would defend the dollar. Another swap agreement was organized between the USA and the thirteen European countries. Table (ii) shows the reserves of the Central Banks expressed in millions of dollars. It must be noted that in addition to figures shown in this table an additional $15

Table (ii)   Central Banks Reserves ($ millions)

Country	1971			1972			1973		
	$	SDR	Gold	$	SDR	Gold	$	SDR	Gold
West Germany	8455	258	3980	12302	493	4426	16837	893	4459
Japan	3188	146	532	13783	307	738	16483	461	801
France	1257	171	3532	3577	378	3825	5059	630	3826
UK	1212	266	1349	5099	642	842	4521	656	800
Switzerland	1932	–	2705	2688	–	3094	3209	–	3094
Italy	2113	77	2887	3030	247	3131	2220	371	3130

billion were also bought by these banks. Out of this sum nearly $10 billion went to the Central Bank of West Germany alone.

Furthermore, the international supply of US dollars had been growing fast since 1969. During the ten years 1969–78, dollar claims by non-residents grew nearly 400 per cent from $78 billion to $373 billion. Many observers feel that this phenomenal increase may have been far in excess of supply and far exceeding stocks. Indications are that the increase in the supply of dollars was definitely faster than the growth of international trade and probably the transaction demand for them.

The dilemma that had developed is as follows: the US out of national interest wished to bring its external 'dollar' position under its own control, while the global liquidity requirements were subject to so many factors, most of which were outside the control of the US. As was shown earlier, the international banking network has its own code of practice when it comes to generating Eurodollar credits and does not necessarily abide by official governmental control.

The reason that these historical facts are presented here, and in chronological order, is to show that the disruption of the world economy after 1973 was not merely due to the adjustment in oil prices during that year and in 1974, but also to the imbalance created by the massive accumulation of Eurodollars. The enormous increase in dollar holding presented a problem, not only of finding a way of funding them, but also to avoid the realization of their inflation-creating potential in the short and medium term. The double

figure inflation that followed after 1974 was a clear indication of the inadequecies of the monetary, and consequently
the economic, policies of the Western industrial countries.

A number of Western politicians and writers came to
terms with this fact. Denis Healey wrote:

> The world inflation of the early 1970's had nothing what-
> ever to do with oil. It was due to the failure of successive
> American administrations to finance the war in Vietnam
> out of current revenue: to the exceptional increase in raw
> material prices because a large number of countries achieved
> unusually high growth rates at the same time; and to a
> series of bad harvests. These factors helped lead to the
> breakdown of the Bretton Woods currency system under
> an American policy for which Treasury Secretary John
> Connally adopted the euphemism 'benign neglect'. The
> resulting currency instability itself added to inflation. So
> inflation was already high and rising by the middle of
> 1973, before the increase in oil prices took place.[4]

A year later C. Fred Bergsten wrote:

> The West German economy is now stagnant, dragging
> down growth and promoting unemployment throughout
> Western Europe . . . But because of the rapid growth in
> government expenditures and budget deficits that this
> growth has caused, West German expansion would have to
> come from more related monetary policy . . . Monetary
> easing should therefore go even beyond the purely cyclical
> needs of the moment.
>
> US policy, however, absolutely precludes such an
> approach in West Germany. Any easing of the West
> German interest rates would trigger a further plunge of the
> DM with unacceptable inflationary results for not only
> West Germany, but also all other countries in the European
> Monetary System.
>
> Similar results will prevail in the developing countries
> with an added twist. A central problem in most developing
> countries is their massive indebtedness, an issue of
> immediate concern to the functioning of the global eco-
> nomy. Yet each additional percentage point in the level of

US, and thus global interest rates, adds about $500 million to the annual current account deficits of Brazil and Mexico and perhaps $4 billion to the deficit of all less developed countries (LDC). As pointed out by the Morgan Guaranty Trust Company in its May 1981 World Financial Markets: 'A one percent point change in interest rates now causes more of a variance in LDC financing requirements than does a one percent change in oil prices.'[5]

The beginnings of a new order

Up to October of the 1973 Arab–Israeli war the Western media, and industrial countries never picked the question of energy as a vital international issue. So long as oil was flowing at rates and prices determined by the multinationals and acceptable to the Western industrial countries, the question of surpluses, inflation and monetarism never arose. When oil producers, members of OPEC, readjusted the oil prices during 1974, suddenly the question of energy came into prominence. Recent events have proved that the real question was never that of a shortage of energy, as much as the sudden financial disequilibrium the price rises created. Money was beginning to flow in an 'uncustomary' direction. It will be a long time before the international community can sort out, beyond any reasonable doubt, as to who caused the snowball of oil price rises and who really benefited economically and politically from the outcome. One thing is now certain, the USA and EEC countries had a good 'scapegoat' to blame just about every ailment of the industrialized countries economy's on the 'rise' in oil prices.

The new situation certainly warranted international recognition, even if only to attract attention to the plight of the less-developed countries.

In May 1974, the Sixth Special Session of the General Assembly of the United Nations adopted what came to be known as the declaration on the New International Economic Order. The international community recognized that the world economy had experienced, in the decade up to 1974, a series of crises in the area of global monetary systems and finance. These crises, although taking place in developed countries, have had severe repercussions on the developing countries because of their greater vulnerability to external economic events. In the area of international monetary systems and development financing of developing countries, the main theme was that developing and developed countries should share equally in the decision-making processes in the major international institutions such as the IMF and the World Bank. Developing countries were also aware of the inflationary trends of the economies of the USA and Europe. The NIEO declaration addressed itself to this aspect by stating:

> Measures to check the inflation already experienced by the developed countries, to prevent it from being transferred to developing countries, and to study and devise possible arrangements within the International Monetary Fund to investigate the effects of inflation in developed countries on the economies of developing countries.[6]

Other objectives of the NIEO declaration in this area were to eliminate the instability of the international monetary system, the uncertainty of the exchange rates, the real value of the currency reserves of the developing countries, the creation of additional liquidity with particular regard to the needs of developing countries and the establishment of a link between special drawing rights (SDRs) and additional development financing in favour of developing countries.[7]

Unfortunately, since May 1974 very little substantial progress has been made in the area of finance and monetary reform. In fact, as new and more conservative administrations took over in the USA and some European countries, the stand of the 'North' became even harder. The view of some developed countries was that the financial intermediation between developed and developing countries, and in particular the deficit economies, should be left to the private sector. The argument was that the private banking sector had proved itself capable of managing and recycling the new surpluses during the seventies. The role of international institutions was seen as to facilitate the adoption of measures that would encourage and help the operations of the private capital markets.

International cooperation in payments adjustment

Pressure from developing countries brought some results in the form of additional facilities for balance of payments, with the idea of improving the recycling of funds for the benefit of countries with limited access to capital markets. The process and mechanism worked well. However, the countries most in need of funds still remained ineligible while only those developing countries who were rated as credit worthy managed to receive substantial volumes of funds. Unfortunately the final distribution remained as skewed as it ever was, and the least-developed countries made very little use of these facilities.

The additional facilities mentioned above were supplemented by considerable improvement in the conditionality of the IMF and in an effort to increase the number of beneficiaries. From the point of view of many developing countries these steps did not go far enough towards providing a satisfactory system of financing payments imbalances.

In terms of facilities the IMF provides a number of options each of which has its own conditionality attached to it. The reserve tranche is provided for balance of payments need and the repayment period is three to five years.

The first credit tranche is provided either in the form of direct purchases or under standby arrangements. The requesting country must present to the IMF an economic programme consisting of fiscal, monetary, exchange-rate, trade and payment policies which reflect reasonable efforts to overcome its balance of payments difficulties. It is obvious that these conditions are open to subjective judgement and there is usually ample room for negotiation and interpretation of member countries intentions. The repayment period is three to five years.

Upper credit tranches are almost always under standby arrangements with specified drawing dates. Drawings are subject to performance criteria which are presented in the 'stabilization' programme by the requesting member country. As in previous conditions, the evaluation criteria relate to such issues as domestic credit policy, prices and incomes policy, government financing, exchange rates, restrictive measures on trade and payments, external borrowing and levels of reserves. If for any reason the country does not meet some of these conditions, further consultations will take place with the IMF before additional drawings are made. The replacement period is three to five years.

Extended Fund Facilities are intended to provide assistance to countries in meeting balance of payments deficits for longer periods and in amounts larger in relation to quotas than under normal credit tranches. Drawings are made in instalments over a period of up to three years and are subject to the condition that the member agrees with the Fund on a programme setting forth the objectives and policies to be pursued during the whole term of the extended arrangement as well as a detailed statement of the measures to be carried out in each twelve-month period. The drawing of each instalment is subject to performance clauses. The repayment is from four to eight years.

Supplementary Financing Facilities are designed to provide supplementary financing in conjunction with other Fund resources to member countries facing payments imbalances which are large in relation to their quotas. Drawings are made under standby arrangements normally exceeding one year and lasting for as long as three years in appropriate cases. The drawings are intended to support programmes adopted under the use of upper credit tranches of the 'Extended Fund Facility', and are subject to the same performance criteria. Repayments must begin not less than three and a half years after drawings, and be completed within a period of seven years.

Compensatory Financing Facilities to operate as support facility to member countries (especially exporters of primary commodities) experiencing balance of payments difficulties due to temporary export shortfalls. The Fund must be satisfied that the problem is short term and largely attributable to circumstances beyond the country's control, and that the member will cooperate with the Fund in an effort to solve its payments problems. The export shortfall for the latest twelve-month period preceding a drawing request is defined on the basis of an estimate of the medium-term trend of the country's exports, but can be modified in the light of judgements concerning its export prospects. Except in the case of emergencies, drawings cannot exceed 50 per cent of a member's quota in any twelve-month period or 75 per cent of its quota in all. The repayment is three to five years.

Buffer Stock Financing Facilities are created to assist in the financing of contributions of international buffer stocks of primary products by member countries with balance of payments difficulties. The commodity agreements must meet appropriate criteria (such as those laid down by the United Nations), and the member is expected to cooperate with the Fund in an effort to solve its balance of payments problems. The repayment period is three to five years (or less in the event of the buffer stock distributing cash to its members).

From balance of payments finance to development aid

The resolution on development and international economic cooperation, adopted at the Seventh Special Session of the General Assembly[8] in 1975, emphasized clearly the issues of real transfers of resources to developing countries for the purpose of development financing. There was a subtle departure from the previous tone of 'immediate relief' finance to a call for development orientated finance.

Developed countries were called upon to make their development assistance substantial, concessional, its terms and conditions ameliorated, its flow more predictable and the whole package untied.

Resolutions like this may reflect the deep feeling of injustice by the developing countries of many past colonial decades. However, after more than five years it does not seem to have helped to bring about an increase in aid level. Many observers believe that such resolutions are so far remote from the realities of everyday politics of the developed countries, that nobody takes them seriously. The international community can achieve a workable resolution only when it can master the art of the possible and abandon the resolutions of the impossible.

The aforementioned resolution demanded that developed countries confirm their continued commitment in respect of official development assistance of 0.7 per cent of GNP. It also called upon those countries who have not yet made such a commitment in respect of these targets to do their best to reach them. The real-life situation was different. European countries' members of DAC failed to achieve more than 0.32 per cent in 1977. Recent figures show that this ratio increased only to 0.37 per cent. Within the group of DAC countries, West Germany, Japan and the USA, were the worst performers. They allocated only 0.20, 0.21 and 0.10 per cent respectively of the increment in their GNP during 1970 to the official development assistance budget. It is also noteworthy that West Germany, Japan and Switzerland, who have experienced substantial surpluses in their balance of payments, have failed to increase their ODA programme. Most OECD countries argue that the idea of allocating funds for official development assistance to developing countries is not appreciated on a national level by the public at large. It is, therefore, not an issue in election campaigns or foreign policy debates. It is unfortunate that the media and some politicians misrepresent the issue as spending the taxpayer's money on unworthy causes, or that such funds can be better employed at home. The message that should get to the public is that the provision of external aid is beneficial both to the donor and recipient of aid and that the developing countries, at worst, are good consumer markets for the goods and services of the industrial countries.

It follows, therefore, that an increase in financial assistance to developing countries may stimulate economic recovery in the industrial countries themselves, especially the export orientated sector. The slogan 'The South as an engine of growth' may be the answer to the widespread recession and unemployment in many developed countries.

Meanwhile, the gap remains wide between the financial requirements for development of developing countries and what DAC countries are willing to allocate for external aid. The rhetorics of the new international development strategy for the 1980s are similar to those made for the 1970s. Very little of the latter's objectives were realized. With conservative administration in the USA and other European countries, the trend seems to be taking a negative turn. It is vital that the international community and the Group of Seventy-seven in particular must use the utmost pressure to reverse current trends with the aim of attaining the 0.7 per cent ODA/GNP ratio as a minimum.[9] Countries such as Denmark, France, the Netherlands, Norway and Sweden, hope to achieve this target by 1985, and some even exceed it. Others are very reluctant to commit themselves, and some even advise against it.

The other group of countries that came to prominence after 1973 was the oil producing and exporting countries. Individually, and through various multilateral institutions, OPEC members undertook massive transfers of resources to developing countries. Between 1974 and 1980, OPEC members, who are developing countries themselves, gave $37,931 million in official development assistance to developing countries. On average, this is equal to 1.97 per cent of the GNP of these countries. If, on the other hand, we take the total official flows, then the ratio goes up to 3.15 per cent of GNP. These figures do not include the flows from OPEC members to the IMF oil facility. Available data for 1974–6 shows that the total official flow rises to 4.6 per cent of GNP.

Table (iii) below shows the OPEC and DAC countries aid performance between 1973 and 1980. It is also interesting to note that OPEC aid goes entirely to developing countries and especially to those with per capita income of $500 or less, while DAC flows to developing countries include Southern European countries like Cyprus, Gibraltar, Greece, Portugal, Spain and Yugoslavia in addition to Israel, which is a large beneficiary, and territories and dependencies of developed countries.

Finally, and even when every target is met by the traditional and the new aid donors, two facts remain unchanged. First, the development needs of the developing countries remains huge in magnitude and beyond the reach of the official bilateral or multilateral aid channels. Secondly, any real effort for development by the developing countries must be self-propelled, in the sense that they should grapple collectively or individually with the sources of capital. This is where governments of capital market countries can help, by

Table (iii) OPEC and DAC countries' aid performance: a comparison, 1973–9

	Net disbursements							
	1973	1974	1975	1976	1977	1978	1979	1980
Total official flows in US$ million								
OPEC	1,746	5,889	8,169	8,137	7,451	5,772	n.a.	n.a.
DAC	11,814	13,494	16,611	16,979	18,008	25,063	25,262	n.a.
as percentage of GNP								
OPEC	1.89	3.35	4.35	3.54	2.70	1.83	n.a.	n.a.
DAC	0.38	0.39	0.43	0.41	0.38	0.44	0.39	n.a.
Offical development assistance in US$ million								
OPEC	1,308	3,447	5,517	5,593	5,856	4,338	6,181	6,999
DAC	9,368	11,302	13,587	13,665	14,696	19,994	22,413	26,719
as percentage of GNP								
OPEC	1.42	1.96	2.94	2.43	2.12	1.38	1.51	1.45
DAC	0.30	0.33	0.35	0.33	0.32	0.35	0.35	0.37

n.a. = not available.
Source: Organization for Economic Cooperation and Development (OECD)/Development Assistance Committee.

facilitating access of developing countries into these markets. The present rules and regulations are so prohibitive that it thwarts any initiative that developing countries may wish to take. Changes need to be implemented into the statutory provisions which limit the extent to which the private institutions of capital market countries can acquire debt securities issued by the developing country borrowers. Other forms of change could be in the area of increasing tax exemption, lowering withholding tax on earnings of non-residents as opposed to those of domestic origin. Finally, many developed countries have recently tightened controls on capital outflow, which adversely affects the capacity of many developing countries to raise funds in the capital markets of these countries.

The spirit of Cancun

As this publication goes to press, the Cancun Summit concluded its sessions and the Co-chairmen gave their impressions of the meeting.

World opinion on the outcome of Cancun differed widely. Some called it a complete failure; others called it a limited and conditional success. No one has yet called it an unqualified success. It definitely was not.

The way this Conference was projected in the Western media was rather misleading. True, it was a meeting between the poor and the rich nations of the world as any fully fledged international meeting would be. It is not true, however, that the poor nations were there to ask for charity. The Third World leaders were there to present a case that is affecting the rich and the poor through decision processes dominated mainly by the rich.

Some leading Western politicians and such other do-gooders believe that the solution to the development problems of the poorer Third World countries is a 'massive transfer of resources'. Some even advocate a North–South Marshall Plan to assist developing countries. The position in many developing countries now widely differs from that of Europe after the war in 1945.

When Europe went to war against Germany and Japan

nearly all the countries involved in the conflict had a sound industrial base with good infrastructure and highly qualified manpower to back it. Their trade lines and counterparts were fully established and some were colonial powers for decades. Even the war itself gave rise to new disciplines, technologies and inventions that were to reflect later on, in the rise of the new industrial Europe. When the Marshall Plan was put into operation and (massive) transfer of resources took place into Europe and Japan, the other basic ingredients for development were already there. Furthermore, the political and economic interests of Europe, Japan and the USA were more in harmony than discord. Trade barriers and protectionist practices were lifted between these countries and the free flow of finance and trade was one of the factors that contributed to the recovery of Europe after 1945. Needless to say, all the important international institutions that were constituted after that date were designed to serve the interest of the then industrial countries.

The situation in the Third World today bears little or no resemblance to that of Europe after 1945. Neither does the international climate appear as conducive as that of post-1945. Many more actors have joined in the international game and the decision-making process are no longer confined to East–West consideration. Even within the same group of countries, national interests now take precedence over regional or community interest. This applies to developed and developing countries alike.

If we take, for example, some of the developing countries who did acquire massive resources (through indigenous means) and see if they are any better off on the scale of development than they were before the acquisition of those massive resources. Most of these countries had either a feudal or agricultural base with hardly any sound manufacturing base, trained manpower or infrastructure. In some of these countries there is total dependency on foreign labour even in the less-skilled areas. In other words, these economies were not geared to absorb massive investment and, in many cases, development programmes came to a virtual standstill because of the bottle-necks in the economy. What applies to these countries is definitely true for many other Third World developing countries who have started the process of development much later as they gradually gained independence and realized their statehood. One exception to this are the few industrialized, among the developing countries, such as Brazil, South Korea, India and Yugoslavia. Massive transfer of resources would definitely help these countries. The question, however, still remains whether these countries, having acquired these resources, proceeded with their development programmes and produced the necessary commodities, would then be able to sell these commodities in the face of trade barriers and protectionist practices. In other words, the package must be complete. Transfer of resources in itself is not sufficient unless there is a change in the overall international trading agreements and the decision-making processes in the corresponding international financial institutions. We realize that development is a complex process, both nationally and internationally, and it is perhaps to the benefit of both developing and developed countries to realize that only by a continued dialogue and the will to help from the position of mutual respect and an appreciation of the interrelated nature of the global economy that perhaps world economic recovery can be realized. No one is naïve enough to believe that such a global recovery was hinging on the Cancun Summit. Nevertheless, it was a forum where a limited but prominent number of North–South leaders heard each other first hand.

The Mexican President said, at the concluding Press Conference, 'that there was no expectation that the meeting would adopt concrete decisions . . . and while views had differed, as expected, participants showed understanding and *political will*'.

Notes

1 Raul Prebish, Third World Lecture, 'Capitalism: the Second Crisis', *Third World Quarterly*, Vol. 3, No. 3, July 1981.
2 R. Triffin, 'The Relationship Between The International Monetary System and Regional Monetary Systems'.
3 EEC countries.
4 Denis Healy, 'Oil Money and Recession', *Foreign Affairs*, Winter 1980, p. 219.

5 C. Fred Bergsten, 'The Cost of Reaganomics', *Foreign Policy*, No. 44, Fall 1981, pp. 32-3.
6 Resolutions adopted by the General Assembly during its Sixth Special Session 9 April-2 May 1974. Supplement No. 1 (A/9559), NY., 1974.
7 These points are fully covered in the main text of the book.
8 Resolution 3362(S-VII), Official Records, Seventh Special Session, Supplement No. 1 (A/10301), N.Y., 1-16 September 1975.
9 See the main text of the book for proposals and schemes for massive resource transfer from developed and other surplus countries to developing countries.

1   AN OVERVIEW*

There is now widespread dissatisfaction with the international monetary system as a framework for trade and payments. This dissatisfaction is shared by those in very different situations and with different points of view. The system has been criticized by peoples and governments from different parts of the world — from the industrialized countries (ICs) and Third World countries including the oil-exporting countries (OPEC). In different ways and for different reasons, each has reason to be unhappy with the present system as shown by the spate of recent reports on the question — e.g., the UNDP/ UNCTAD Report, the Brandt Commission, the Report of the Committee of Experts of the Commonwealth Secretariat, and the South–North Conference at Arusha.[1]

This study attempts to identify the main sources of dissatisfaction and major areas for reform, and to review and assess alternative proposals. How one looks at as broad an issue as the international monetary system which directly or indirectly affects most economic activities, obviously depends in large part on the question of whose interests one is primarily concerned with. This review takes the interests of the least developed countries (LDCs) and the interests of development as the major consideration. However, any realistic suggestions for reform must also take into account the interests of the other major parties involved in the system. In many (but not all) areas LDCs seem powerless on their own and reform can only emanate from the ICs and/or OPEC. OPEC on the other hand has always regarded itself as part of the Third World in any process of global negotiations. Moreover, a monetary system which leads to a steady expansion of world demand and assists in solving the problems of recession/inflation in ICs, and creates conditions for a stable outlet for international monetary surpluses, is likely to be in the interests of global development. Thus while we take development as the major objective, a central assumption is that any reform must also be in the interests of the relevant and significant decision makers internationally. One critical weakness of some of the proposals for reform appears to be that they ignore this requirement.

The Western industrialized countries and the Third World are composed of countries with often divergent interests. For example, within the Third World a distinction is made between OPEC and other developing countries. Within OPEC there is a significant distinction between the oil-exporting countries which are in substantial surplus on current account and those who are not. There are major differences within the other groups which become of considerable relevance in assessing the likelihood of support for particular reforms, as we shall see below.

During the past decade or so a series of developments — political and economic — have led to the current financial disarray and the powerful sense of dissatisfaction with the ruling system. Much of the disarray has been attributed to the collapse of Bretton Woods. The Bretton Woods era (1945–71) certainly witnessed a massive — possibly unparalleled — growth in world trade, combined with a stable payments system and up to the end of the 1960s a fairly low rate of inflation in the industrialized countries. The success of Bretton Woods however — in terms of its stability and acceptability — was not so much due to the particular institutions and rules of the game then adhered to (which themselves contained inherent contradictions),[2] as to an underlying favourable set-up which was well designed for the economics and politics of the underlying situation. The Bretton Woods system collapsed when the underlying economic situation changed. A major underlying cause of international monetary problems today is that institutions have not adapted to the new situation. There is thus a form of institutional lag — hence the spate of proposed reforms.

Apart from this lag — which unavoidably accompanies any major change in world economy — there are some special problems today. First, problems of the world economy appear to be more intractable than those in the Bretton

Woods era. The problems of inflation and unemployment in industrialized countries together with a threatened natural resource shortage have produced divergent interests in the world economy. It is not clear that there exists an equilibrium satisfactory to all. parties. Institutional reform, though necessary, may not be able to counter underlying disequilibrium.

Secondly, earlier periods of stability (e.g. the UK dominated Gold Standard and the US dominated Bretton Woods system) have been monocentred, in the sense that there was a single dominant economy whose financial institutions, currency and military force also dominated the international monetary system. Thus during the nineteenth century, the UK simultaneously provided the financial mechanisms, the trade surpluses and the capital goods involved in overseas investment, as well as being dominant from a military point of view. The US filled a similar role after World War Two. Recently however there has been a major geographic fragmentation and division so that financial institutions, current account surpluses, capital goods production and military power are all located in different places, causing a form of monetary schizophrenia. Although the US and the UK still retain dominance in financial institutions, the current account surpluses are located in the OPEC countries and other OECD countries. Capital goods capacity on the other hand is spread around the world, especially in OECD and in some newly industrializing countries but not in OPEC. Absorptive capacity for these surpluses seems, however, mostly to be located in Third World countries. While, historically, military power reinforced economic power in the cases of the UK and US, today the economically strong industrialized countries — Germany, Japan — are militarily weak as are those in possession of financial surpluses. The polycentred nature of power produces uncertainties and disequilibrating mechanisms, but also offers potential for reforms. Moreover, to complicate any institutional reform designed to overcome the schizophrenia, the geographic location of current account surpluses and deficits varies substantially over time, with for example Germany and Japan in surplus one year and in deficit the next. Any satisfactory new mechanisms must allow for this instability.

Thirdly, the Third World has acquired a considerable political voice, if not power, and will no longer concur automatically with any situation that advanced countries find acceptable. This, together with the consensus that development and poverty eradication are important international policy objectives, considerably complicates the requirements for reform. For the first time the distribution of international resources between rich and poor nations is an important aspect of the international monetary system. Thus, though institutional lag forms an important aspect of the situation it is by no means the only source of difficulties.

This study considers changes in the financial system which might lead to a more satisfactory working of the system in the 1980s, particularly from the point of view of the Third World. Many of these changes can only occur if they have the support of other parties — the industrialized countries in some cases, OPEC in others. The need for such support limits and shapes potential changes. Other changes may be effected by the Third World itself: the practicability of these changes depends on cooperation among Third World countries. The study covers the following major problem areas:

1   Issues relating to *recycling* from countries in surplus on current account to deficit countries. A healthy world economic situation is likely to contain some countries in long run surplus on their current account, with others in long run deficit, permitting the less developed countries to invest more than they save, while the more developed countries save more than they invest. In general it is to be expected that LDCs would be in current account deficit and DCs in surplus — this should be a major mechanism for development. But clearly, such a situation must be accompanied by some financing mechanism (or recycling mechanism) which produces an appropriate distribution of surpluses/deficits and avoids short-term crises. A recycling problem arises where financial mechanisms are inadequate so that what would be the appropriate level and distribution of surpluses and deficits in the light of each country's objectives and their savings and investment potential is not realized because of deficiencies in financial mechanisms. Since the early seventies,

with the emergence of the large OPEC surpluses, the recycling problem has arisen in a new form. During the seventies the private sector — especially US banks — filled the institutional need created by the sudden emergence of surpluses in a new part of the world. But while the resulting world economic situation was much better than in the absence of any such private mechanisms, there were various defects in the situation.

Chapter Two considers how the system operated in the 1970s and prospects for the 1980s, pointing to the areas where reforms are needed. Chapter Three discusses institutional alternatives, both in the international public sector and the private sector. Chapter Four identifies new financial mechanisms that might improve the recycling process. Chapter Five focuses on the problems of the poorest countries, which received only a fraction of the total external finance available in the 1970s, and considers various ways of increasing their access to finance.

2 The question of *conditionality*. The conditions (that is policy changes required of borrowing countries) for IMF financial support are playing an increasingly important role as more and more countries are forced to have recourse to those IMF facilities where strict conditions obtain and as other financial sources make their own actions dependent on IMF approval of country policies. Chapter Six examines the justification for conditionality and explores whether Third World countries could or should seek alternative conditionality.

3 The level of international reserves, and their distribution, is in part the result of a series of uncoordinated and unplanned events: the amount of dollars held overseas depends on the size of the US deficit, while their value depends on the exchange rate for dollars; the appreciation of gold has enormously increased the value of gold reserves, with a somewhat arbitrary distribution depending on the initial gold holdings; the Special Drawing Rights (SDRs) are the one planned element in international liquidity, but they account for only about 4 per cent of the total reserves. The LDCs find the present system

unsatisfactory for a number of reasons: the arbitrary distribution of gains and losses in capital values, which despite the
arbitrary nature, has tended to disfavour LDCs who hold a
large amount of dollars and little gold; while the major industrialized countries, especially the US, are able to finance
a deficit by printing dollars. Chapter Seven considers the
merits of a commodity reserve currency and considers ways
of extending the role of the existing system of SDRs.

4 *A world view.* Discussion of the international economic
system, of adjustment, the IMF and conditionality and of the
role of an international currency all point to a lacuna in the
world system — the absence of any systematic world economic
management. Chapter Eight summarizes the case for having
more economic analysis and management at the global level
and considers how far the existing lacuna is due to an institutional gap and how far to political problems.

5 *South–South monetary arrangements.* To a large extent
discussions about the international monetary system have
been directed to North–South arrangements. But this is one
area where the Third World can also act on its own, and does
not need to persuade the North. Deficiencies of South–South
monetary arrangements cause biases in financial flows, leading to parallel biases in trade. Chapter Nine identifies and
discusses alternative South–South monetary arrangements.

6 *Action for the 1980s*: Chapter Ten brings together the
proposals made in the previous Chapters.

There are two significant aspects of the international
monetary system today that we deal with only in passing:
one is the debt problem and issues of debt rescheduling, the
other is the question of exchange rates. These questions are
discussed only as they impinge upon the issues we deal with
more centrally. These omissions are due to constraints of
time and the fact that there have been a number of recent
reports on these issues.[3]

Notes

* We are very grateful for research assistance from Platon Tinios and Alan Robinson. During the course of this study we benefited from advice and comments from a large number of people. We are especially grateful to Carlos Diaz Alejandro, Graham Bird, Sidney Dell, Gerry Helleiner, Tony Killick, Michael McWilliam, Gustav Ranis, Paul Streeten, and Simon Teitel, as well as to officials at the World Bank and International Monetary Fund.

1 See S. Dell and R. Lawrence, *The Balance of Payments Adjustment Process in Developing Countries*, Pergamon, 1980 which reports on the UNDP/UNCTAD project; the Brandt Report 'North-South: A Programme for Survival', Pan Books, 1980; Report by a Commonwealth Group of Experts: *The World Economic Crisis: A Commonwealth Perspective*, 1980; and report on the South-North Conference, Arusha 1980, in *Development Dialogue*, 1980, 2.

2 See R. Triffin, *Gold and the Dollar Crisis*, Random House, 1960.

3 On debt and debt rescheduling see C. Hardy, Background Paper; N. Hope, 'Development in and Prospects for the External Debt of the Developing Countries − 1970-80 and Beyond', World Bank Staff Working Paper (forthcoming); G. K. Helleiner, 'Relief and Reform in Third World Debt', mimeo, 1978; on exchange rate policy in a world of floating rates, see G. K. Helleiner, 'The Impact of the Exchange Rate System on the Developing Countries: a Report to the Group of Twenty-Four', 1981; G. K. Helleiner, Background Paper; D. Brodsky and G. Sampson, 'Exchange Rate Variations Facing Individual Industries in Developing Countries' and 'The Sources of Exchange Rate Instability: Dollar, French Franc, and SDR Pegging Countries', mimeo, 1980; W. Branson and L. Katseli-papaefstratiou, 'Exchange Rate Policy for Developing Countries', Economic Growth Center, Yale, Discussion Paper No. 300, November 1980; *Foreign Exchange Markets Under Floating Rates*, Group of Thirty, 1980; M. J. Stewart, 'Floating Exchange Rates in the 1970s and their impact on the World Economy', FMM (80) 9, Papers for Commonwealth Finance Ministers Meeting, September 1980.

2 RECYCLING IN THE 1970s AND PROSPECTS FOR THE 1980s

Introduction

The 1973–4 oil-price rise led to a number of structural and policy changes in the world trading situation and in financial markets. The immediate consequence was a noticeable trade surplus among the oil-exporters of more than $60 billion, paralleled by similar deficits among oil-importers. While the world has seen large trade surpluses and deficits before, there were several features of this situation which made it unique and created particular problems. First, the 'overnight' quality of the change. Secondly, the new surplus countries lacked financial capital markets or financial expertise to enable them to 'lend' the surplus directly to deficit countries in the way that historically the major surplus countries (e.g. 19th century Britain and 20th century USA) have done. Thirdly, to the extent that the new deficits were located in developing countries, there was limited capacity to adjust, other than by deflation, and with very little potential to offset the oil-deficit by selling exports, particularly in the context of depressed world demand.

Despite these features of the situation, the world did get through the crisis without catastrophic deflation. First, a substantial part of the surplus oil revenue was absorbed in the oil-exporting countries themselves, through increased development expenditure and purchase of armaments. Secondly, the international banking sector succeeded in 'recycling' a substantial proportion of the funds from the surplus oil-exporting countries to the deficit oil-importing countries, particularly to some of the newly industrialized developing countries. As a result, the exports of many of the oil-importing ICs maintained a reasonable growth, and a number of LDCs, despite substantial current accounts deficits, achieved impressive rates of growth in gross national product. In this process of international financial adjustment, international banks played a significant role, while the official institutions — the IMF, the World Bank and the traditional aid donors — made a much smaller contribution.

The experience of the 1970s has in some quarters been interpreted as suggesting that recycling can with confidence be left to the commercial sector and that, therefore, there is no need for new international institutional arrangements. But before coming to that conclusion we need to answer two sets of questions: firstly, how satisfactory was the recycling process in the 1970s and secondly, will the 1980s be simply a replica of the 1970s or will changing circumstances make new demands on the system, which the institutions of the 1970s are unlikely to be able to meet.

The adjustment process in the 1970s

The adjustment process in the 1970s took a number of forms: the size of the OPEC surplus was substantially reduced from 1974 to 1978 as a result of the rapid growth in imports among OPEC countries which were about $20 billion in 1973 and $100 billion by 1978, and also because of a slow-down in the growth of oil imports of the oil-importing countries, with a slow-down in economic growth and energy saving and energy substituting activities.

Thus the growth of GNP per head for the industrialized countries was 2.4 per cent p.a. in the 1970s compared with 3.9 per cent p.a. in the 1960s; among LDCs the slow-down was much less, with a growth in GNP per head of 2.7 per cent p.a. in the 1970s among oil-importing LDCs compared with 3.1 per cent p.a. in the 1960s. For the major industrialized countries, the quantity of net oil imports was the same in 1978 as in 1973.[1] Inflation in the ICs also eroded much of the increase in the real price of oil. The OPEC surplus thus fell dramatically from 1974 to 1978.

As Table 2.1 shows, by 1978 the oil-surplus had been reduced to negligible proportions ($5 billion). However, it is important to note that this was due to the successful

Table 2.1   Balance of payments on current account: surplus (+) and deficit (−) ($ billion)*

	Oil-exporting countries	Industrial countries**	Non-oil LDCs
1973	+6.6	+18.2	−11.3
1974	+67.8	−13.2	−36.9
1975	+35.0	+16.2	−45.8
1976	+40.0	−2.1	−32.1
1977	+31.7	−5.1	−28.0
1978	+5.0	+30.8	−36.2
1979	+68.4	−10.6	−54.9
1980	+115.0	−51.5	−68.0

*Totals do not add to zero because of errors, omissions, other asymmetries in reporting, plus balances of listed groups with other areas, mainly USSR and other countries of Eastern Europe which are not members of the IMF and the People's Republic of China.

**Excludes 'official transfers'.

Source: IMF, *World Economic Outlook*, Washington, 1980, Table 11.

adjustment − in terms of current account balances − of the industrialized countries whose deficit was eliminated in a very short period and which experienced a substantial surplus by 1978 (of $31 billion), whereas the non-oil developing countries continued to run very large deficits ($36 billion) in 1978. On average 20 per cent of the import bill of LDCs is due to oil imports while 80 per cent consists of imports of other services and commodities from ICs.

The deficits at this time among LDCs contained two elements: the 'normal' development deficit as more developed capital-surplus countries lent to less developed capital-deficit countries; and the special deficits caused by the oil-price rise. The latter itself has two elements − the direct impact of rising energy prices on the import bill and the indirect impact on their trade balances. These included depressed export earnings (as a result of recession among industrialized countries) and increased import expenditure (as a result of those increases in the price of manufactured imports induced by the rise in price of oil). In the process of eliminating trade deficits the industrialized countries increased the indirect element in the deficits of LDCs.

Despite the near elimination of the OPEC surplus by 1978, there remained a very substantial need for financial recycling, but the nature of the required financial flows had changed from being primarily a matter of securing the movement of funds from the OPEC countries to ICs and other LDCs to one of recycling from the industrialized countries to the developing countries. Although the deficits of the oil account among industrial countries remained very large, expansion of exports to OPEC and LDCs enabled them to achieve an overall surplus on current account. The LDCs remained in substantial deficit with both ICs and OPEC, their deficits with ICs being greater than those with OPEC.

In 1979–80 reflation in the ICs plus a further oil-price rise re-created the 1974 situation with both the ICs and LDCs having sizeable current account deficits. Thus throughout the period, there was a need for the movement of a very large quantity of funds to finance the deficits of the LDCs.

A major element in this process of adjustment was, therefore, financial flows from surplus to deficit countries, permitting the deficit countries to finance their deficits. The availability of such finance constituted another form of adjustment: in the absence of such finance the only way the LDCs would have been able to adjust was through severe deflation which would have reduced their import demand from ICs, causing additional adjustment problems for the industrialized countries. Table 2.2 shows LDC sources of finance in absolute terms, while Table 2.3 shows the proportionate importance of different sources of finance.

The three major sources of finance in the 1970s for LDCs were direct investment and other non-debt-creating transfers, net long-term borrowing from official sources and net long-term borrowing from private sources. The first item does not respond to short-term balance of payments needs; it depends on long-term investment strategies of multinational companies and host governments and aid policies of donor governments. While in money terms the absolute amount transferred in this way grew during this period, its significance as a source of finance dropped significantly from

Table 2.2 The finance of LDC deficits in the 1970s ($ billion)

	1973	1974	1975	1976	1977	1978	1979	1980
Need for Finance:								
1. Current a/c deficit	11.3	36.9	45.8	32.1	28.0	36.2	54.9	68.0
2. Accumulation of reserves	9.7	2.1	−2.0	12.8	12.0	18.0	11.6	8.8
3. TOTAL financial requirements	21.0	39.0	43.8	44.9	40.0	54.2	66.5	76.8
Sources of finance:								
4. Financing through transactions that do not affect net debt position*	9.2	12.2	11.4	11.7	13.6	15.3	19.4	20.5
5. Net long-term borrowing – official	5.5	9.6	11.4	10.2	14.4	16.3	15.9	19.1
6. Net long-term borrowing – private	6.4	9.6	14.9	17.2	17.0	21.0	26.2	26.9
7. Fund credit and short term borrowing from other monetary authorities	0.3	1.6	2.4	4.3	0.5	0.7	0.7	1.6
8. Other short term borrowing and errors and omissions	−0.4	5.5	3.7	1.5	−5.5	0.9	4.3	8.7

*Includes net direct investment, unrequited transfers received by governments, SDR allocations and valuation adjustments.
Source: World Economic Outlook, op. cit., Table 19.

44 per cent to 27 per cent of the total. While it affects the total requirements, it cannot be expected to play any systematic role in balance of payments of finance, though aid should perform this function for the poorest countries. Both net long-term official borrowing and private borrowing made a very substantial contribution to recycling; however, in proportionate terms the private sector made the largest contribution and also rose most during the period. While the proportion of total finance from official long-term sources dropped slightly (from 26.2 to 25 per cent between 1973 and 1980),[2] the proportion of private finance rose from 30.5 to over

Table 2.3   Proportionate significance of sources for LDCs

	1973	1975	1980
1. Direct investment and other non-debt affecting transfers	43.8	26.0	26.7
2. Net long-term borrowing – official	26.2	26.0	24.9
3. Net long-term borrowing, private of which	30.5	34.0	35.0
– financial institutions	19.0	21.0	21.2
– bond issues	2.4	0.5	
– suppliers credit	1.9	2.5	14.0
– other sources	7.1	9.8	
4. Use of Fund credit and borrowing from other monetary authorities	1.4	5.5	2.1
5. Other short-term borrowing and errors and omissions	−0.2	8.4	13.1

Source: World Economic Outlook, op. cit., Tables 19 and 20.

35 per cent. The private sector – with financial institutions (i.e. bank finance) dominating – clearly played a very critical role in the recycling process and thereby in protecting developing countries against the full shock of adjustment which might otherwise have occurred.

The significance of the private sector in financial flows to LDCs in the 1970s is brought out more clearly in Table 2.4, which includes private non-guaranteed debt as well as the publicly guaranteed debt included in Tables 2.2 and 2.3. Private sources accounted for 53.6 per cent of net flows of medium- and long-term capital[3] in 1970, 69.1 per cent in 1973 and 71.9 per cent in 1980. By 1979, private debt accounted for 64.1 per cent of outstanding (medium- and long-term) debt, compared with 45 per cent in 1970. The big increase came from private financial institutions (i.e. bank lending) which accounted for nearly 35 per cent of outstanding debt in 1979 compared with 10 per cent in 1970.

Table 2.4   Medium and long-term external debt of non-oil LDCs

Outstanding debt ($b)

	1970	(as % total)	1973	1979	(as % total)
Public debt					
Concessional, bilateral	22.6	(35.6)	34.8	71.6	(18.9)
Official export credits	4.3	(6.8)	6.2	21.0	(5.6)
Multilateral loans	8.0	(12.6)	12.9	43.2	(11.4)
Private					
Publicly guaranteed:					
Suppliers credits	7.0	(11.0)	10.5	21.5	(5.7)
Financial institutions	6.3	(9.9)	18.7	131.0	(34.6)
Bonds	3.2	(5.0)	4.7	15.5	(4.1)
Other	1.1	(1.7)	1.2	1.1	(0.3)
Private, non-guaranteed	11.0	(17.3)	25.7	73.4	(19.4)
TOTAL	63.5		114.8	378.3	

Proportions of net flows to LDCs (%)

	1970	1973	1979
Official sources	46.4	30.9	28.1
Private sources	53.6	69.1	71.9

Source: N. Hope, 'Development in and Prospects for the External Debt of the Developing Countries – 1970–80 and Beyond', World Bank Staff Working Paper (forthcoming), Tables 1a and 2a.

In contrast, the international public financial institutions made only a small contribution to the net flow of finance. The Fund and other monetary authorities contributed 3.1 per cent of the cumulative finance needed between 1973 and 1980, and this at a time when the LDCs as a whole were in severe financial difficulties and the Fund contribution might have been expected to be greatest.

The apparent success − particularly notable for being unplanned and uncoordinated − of the commercial sector in recycling funds in the 1970s has led some observers to believe that the market mechanism, the 'invisible hand', can be relied upon to do the same job in the 1980s without any major institutional change. This was the view, at least for 1980, for example, of Fred Bergsten of the US Treasury:

> In a comprehensive US statement on the recycling of the OPEC surplus, Mr Fred Bergsten claims that private capital markets plus new resources and commitments of the IMF and the World Bank are quite capable of coping with a deficit of around $70 billion for the industrialized countries and $50 billion for oil-importing developing countries.[4]

In a similar vein, the British Foreign and Commonwealth Office states that 'the Government believe . . . the international capital market can continue to play the primary role in recycling'.[5]

Others have questioned this rather complacent view, as will be discussed below. Whether it is a reasonable view to take − for the longer term, and not just for the 1980s − depends on a number of factors, including the likely magnitude of the problem in the longer term and on the capacity of the market, both lenders and borrowers, to repeat the 1970s performance in the 1980s. But before considering these questions, there is an important prior question to be answered about the 1970s: was the recycling process really as satisfactory as a bland look at the aggregate figures suggests?

How satisfactory was recycling in the 1970s?

Closer examination of the 1970s suggests a quite large number of reasons why one would not, without serious qualification and major institutional change, recommend the 1970s as a model for future recycling processes: these include the quantity of funds recycled; their distribution between countries; the overt price and the hidden conditionality involved; their effect on the development process; the heavy indebtedness that resulted; and the possible dangers that have developed to the stability of the world banking system.

An important aspect of the logic of accounting is that surpluses and deficits taken together for the world as a whole must be equal,[6] and the deficit countries must in fact find some source of finance for their deficits. It therefore does not follow from the fact that some countries had surpluses in the 1970s and others deficits, and that the deficit countries found finance for their deficits, that the total quantity of funds recycled was at an ideal or desirable level. The financial system may lend itself to too high or too low a level of recycling, as compared with a desirable level. If too much finance is available – as compared with the desirable outcome – then countries may adjust too little and run deficits which are not sustainable in the long run; alternatively, if too few potential recycling mechanisms are available, surpluses and deficits will be lower than desirable. When too few funds are available, countries will have to take deflationary or restructuring action to reduce the deficits to that level for which potential funds are available.

In practice, it is not possible to estimate precisely what the desirable level of international financial flows would be; indeed observers would differ about this depending, among other things, on their view of the relative significance of economic growth and controlling price inflation as objectives of economic policy. None the less, there is strong support for the view that – despite the very large sums involved in recycling – *the total quantity of funds recycled in the 1970s was too low*. As Table 2.5 shows, economic growth in the 1970s was significantly lower than in the 1960s for ICs and low-income LDCs.

For ICs, developments in the 1970s were to a large extent the result of their own policy decisions and were not constrained by the availability of finance. ICs chose to operate their economies at a rather lower level of growth in order to combat inflation and reduce the power of OPEC to impose price increases. As a group, although perhaps not for each individual country, ICs could have run their economies at a higher level of demand with consequently higher levels of trade deficit, without meeting financial constraints. Hence, the availability of finance was not a major problem during this period for these countries. But LDCs are constrained by the availability of external finance: some LDCs (middle-income newly industrializing) were able to borrow in the international markets and were not constrained by finance. But other LDCs, especially low-income LDCs, were forced to limit their development plans because of lack of finance to meet their deteriorating payments situation: lack of access to finance, worsening terms of trade and depressed export markets as a result of the depressed levels of demand in ICs meant that they had to restrict levels of activity.[7]

Table 2.5   Rate of growth of GNP per head, per annum (%)

	1960–70	1970–80
LDCs:		
Low-income	1.6	0.9
Middle-income	3.6	3.1
Industrialized countries	3.9	2.4
Oil exporters	2.8	3.5

Source: World Development Report, 1980, World Bank, Table 2.8.

Undoubtedly, the deflationary pressures would have been much stronger in the absence of the commercial sector's recycling. Moreover, the depressed level of activity in OECD countries (see the unemployment figures in Table 2.6 which show a significantly higher level in each country in the late 1970s than the early 1970s) is in part, possibly large part, a consequence of deliberate policies on the part of the ICs. However, the slow-down in world activity, the rise in unemployment, together with the increased moves towards protectionism suggest inadequate expenditure in the world as a whole and this in turn suggests that OPEC surpluses should have been higher and the rest of the world's deficits higher than that actually recorded for a satisfactory level of world economic activity. A major weakness of the current world monetary system is that no single authority has the responsibility, at a world level, for ensuring adequate world demand.

Individual private banks cannot perform that function and international public institutions do not.

Table 2.6   Unemployment rates in OECD countries (%)

	US	Canada	Japan	France	Germany	Italy	UK
1973	4.7	5.6	1.3	2.6	0.9	6.3	3.0
1975	8.3	7.0	1.9	4.1	3.6	5.8	3.9
1977	6.9	8.0	2.0	4.9	3.6	7.1	6.1
1979	5.7	7.4	2.1	5.9	3.2	7.6	5.8
1980	7.0	7.5	2.0	6.3	3.2	7.5	7.4

Source: National Institute Economic Review, February 1981, p. 50.

The commercial sector's contribution was very much greater in gross terms than net. Between 1973 and 1979 gross private sector disbursements to LDCs amounted to $327.1 billion; deducting amortization, cumulative lending was $183.9 billion; cumulative interest payments were equivalent to over a third of this sum ($65.9 billion).[8] The contribution to the net flow of funds was also reduced by LDC accumulation of assets in the Eurocurrency market. Killick concludes that 'To a substantial extent, therefore, the banks were merely relending LDC deposits − a useful service but not a major contribution to recycling'.[9]

The distribution of commercial lending

Commercial sector lending in the 1970s was heavily concentrated among middle-income countries (see Tables 2.7 and 2.8). According to OECD data for 1978, middle-income countries received nearly three-quarters of the bank lending and bonds, while low-income countries received under 5 per cent of the total. This concentration contrasts with the distribution of official flows (concessional and non-concessional) which to a greater extent went to low-income countries.

In terms of the balance of assets and liabilities with the Eurocurrency market, it is estimated that in March 1980,

Table 2.7 Distribution of financial flows ($m.), 1978

Recipient:	All LDCs	% of total	Low income*	Newly industrializing	Other middle income
Types of finance:					
Concessional					
ODA	23,450	29.5	13,440	501	8,892
Non-Concessional					
Bank lending	22,514	28.3	1,053	11,625	4,992
Bonds	3,027	3.8	115	1,832	418
Export credits	12,247	15.4	1,226	2,032	3,234
Direct investment	11,833	14.9	872	5,436	3,509
Other (mainly official)	6,538	8.2	2,203	1,395	2,574
TOTAL	79,609	100	18,910	22,819	23,619

*For definition of 'low income' see Chapter Five.
Source: OECD Development Cooperation, 1980, Table IV–10.

Table 2.8 Share of financial flows among LDCs, 1978

Recipient:	Low income	Newly industrialized	Other middle income	Unallocated
Concessional				
ODA	57.3	2.1	37.9	2.7
Non-Concessional				
Bank lending	4.7	51.6	22.2	21.5
Bonds	3.8	60.5	13.8	21.9
Export credits	10.0	16.6	26.4	47.0
Direct investment	7.4	45.9	29.7	17.0
Other (mainly official)	33.7	21.3	39.4	5.6
TOTAL	23.8	28.7	29.7	17.8

Source: OECD Development Cooperation, 1980, Table IV–10.

low-income countries had a small positive balance ($3.5 billion), middle-income countries had net liabilities of $17.1 billion and upper-income LDCs had a negative balance of $59.2 billion.[10]

Within the middle-income category, there was also heavy concentration, with the newly industrializing countries receiving the bulk of the funds. In 1979, the 13 major borrowers accounted for 68.2 per cent of debt from private sources, while the four largest borrowers accounted for 44.1 per cent of private debt.

Those countries that were able to borrow substantially were able to maintain higher rates of growth of imports and of GNP per head than those countries which had lesser access to commercial markets or to other sources of finance for imports. This has already been indicated in the data showing a much more marked deterioration in growth rates among low-income LDCs, than middle-income LDCs who had greater access to private financial markets. The UNDP/UNCTAD study of adjustment provides more detailed evidence:

Table 2.9 Import capacity and economic performance of non-oil developing countries (unweighted averages of average annual percentage growth rates)

	annual % increase in GNP		annual % increase in domestic investment	
	1965–73	1973–6	1965–73	1973–6
30 countries with sustained or improved growth of import capacity*	4.3	5.3	6.1	15.3
40 countries with diminished growth of import capacity**	4.9	2.9	5.3	4.3

*Countries having an average annual rate of growth of import volume in 1973–6 equal to or greater than that experienced during 1965–73.

**Countries having an average annual rate of growth of import volume in 1973–6 below that experienced during 1965–73.

Source: Dell and Lawrence, op. cit., Table 2.11.

The distribution of commercial lending is much more concentrated on a few upper- and middle-income LDCs than official lending. Among low-income LDCs, official long-term debt accounted for 51 per cent of their total balance of payments finance in 1980 compared with 1 per cent financed by long-term private flows, whereas the major exporters of manufactures received 24.4 per cent of their finance from official sources and 32.1 per cent from private sources. The growing significance of the private sector in recycling thus led to a proportionately greater amount of funds to finance imports for middle-income LDCs, and less for lower income LDCs, and consequently enhanced the relative performance of middle-income LDCs.

Conditions of commercial lending

Despite some lengthening in recent years, much of commercial lending is of very short maturity. At the end of 1979, LDCs had $79.8 billion outstanding borrowing of less than one year maturity and $115.8 billion of more than one year.[11] The longer term loans involve fluctuating interest rates which change every 3–6 months following fluctuations in the London Inter-Bank Offer Rate (LIBOR). Further fluctuations, for particular countries, are caused by fluctuations in the spread in relation to LIBOR. Such variability can considerably complicate forward planning since very substantial sums of money are sometimes involved.[12]

The interest charged is on average higher and the maturity period shorter than finance from other (official) sources. In 1979 interest on official debt was 4.9 per cent, compared with 11.7 per cent for private source debt; average maturity for official debt was 24.4 years with a grace period of 6.4 years. For private debt, average maturity was 8.9 years with a grace period of 3.7 years.[13] Thus the switch to private sources of finance has led to a considerable hardening of the overall terms received by LDCs. The relatively short-term nature of many loans involve rollover problems which can be severe especially where bunching occurs. While in normal circumstances the rollover may present no problems, it can provide an opportunity for a crisis of confidence in a particular country.

It is sometimes claimed that many countries prefer the unconditional nature of commercial credit to the conditions imposed by the IMF and this is a major reason why so little use was made of IMF facilities in the 1970s. This has been explicit in the case of Brazil. But it has also been claimed that commercial lending involves a sort of 'hidden conditionality' which may be at least as bad from the point of view of recipients and, because it is hidden, is more difficult to dispute or publicize.[14] According to one experienced banker[15] 'Private bank "conditionality" is unavoidable'. These conditions are summed up as being those government policies which 'keep them creditworthy for international borrowing'. There is a certain amount of circularity involved here, since, according to Friedman, exclusive reliance on various objective indicators (e.g. balance of payments) is rejected by most banks in favour of confidence about creditworthiness. This vague and judgmental criterion, together with a herd instinct among bankers, may give undue influence (positive or negative) to random developments.

Countries very dependent on commercial borrowing may condition their policies — e.g. towards international reserves, and the private sector especially multinational companies, some of which have close links with the international banks — to maintain a good credit rating.[16] But the very wide variety (politically and economically) of countries to which the commercial sector lends suggests that conditions imposed relate more to banks' confidence in repayment than to politics. However, in any single country a number of banks may be involved, so a country's credit rating with any one bank depends not only on the objective prospects for the country but also expectations about the confidence and policies of other banks, although syndicated lending permits a common bank view. Thus 'politics' and other confidence factors may enter conditionality through expectations about other lenders' behaviour. For official loans (e.g. the World Bank), the assessment is to a much greater extent confined to 'objective' variables, e.g. the likely behaviour of exports, imports etc. Of course individual countries may gain by the more complex determinants of commercial lending; it is unlikely, for example, that either S. Korea or Brazil would have been able to spend their way out of the crisis of the 1970s if they had had to rely exclusively on official sources of finance. But countries may also lose when there is a crisis of confidence among commercial lenders, or when there is general (and self-justifying) consensus that a country is not creditworthy, such as appears to be believed about many low-income countries.

Increasingly, the commercial sector has made its lending conditional on IMF approval of a country's policies, thus adding IMF conditionality to their own. This was the case, for example, in Turkey and Jamaica. But in Turkey, when the IMF did reach agreement, the commercial sector used the IMF facilities as an occasion to withdraw money, rather than lend.[17] The higher interest rates charged by the private sector may in normal times be regarded as the cost of avoiding IMF style conditionality. But when (as with rescheduling arrangements) IMF approval becomes necessary to secure private banks' commitment, countries are faced with both high interest and high conditionality. Moreover, the normally amorphous implicit commitment of the private sector to provide support if IMF approval is forthcoming cannot be relied upon always to be effective in practice. A more formal agreement would do so, but would then tie private lending firmly to IMF conditionality, which would limit the options for some countries.

Developmental effects of commercial lending

Commercial lending affects development through its distribution and through the use made with it by those who receive it.

The bias in distribution has already been noted. While an oil-price rise affects very poor countries both directly and, perhaps to a greater extent, indirectly (via deteriorating terms of trade for their exports to ICs), the recycling of funds via the commercial sector tends to leave them out. The World Bank has suggested that this situation will continue throughout the 1980s: 'the poor countries cannot borrow much capital on commercial terms, nor would it be prudent to do so . . . these countries may find their options increasingly restricted by a key constraint — their credit-worthiness'.[18]

As far as the recipients are concerned, heavy commercial borrowing may have positive or negative effects on development depending on the use that is made of it. Borrowing that is used to raise investment rates, develop export potential or raise productive consumption can raise the growth rate (or avoid a fall) both in the short and long term. This appears to be the case in S. Korea, which used the heavy borrowing in the 1970s to raise investment and exports, and whose growth in GNP actually accelerated.[19] Borrowing, on the other hand, may be used to finance unproductive consumption (public and private) and military expenditure and may simply postpone adjustment policies. A notorious example is Zaïre. The low profile and complex nature of commercial bank conditionality means that in general there is very little assurance that commercial lending will be used productively rather than unproductively.

Furthermore, many LDCs have projects with high social rates of return which cannot easily be appropriated, either through the market or through taxation, in a form appropriate for commercial repayment. Where this is so, LDCs may have less commercial creditworthiness than the social return on projects would justify, and the countries themselves may be reluctant to resort to commercial borrowing, even though such funds could be productively used within their economies.

Country indebtedness and international stability

As a result of the growth in borrowing and rising interest rates, debt service ratios on public and publicly guaranteed debt rose throughout the 1970s for non-oil developing countries as a whole from about 9 to about 11 per cent. The rise was not dramatic, in view of the considerable borrowing, nor to very high levels. As Table 2.10 shows, the experience of different groups of countries differed.

Low-income countries as a group actually experienced a fall in debt service ratios, though this was wholly due to the experience of India. Excluding India, low-income countries' debt service ratio was constant throughout the period. From this point of view therefore the low-income countries started the 1980s in a strong position. Among middle-income countries, there is a marked divergence between exporters of manufactures, whose average debt service ratio did not rise very sharply, and other middle-income countries which experienced a larger rise in their debt service ratio despite the fact that the increase in their debt was much smaller in absolute terms and somewhat smaller in proportionate terms. Borrowing as such does not cause a debt service problem: it depends on what is done with the loans. Clearly, to the extent that they are accompanied by a rapid growth in exports, the debt service ratio need not worsen. However, the use of this ratio as an indicator of potential debt problems — as is the near universal practice — biases the results in favour of exporters and against countries with a similar overall balance of trade which have emphasized import substitution.

High debt service ratios in particular countries may cause these countries problems in future borrowing. If they lead to default, they may also threaten the stability of the international banking system, and could result in a *multiplied* contractionary process. For example Lipton estimates that a default of say $10 billion could lead to a reduction in total lending of $50 billion, thus being responsible for major deflationary pressures. Provisions for some defaults, without instituting contractionary activity, must be allowed for in normal international bank operations. So the multiplier effect Lipton posits will only occur in the event of an abnormal amount of defaults.[20]

The number of countries in arrears on payment on current account has risen from 3 in 1974 to 22 at the end of 1980.[21] There has been a significant increase in the number of countries seeking debt relief and in the amounts involved since 1975. The resulting multilateral negotiations have involved rescheduling of debt rather than default. In general, the creditors have not been losers.[22] These average figures conceal very sharp differences between countries: a number of heavy borrowers recorded very sharp increases in debt service ratios.

Table 2.10 Debt and debt service ratios for non-oil LDCs

	1973	1976	1979	1979 1973
1. *Low-income countries*				
Debt service ratio*	13.3	10.7	10.7	80.5
Debt $b.	19.8	29.6	40.4	204.0
2. *Low-income excluding India*				
Debt service ratio	10.4	10.7	10.8	100.0
Debt $b.	9.2	16.2	24.8	270.0
3. *Middle-income, major exporters of manu-factures*				
Debt service ratio	12.8	13.4	16.6	129.7
Debt $b.	40.2	78.5	142.7	355.0
4. *Other middle-income countries*				
Debt service ratio	12.3	12.8	18.0	146.3
Debt $b.	20.4	34.2	67.9	332.8

*ratio of interest payments plus amortization to exports.
Source: N. Hope, op. cit., Tables 8a, 8c, 9a and 10a.

For most countries with 'high' debt service ratios, no major problem has arisen, although where problems have arisen they have tended to be concentrated among countries with debt service ratios of over 20 per cent.[23] The many complex links between banks (with for example syndicated loans being the norm) in some ways increase the potential effects of default but they also mean that the international community is under considerable and mutual obligation to prevent it.

The high level of borrowing in the seventies — especially from the commercial sector — has clearly increased both the possibility and the effects of any default. This must be a consideration in assessing the need for new mechanisms; but from the evidence to date it would appear that the major risk is to the plans of particular countries rather than to the world at large. Projections for Latin America as a whole — a

Table 2.11   Debt service payments on public and publicly
guaranteed debt as a percentage of GNP and exports

Countries (in ascending order of income per capita)	GNP in:		Exports of goods and services in:	
	1970	1978	1970	1978
India	0.9	0.8	20.9	9.4
Zaïre	2.0	6.5	4.4	31.3
Pakistan	1.9	2.1	21.6	12.2
Indonesia	0.9	3.1	6.9	13.0
Egypt	4.1	8.7	28.7	22.2
Zambia	3.2	7.1	5.5	20.8
Bolivia	2.2	8.5	10.9	48.7
Philippines	1.4	2.8	7.5	13.4
Peru	2.4	7.4	11.6	31.1
Korea, Republic of	3.1	3.9	19.4	10.5
Algeria	0.8	5.9	3.2	20.9
Mexico	2.1	6.9	23.6	59.6
Panama	3.0	25.2	7.7	39.2
Taiwan	1.4	2.6	4.5	4.4
Chile	3.1	7.3	18.9	38.2
Costa Rica	2.9	7.2	9.7	23.0
Brazil	0.9	2.2	13.5	28.4
Uruguay	2.6	8.7	21.5	45.7
Argentina	1.9	3.5	21.5	26.8
Portugal	1.3	1.1	4.4	3.7

Source: World Development Report, 1980, Table 13.

region which borrowed heavily in the 1970s – indicate that
the future trajectory appears manageable.[24]

Prospects for the 1980s

The oil-price rise of 1970 and 1980 has re-created the 1973–4
situation of financial surpluses among OPEC countries and
deficits in ICs and LDCs (see Table 2.1). It is estimated that the
OPEC surplus will be running between $100 and $120 billion
in 1980. In real terms, the size of the current OPEC surplus
and the deficit among LDCs in 1980 was comparable to that
of 1973–4. But it has been argued (although with less force

recently) there are significant differences between the 1970s and 1980s which may lead to more general problems in the 1980s than those experienced in the 1970s.

Many observers, including the IMF, the World Bank, the Bank of International Settlements and the Group of Experts appointed by the Commonwealth Secretariat, have suggested that the OPEC surpluses are likely to be more persistent in the 1980s. In the first place, it is argued that the rate of growth of imports of OPEC countries will be slower than in the 1970s.[25] Secondly, it is believed that OPEC will try to resist any deterioration in the terms of trade similar to that which helped reduce the surplus between 1974 and 1978: a stable or increasing real price of oil was suggested as likely. However recent developments challenge these views. In the first place there has been downward pressure on oil and therefore prices, partly due to considerable energy saving on the part of developed countries. Secondly, there are few signs of the supposed slackening in OPEC imports from the ICs of manufactures and services. But if the industrialized countries resume economic growth, this would bring renewed upward demand on oil and therefore create further surpluses.

The net effects on OPEC surpluses and on LDC deficits are difficult to predict. The Commonwealth Group of Experts predicted a cumulative deficit among non-oil LDCs of $400 billion from 1979 to 1983. But a recent study[26] estimates an OPEC surplus of $68 billion in 1981 with reduction to a zero surplus by the end of 1982. However, to the extent that the OPEC surplus is reduced as a result of reduced activity in the ICs, LDC deficits may not be much affected since the effects of a lower price of oil may be offset by worsening markets in ICs. The World Bank predicts a current account deficit among LDCs of $95 billion in 1985 and $173 billion in 1990 for the 'High' case (and $84 billion and $130 billion in 1985 and 1990 in the 'Low' case).[27] It is difficult to make precise comparisons with the 1970s because of price changes, but with these figures it seems likely that the orders of magnitude for LDCs may not be all that dissimilar to the 1970s when, as noted earlier, they experienced a large deficit throughout the period, despite the reduction in the OPEC surplus. Whether or not a persistent OPEC surplus poses greater problems for

the LDCs in the 1980s than developments did in the 1970s
may depend in large part on IC reaction to more persistent
OPEC surpluses. There is little point in making too much of
these projections which are based on a host of dubious
assumptions. However, one can conclude that for any reasonable growth prospects for LDCs there will be a need for a
very large amount of balance of payments finance throughout the 1980s. However, the sums involved are not all that
much larger in real terms, according to present estimates,
than those which were achieved in the 1970s.

It has been strongly argued also, that the commercial
sector will not be able to repeat its recycling performance of
the 1970s. This conclusion is summarized by the World
Bank: 'The extraordinary expansion of private commercial
lending to developing countries that took place in the 1970s
is unlikely to be repeated during the current adjustment'.[28]
This view is echoed by most commentators with varying
degrees of emphasis.[29] This would be a highly significant
conclusion in relation to whether new mechanisms are
required. It is therefore important to explore its basis,
particularly given the fact that the funds will be available so
long as the surpluses persist and that 'financial' intermediaries
make money from borrowing these funds and on-lending
them. Doubts about the magnitude of commercial recycling
arise at each of the stages of the recycling operation – the
willingness of the ultimate lenders to lend, of the ultimate
borrowers to borrow and of the financial intermediaries to
perform the operation.

(a) OPEC – the ultimate lenders. It is claimed that OPEC
dislike lending via the commercial banks for a number of
reasons. First, because with inflation the real return is near
zero and sometimes negative, they would do better investing
in assets whose value may increase with inflation (e.g. equities,
real estate), or 'keeping the oil in the ground'. There is
evidence of increasing OPEC diversification into equities.[30]
But unless this affects real variables (e.g. investment), such
activity will release other funds for on-lending. The 'keeping
the oil in the ground' option is a complex one depending on
politics as much as economics, but in the short term might,
in any event, tend to raise the real price of oil and therefore,

given the low demand elasticities, the surpluses and the funds available for lending. Secondly, OPEC are said to dislike losing control over their money, and prefer to lend it directly themselves using their own banks, a view which gathered force as a result of the US freeze of Iranian assets.

Recycling of the OPEC surpluses is likely to be complicated by an increasing diversification of OPEC foreign assets away from bank deposits and into investment in equities, gold and long-term bonds.

(b) LDCs — the ultimate borrowers. Very high levels of debt among some middle-income countries may limit their willingness to continue to borrow as much as before, while much publicized difficulties of a few countries could deter other countries from getting in the same situation. Among low-income countries, the cost of borrowing may act as a severe deterrent. One reaction of the banks to increasing exposure and reduced confidence is to widen spreads, raising interest rates to LDCs.[31] But the very stringent domestic deflation that may be necessary for countries who do not borrow, may well counterbalance these effects. Moreover, the countries who are heavily indebted have to borrow more in order to meet their obligations. Thus Brazil is an example of a very heavily indebted country which is actively seeking new loans. So long as the increase in export earnings exceeds the increase in amortization and interest payments, continued borrowing may be associated with reduced debt service ratios. It seems unlikely that LDC willingness to borrow will be a serious constraint.

(c) Financial intermediaries. It is said that some banks are becoming more cautious about undertaking a large amount of recycling.[32] For one reason, some established banks are beginning to face balance-sheet ratio problems; OPEC deposits are at very short notice, while the loans are typically of longer maturity.[33] Unless OPEC can be persuaded to transform their deposits into longer-term assets, this could limit the lending capacity of some banks without an expansion of their capital base. Moreover, very heavy exposure of particular banks in particular countries may limit their lending to these countries. National regulatory authorities, fearful of bank collapses, are beginning to intervene more actively to constrain lending.[34] In 1979–80 Central Bank Governors of the main industrial countries agreed that more supervision was required.[35] It is also felt that the Iran freeze will make banks 'much more chary about becoming unduly dependent upon major OPEC deposits as a basis for term lending'.[36]

It is difficult, perhaps impossible, to know how much this type of factor is actually going to affect bank lending. After all, in 1973–4 similar cautious talk was heard but in fact the market did lend huge amounts. This seems likely to be the situation again in the 1980s. While there is some evidence, however, that in 1979–80 some banks refused to participate in some syndicated loans,[37] the latest BIS data indicates that bank lending to non-oil LDCs was 20 per cent more in the first 9 months of 1980 than in the corresponding period a year earlier. Despite the talk of 'overexposure' the US banks are actively seeking new business in Latin America, where they derive a large proportion of their profits.[38] Changes in the regulations of US banks are likely to increase some banks' potential participation in international lending. Moreover, new banks from Europe and Japan are becoming active in recycling.[39] In addition, there is a rapid expansion of Arab financial institutions, including wholly-owned banks, joint ventures and aid institutions.[40] Diversification of OPEC funds has been quite marked recently. The dollar's share of OPEC deposits with the main financial centres (US, Japan and Europe) is estimated to have dropped to about 60 per cent, in contrast just after 1973 dollar deposits are estimated to have accounted for 80 per cent. One estimate suggests that less than half of the 1979 OPEC surplus went to the 'North' financial centres.[41] Thus, possible limits to the growth in lending by major US banks may have little effect on bank lending at a world level.

Direct borrowing by issuing bonds is an alternative to borrowing via the commercial banks. In the 1970s this was only undertaken by a few well established countries[42] and accounted for only a small proportion of private lending (9.6 per cent from 1974 to 1978 of net LDC long-term borrowing)[43] from private sources, but this proportion was rising (from 7.8 per cent in 1973 to 17.1 per cent in 1978). There was a fall in LDC bond issues in 1979 with less than

3 per cent of LDC private borrowing being met by bonds. This fall continued into 1980 due to a rise in interest rates.[44] But if the commercial banks become much more cautious in their lending, and if markets are liquid through the effects (direct or indirect) of OPEC surpluses, the bond market may offer an alternative recycling mechanism. With volatile interest rates, bonds will only be attractive if they include provision for flexible interest payments.

Is there a need for a new recycling mechanism?

Despite much pessimistic talk about the ability of the market to function again as it did in the 1970s, there does not seem all that much objective reality about the talk. If the surpluses persist then there will be funds available to lend, borrowers in need of finance and money to be made by the commercial sector from performing an intermediary function. But as one group of banks slows down, for the reasons mentioned above, and another takes over there could be a temporary slow-down, as there often is in the handover in a relay race. This is the conclusion of McWilliam:[45]

A likely consequence will be a broadening of the market in the sense that a new generation of international banks will both be soliciting OPEC deposits and recycling them in balance of payments lending. *But this could well take some time to become effective.* [Our italics.]

A slow-down might also occur because of a search for new *borrowers* as old borrowers find they are unable to expand their exports sufficiently to keep debt servicing within manageable limits. If there were such a slow-down it could have serious effects on the world economy and the prospects of particular economies. A potentially temporary lag in their ability to borrow may cause countries to cut expenditure which then has multiplier effects on the world economy. Such effects will ultimately reduce both surpluses and deficits, the funds available for lending and the sums countries want to borrow: balance will be achieved but at a lower level of world activity.

In our view, fears that there will be much of a slow-down

in commercial lending to LDCs have been exaggerated. With excess liquidity in the system and willing borrowers, the commercial sector will continue to lend very large amounts of money, with diversification among both lenders and borrowers. None the less, to rely too heavily on the commercial sector to carry out the major recycling function involves dangers; a hiccup in the system can lead to major contractionary forces. In addition, commercial section recycling leads to an unbalanced distribution of world resources, with very little for low-income countries.

Thus a look at prospects for the 1980s suggests the need for additional mechanisms because one cannot rely on the uncoordinated efforts of the private sector to recycle at the level and with the speed required to prevent major international deflationary shocks. Moreover, while the system appeared to function well in the 1970s, closer inspection has revealed very major defects — defects which are likely to be repeated unless there is some major institutional change in the 1980s. So long as there is a significant possibility of crisis, panic and multiplied contraction, there is a need to provide an institutional response to such a situation — a safety net.

Desirable characteristics of recycling mechanisms in the 1980s

The discussion of events in the 1970s and prospects for the 1980s suggests certain functions which need to be filled by public financial institutions.

1   To ensure an adequate overall level of recycling from the point of view of the world situation. This would involve taking a world view about surpluses/deficits and likely flow of funds and then ensuring, directly or indirectly, that sufficient financing/recycling occurs.

2   To overview, supervise and fund a growing proportion of total recycling so as to achieve:

(a) a higher (and more predictable) overall level of recycling than seems likely leaving the main task to the private sector;

(b) lower levels of interest rates, especially to some borrowers, through the pooling of risks which would be involved;

(c) lending to countries, which is planned on a medium-term basis, and related to a number of 'objective' economic factors rather than 'confidence' which can lead to large increases/decreases in lending to particular countries;

(d) medium-term lending (5–10 years) and systematic 'roll-over' provisions;

(e) improved country distribution, so that (i) a few countries do not receive most of the funds; and (ii) there is access to funds for low-income countries on terms which they can pay.

The following chapters consider reforms which might contribute to these requirements.

Notes

1 This aggregate figure conceals big differences among countries. The UK became a major producer during this period. The Common Market countries and Japan all showed a big drop in oil imports, but the US showed a big increase.

2 The figures for 1980 are in part estimates – they are derived from the IMF, *World Economic Outlook*.

3 Medium and long-term is defined as debt having an original maturity of more than one year.

4 Reported in *Financial Times*, 16 June 1980, 'Markets "can cope" with OPEC surplus'.

5 'The Brandt Commission Report', Memorandum prepared by the FCO for the Overseas Development Sub-Committee of the Foreign Affairs Committee, July 1980.

6 Because of 'errors and omissions' the two do not in practice precisely balance: recorded 'deficits' exceed recorded 'surpluses' by a significant amount.

7 S. Dell and R. Lawrence, *The Balance of Payments Adjustment Process in Developing Countries*, Pergamon, 1980.

8 N. Hope, op. cit., Table 29.

9 T. Killick, 'Only Select Borrowers Benefit', *Financial Times*, 7 November 1980.

10 T. Killick, op. cit., Table II.

11 M. McWilliam, 'Non-oil LDCs and the international capital markets', *Standard Chatered Review*, September 1980.

12 See S. Griffiths-Jones, 'The Growth of Multinational Banking and the Euro-currency Market and their Effects on Developing Countries', *Journal of Development Studies,* January 1980; she estimates that the rise in interest rates in 1978 added $4 billion to LDCs obligations p.a.; Brazil's unplanned additional burden was $1 billion.

13 N. Hope, op. cit.: the figures are for medium- and long-term debt, i.e. debt having an original maturity of more than one year.

14 A. Fishlow, 'Latin American External Debt: Problem or Solution', mimeo, 1981, points to an asymmetry in private capital markets which impose little interference in good times, but in bad times they involve considerable limitations.

15 I. Friedman in W. Cline and S. Weintraub, eds, *Economic Stabilisation in Developing Countries*, Brookings, 1981.

16 Friedman, op. cit., argues that banks would tend to add to IMF conditionality a number of points, including that the country should 'end undue government interference in the market mechanism' and 'eliminate or reduce laws that discriminate against foreigners'. See Cline and Weintraub, op. cit., p. 246.

17 See *Financial Times*, 13 November 1980. An IMF official is quoted as saying 'We did not make major loans to Turkey just so that the banks could get their money out'.

18 *World Development Report, 1980,* op. cit., pp. 25-6.

19 S. Griffiths-Jones, 'Adjustment Policies in the 1970s'. Background paper for Marlborough House Seminar on Adjustment Policies, November 1980.

20 M. Lipton, 'World Depression by Third World Default?' for Freidrich–Evert–Siftung 'Brandt Symposium', mimeo, 1980.

21 G. K. Helleiner, 'Comment on A. Fishlow's paper', mimeo, 1981.

22 C. Hardy, Background Paper.

23 G. Feder *at al., Estimation of a Debt Service Capacity Index*, World Bank, mimeo, Washington, 1979.

24 A. Fishlow, op. cit.

25 *World Economic Outlook*, 1980, p. 27.

26 A. Stoga of First National Bank of Chicago quoted in *Financial Times*, 17 July 1981.

27 *World Development Report, 1981*, Table 2.4. See Chapter 3, p. 39 for definition of 'High' and 'Low' cases.

28 *World Development Report, 1980*, op. cit., pp. 10-11. *World Development Report, 1981* is less sure of this conclusion but still predicts a lower rate of increase of commercial lending in the 1980s than the 1970s.

29 See IMF, *World Economic Outlook*, 1980, op. cit.; Lipton, op. cit.; Morgan Guaranty Trust, *World Financial Markets*, September 1980; Report by a Commonwealth Group of Exports, op. cit. P. Oppenheimer, 'Financial Implications of the Energy Problem', mimeo, 1980.

30 See D. Marsh, 'OPEC's Grand Juggling Act', *Financial Times*, 14 October 1980.

31 See McWilliam, Oppenheimer and *World Development Report, 1980*, op. cit.

32 See C. Hardy, 'Commercial Bank Lending to Developing Countries: Supply Constraints', *World Development*, February 1978.

33 'There is much greater consciousnes of balance sheet ratios, which will tend to place limits on a massive accrual of deposits through the commercial banking system', McWilliam, op. cit., p. 5.

34 For example, both US and German authorities are demanding *consolidated* balance sheets from banks with international activities to prevent offshore evasion of national regulations.

35 Oppenheimer, op. cit., p. 18.

36 McWilliam, op. cit., p. 5.

37 Oppenheimer, op. cit., p. 18.

38 See 'Chase's Big Push in Latin America, Bank's move to tap region's rapid economic growth', *Herald Tribune*, 24 November 1980.

39 See *Financial Times*, Supplement on Japanese Banking and Finance, 3 December 1980; D. Marsh, op. cit.; 'Euromarkets – 1980', *Herald Tribune*, November 1980.

40 D. Marsh, op. cit. and 'Bypassing Euromarkets', *South*, No. 2, November 1980.

41 Marsh, op. cit.

42 In 1979 Brazil, Argentina, Mexico, Algeria, Malaysia, Thailand, the Philippines and S. Korea raised money by issuing international bonds.

43 IMF, *World Economic Outlook*, Table 19.

44 'Eurobond problems for Third World', *South*, November 1980.

45 McWilliam, op. cit., p. 6.

3 TRANSFER OF RESOURCES: INSTITUTIONAL ALTERNATIVES[1]

Recent developments in the world economy mean that a very large flow of financial resources to LDCs will be required in the 1980s if developing countries are to experience a significant and sustained rise in per capita incomes.

Requirements for external finance among LDCs depend on world economic developments as well as LDCs' own growth strategies. The World Bank has made projections on the basis of two sets of assumptions. In the 'Low' case there is an 'unsuccessful [world] adjustment in 1980–85; though payments in balances are reduced growth remains depressed, and inadequate foundations are laid for recovery after 1985'.[2] According to the 1981 projections, in the Low case, GNP per capita among ICs grows by 2.3 per cent p.a. between 1980 and 1990; among low-income developing countries GNP per capita growth would grow by 0.7 per cent p.a., while among low-income countries in Sub-Saharan Africa per capita incomes *fall* by 1 per cent p.a. Middle-income oil importers are projected to grow by 2.1 per cent p.a. The 'High' case 'represents a much more successful adjustment' such that ICs are able to maintain a higher level of demand and rate of growth; IC income per head grows by 3.1 per cent p.a. Over the decade, middle-income LDCs' GNP per capita grows by 3.4 per cent p:a. and low-income oil importers by 1.8 per cent p.a., but growth in incomes per head in low-income Sub-Saharan Africa remain stagnant at 0.1 per cent p.a., 1980–90.

In the High case the World Bank estimates financial requirements among LDCs as $75.3 billion in 1980, rising to $124.4 billion in 1985 and $206.7 billion in 1990. At constant prices, the 1990 estimate represents a 40 per cent increase over the 1980 (actual). It should be emphasized that these estimates are not based on what would be required if LDCs were to grow as rapidly as feasible, given limits on physical and human resources and immediate consumption requirements. Estimates of this latter sort − taking some target growth rate for LDCs and estimating savings and foreign exchange gaps − would certainly produce much larger foreign exchange requirements. The World Bank figures are rather estimates of what they consider a feasible path, in the light of assumed developments in the world, given problems for LDCs in securing adequate finance. Even so the Bank produces very high figures for financial requirements. Yet these high figures involve slow growth in per capita incomes, especially among low-income countries.

The accuracy of these estimates, within broad limits, is rather unimportant. What is important is that very substantial financial flows will be required in the 1980s to maintain quite modest growth rates among LDCs. To achieve optimum growth would require even more substantial flows.

The last chapter concluded that a satisfactory outcome was unlikely, if the resource flows were to be left to the private sector without any additional intervention. This chapter considers various new mechanisms/institutions that have been proposed for the 1980s to add to or support the operations of the private sector. As indicated in the last chapter, the 'recycling' question raises a number of issues and this chapter concentrates on the general question of securing a sufficient quantity of financial flows. Later chapters consider other important issues, particularly that of the distribution of flows.

Types of resource flows

One needs to distinguish at the outset between aid (i.e. flows of funds on concessional terms) and commercial flows (i.e. funds generating a 'commercial' rate of return to lenders). The distribution is not to be identified with an institutional distinction in the form of financial flows. Commercial institutions may be responsible for concessional flows when they receive public guarantees or subsidies, while public institutions (e.g. IBRD) may lend on commercial or near commercial terms.

Aid

From the point of view of developing countries, perhaps the best mechanism for the transfer of resources is Official Development Assistance (ODA) which takes the form of grants or loans on highly concessional terms. But although the developed countries as a whole are currently contributing only half the target figure of 0.7 per cent of GNP to ODA, the prospects of any substantial increase in this percentage are bleak. Partly because most OECD countries are running balance of payments deficits, but mainly because tight controls on public expenditure are very widely regarded as a crucial element in anti-inflationary policies, there is little disposition in the North to increase — or in some cases even maintain — real levels of development assistance. President Reagan has announced his intention to secure a substantial reduction in real aid flows; in the UK aid fell from 0.51 per cent of GNP in 1979, to about 0.34 per cent in 1980, while other normally generous aid-givers (e.g. the Dutch) have announced that they intend to hold aid constant in real terms in the near future. However, Japanese aid is growing and is planned to increase quite substantially. In the last few years OPEC has given around $5 billion p.a. as aid. This is a much higher proportion of GNP than OECD countries. In 1979 ODA from Saudi Arabia amounted to 3.1 per cent of GNP; it was 5.1 per cent in Kuwait, 2.9 per cent in Iraq and over 5 per cent in UAE and Qatar.[3] OPEC aid amounted to 17 per cent of total ODA in 1979. None the less OPEC aid over the next decade is unlikely to alter the general picture of a rise in ODA on a scale too small to make a significant contribution to the South's need for additional resources.

It can be assumed that a massive increase in aid cannot be relied upon to secure the desired resource transfer. This is an important conclusion underlining much of the remainder of the discussion. In itself it is sufficient to make irrelevant proposals (e.g. that in the Brandt Report, discussed below), which assume a substantial increase in aid. This does not mean that aid becomes irrelevant; it may be used to finance interest subsidies and guarantee schemes, and it is one of the only sources of finance for the poorest countries. However, no scheme is likely to be viable which assumes a massive increase in aid. If this aid pessimism proves incorrect, it would be easy to generate schemes which make use of aid.

The dire prospects for low-income countries are a powerful justification for more aid. Moreover, there is some validity in Brandt commission-type arguments that a substantial increase in aid could contribute to export demand and thus increased growth in ICs and could therefore be of substantial mutual gain. It sometimes appears to be suggested that because OPEC has financial surpluses and some ICs do not, the major aid obligation falls on OPEC rather than on the ICs. This suggestion is misconceived. The obligation to transfer resources on concessional terms to meet the needs of poor countries falls on countries broadly in proportion to their wealth, as indicated by their per capita incomes, not in accordance with surpluses on the current account of countries' balance of payments.

Flows on commercial terms

Given the poor prospects for aid, it follows that the bulk of funds will have to generate some form of commercial return for the lenders. This in turn means that borrowers will need to pay commercial rates of interest, except to the extent that aid of one type or another is used as some sort of subsidy. However, as the Chart below indicates, this does not mean that there is a unique way, institutionally, in which the funds are borrowed or disbursed.

The Chart presents a rather simple view of the alternative institutional arrangements for transferring funds from surplus to deficit countries in order to provide a framework in which to consider alternative proposals.

As shown in the Chart, funds from surplus countries may go to deficit countries via the commercial sector (mainly banks) or via the international public sector. Before discussing the various alternatives, it may be helpful to make a few background comments:

1   The Chart shows how funds need to move to deal with the recycling problem — viz. the movement of funds from

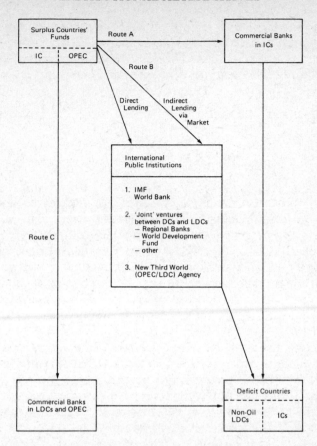

Fig. 3.1 Alternative Recycling Institutions

surplus to deficit countries. For concessional resource flows funds also move from ICs (who may be in deficit) to LDCs in deficit.

2 The choice between routes is complicated by the fact that the location of surpluses and deficits is changing over time. As shown in the last chapter, for example, in 1973–4, the surpluses were almost exclusively in OPEC countries (as they are again today) and the industrialized countries (ICs) were in deficit, as well as the non-oil LDCs. But in the course of the 1970s, the OPEC surplus was more or less eliminated,

the ICs re-established a large surplus, while the non-oil LDCs remained in deficit throughout the period. This situation may well recur in the 1980s. Thus institutions will need to have the required flexibility to deal with such changes.

3   In the seventies, the bulk of the funds went via the industrialized countries' commercial sector, as discussed in the last chapter. This is likely to be the situation in the 1980s too, but doubts about the viability and desirability of this route are behind the analysis of alternatives to be discussed below.

4   The ultimate lenders, the ultimate borrowers and the financial intermediaries all influence the route chosen. Thus part of the reason for the minimal use of the IMF in the seventies lay in LDC reluctance to ask for funds in view of the strict conditionality imposed;[4] moreover rather slow institutional response on the part of the public international institutions also limited use of this route, in contrast to the rapid and massive response of the IC commercial sector. But the ultimate lenders have much the most power of choice. In the seventies it was the fact that they placed the bulk of their funds on the market in industrialized countries that permitted the IC commercial sector to play the role it did. Potentially the surplus countries have considerable power to alter the route simply by altering their placement of funds. This power is of course much larger if the surplus is in the hands of the governments of the surplus countries, rather than in the hands of private individuals. In general, the funds are mainly in government control in OPEC countries, but to a much lesser extent when the surpluses are located in industrialized countries. While the surplus countries can change the mechanisms used for recycling by changing their distribution of funds, their ability (and even more willingness) to do so depends on the institutional alternatives before them. Thus in the seventies, they really had rather little choice because the LDC/OPEC commercial sector was undeveloped and the international public institutions had limited capacity. In the longer run, the surplus countries can help widen the alternatives by building up institutions, but in general being recently underdeveloped countries,

their capacity to build institutions is limited. Hence institution building — on the part of the developed countries, the LDCs as well as OPEC — can potentially play an important part in influencing the route funds take. This institution building is not just a matter of developing or expanding alternative institutions, but also of changing the financial instruments available in such a way as to make them more attractive from the point of view of lenders, borrowers or both.

5   The picture in the Chart is fundamentally misleading in one respect — viz. in presenting *given* surpluses to be transferred to finance *given* and equal deficits. In fact, the size of surpluses and deficits is influenced by the system of international finance, which may permit countries to finance larger (or smaller) deficits and thus generate larger or smaller surpluses. A sufficient level of finance for LDCs is one that permits them to grow as fast as they wish in the light of their absorptive capacity. For developed countries, a sufficient level of finance is one that permits them to expand demand at a level which would be considered desirable in the absence of external financial constraints.

For the most part developed countries have not been subject to financial constraints in the sense that most of them could borrow as much as they wished. But many LDCs have met financial constraints. A very important consideration in thinking about institutional alternatives is the extent to which they permit sufficient finance.

It is difficult to define precisely what would constitute 'sufficient' finance. One approach is to assess each country's growth potential in the light of its own resources and derive a 'foreign exchange' requirement as an assessment of the foreign exchange gap which would occur if the country grew at the rate dictated by its own potential, given the prospects for exports. But this implies that each country has a unique growth potential, independent of the availability of foreign resources. To the extent that foreign and local resources are substitutable, this cannot be assumed.[5] At a country level, one might establish how much foreign finance each country could use sufficiently well to generate a rate of return at least as high as commercial interest rates. If a country has more limited access to external finance than that then clearly there are deficiencies in the availability of finance.

But this — although it probably would suggest some deficiency in finance for some countries — is not all that is meant by 'insufficient' finance. Three other aspects are involved: first, at a country level, despite the difficulties of identifying growth potential independently of availability or foreign finance, there is some sense in looking at the question in this way. If countries have experienced a sustained growth in GNP per capita of say 1.8 per cent p.a. (taking the actual figures for low-income developing countries from 1960 to 1970), this would suggest — unless there is some dramatic change in their absorptive capacity — that they could maintain such a growth rate. If external developments depress this growth to below 1 per cent p.a. (as they did for this group of countries for 1970–80 and are expected to do so again for 1980–90), there is a strong presumption that the availability of external finance is constraining growth: sufficient finance, in these cases, would permit a continuation of the 1960–70 growth rates. At a country level (or even regional level), countries would find it impossible to pay commercial rates of return on the sort of level of finance defined in this way as sufficient, so one cannot blame the commercial sector for providing insufficient finance, nor look to it to provide sufficient levels of finance in the future. But the approach is none the less useful in estimating the sort of level of finance that would be approximately adequate.

In order to generate returns which would enable countries to pay commercial rates, considerable transformation of individual economies may be necessary. Such a transformation requires substantial investment as well as other changes in policy and in many cases will not occur in a situation of depressed investment and growth. Hence the second aspect of 'sufficient' finance at a country level is the provision of enough medium-term finance to enable countries to undertake the necessary structural adjustment. It is clear that many countries, especially in Africa, have not been receiving sufficient finance for medium-term adjustment and thus their prospects instead of improving actually appear to worsen over time, as indicated by the negative growth projected for Sub-Saharan Africa during the 1980s. Thirdly, there is a fallacy of composition looking at the problem of sufficient finance country-by-country. At a world level, greater finance would involve a greater growth in world markets and would thus permit each country to generate greater returns on its projects and hence improve each country's ability to service commercial debt. To assess sufficient finance at a world level involves assessing world productive potential.

The real problems of definition briefly discussed here should not prevent consideration of the very important question of the appropriate or optimal level of surpluses/ deficits and financial flows both at a world level and at the level of individual countries. In each case, an attempt needs to be made to assess surpluses/deficits and financial flows necessary to achieve what appears to be a reasonable growth rate in the light of countries' own capacities and resources and their needs. If such an exercise produces a requirement for additional finance over and above that forthcoming, this provides strong *prima facie* evidence that levels of financial flows are inadequate. This appears to be the case, for example, for Sub-Saharan Africa.

LDC financial requirements are greatly influenced by economic policies in ICs. With rapidly expanding demand among ICs, LDC export earnings increase and consequently so does their capacity to import, for any given flow of external finance. With a lower level of demand for exports from ICs, LDCs need more finance to permit the same rate of growth of imports. Since LDC total overall growth potential is broadly constrained by the rate of growth of their imports, their need for external finance is greater the lower growth in ICs. This is the opposite combination of developments from that shown in the World Bank projections, where higher growth among ICs is associated with higher financial flows to LDCs. This contradiction is explained by the fact that with lower growth in export earnings, which follows from lower growth among ICs, LDC capacity to service debt and therefore to borrow is reduced. While the

World Bank projections are therefore realistic, they clearly reveal the deficiencies of the financial system which offers *more* finance when it is *less* needed. The same is true for individual countries: those whose export prospects are weakest, and therefore whose need for external finance is greatest, get least finance.

6   In the short run, certainly, and in the long run, probably, the choice is a matter of *balance*, i.e. of changing the proportions of funds which move in one route compared to another, rather than making exclusive use of a particular route. For example, it is extremely unlikely over the next ten years that the route via the commercial sector in ICs would or should be completely eliminated and replaced by a single new public institution. A variety of channels is desirable both from the point of view of the lenders and the borrowers. The lenders require diversification of their portfolio in order to spread risks. The borrowers benefit from diversity too, so that they are not entirely dependent on the decision of a single institution. Moreover, specialized institutions can better cater to specific needs.

7   Institutional changes and interventions of various sorts are partly directed towards changing the route, partly to changing the effects of use of a particular route, e.g. changing the way in which the commercial sector distributes funds.

8   There is a complex question of *additionality* which is related to the previous comments. On the one hand, it is likely that new institutional channels may displace existing channels, e.g. funds available on the market may go to international public institutions rather than the commercial sector, or the placement of commercial funds may be altered away from IC institutions to LDC/OPEC institutions. On the other hand, as pointed out in 5 above, it is wrong to assume a given level of surpluses/deficits. New institutions can add to the total financial flows in the world economy. In any particular case, it is extremely difficult to assess the likely displacement as against additionality. However, additionality is more likely (i) the greater returns (in level and security) offered to lenders and therefore the more likely they are to

find maintaining a surplus attractive. However, some analyses[6] suggest that the OPEC surplus countries do not have all that much control over the size of their surpluses, and in any case do not determine its size on purely economic grounds, so this argument may be overplayed; and (ii) the more the finance available to deficit countries permits them to operate their economies at a high level of demand and to maintain long run deficits.

Existing institutions may not be capable of dealing with a substantial expansion in activities. Consequently, in a dynamic setting, when significant potential growth occurs in lending and borrowing, the potential increase may not be realized without institutional change. In this sort of situation — which many think to be an accurate representation of the 1980s — new institutions are likely to create additional flows, where these are defined as flows over and above what would have occurred without institutional innovation.

Proposals for change

The starting point of all proposals is that continued near-exclusive reliance on the IC commercial sector, as in the seventies, is unsatisfactory for the sort of reasons discussed in the last chapter, viz.

(a) the level was inadequate;
(b) the distribution among LDCs was unsatisfactory;
(c) it led to potential instability in the world financial system;
(d) the real return on financial assets for surplus countries was low, often negative;
(e) there is some feeling, strong among LDCs and more qualified in OPEC, of dislike for so much of the surplus going through IC dominated institutions.

Not all proposals are directed at all of these issues. It is helpful to distinguish between proposals for new (or expanded) institutions, and those for new financial instruments, although in practice many of the proposals embody both. This chapter considers alternative institutions; the next chapter, new financial instruments.

Institutional proposals

An expanded role for the IMF?

In the 1970s, the IMF made a very small direct contribution to net financial resource flow in comparison with the magnitude of the problem:

Table 3.1 ($ billion)

	1973	1974	1975	1976	1977	1978	1979	1980
Non-Oil Developing Countries current a/c deficit	11.3	36.9	45.8	32.1	28.0	36.2	54.9	68.0
Net use of Fund credit + short-term borrowing by monetary authorities from other monetary authorities	0.3	1.6	2.4	4.3	0.5	0.7	0.7	1.6

Source: World Economic Outlook, IMF, 1980, Table 19.

Various new facilities were introduced during the 1970s. These included the Oil Facility to assist countries in paying for the increase in the price of oil. This facility only lasted a short period. The Extended Fund Facility (EFF), was also introduced in 1974, and was a medium-term financial facility. The additional facilities were too small in magnitude to make an adequate contribution to the finance of LDC deficits. Moreover, the EFF was subject to strict conditionality.

One mechanism which has been proposed for transferring resources is the establishment of a Medium-Term Facility in the IMF.[7] Such a facility would enable developing countries to adjust more gradually than is permitted under present Fund procedures to structural balance of payments problems which have arisen through factors outside their control, and thus avoid or minimize cuts in imports which would adversely affect both their own development programme and the course of world trade. Drawings on the new facility would be on first credit tranche conditions[8] (as was the case with the Oil Facility): countries would be required to make reasonable efforts to solve their structural balance of payments problem in a way that did not disrupt their development programme. Repayments of drawings would not need to be completed until 10 years after the date of the first drawing; and the interest rate on drawings charged to poorer borrowers could be subsidized, perhaps from a special account subscribed to by high-income members of the Fund, or out of the proceeds of further gold sales by the Fund.

The proposed new facility has a number of advantages: it represents a realistic response to the fact that many developing countries suffer from structural imbalances which need to be adjusted to more gradually than is permitted under traditional Fund procedures and it would have different and less deflationary conditionality than the Extended Fund Facility; it is technically feasible; and it could be brought into operation fairly quickly. But there are some problems. Developed countries may not see the need for such a low conditionality facility, particularly now that repayments under the Extended Fund Facility can be made over a period of up to 10 years, and now that the World Bank is beginning to move into the field of structural adjustment programmes. Some developing countries may be less in favour of a new facility made available through the Fund – which they see as dominated by developed countries – than of one made available through some new institution in which they have a more equitable share of the decision-making. Another aspect to be considered, in the context of a substantial transfer of resources, is the revolving nature of the new facility requiring repayments of principal to be completed within 10 years. Finally, there is the question of how the concessional element in the facility would be financed, which of course applies to any proposal involving concessional elements.

Recent developments in the operation of the IMF have gone some way to meeting the demands for a Medium-Term Facility. Quotas have been increased by 50 per cent, while the limit on loans has been increased to 650 per cent (of old quotas) or 450 per cent of new quotas.[9] The repayment period has been extended to 3 years. The conditions on which IMF loans are extended have been changed somewhat and supply conditions are included as well as demand (see Chapter 6). There is also a plan to charge lower interest to low-income countries on the Supplementary Financing Facility. These changes should increase the contribution the IMF makes to the flow of financial resources. In order to meet its new commitments, the Fund is proposing to borrow from $6 to $7 billion in 1981, either directly from surplus countries, and/or indirectly via the market. However, although this represents a very large increase in relation to performance in the 1970s, it is not so large in relation to the anticipated LDC deficit. The Fund might contribute at most about 10 per cent to a deficit of around $70 billion in 1981, but after that, unless there is a dramatic change in the Fund's role, its *net* contribution will necessarily diminish.

As it has developed historically, the Fund represents essentially a *temporary* financing facility, providing funds while countries adjust to a new situation and eliminate their deficits. The definition of temporary has been extended and countries given more time to adjust. But the time horizon of the Fund is still shorter than the time many LDCs feel is necessary to achieve structural adjustment. Hence the demand for a Medium-Term Facility.

Apart from its direct contribution, it is widely believed that the Fund could (and to some extent does) play a substantial indirect role by providing encouragement to the private sector to lend funds to countries with whom it has arrangements, operating, in a very informal way, a type of indirect guarantee mechanism. However, as noted earlier, developments do not always work that way and sometimes a Fund agreement can become an occasion to withdraw funds (as in Turkey). At other times, it certainly acts as a signal for private sector involvement (Jamaica). There is some evidence for 1971-9, of a positive correlation between drawings on the Fund and borrowing for the Eurocurrency markets for developing countries as a whole.[10]

To make sure of the indirect mechanism via the private sector would require more formal agreement between the Fund and the private banks than occurs at present. But that sort of arrangement would give the Fund power disproportionate to its own resources, which might limit the freedom of manoeuvre for many countries. This would certainly be the attitude of countries like Brazil who have been successful in attracting private funds without Fund arrangements. Other countries might welcome some objective assessment of their prospects to help inform others, such as private banks, whose assessments tend to be based on rather limited information. But differences in general philosophy between the Fund and many LDCs (discussed in Chapter Six) mean that the Fund assessment is generally not regarded as fulfilling this function adequately.

The World Bank

While the Fund expertise lies in short-term balance of payments management, the Bank's project and country specialism would seem to make it a better vehicle for medium- to long-run financial transfers.

A number of proposals have been made which involve cooperation between ICs and OPEC in order to secure a sizeable movement of funds to LDCs, using the World Bank as the administrative vehicle of the transfer. The Venezuelan proposal, the Mexican proposal and the OECD/DAC proposals are all of this type. Each involves the World Bank and associated institutions borrowing very substantial sums from the ICs and OPEC (generally on the market, rather than directly from governments) and relending to LDCs. In each proposal ICs or OPEC or the World Bank provide some sort of guarantee, thus making the proposal attractive to lenders, but at the same time involving a cost to the guaranteeing institution which might be at the expense of other forms of financing.

Venezuelan proposal:[11] The aim would be to transfer something like $16–20 billion a year, for five or ten years, from OECD and OPEC countries to developing countries. The funds would be made available on a long-term basis, varying from 12 to 20 years. Funds would be raised in two different ways. Of the total, something like 75 per cent would be raised by selling 'OPEC Development Bonds' in international capital markets; OPEC countries themselves would agree to purchase a quarter or so of these bonds, and would act as 'first guarantor' of the bonds taken up by private investors. The remaining 25 per cent of the money would be subscribed by developed countries, out of existing or increased aid allocations. In consequence, a quarter or so of the total funds could be channelled to basic needs projects in the least developed countries on concessional terms; the remainder would be lent at market rates, but at a 12–20 year maturity, to bankable projects in other developing countries. In both cases, funds would be disbursed through the World Bank family.

Mexican proposal:[12] The Mexican proposal is rather similar to the Venezuelan proposal. Its main objective is to match the excess capacity in the capital goods industries of developed countries with the need for investment goods among LDCs. It was proposed to establish a fund of $15 billion, to be disbursed over a three to five year period in the form of loans with a maturity of 15 years or so. The fund would be financed by the issue of 15-year bonds on the international capital markets, and these bonds would be guaranteed by the governments of developed (and perhaps some developing) countries. The incentive to governments either to subscribe to the bond issue themselves or to guarantee the value of bonds taken up by private institutions would be that the loans made to finance projects or sector programmes in developing countries could only be used to purchase capital goods from other developing countries or from developed countries whose governments had contributed to the bond issue. Thus the presumption is that the prospect of additional output and employment in their capital goods industries would persuade these governments to provide guarantees, particularly since loans would only be made on projects which the World Bank or other managing institution expected to yield an acceptable rate of return, thus rendering remote the likelihood of guarantees actually being called on.

OECD/DAC proposal:[13] Like the Venezuelan and Mexican proposals, the essence of this scheme is to increase the flow of non-concessional private capital to developing countries by providing it with a form of guarantee. In this case the focus would be on the private international banks, which would be encouraged to expand their loans to developing countries by associating such loans with World Bank lending under an extended provision of 'co-financing'. The security of private funds lent to developing countries through this mechanism would be enhanced by the 'cross-default' provisions, which would stipulate that defaulting on the private element in the package would be deemed a default on the World Bank component as well, with the serious consequences for the defaulting country which that would entail. Loans would be made on commercial terms to projects in developing countries which promised an acceptable rate of return.

All three proposals have rather similar advantages and weaknesses; the major advantage is to secure a substantial flow of funds to LDCs on a systematic basis. Each is technically feasible. But in so far as the schemes require commercial returns (which is their main element), they are liable to involve a distribution biased in favour of middle-income countries as with existing commercial lending; to the extent that they involve subsidized elements for concessional finance for low-income countries, there is no guarantee that finance of this concessionality will be additional to existing aid flows. The proposed guarantees may also be at the expense of other lending and aid. Moreover, the lending on commercial terms may not itself be additional but may consist of a diversion of existing bank commercial lending to LDCs. None the less, the distribution of flows under these schemes, the terms on which the flows occur and the projects to which they go, are likely to be an improvement compared with private bank lending, while some additionality in flows should occur. Probably the most significant problem is that there appears to be little support for any of the schemes from either OPEC or the ICs, so that although they have been around in international negotiations for some time none of the schemes has got anywhere operationally.[14]

Current developments in the World Bank indicate some of the difficulties of using the World Bank as a vehicle for massive resource transfer. Between 1977 and 1980, average lending of the World Bank (including IDA) was $9.25 billion. Lending is expected to rise to $15 billion by 1985, as a result of the doubling of the capital contribution.[15]

A change in the gearing ratio of the World Bank from its excessively cautious 1:1 to, for example, 1:4 would permit rather painless expansion, but at this stage it seems likely that the developed countries (who have 65 per cent of the votes on the Board of Directors) are likely to veto any such change. The Bank is limited in any role of guarantor because under its constitution a guarantee is counted against its lending capacity. The World Bank would be a potentially convenient institution for massive resource transfer if the ICs, which dominate it, wanted such a transfer. But while they are in a deflationist and ultra-cautious mood, a good deal of the resource transfer will have to go through other institutions. There are other problems about using the World Bank. The Bank's expertise is in project finance. But the balance of payments deficit of LDCs calls for programme finance rather than project finance. The Bank has moved into this area in a small way, with structural adjustment loans. But so far in most cases rather stringent conditions have been exacted and few countries have been granted such loans. Expansion of the World Bank via the increased capital subscription and perhaps some change in the gearing ratio will make some contribution to the transfer of resources. But it is unlikely, with its present constitution and directors, to play the sort of role envisaged in the proposals just discussed.

The domination of the developed countries in the constitutions and bureaucracies of the World Bank and IMF represent both an advantage and a defect in the current world situation. The rather cautious and conservative attitude that IC domination secures makes these institutions appear to be a very safe vehicle for resource transfer and therefore attractive to lenders, including OPEC. Yet their power structure does not reflect the new distribution of financial power, while it is in direct conflict with NIEO claims for more power for the Third World. Moreover, industrialized country caution about expansionary resource transfers limits the potential of institutions which they control in providing a vehicle for the required transfers.

Thus while there is a case for expansion of transfer via these institutions, there is a strong case for exploring other institutional mechanisms, particularly those in which OPEC and the Third World more fully participate. Greater participation by the Third World in financial institutions may not change the way these institutions operate. But it is likely to make their activities (e.g. conditionality) more acceptable to the countries concerned.

Energy affiliate: this was proposed as an affiliate institution to the World Bank, which would involve a substantial flow of resources (total lending of up to $30 million was proposed) for energy projects in the Third World. As an affiliate, it would avoid some of the rigidities imposed by the World Bank constitution. It was intended to have a different voting structure with a greater representation for OPEC and the LDCs (one-third, one-third, one-third was envisaged for ICs, OPEC and LDCs).[16] The negative attitude of the US administration has prevented this proposal coming to anything, at least for the moment. At recent discussions, some OPEC countries have also been critical of the proposal. While the actual proposal may not come to anything, the idea contained interesting possibilities which could be revived in future proposals. First, the concept of an affiliate relationship permits use to be made of the World Bank's prestige in financial markets and expertise without constraining the institution as much as would be the case if it were fully part of the Bank. Secondly, more equal participation by each of the major groups avoids the problems related to near complete domination by the developed countries or those that might arise with an institution which had no IC participation. Thirdly, there is clearly a role for institutions with sectoral specialism.

The Regional Banks

There has been a marked difference in the role of the different Regional Banks. The Inter-American Development Bank has been the most significant source of funds, then the Asian Development Bank, while the Arab and African Banks have played a rather small part in quantitative terms.

The experience of the various Regional Banks has been very different and they have differing degrees of potential for expansion. The Inter-American Bank has been by far the most successful: it is long-established, able to borrow substantial amounts of finance and it is controlled by the

Table 3.2

	Capital, end 1980 ($ b.)
Inter-American Development Bank	15.1*
Asian Development Bank	9.5**
Arab Bank for Ec. Dev. in Africa	0.7
African Dev. Bank	1.6**
TOTAL	26.9
World Bank	40.0***

*Future commitments will raise this to $19.6 billion.
**1979
***1980 — to be doubled to $80 billion in 1981.

Table 3.3   Disbursements ($b.)

	Starting date	Cumulative to end 1980	Disbursements in 1980
Inter-American	1959	10.5	1.4
Asian	1966	2.5*	0.5*
Arab	1973	0.2	0.05
African**	1964	0.6*	0.2*
TOTAL		13.8	2.15
World Bank	1945	80.0	5.8

*1979.
**Includes African Development Fund.

developing countries of the region. The agreed expansion of
its capital resources will allow it to make a major contribution to the needs of the region. The Asian Development
Bank has the potential to increase lending and borrowing if
the member countries and in particular Japan consent. The
African Bank has been least successful, being constrained by

political and administrative difficulties and unable to speed up the disbursement of funds in project lending. The African Bank has not yet attempted to borrow in international markets and maintains a low gearing ratio. The Arab Bank is more of an aid agency than a development bank, receiving funds directly from members rather than borrowing and a large part of disbursements involve a high concessional element.

In principle, the Regional Banks are joint ventures or cooperatives, giving an important (sometimes majority) decision-making role to the net recipient LDCs in the region. In the Inter-American Development Bank, for example, the regional developing countries have 56.2 per cent of the votes.

Some of the Banks have gone in for a wide variety of schemes such as co-financing (with other public or private institutions) and supervised credit (in which the Bank prepares the project and seeks outside finance) which increases the leverage of Bank resources.[17]

Expansion of the Regional Banks could be one significant element in the system of resource transfers. The advantage is that they are less dominated by the industrialized countries and have greater LDC participation. Clearly, this is a more feasible path in the case of the Inter-American Bank than in the weaker institutions, where 'institution building' will need to precede expansion. A doubling of current disbursements would mean an annual flow of over $4 billion, which would represent a significant contribution to the transfer of resources. Such an increase might need to be accompanied by a move towards programme finance for part of the disbursements.

A World Development Fund

The Brandt Commission pinpointed the case for a new institution: 'What is needed essentially is a bridge between the long-term project financing available from such institutions as the World Bank and the short-term adjustment finance available from the IMF'.[18] The solution it proposed was an institution that 'might be called a World Development Fund'. It would have universal membership, and would thus offer an opportunity for developed and developing countries to cooperate on a basis of more equal partnership. The main thrust of the new organization would be in the direction of programme lending, including support for measures to increase trade among developing countries, to undertake exploration for minerals, etc. So far from competing with the World Bank and the IMF, it would 'complement and complete the existing structure'.[19] Its long-term programme lending would help the disbursement of World Bank lending held up by the shortage of domestic resources, and could also help to keep countries from reaching the kind of crisis situation in which they have to go to the IMF for balance of payments adjustment finance. Many of the new Fund's operations would involve co-financing arrangements with the World Bank and the Regional Development Banks, and the bulk of its lending would go through regional and sub-regional institutions.

The crucial point about the World Development Fund, as envisaged by the Brandt Commission, is that the great bulk of its resources would come from government contributions, and not from private institutions seeking a market rate of return on their investment. It was envisaged that these contributions would flow from a rapid move towards the 0.7 per cent target for ODA by all those countries committed to it, and an increase in the target to 1 per cent of GNP by the year 2000; and, more generally, by the introduction of 'automatic mechanisms' which would yield revenue from a wide range of countries on a basis which took progressive account of their wealth. A levy on international trade with built-in adjustments to ensure that its incidence was equitable in relation to different countries' GNP would be one possible way of putting this idea into practice.

With this method of financing the World Development Fund, the predominance in its operation of long-term programme lending makes good sense. It would be relieved of the need — imposed on the World Bank by the requirements of the private investors who provide much of its funds[20] — to concentrate on projects which yielded a commercially acceptable rate of return. It would also be relieved of the need — imposed on the IMF by the traditionally short time horizon within which it operates — to provide programme assistance only on strict conditions which promise a speedy return to balance of payments equilibrium. It should, in fact, be able to fill the role allotted it — that of bridging the gap between long-term Bank project financing and short-term IMF programme financing.

The success of a World Development Fund would depend on the willingness of Northern and OPEC countries to provide official development assistance, in one form or another, on a much larger scale than at present. Without such willingness, the World Development Fund as envisaged would be stillborn. In this event, one would be forced to accept that any substantial financial resource flow to the South would depend on satisfying investors in the North and OPEC that their money was being lent on terms that promised a secure and commercially acceptable rate of return.

If we assume that ODA is unlikely to be a substantial source of resources, then the World Development Fund would have to be rather different than that envisaged by Brandt, since it would need to generate a commercial return on its activities. But there could still be a role for such an institution which would operate largely on commercial terms, but would provide medium-term finance, mainly on a programme basis, thus filling the gap identified by the Brandt Commission.

Other New 'World' Agencies

Various other proposals have been made to develop new institutions to contribute towards recycling, which are in the nature of joint ventures between DCs, LDCs and OPEC, rather than dominated by any one party. One example is that proposed by UNIDO, 'A Global Fund for the Stimulation of Industry'.[21] This Fund would be a financial intermediary in the market for channelling funds to industrial development in the developing countries. The capital base would consist of capital subscriptions by members, only a small proportion of which would be called-up. It is proposed that the voting structure should be roughly equal for each of the three major parties — ICs, LDCs and OPEC. An interest subsidy element is proposed for up to 25 per cent of the lending for the least developed countries. It is

proposed that this subsidy might be financed by IC government subscriptions.

The Case for a Third World Development Agency

One of the most promising proposals is that of Algeria and
Venezuela for a new institution, a Third World Development
Agency, based on the OPEC Special Fund (now OPEC
Fund for International Development) created in 1976.[22] It
would recycle OPEC surpluses *directly* to the Third World.
It could mobilize the international capital market to channel
more funds to the LDCs. It could make some contribution
to neutralizing the harmful effects of the oil-price increase
on poorer LDCs by providing grants and subsidies, in a
coordinated way. It could assist the energy development
programmes in LDCs and generate real investment opportunities for OPEC in joint ventures with LDCs. Through these
and other measures, it would strengthen the solidarity of the
LDCs. It might also help to strengthen the South in a North–
South negotiation.

The underlying rationale of the new Agency as envisaged
in the Algerian–Venezuelan proposal 'would be its ability
to strengthen the solidarity of OPEC countries and other
developing countries by *pooling their credit capacities* for
the benefit of all developing countries'.[23] More specifically,
it would 'provide funds for general development projects —
particularly those projects likely to promote trade amongst
developing countries and lessen their dependence on imported
energy'. Funds would be provided on both concessional
and non-concessional terms: 'the conditions of financing
should be suited to the general economic situation of each
country, its degree of dependency on imported energy, and
the situation of its balance of payments', and for the promotion of certain projects, 'specially adapted terms will be
given to those countries which are worst affected or least
developed'.

It is proposed that the authorized capital of the Agency
would be $20 billion, though this amount could be increased
from time to time. Half this capital ($10 billion) would be
paid in, and the other half would be callable. On the basis of
the implicit guarantees represented by this paid-in and

callable capital, bonds would be issued in international capital markets at commercial rates of interest, though it is envisaged that initially a significant proportion of the bond issue would be taken up by the OPEC countries themselves.

The strength of the Algerian–Venezuelan proposal lies in the fact that OPEC unquestionably has the resources to subscribe to the Agency on the scale contemplated; that such paid-in and callable capital subscriptions should act as a sufficient guarantee for additional private sector capital, possibly on a substantial scale, to be invested in the Agency's bonds; and that explicit provision is made for the subsidization of the interest rates charged to developing countries in appropriate cases. Detailed features of the mechanism, however, need to be worked out and agreed on: how the capital subscriptions are to be allocated between OPEC members, what proportion of the subscribed capital should be used for subsidies, what degree of subsidy should apply to which categories of projects and countries, etc. In addition to callable capital, it might be necessary to have joint and several guarantees by the subscribing countries to raise capital on the market. In principle, however, it seems clear that given an OPEC commitment to it, the proposed mechanism is eminently viable, and could promote a significant increase in the volume of resources transferred to non-oil developing countries. The hope of its sponsors that the new body would strengthen the solidarity of Third World countries might well be realized, since from the start it would be set up, financed and operated by Third World countries themselves — unlike the IMF and World Bank, which were set up, and are still dominated by, a handful of developed countries. It would be concerned entirely with the problems of Third World development and for the sake of its own viability would seek out genuine investment opportunities producing real and sustained growth in those countries, and not just short-term adjustment. At the same time, it would be a mistake to exaggerate the say, which borrowers, rather than lenders, are likely to have in the lending policies and conditions of the proposed Agency, even if both groups do belong to the Third World. In the functions allotted to the Agency, the interest of the lenders has to be fully taken into account, while borrowers will have to ensure repayment by adopting measures to generate resources and secure foreign exchange.

In order that the Agency becomes a genuine Third World Development Agency, and not only an extension of the OPEC Fund, it should be possible to broaden the scope of this Agency beyond that suggested in the Algerian–Venezuelan proposal.

First, its capital subscription could be open to non-OPEC countries also. If the concessional element in its operation is not too great, several middle-income LDCs may find subscribing to its capital attractive. Non-OPEC LDCs could be given the option of subscribing less to paid-in capital and more to callable capital. This would increase their contingent liability without detracting much from their current foreign exchange resources. The formula for calling their capital, when necessary, could be determined so far as not to impose too great a burden at a time of severe foreign exchange shortage. It should of course be realized that too great an emphasis on callable capital in relation to paid-in capital may reduce the credibility of this Agency in the market. On the other hand, diversifying the number of countries subscribing to and guaranteeing its capital reduces the risk of default. In this way the capital base of the Agency could be significantly expanded, and it should be able to raise substantially more funds in the international capital markets on the basis of the implicit guarantees. Participation of a number of non-oil LDCs would increase their stake in the Agency, and would make it easier for the Agency to impose conditionality on the borrowers, which may be necessary to protect the lenders' interests.

Secondly, the Agency could support joint ventures among a number of LDCs. Since OPEC countries are mainly dependent on a single exhaustible resource, they are looking for investment opportunities in other kinds of real asset to provide security of supply of some of their basic requirements. Accordingly, several projects involving product-sharing in agriculture, or minerals and metals, have been worked out between LDCs and OPEC. There is scope for similar activities, extended to trade, manufacturing and commerce, where LDCs and OPEC countries can participate in investment, production marketing and buying arrangements. To the extent that the Agency promotes this kind of activity, it will ensure a real rate of return on OPEC investments, allowing the OPEC countries to convert their ownership of a single exhaustible real asset into command over a number of real resources, while benefiting the LDCs by expanding their investment and production.

Thirdly, the Agency might promote collective self-reliance among LDCs more directly as an instrument of power or leverage in North–South relations to extract more concessions from the Northern industrialized countries. It would be similar to what President Nyerere has described as the 'Strike Fund' of the Third World countries. In many cases of financial arrangements, mineral exploration or industrial expansion, LDCs have to accept highly unequal terms from multinational corporations dominating these fields because of a lack of alternative competitive sources of finance. The Agency, by providing a readily available alternative source, may help to improve these terms in favour of the LDCs. In areas such as commodity arrangements, the Common Fund and producers' associations, financial support from this Agency could also strengthen the bargaining power of the LDCs. In addition, the Agency may support monetary arrangements among LDCs, as described in Chapter Nine of this Report. All these would strengthen the instruments of South–South cooperation and trade, helping LDCs to protect themselves from the unequal relationships of international trade between developed and developing countries.

Whether or not this Agency could be expanded in its scope, participation and operation, along the lines suggested, will ultimately depend on the importance that the OPEC countries attach to the solidarity of the Third World. But even if conceived on a more limited scale, the Fund could play an important role in recycling funds to the non-oil LDCs.

The viability of this Agency, and its attractiveness to its capital subscribers among LDCs, including the OPEC countries, would of course improve if its operations are run commercially yielding a competitive financial return. But in many cases low-income countries and the poorer of the middle-income countries need loans on concessional terms. If strengthening the solidarity of the LDCs is one of the aims of this Agency, it cannot ignore the interests of the poorer LDCs. It would be necessary for the Agency to strike a balance between its concessional and non-concessional activities, so that the interests of the maximum number of LDCs can be served, without making it financially unviable.

The main difficulty in expanding concessional operations is the need for concessional funds. Periodic replenishment of the Agency's concessional funds might come from the OPEC countries, whose development assistance as a percentage of GNP is much greater than that of the developed countries. If this percentage remains at its present level, the volume of development assistance from OPEC countries will grow quite significantly. If some proportion of the development assistance funds from OPEC is channelled through the Agency, it would ensure its ability to provide concessional funds to poorer LDCs.

The OPEC countries have often argued that the responsibility for helping the poor countries should be borne mainly by the developed industrialized countries, since the OPEC countries themselves are developing countries and their current surplus funds are temporary and will disappear when oil resources are exhausted unless they can build up other assets and modernize their economies. To this is often added the somewhat political argument that the underdevelopment of the LDCs is due to the inequities in the international economy, perpetuated by the policies of the developed countries, and therefore should be eradicated mainly by assistance from the developed countries. Such arguments would have a much greater appeal if the OPEC countries undertook the responsibility of redressing the difficulties created by the rise in oil prices for the LDCs, at least for the low and middle-income countries.[24] The World Bank estimates that the cost of net oil imports of the low-income countries will be $6 billion in 1985 rising to $11.1 billion in 1990, as against $3.3 billion in 1980.

A number of problems would arise in setting up and operating the new Agency. Some of these, such as the need to recruit or train staff qualified in project appraisal etc., would merely be a matter of time. Others raise more fundamental issues which require balancing the requirements of operational convenience and financial viability and its ability to serve its main objectives. How far, for example, would the Agency concentrate its lending on identifiable projects which promised a satisfactory rate of return, and how far on satisfying the more general needs of non-oil developing countries, such as support for measures reinforcing regional integration, expenditure on broad measures of social development, or the financing of balance of payments deficits? It may be argued that the greater the emphasis on programme lending, the greater the need to avoid competing with the World Bank for viable projects whose total number may prove difficult to expand at the rate necessary to absorb the sums available, If, however, the main emphasis is to be on long-term programme lending, the same question arises as in the case of a major expansion of programme lending by the World Bank: what conditions are to be applied and what performance indicators are to be monitored? Tight conditions will reduce the ability of many developing countries to benefit from the activities of the new Agency. Loose conditions, on the other hand, may damage the credibility of the Agency's bonds, and significantly reduce the amounts of capital it can raise.

This dilemma should not prove insoluble, and should be easier to solve the greater is the amount of concessional funds that OPEC countries are willing to make available to the new Agency. Thus in the ultimate analysis the effectiveness of the new Agency is likely to depend on the commitment and generosity of its OPEC subscribers.

Joint Investment Fund among Gulf States: Six Gulf States[25] are planning to launch a joint investment fund with capital of between $3 billion and $6 billion to concentrate on investments in projects in developing countries.[26] The fund is to be set up under the aegis of the Gulf Cooperation Council. The investments are intended to be on commercial terms. This Fund could provide the initial basis for a Third World Development Agency.

LDC/OPEC Banks

The third alternative route is to make greater use of commercial banks in OPEC and LDCs. In the early 1970s this sector was almost non-existent, but during the past decade it has grown very rapidly, especially the Arab banking sector. The first large banks with major Arab participation consisted of consortia which made use of Western financial knowhow and management. For example, the Union des Banques Arabes et Françaises (UBAF), which has an asset base of $6 billion, La Banque Arabe Internationale d'Investissement — owned 50 per cent by an Arab holding company and 30 per cent by the Credit Lyonnais — has an asset base of $1 to $5 billion. These banks are as large as the two smaller Regional Banks, and are expanding fast. UBAF's net income tripled in 1979. The consortia are an intermediate stage. More recently Third World international commercial banks have developed. The Gulf International, established in 1977 was the first completely Arab owned international bank. In 1980 it became one of the fifty largest managers of syndicated loans on the Euromarket. In 1980 the Arab Banking Corporation was established. Arlabank, established in 1978, is a Third World commercial bank with 60 per cent Arab shareholding and the rest Latin American. In 1979, it approved loans of $2.3 billion. While most of the Arab banks tend to specialize in moving funds within the region (e.g. with loans to Jordan and Morocco by the Arab Banking Corporation), increasingly loans are made to other Third World countries. Gulf International's customers include Nigeria, S. Korea, the Ivory Coast and Brazil. Arlabank lends heavily to Latin America.[27] Joint ventures between banking or investment companies and individual LDCs provide a vehicle whereby the financing institution can acquire some equity interest in LDC productive ventures, while sharing the risk with the LDC. Such joint activities are becoming increasingly common, offering a source of risk capital to LDCs and a potentially attractive use of funds to OPEC countries.

These developments are expanding very rapidly and will account for a growing proportion of recycling during the

1980s. Collaboration between commercial institutions and public ventures such as the Regional Banks and the proposed Third World Development Agency in co-financing may reduce the risk to the lenders while increasing access to finance among borrowers. The total magnitude of direct commercial recycling from OPEC to non-oil LDCs could expand to a scale similar to the activities of the regional banks.

Some conclusions on institutional alternatives

The dominance of the IC commercial banks in recycling in the last decade was partly a reflection of the lack of institutional alternatives; the other routes were incapable of doing more than a limited amount. The commercial sector in the LDCs was undeveloped; the IMF, the World Bank and the Regional Banks responded slowly and were only able to transfer a small amount of the total funds. For the eighties, the institutional alternatives are already greater; the commercial sector in OPEC/LDCs has developed; the IMF, the World Bank and the Regional Banks all have already expanded their recycling capacity considerably and are planning for further expansion. Changes already underway in the major international institutions are going to increase their capacity to transfer resources considerably; the IMF contribution may rise to $3–4 billion per annum in the period 1980–5; the World Bank's net disbursements to around $7–8 billion;[28] the Regional Banks to $3–4 billion, or a total of around $13–15 billion (i.e. nearly one-fifth of total non-oil LDC balance of payments requirements). Together with bilateral aid, the total *public* transfers might come to around 40 per cent of the total LDC deficit estimated by the World Bank for the 'High' case.[29] *This still leaves over half of the recycling to be handled by the commercial sector.*

There is a strong case for further institutional innovation. There are problems — discussed in the last chapter — about over-reliance on the commercial sector. Moreover, political objection has been voiced to permitting the funds originating in OPEC to be distributed almost exclusively by institutions dominated by the ICs. Further expansions of the World Bank and IMF would be one possibility; but while planned expansion in these institutions is obviously useful, they remain largely IC dominated and their existing structure makes them unsuited to play a very much larger role; in the case of the IMF this is because programmes are largely conceived as short term and temporary balance of payments support; in the World Bank project finance dominates. Thus there remains a medium-term financial gap, as noted by the Brandt Report.[30] Expansion of the Regional Banks (over and above that already envisaged) could make a significant (although limited) contribution to the recycling required. But although they are much more 'joint ventures' with the Third World than the World Bank, their finance, like that of the World Bank, is largely project oriented. Even with a quite large expansion of the Regional Banks, there would still be a case for new global institutions. As noted above, these could be of two types; a new institution (e.g. the Brandt Commission World Development Fund or the proposed energy affiliate) with equal participation of the ICs, OPEC and the Third World; or a new Third World Institution such as the proposed Third World Development Agency, which consists of a partnership between OPEC and the non-oil LDCs.

The choice between these two is largely for OPEC surplus countries to make. With a sufficient commitment of Funds they are in a position to make or break any proposal. The proposal for a Third World Development Agency is obviously attractive from the point of view of Third World solidarity. But so far, despite talk, it seems that OPEC likes to have IC participation or even dominance in the investment of the bulk of their funds, so as to ensure their security. But while they may gain financial security from this, they lose power. In the first chapter an institutional lag was noted between the acquisition of financial power by OPEC and institutions to permit them to recycle directly as the ICs did in the past. Initially this institutional lag was the natural result of the sudden development of financial surpluses among previously undeveloped countries. But now, as proposals for new institutions abound, it is more a matter of decision for OPEC countries. In large part the institutional lag could be eliminated if OPEC made a commitment to support a new institution.

There is a strong case for encouraging the development of a multiplicity of institutions, expansions of the existing institutions as well as the development of new ones. This prevents domination by one or two institutions and permits flexibility of response, necessary in a changing world.

Notes

1 This chapter draws heavily on the background paper prepared by Michael Stewart.

2 *World Development Report*, 1980, World Bank, p. 6. *World Development Report*, 1981 states that 'The High case reflects the view that the industrial countries will be relatively successful in meeting these challenges' [i.e. in making structural adjustments to boost productivity growth, economize on energy and stimulate its production and to 'find some way of containing inflation while growing fast enough to reduce unemployment'.].

3 *Development Co-operation*, 1980 Review, OECD, p. 127.

4 Quite a number of LDCs did not even make use of low-conditionality IMF facilities in the 1970s. See G. Bird, 'The IMF and the Developing Countries: Evolving Relations, Use of Resources and The Debate over Conditionality', ODI Working Paper No. 2, March 1981.

5 See V. Joshi, 'Saving and Foreign Exchange Constraints', in P. Streeten (ed.), *Unfashionable Economics: Essays in Honour of Thomas Balogh*, Weidenfeld and Nicholson, 1970.

6 See e.g. R. Mabro, Background Paper.

7 See S. Dell and R. Lawrence, *The Balance of Payments Adjustment Process in Developing Countries*, Pergamon, 1980, p. 138, and 'Outline for a Program of Action on International Monetary Reform', Group of Twenty-Four, September 1979, item C, p. 10.

8 The first credit tranche corresponds to the first 25 per cent of a country's quota, beyond the gold tranche and is available after discussions with the country, with few conditions attached.

9 There is some lack of clarity about the present limits; some argue that the limit is 650 per cent, but elsewhere the figure of 450 per cent is used.

10 See G. Bird and T. Orme, 'An Analysis of Drawings on the International Monetary Fund by Developing Countries', *World Development*, forthcoming.

11   This proposal was outlined by President Perez at a press conference after the December 1977 meeting of OPEC Ministers at Caracas. It should not be confused with the proposal submitted by Algeria and Venezuela to the December 1979 ministerial meeting in Caracas, which is discussed later in the Chapter.

12   Proposal put forward by the Mexican government at the meeting of the Development Committee in Mexico City, April 1978.

13   *A Proposal for Stepped-Up Co-Financing for Investment in Developing Countries*, OECD, Paris, May 1979.

14   For more detailed discussion and assessment of the schemes, see Michael Stewart, Background Paper.

15   Net disbursements, deducting payment of interest and repayment of principle, which constitute the actual resource transfer are much lower than these figures for gross lending at $2.6 billion in 1979.

16   This is the voting structure of the International Fund for Agricultural Development.

17   See e.g. T. C. Ho, 'Co-financing', Asian Development Bank, mimeo, 1978.

18   Brandt Commission Report, *North–South: A Programme for Survival*, Pan, 1980, p. 234.

19   Ibid., p. 253.

20   The World Bank raised $5.2 billion by borrowing in 1980.

21   See *Industry 2000: New Perspectives*, UNIDO, ID/CONT. 4/3, 1979, pp. 21–2.

22   Joint Proposal by the Algerian and Venezuelan Delegations on the Need for Additional Financial Cooperation between OPEC Member Countries and Other Developing Countries, submitted by Algeria and Venezuela to the meeting of OPEC ministers held at Caracas in December 1978.

23   Abdelkader Sid Ahmed, Background Paper.

24   See introduction for the counter arguments.

25   Saudi Arabia, Kuwait, Bahrain, Qatar and the UAE.

26   According to the Kuwaiti Minister of Finance, Mr Abdul-Latif Youseff al-Hamad, in a speech reported in the *Financial Times*, 1 July 1981.

27   See D. Marsh, 'OPEC's Grand Juggling Act', *Financial Times*, 14 October 1980; and 'Bypassing Euromarkets', *South*, No. 2, November 1980; 'Impressive Force in the Market' by J. Makinson, *Financial Times*, 25 June 1981 on the growth of Arab consortia.

28   In 1980, World Bank (and ODA) disbursements were $5.8 billion, corresponding to a net transfer of resources (deducting repayments of principle interest and other charges) of $2.6 billion.

29   These estimates are in accord with recent projections of the World

Bank which shows the 1985 deficit of LDCs (in the 'High' case) being financed by ODA (33 per cent), non-concessional official finance (11 per cent), direct investment (13 per cent) and commercial lending (44 per cent). See *World Development Report*, 1981, Table 2.4.

30 See also D. Avramovic, Background Paper.

4 NEW FINANCIAL MECHANISMS

This chapter considers proposals for new financial mechanisms which have been proposed in order to improve resource transfers. While some of these mechanisms are − as proposed − tied to particular institutions, in theory they could be associated with a range of institutions. Three types of instrument are considered: indexation of financial assets; protection of financial assets against exchange risk; and guarantees to lenders against borrower default. A fourth proposal for an interest subsidy is considered in the next chapter, as its prime intention is to help low-income countries.

1. Indexation of financial assets

The proposals here may be divided into two categories. First, proposals to index OPEC financial assets in order to ensure a steady supply of oil and investment from the OPEC countries to the rest of the world. Such a proposal has been put forward in concise terms by Dr. Gutowski.[1] Second, proposals to index loans made to LDCs, designed to improve access and particularly maturity of LDC borrowing. An example is the proposal of Williamson.[2] While there is some overlap in the two types of proposal, there are also big differences, and they will be discussed separately.

Indexation of OPEC financial assets − the Gutowski proposal: This is a proposal for a triangular agreement between the West, OPEC and the LDCs, although the main actors are OPEC and the West. OPEC would agree to supply oil at a uniform price; this price will not increase by more than 2 per cent p.a. in terms of the price of manufactures.[3] The West would agree to provide a bond for OPEC investment (of $40 billion p.a. denominated in SDRs) whose return would be indexed to be equal to the rate of increase in the price of oil. One-eighth of the proceeds from the bond ($5 billion) would be paid into a fund for concessional lending to LDCs.

In theory all three parties might gain from the agreement. Clearly the industrialized countries (and the LDCs) would gain if they secured steady supplies of oil and a steady (and limited) price increase. Compared with zero or negative real returns on past investment, OPEC would gain from interest indexation. However, if the higher interest rates now ruling persist such indexation might not raise returns to OPEC. LDCs would gain from concessional loans, assuming that they add to and do not displace existing concessional flows, as well as from a stabilization of the world economy.

It is argued that the effective choice, at the margin, for OPEC surplus countries, is between keeping oil in the ground and accumulating financial assets. So long as decisions at the margin are taken on economic grounds then indexation of financial assets may be necessary to ensure steady supplies, so that real returns on financial assets bear some relation to the change in oil price. But the proposed triangular contract is likely to founder on OPEC's insistence that they should control the supply and price of oil. This is regarded as non-negotiable.[4] Moreover, the potential gains to OPEC are not certain: a maximum is put on the trend change in the price of oil (although there is a provision for a price increase if spot oil prices are above the maximum for 6 months), but not a minimum; whether or not they gain from the proposal indexation of interest on financial assets depends on what happens to inflation and nominal interest rates. From the point of view of ICs, the gains are also uncertain, while there are substantial costs. On the one hand, it is known that OPEC, and especially Saudi Arabia, does not want to disrupt oil supplies drastically because they recognize the effects on world economic stability. From this point of view indexation of oil prices may not be necessary. On the other hand, it is unlikely that the various members of OPEC would wish to abide by the scheme at times of crisis, when large gains might be made by by-passing it. ICs could incur substantial costs in relation to indexation of financial assets and concessional lending to LDCs. Further objections from the point of view of the ICs[5] are that once indexation was accepted for oil it would be difficult to resist indexation for other primary commodities and that the scheme would involve excessive intervention in commodity and financial markets. On financial markets the scheme 'would considerably distort and falsify capital flows'.

A major weakness in the logic behind the scheme is that it assumes OPEC decisions are taken purely in relation to the economic costs and benefits to the countries concerned, taking a long-run view. This is wrong for both high population, high absorbers among oil producers and the low absorbers. The high absorbers, for example Nigeria or Mexico, are under considerable pressure to maximize short-run revenue from oil to finance expenditure and therefore any scheme related to financial assets is rather irrelevant to them. Decisions by the low absorbers are also taken in a political context in which the interests of the current decision-makers may have considerable weight, as against the long-run interests of the country as a unit. From this point of view, current revenue — even if invested in rather poor financial assets — may be preferable to keeping the oil in the ground, which may not make much sense as a personal investment.

Less developed countries are rather marginal in this scheme, since the concessional flows to LDCs are tacked on to the scheme, not an intrinsic part of it. But they would stand to gain substantially, albeit indirectly, if the scheme succeeded in stabilizing and raising world economic activity, by ensuring predictable rises in the oil price and uninterrupted supplies. Our main doubts about this scheme is whether it would succeed in these aims, given the highly political nature of decisions about oil prices and supplies. However, some attempts have already been made to negotiate for a steadier supply and more predictable and gradual changes in prices of oil. Efforts along this line should continue. The scheme considered contains the elements for negotiation but in its present form it is an unlikely contract.[6]

Indexation of LDCs loans:[7] It is well established that much LDC borrowing from the private sector is of short maturity. This, together with high nominal interest rates because of high expected rates of inflation, means that the debt service ratio seems high, even though the level of debt in real terms is not particularly high by historical standards.[8] Short maturity means that LDCs are vulnerable to reduced confidence when they seek to 'rollover' their debt; the high debt service ratios give rise to such lack of confidence. Thus many countries are threatened with financial crises, even though their underlying situation may not warrant it.

The proposal for an indexed bond for LDCs is directed at lengthening maturities and thus reducing debt service ratios, so helping to avoid the problems caused by short maturities. The lack of long-term lending and borrowing is attributed to the risks that arise for both lenders and borrowers from unexpected variations in the inflation rate. 'What is needed is a financial technique that will insulate the real value of debts, and also the effective maturity of debt, from unexpected variations in the rate of inflation.'[9] Williamson proposes that some international financing institution (preferably an existing one, e.g. the Fund or the World Bank, or a new one) issues a bond of 50 year maturity denominated in SDRs, with a real interest payment and redemption value which is indexed to some price index, such as a weighted wholesale or retail price index of a number of leading countries. The bonds would be issued on behalf of a group of LDCs, thus leading to risk spreading. A partial guarantee given by the issuing authority would further reduce risks to lenders. Borrowers' repayment would be related to their share in the issue, modified by any unexpected improvement/worsening in their terms of trade as compared with a 'normalized' movement in the terms of trade of the group of borrowing countries as a whole.

It is argued that such a scheme would permit a larger flow of lending to the LDCs, at longer maturities, without an increase in the risks faced by lenders. Oil exporters with large financial surpluses would find the bonds attractive since they would guarantee a real return, would minimize risks and would promote development. The South would benefit from long-term lending and the banking system of the West would be strengthened by a reduction in the risk of default by an LDC sparking off a financial crisis. The Williamson plan does not suffer from the same objections as the Gutowski/Roth plan since it avoids the complex oil pricing and production agreements and it adopts a market solution which could be implemented more quickly than any scheme calling for negotiation on a large number of issues.

A substantial objection to the scheme, from the point of view of LDCs, is that on the whole inflation has tended to help debtor countries, reducing the real value of their debt, so that for quite long periods they have paid zero or negative real interest rates. A scheme such as this would make it impossible to avoid the burden of debt by inflation. Whether or not this is an important objection depends on what is expected to happen to inflation and interest rates. Nominal interest rates are now well above the rate of inflation, but this could be temporary, to be attributed to a short-term wave of monetarism that is sweeping industrialized countries. The gains from long-term borrowing for LDCs might out-weigh the losses from increasing the real burden of debt. So long as the new bond remains optional, leaving LDCs with other options, then the force of this objection is weakened. However, it seems likely that the existence of an indexed bond of this kind would tend to make other non-indexed borrowing less attractive, so that countries would have to adopt indexation or to raise their interest payments on non-indexed assets. It seems likely that — if introduced on any scale — such an indexed bond would tend to push up the real cost of borrowing across the board, at least compared with past experience. That being so, it would be necessary to consider carefully whether the gains from long maturity would outweigh these costs.

A further objection is that the newly industrializing countries, who have so far been successful in raising com-mercial loans, may still be able to gain a sufficient volume of bank loans by themselves and may be unwilling to partici-pate in a scheme sharing risks with less creditworthy LDCs which would tend to raise their interest payments. Williamson concedes this point but argues that the existence of guarantees will reduce the cost of borrowing through the scheme. For this to be the case, the guarantees would have to be financed independently of the scheme.[10] Guarantees also tend to involve a bias against countries who previously could borrow without them (see discussion below).

It seems likely that an indexed bond would tend to increase the cost of borrowing, not only to those countries associated with it, but also to other countries. If it is introduced when interest rates are generally high, it would tend to maintain high rates over the life of the bond. If offered when interest rates were low (in relation to inflation), it would tend to raise the cost of borrowing. There would be gains in terms of increased maturities. The value of such an instrument then depends heavily on how burdensome short maturities are. The view presented here is that short maturities do not normally create much of a problem. Where they do (when countries are in acute difficulties) the country's difficulties would not be substantially affected by longer maturities because at such times countries are normally seeking additional capital, not only meeting rollover requirements.

One aspect of the Williamson scheme deserves further consideration, that is the proposal to adjust repayment obligations (both interest and amortization) according to movements in the terms of trade. This feature would help countries suffering from particularly adverse movements in their terms of trade by reducing their debt service obligations in those years. This complicates the scheme, and is not an essential part of it, but does contribute to the solution of a very real problem of debt servicing for countries with greatly fluctuating terms of trade. This aspect of the scheme need not be confined to this particular scheme, but should also be considered in relation to other lending such as the normal lending of the IMF or the World Bank. If a satisfactory scheme were devised for all public lending, it could make a real contribution to countries whose difficulties are associated with adverse movements in the terms of trade.

But problems arise in defining the type of movement in terms of trade which would qualify for reduced repayments or would justify increased repayments. Williamson emphasizes 'unexpected' movements, but there is no particular reason why unexpected movements should justify compensation while expected movements do not. Moreover, his particular measure — the movement of a country's terms of trade in relation to the movement of the terms of trade for a group of LDCs — does not qualify as a measure of 'unexpected'. Williamson's measure helps countries with particularly strong adverse movements, and this help would be at a cost to countries whose terms of trade might also have moved adversely but less than the average movement. Rather than tying movements to what happens to one country's terms of trade in relation to a group of LDCs, it would be preferable to look at each country's terms of trade individually. Two types of adjustment would in principle be possible. First, adjustments to compensate for fluctuations so that a country became liable to higher payment (for interest and amortization) when terms of trade were in a cyclical upswing and to lower payment when they were in a cyclical downward swing. There would be strong justification for this sort of adjustment. Secondly, it would also be possible to adjust according to trend movements in the terms of trade. While the first adjustment (for fluctuations) should alter the timing but not the total payments any country made, the second (trend) could involve a real change in countries' liabilities according to their particular long-run fortunes, with some countries gaining and others losing. For this reason the second (trend) adjustment while also justified, is liable to be opposed by those who believe they will be the losers. At this stage we believe there is strong justification for further investigation of both types of adjustment to apply to all international public lending.

2. Protection of financial assets against exchange risk[11]

In a world of fluctuating exchange rates, OPEC countries suffer two types of exchange risk: one in their terms of trade, as the $-denominated oil price fluctuates with fluctuations in the dollar exchange rate; secondly, in relation to the value of their financial assets held overseas. Greater short-term exchange rate turbulence, that has accompanied the move towards flexible exchange rates, particularly increases the risks arising on short-term financial investments. Short-term commercial bank deposits account for about half OPEC foreign investments.[12]

There are a variety of ways in which currency diversification in short-term investments could reduce these risks. Some involve a market solution, for example where overseas banks offer depositors a variety of currencies. In addition OPEC themselves diversify directly by investing in a range of currencies. The Commonwealth Group of Experts proposed a rather roundabout method whereby Central Banks would take on the exchange risks.[13] Helleiner proposes a much simpler and more direct route: that financial assets are denominated in SDRs (or some other currency bundle).

To the extent that fear of exchange rate fluctuations is inhibiting OPEC from accumulating and investing in financial assets, the provision of SDR-denominated financial assets might encourage a greater total amount of recycling, and a different distribution of those assets. Whether or not such a change would make any direct contribution to recycling towards LDCs depends on whether problems of exchange risk are inhibiting recycling to LDCs, directly or indirectly via the commercial markets. It is difficult to be categorical about this, but it is unlikely that they form a very important influence on the total borrowing of LDCs. On the other hand, a scheme to denominate assets in SDRs could be accompanied by a special scheme for on-lending (or guaranteeing loans) to LDCs,[14] along the lines discussed, for example, in the previous chapter. SDR denomination might make schemes to borrow from OPEC and on-lend to LDCs more attractive to OPEC. As far as LDCs are concerned, they too would enjoy a reduction in exchange rate risks if borrowing and repayment obligations were denominated in SDRs. The actual payments obligations would be greater (or less) than without such denomination depending on the actual movement in the SDR exchange rate. Thus while exchange rate risks would be reduced, for both lenders and borrowers, in terms of actual payments for any given loan this is a zero-sum game in which any gains (losses) made by lenders through changes in exchange rate are precisely offset by losses (gains) made by borrowers. However, both lenders and borrowers reduce their risk, so that to that extent they both gain.

Exchange rate risk is also a possible cause of the short

maturity of much of OPEC investments. Hence any scheme which reduces it may help lengthen maturities. SDR denomination of financial assets could reduce speculative movement of financial assets and the resulting exchange rate instability, and make some contribution towards achieving a steadier flow of recycled funds with more direct recycling to LDCs. The gains are not likely to be very large, but SDR denomination should be one aspect of any new recycling scheme, of the sort discussed in the preceeding chapter.

3. Guarantees

Many of the proposals for changes in recycling involve guarantee facilities for some part of the recycling to LDCs. This was an element, for example, in the Mexican and Venezuelan schemes discussed in Chapter Three and of Williamson's bond. There are a variety of ways in which LDCs may be 'underwritten' by the international financial system: some are formal, some are informal. Informally, the existence of some 'lender of the last resort' liable to bail out countries when in difficulties operates as a powerful guarantee. The role of the IMF — and its expanded facilities — can be seen as a *de facto* guarantee mechanism. Knowledge about official debt rescheduling activities operating via the Paris Club constitutes another informal guarantee. While these all underwrite a country's general repayment capability, they do not guarantee repayment in particular cases. Proposed facilities for guarantees are intended to achieve this and thereby to extend a country's access to the commercial sector.

Two types of formal guarantee mechanism may be distinguished: one is an underwriting of a borrowing/lending institution, thus enabling it to borrow (and lend) more and on better terms than without some underwriting. The callable capital of the World Bank acts in this capacity to make the World Bank in a strong position to borrow and lend. In the proposal in Chapter Three, it was suggested that the OECD or OPEC would offer similar backing for the new lending schemes. A second type of guarantee mechanism is a facility which directly guarantees in part or whole the repayment of loans made by some outside body, e.g. by the commercial sector. The first type of guarantee or backing would be necessary for expanding lending through the international public sector; the second type would be suitable if it is desired to make substantial use of the commercial route, while extending its quantity and changing its distribution. The second type of facility seems necessary as well as the first for two reasons: first, even with a large expansion in the public route, there will remain very substantial commercial sector recycling in the eighties, as shown in Chapter Three. Secondly, the uncertainties about the total level and uneven distribution of commercial finance among countries remain serious defects of this route. These defects might in part be corrected by the use of guarantee facilities, which could extend commercial sector activities to countries which have previously had little access because they were thought to be 'poor' risks. The net effect would tend to be to redirect commercial lending away from the 'good' risks, who currently have access to unguaranteed funds. They too might be forced to obtain guaranteed loans.

A guarantee facility for commercial loans. Zolotas[15] has put forward one such proposal, describing it as an international loan insurance fund. In his scheme the fund would be operated by the World Bank and IMF with membership being open to all IBRD member countries. Guarantors would be the IBRD, IMF, OPEC and the developed countries – each guarantor being assigned a quota (denominated in SDRs) to determine the limits for capital calls on the guarantors. The liability of the fund would be limited to a multiple of the capital of the fund. Guarantees would be extended to loans for balance of payments support and for development projects. Guarantees would cover a percentage of loans which could vary for different countries according to their access to capital markets. It is proposed that the recipients pay part of the cost of the guarantee by paying interest on the loan at the rate ruling in the absence of a guarantee. The difference between this and the actual rate of interest charged in the presence of a guarantee would be paid by the lender to the insurance fund, which would thus accumulate reserves, increasing its total guarantee capacity.

To consider the implications of such a scheme it is helpful

to distinguish 'rational' and 'irrational' perceptions of risk. To the extent that commercial bankers are holding back because of some irrational perception of risk, due to a lack of knowledge of the countries concerned, for example, the facility would not increase the proportion of bad debts. But even in this case, there are bound to be some bad debts. These will be met by the fund, instead of by the commercial sector, which should have the effect of increasing the profits and/or improving the terms on which the commercial sector extends loans. There will tend to be some displacement – in relation to both terms and total access – from countries which previously had access to (unguaranteed) commercial loans towards countries which had limited access. To the extent that countries which previously had access to unguaranteed facilities continue to make use of them, they are likely to suffer worse terms and perhaps diminished access. Their share of guaranteed facilities is likely to be lower than their previous share of unguaranteed facilities unless the total flow of finance to LDCs increases sufficiently to offset this. In the Zolotas scheme their terms may not be affected; in other schemes they will tend to have to pay more to contribute towards covering the risks of the previously unguaranteed. A scheme might also cover loans for genuinely more risky investments (where previously commercial bankers had held back because of rational perceptions of risks). In this case the bad debt ratio would rise.

The potential gearing ratio of the facility – between callable capital and guarantees offered – depends on the bad debt ratio. The commercial sector, with no guarantees, is able to operate a gearing ratio of $1:26$[16] and make profits, with loans extended on the basis of its perceptions of risks. To the extent that the facility does not extend to genuinely worse risks, then it too can use a similar high gearing ratio. But to the extent that the scheme extends to genuinely more risky investments, then the gearing ratio would have to fall, diminishing the total guaranteeing capacity of the institution.

In practice some combination (covering irrational and rational risks) is likely and desirable. But to bias the scheme in favour of fairly low risks, may involve limiting its coverage mainly to middle-income LDCs, rather than very low-income LDCs, leaving other schemes to meet the problems of the poorest countries (see next chapter). In addition, if the guarantee scheme were operated in combination with some form of *conditionality* (either of the macro or micro-project variety) this could reduce the proportion of bad debts on the (unproven) assumption that conditionality reduces bad debts. This would have the major disadvantage for many LDCs of introducing conditionality into areas which have previously been rather unconditional. The conditionality need not be of the Fund variety.[17] Some extension of conditionality might be a necessary cost of extending commercial sector coverage.

One proposed scheme for guarantees[18] would direct the guarantees to 'threshold countries', i.e. middle-income countries engaged in structural adjustment programmes designed to enable them to gain direct access to financial markets. The main idea is to supplement IMF and World Bank resources available to such countries by partially guaranteed non-concessional funds.

Any guarantee facility is likely to alter the distribution of financial flows between countries, and possibly between projects. It could also alter the total quantity of funds available for lending to LDCs. These effects will vary according to the precise details of the scheme. It is none the less worth considering them at a general level. Probably the most important question is the effect on the total flow of funds. In so far as guarantees raise the total funds available to LDCs significantly the distributional effects become of lesser significance. Whether or not a guarantee facility would raise the total flows to LDCs is very difficult to establish. In the first place it would depend on whether the funds which financed the facility were *additional* to funds available for development (e.g. whether they were a substitute for or an addition to a country's subscription to, say, the World Bank). If the financing funds were additional, then this is a sufficient reason for expecting some additional flows to LDCs. But there is no very good reason to expect them to be additional, so the next question is whether without additionality, a guarantee facility could, by operating a sort of banking multiplier, generate a larger amount of loans than if the finance were used directly for lending. Any lending facility can (as the commercial banks do) generate a much larger total lending than its capital base. Among commercial banks gearing ratios of over 20 are common. It is unlikely that a guarantee facility would be able to achieve a higher gearing ratio. Hence there is no reason to suppose that it would out-perform (quantitatively) a direct lending facility if the latter were operated with commercial gearing ratios. But the public lending facilities — the World Bank and Regional Banks — are limited (by constitution) to a 1:1 gearing ratio. A guarantee facility could then be viewed as an alternative to raising the gearing ratio of these public banks, an alternative which has the possible advantage for ICs of making use of their commercial sectors as compared with the use of the World Bank.

Against this, for LDCs, the lending involved is likely to be more expensive and less developmental in orientation than an international public lending facility. Given the current rather conservative attitude towards changing the gearing ratio of the World Bank, the use of a guarantee mechanism may be seen as a more feasible alternative in the short run. With their present constitution, the facility could not be administered by the World Bank or Regional Banks without reducing their lending capacity by an equal amount. However, a small change in their Charters could alter this. A higher gearing ratio — achieved directly or via a guarantee mechanism — does not ensure that total flows of finance to LDCs are increased since what may happen is that funds which were previously lent without guarantee directly by the commercial sector, are now diverted to the new facility. Some diversion seems unavoidable, but it seems probable that some additional lending to LDCs would also result.

While there are many unknowns, then, our conclusion is that a guarantee facility could increase total flows, but by no more than could be achieved by a public lending facility which had a high gearing ratio. In many ways (especially from the point of view of the quality of lending and country distribution) the latter is to be preferred. But since it is rather unlikely, a guarantee facility may be the most feasible solution. The distribution of flows of finance is likely to alter following the introduction of a facility. Here the precise effects very much depend on the nature of the scheme. In general, countries which have had little difficulty in raising unguaranteed loans will tend to lose proportionately (whether they lose absolutely depends on the effects on total flows), while countries which have had more limited access to the private sector than they would have liked and which would qualify for guarantees under the scheme would tend to gain. Countries which previously have had access to unguaranteed loans may find it difficult to continue to get these in similar quantities and find it necessary to pay a higher price and/or join the guarantee scheme. These effects could be offset if a higher total flow of finance results.

A change in distribution of finance away from the countries which have previously got the bulk of the funds is one of the aims of introducing a guarantee scheme — since the rather concentrated distribution has been a major defect of commercial flows. But such a change may well give rise to opposition from potential losers. Moreover, the new distribution will be unlikely substantially to favour the low-income countries who were the chief losers in the 1970s. This is because the problem, for many low-income countries, is not so much access to capital markets as unwillingness/inability to pay the terms required. These terms will not be significantly altered by a guarantee scheme.

How a guarantee scheme affects the distribution as between projects will depend in part on the administration of the scheme. Some schemes involve public assistance in identifying and vetting projects (e.g. by the Regional Banks), which may alter and improve project selection. Without such additional intervention, the selection of projects could worsen, through a type of 'moral hazard' process, because with the guarantee there will be less incentive for the commercial sector to be careful about project selection.

Conclusions on guarantees

A scheme to use public money to provide guarantees for commercial sector lending to LDCs is a second best way of generating financial flows. It would be preferable to increase the lending capacity of existing (or new) public institutions by raising their gearing ratios to high levels. Assuming this expansion is not feasible, a guarantee scheme could contribute to an increase in total financial flows to LDCs and might improve its distribution within the category of middle-income countries, but it would be unlikely to do much for low-income countries. Among middle-income countries, the existing distribution has not been too bad; while a few countries have received most of the finance, these have also been the largest countries in terms of population and GNP.

There would be a cost for the 'losing' countries who would probably have to pay more for less finance with the scheme. Any improvement in distribution would be more likely if a guarantee scheme involved an international public institution — the World Bank and/or Regional Banks — in identifying projects/programmes which would qualify for guarantees or partial guarantees. This would also make it likely that the scheme improved rather than worsened project selection.

A guarantee scheme is not the panacea some proponents have suggested, but with appropriate administration, it could play a role in improving the distribution and raising the quantity of commercial sector financial flows.

Conclusions on new financial mechanisms

We do not find that any of the proposed new mechanisms will offer a simple panacea. The proposed 'triangular' agreement between OPEC, ICs and the Third World is likely to be ineffective in producing its desired effect — a steady supply of oil at a slowly rising real price — because neither producers nor consumers would be prepared to meet the requirements of the agreement. This proposal has little to offer the Third World directly. Indexation of LDC bonds could permit a lengthening of maturities, but at a cost which borrowing countries may not believe worthwhile. SDR denomination of financial assets would reduce risk, but is unlikely to make a major contribution to the recycling process. A scheme to guarantee commercial sector loans to LDCs would be less satisfactory than an equivalent expansion of lending through existing or new public development agencies. But assuming any such expansion will be limited in size, a guarantee scheme could provide a useful supplement which might add to the total flows of finance to LDCs and improve their distribution. Such a scheme would need to be administered by a public development agency which assists in project/programme identification.

Expansion of direct lending facilities (for example through the proposed Third World Development Agency) and improving the distribution of commercial flows (through a guarantee mechanism), will for the most part help the financial problems of middle-income countries, where there is a potential capacity to service debt, and the major obstacles to increased financial flows are institutional. There has been an uneven flow of finance among middle-income countries. The eleven major middle-income borrowers accounted for nearly 60 per cent of the total debt from private sources among all developing countries in 1979.[19] These eleven countries had 42 per cent of the population of middle-income countries and 55 per cent of the GNP.[20] The remaining forty-one middle-income countries with 58 per cent of the population and 45 per cent of the GNP of middle-income countries received a disproportionately small proportion of private financial flows, especially in relation to their population share but also in relation to their income share. There is therefore some significant potential for improving the distribution of financial flows among middle-income countries. But the major malfunctioning of the international financial system has been the very small proportion of finance received by low-income countries. The mechanisms considered above will not be capable of doing very much for the poorest countries, where the capacity to service commercial debt is limited. The problems of the poorest countries – and possible solutions – are considered in the next chapter.

Notes

1 A. Gutowski, 'Sketch for a Contractural Agreement between Oil-Exporting States and the Oil-Importing States', Institute for

Economic Research, Hamburg, mimeo 1980, and *Financial Times*, 23 May 1980.
2 See J. Williamson, Background paper.
3 Described as 'finished products' in the proposal.
4 See the discussion of R. Mabro, Background paper. This point was also made by all those connected with OPEC at the Oxford Workshop and also by O. Schlecht, 'Outline for a contractural agreement between OPEC, the industrialized countries and the developing countries, an opinion', Bonn, mimeo, 1981.
5 See Schlecht, op. cit.
6 'In general, the main objection to the Gutowski/Roth approach is that the authors assume a broad identity of interest between the member countries of the individual groups — OPEC, the industrialized countries, and the developing countries. But in reality this is not the case: conflicts of interest exist — among the OPEC countries as well — which are sometimes acute, according to their political and economic positions.' Schlecht, op. cit., p. 3.
7 See J. Williamson, Background Paper.
8 Ibid., and Fishlow, op. cit.
9 Williamson, op. cit.
10 Williamson proposes the guarantees should be financed in part by the upper-income LDCs as they 'graduate' from aid recipients to aid donors.
11 See G. K. Helleiner, Background Paper.
12 *Bank of England Quarterly Bulletin*, March 1981.
13 *The World Economic Crisis*, Report by Group of Experts, Commonwealth Secretariat, 1980, p. 25.
14 This is an aspect of the Commonwealth Group of Experts scheme, but not that of the Group of Thirty, which makes a similar recommendation. See Group of Thirty, *Reserve Assets and a Substitution Account: Towards a Less Unstable International Monetary System*, February 1980.
15 X. Zolotas, 'The Case for an International Loan Insurance Fund', *The Banker*, November 1980.
16 This is the ratio of capital:assets of the top 50 banks in the list published by *The Banker*, June 1980.
17 See Chapter Six for a discussion of conditionality.
18 M. Camdessus, 'Introduction of New Guarantee Systems', mimeo, April 1981.
19 N. Hope, op. cit.
20 *World Development Report 1980*, figures for 1978.

5   RECYCLING TO THE POOREST COUNTRIES

In the 1970s the low-income countries obtained very little commercial finance. Although they received a fairly high share of ODA, their total access to external finance was small compared with middle-income countries. Consequently, they were forced to curtail development plans and real income growth slowed markedly. It is likely that a similar situation will occur in the 1980s, so that they will fall further behind the rest of the world. A major challenge for the 1980s is to redirect resources towards these countries. This chapter examines possible changes in the international system of resource transfer that might help to do so.[1]

The 1970s

The low-income countries' share of external finance received by all non-oil LDCs fell in the 1970s from 16.9 per cent (1973) to 14.3 per cent (1980)[2] – see Table 5.1. Moreover the situation was not equitable at the beginning of the period, for their share of external finance was below their share of GNP and substantially below their share of population (estimated to be 59.7 per cent in 1978[3]). These figures include India, which receives substantially less external finance per capita than other low-income LDCs. This is illustrated in Table 5.2. In 1978 total external financing receipts per head were $2 in India, and $25 for other low-income countries; whereas among middle-income LDCs receipts were $65.3 among the newly industrializing countries (NICs) and $55.9 among other middle-income LDCs.[4]

The drop in share of external finance received by low-income countries was due to their low (and falling) share of commercial loans, during a period when these became an increasingly important part of total flows. While low-income

Table 5.1   Major flows of external finance to non-oil LDCs 1973–80

(1978 $ b.)

	1973	1978	1980
All LDCs:			
ODA	9.4	11.6	13.6
Private direct investment	5.3	4.8	4.7
Commercial loans	14.3	30.3	27.8
TOTAL	29.0	46.7	46.1
Low-income LDCs:			
ODA	4.1	5.1	5.7
Private direct investment	0.2	0.2	0.2
Commercial loans	0.6	0.9	0.7
TOTAL	4.8	6.2	6.7
% share of low income in:			
ODA	43.6	44.0	41.9
Private direct investment	3.8	4.2	4.3
Commercial loans	4.2	3.0	2.5
TOTAL	16.9	13.3	14.3
Population, 1978		59.7	
GNP, 1978		23.7	

Source: World Development Report, 1981, Table 5.1.

LDCs' share of commercial loans fell to 2.5 per cent of commercial loans to all LDCs, commercial loans rose from 49 per cent to over 60 per cent of total flows (excluding short-term borrowing) to LDCs between 1973 and 1980. Low-income countries maintained their share of ODA (at over 40 per cent).[5] The reason for the fall in low-income countries' share of commercial loans was due to a quite dramatic fall in their share of *private* capital flows;[6] their share of official (non-concessional) loans rose during the period;[7] at the same time private commercial loans increased relative to official.

While, relatively, low-income countries' access to external finance was reduced their *need* rose as a result of a strong

Table 5.2 Total external financing receipts of LDCs, 1978

	TOTAL		ODA*	
	$ per capita	as % GNP	$ per capita	as % GNP
Low-income:	14.0	6.8	10.0	4.8
of which				
India	2.0	1.2	2.1**	1.2
Least developed	18.5	10.2	15.8	8.7
Low-income ex-India	25.0	10.4	17.2	7.2
Middle-income:				
Newly industrializing	65.3	3.5	1.4	0.1
Other	55.9	6.8	21.0	2.6

*Official development assistance is defined as grants, loans or technical assistance which are undertaken by the official sector with the aim of promoting economic development and welfare as the main objectives. To qualify as ODA financial flows must be at concessional terms which for loans entails at least 25 per cent grant element. On this definition 'hard' loans by the World Bank and regional development banks do not qualify as ODA.

**Since 1976 India's receipts of ODA have been larger than total receipts due to a large payments deficit and a deficit on non-ODA capital flows.

Source: OECD, *Development Co-operation*, 1980, Table IV–9.

adverse movement in their terms of trade following the oil price rise of 1973–4. They suffered directly from the rise in the price of imported oil. Indirectly they suffered from the price rise in manufactured imports, due to the oil price rise, while markets for exports were depressed as a result of the subsequent world deflation, with the result of a deterioration in the terms of trade between primary (non-oil) products and manufactures. The real value of their export earnings — in terms of the price of imports — fell during this period by 1 per cent per annum 1973–9 although the volume of exports increased by 2 per cent per annum.

Between 1970 and 1980, the terms of trade of low-income oil importers deteriorated by 16 per cent *vis-à-vis* industrialized countries, while those of middle-income countries improved by 2 per cent.[8] It is worth emphasizing the significance of the indirect effects because it means that policies for direct alleviation of additional cost of oil (e.g. through OPEC providing low interest loans for oil purchases as Venezuela and Mexico have)[9] can only partially offset the deterioration in trade balances.

The net result of these direct and indirect effects taken together was a very large reduction in the real purchasing power of exports: among all low-income importers the export purchasing power net fell from $16.2 billion in 1970 to $11 billion in 1980. The fall was most marked for African countries – from $7.4 billion to $3.7 billion, i.e. halving the real purchasing power of exports net of fuel imports.[10]

The combination of reduced export earnings and limited access to external finance led to a very sharp reduction in the growth of imports among low-income countries from 4.1 per cent per annum 1967–72 to 0.75 per annum 1973–80.[11] (In contrast among LDCs as a whole import volume rose by 6.7 per cent per annum 1973–80, compared with 7.6 per cent per annum 1967–72.)[12] The sharp reduction in growth of imports involved a reduction in growth of *all* types of expenditure – private consumption, public consumption and investment. Growth in per capita incomes slowed down from 1.6 per cent per annum to 0.9 per cent per annum.[13]

It is often suggested that low-income countries have limited access to commercial borrowing because the commercial sector correctly judges that they will not make 'good' use of the funds and will therefore not be in a position to meet the repayment obligations. In one way this position was vindicated by the events of the 1970s which showed that middle-income countries did, on the whole, make good use of borrowed funds in that they did create a repayment capacity, while the slow growth among low-income countries is taken as proof that they lacked the potential to make such 'good' use of funds. But growth among low-income countries was undoubtedly import restrained during this period. In one way it is remarkable that with such a dramatic drop in the rate of increase of the volume of imports, the fall in the growth rate was so much less marked. Comparing the proportionate fall in growth in imports with the proportionate fall in growth of per capita incomes, low-income countries did much 'better' than middle-income countries in maintaining income growth. To the extent that growth among low-income countries was import-restrained, growth would have been higher had more external finance been available. It follows from this that low-income countries would have enjoyed some positive returns from greater finance and would therefore have generated some repayment capacity. It does not follow — without much more detailed investigation — that they could have generated a 'commercial' return (especially given the problems that sometimes arise in transforming social returns into the foreign exchange needed to service debt), but it does suggest that they could have created some servicing capacity. This conclusion is, of course, highly relevant to policy recommendations for the 1980s, since it means that grant aid is not the only viable way of transferring resources to low-income countries.

Prospects for the 1980s

Without any major change, the prospects for low-income countries in the 1980s are poor. In the World Bank's High case, growth in income per head among low-income countries is expected to be 1.8 per cent per annum from 1980 to 1990 compared with 3.4 per cent per annum for middle-income countries.[14] In the more realistic[15] Low case, growth in per capita income is expected to be 0.7 per cent per annum for low-income countries (2.1 per cent per annum for middle-income). In each case the prospects for sub-Saharan Africa are particularly poor with a decline in per capita income in the Low case and stagnant income per head in the High case. Slow growth among low-income countries is attributed to slow growth expected in export earnings for 1980–5 due to the stagnant world economy and limited access to commercial capital. Current account deficits for low-income countries are projected in the High case to rise (at 1978 prices) from $8.6 billion in 1980 to $12 billion in 1985 and $15 billion in 1990.

Deficits of this magnitude will be difficult to finance, on

the assumption that these countries have limited access to commercial funds. The World Bank states that they could only be financed with a higher level of aid and a greater proportion of that aid going to low-income countries. Yet these deficits are really too small in the sense that they permit only very slow growth. Thus there is a major financing/recycling problem for low-income countries in the 1980s. The rest of this chapter considers ways of tackling this problem.

External finance for low-income countries

It has already been pointed out that the prospects for any substantial increase in aid are very poor and no solution should rely on this. According to the DAC Chairman's Report:

> it would be unrealistic to expect in the years to come a major increase in the ODA/GNP ratio for DAC countries collectively in the absence of new political decisions . . . Contrary to what happened in 1973–1974 after the first steep rise in oil prices, there is so far little evidence to expect a similar upsurge in OPEC aid after the sharp increase in oil prices in 1979.[16]

At best it seems that aid may maintain its present proportion of OECD/OPEC income. With a 3 per cent annual growth in income this would involve a 34 per cent increase in aid in real terms over the decade. If low-income countries receive a constant or slightly rising share of this aid, it will be insufficient to meet their needs.

The immediate needs of low-income countries for external finance are not very large in relation to total flows. It is estimated that a sum of $2.2 billion would have been required in 1980 to maintain energy imports at 1978 levels, but this does not cover indirect effects of a slow-down in world demand.[17] With the current proportion of aid going to low-income countries, total aid would need to increase by $4.9 billion or 17.5 per cent of 1979 levels to achieve an extra flow of $2.2 billion to low-income countries. If the proportion of ODA rose to 0.45 per cent of GNP this would permit an additional aid flow to low-income countries — again assuming no change in the proportion of the total they receive — of $3.2 billion (1979 calculations) making some contribution to indirect as well as direct effects of the change in oil prices.[18]

These calculations assume that the additional aid all comes from the OECD countries. The additional costs for energy among low-income countries could also be met by grants from OPEC to meet these costs, or by loans on very favourable rates, as is already done partially by some OPEC countries.[19] Total costs of importing oil among low-income countries were estimated to be $3.3 billion in 1980 rising to $11.1 billion by 1990.[20] These sums are high in relation to current flows of OPEC aid (at $5.2 billion in 1979), but not in relation to the OPEC surplus of $115 billion in 1980.

The aid proportion

In 1979 the share of low-income countries in net ODA disbursements was about 45 per cent having dropped slightly during the 1970s.[21] The share of DAC bilateral aid going to low-income countries fell sharply between 1970 and 1978 and was 38 per cent in 1978.[22] At current aid levels a switch of 10 per cent in the share of total ODA involves about $2 billion, or one-fifth of the current account deficits of low-income countries in 1980.

A switch of aid so that two-thirds went to low-income countries would increase their receipts by about $4 billion at 1980 values. This seems a reasonable proportion to aim for by 1985 if aid does not rise as a proportion of developed countries' GNP, and one that would be sufficient to meet much of the financing needs of low-income countries. Of course any such switch would have to be at the expense of middle-income countries, involving a corresponding reduction in their share of aid receipts. But it should be pointed out that given their higher income, there is considerable justification for such a switch; moreover, as a proportion of their total external receipts, a $4 billion cut would amount to only 8.6 per cent of middle-income receipts; but the cut would mainly fall on middle-income countries other than

NICs (since NICs receive very little aid) and for these countries it would amount to a 17 per cent cut.

For a number of reasons middle-income countries find it easier to attract commercial funds than low-income. While the distribution of commercial funds among middle-income countries was uneven in the 1970s (see Chapter 2) the sort of measures suggested in earlier chapters — new financial intermediaries, expansion of World Bank and Regional Bank (hard) lending and new guarantee facilities — would all be especially suited to secure a transfer of funds to (non-NIC) middle-income LDCs. These schemes could very easily offer such countries very much more than the proposed 17 per cent cut in external finance (although probably at higher cost). Moreover, even without such schemes, these countries are already beginning to get commercial funds as the banks seek to diversify their lending.

A big increase in aid to low-income countries either as a part of a general increase in aid, or through a *substantial* switch in the aid proportion going to low-income countries is the best solution to their problems in the 1980s, leaving other schemes to deal with the problems of middle-income countries.

However, while a two-thirds proportion should be an immediate aim, it would be naive to think that it is very likely to be achieved. In the seventies, despite the prominence of 'Redistribution with Growth' and 'Basic Needs' as development strategies, there was a drop in the proportion of aid going to low-income countries. In 1978 only 7 DAC countries gave less than 55 per cent of their bilateral aid to low-income countries, but these 7 included the US, France, West Germany and Japan.[23] Together these 4 countries accounted for 68 per cent of DAC bilateral ODA.[24]

In each case there are special political reasons for high levels of ODA going to some middle-income countries. For example, France concentrates aid on ex-Colonial territories; Germany gives a large proportion to Turkey (16 per cent); 44 per cent of the US's bilateral aid goes to Egypt and Israel.[25] It is unlikely that there will be much shift in these patterns; indeed, the Reagan administration's 'cost-benefit' attitude to aid and its advocacy of the idea that aid should be used as a political weapon is likely to lead to a shift away from low-income countries, which are often viewed as lacking international political significance. The Stockman memorandum, putting forward an aid-cutting programme to the Reagan administration, argued that 'The reductions in aid would mainly affect the poor countries of Africa and the Asian sub-continent'. In the UK aid cuts are also falling disproportionately on low-income countries. In 1979, 77 per cent of OPEC aid was accounted for by bilateral grants and loans. Syria and Jordan were the main recipients, receiving 51 per cent of OPEC aid; together with aid to Gaza, the West Bank and the Palestinians these countries accounted for 60 per cent of the total. The largest non-Arab recipients, India and Pakistan, received $100 million together or 2.2 per cent of OPEC aid.[26]

In so far as bilateral aid fails to make a sufficient contribution to the two-thirds target, there would be a strong case for having a much higher target for multilateral aid, where the political constraints are less strong. Multilateral (concessional) flows account for about a quarter of total ODA; about three-quarters already goes to low-income countries. If this ratio were increased to around 90 per cent, it would add about $1 billion to the receipts of low-income countries.

It is clear that a large part of the needs of low-income countries could and should be met from aid. It would require only a relatively small proportionate increase in aid flows to meet their needs, if all the extra aid went to low-income countries: a 14 per cent increase in total aid would raise flows by $4 billion (1979 values), or over half low-income countries' current account deficit. If the general aid pessimism proves correct, a similar additional flow could be achieved by aid-switching. Either an overall increase or a substantial switch in aid (or some combination) to achieve the extra aid flows is the best solution to the problems of low-income countries in the 1980s. It would be useful to have a target for the proportion of aid that should go to low-income countries, in addition to the overall aid target. In the analysis above we suggested two-thirds as a reasonable target for the 1980s, which would be justified not only by considerations of poverty and basic needs but also by the very limited access low-income countries have to other forms of external finance compared with middle-income countries.

Increasing aid leverage

While extra aid is the best solution, in case this is not forthcoming it is worth considering ways in which low-income countries might increase the effects of aid in generating external resources. The same amount of aid − from a donor's point of view − can generate a greater resource flow, in the short run, if aid is combined with other forms of finance. The range of schemes that might achieve this have more to offer low-income countries than an attempt to increase their access to pure commercial finance.

One proposal often made is that aid should be used to provide an interest subsidy, so as to reduce the cost of commercial borrowing. It is estimated that $1 in cash could be used to generate a 4 per cent interest subsidy for $4 in lending.[27] An interest subsidy only permits greater resource flow in the short term, since it permits today's aid to 'go further' but pre-empts future aid, for payment of the subsidy, thus reducing the resource effect of tomorrow's aid. It only makes sense, therefore, if it is believed that the current need for capital flows is more critical than the future need; i.e. if it is believed that removal of a foreign exchange bottleneck today would reduce future bottlenecks, for example, by creating foreign exchange earnings. But in such a situation, the prospective foreign exchange earnings should permit the country to service a commercial loan.

Co-financing with the commercial sector is another way in which the resource transfer effects of aid can be increased. Here the fact of official commitment to a project, the technical project appraisal functions the official donor performs and cross-default clauses may help attract commercial finance and improve its terms. For low-income countries this is probably more beneficial in 'multiplying' the effects of aid than interest subsidies, because it provides technical assistance in the form of project identification and appraisal and secures access to commercial finance. Co-financing has been an important element in World Bank finance: in the financial year 1979, 47 per cent of Bank loans involved some element of co-financing and funds provided by co-lenders amounted to 32 per cent of total Bank lending. But most of this co-financing was with other aid donors, designed to spread risks, reduce procurement tying and, more recently, assist OPEC in project identification. Quite a substantial amount involved official export credit agencies. Co-financing with the commercial sector has been smaller. In 1979 there were 18 co-financing operations with commercial banks, supplying $1.3 billion to 13 countries. But some assessments suggest that past co-financing operations have not significantly increased the volume or improved the terms of commercial bank loans, although the Bank has helped to introduce new banks to lending to LDCs (e.g. in co-financing operations with Japanese banks). Altogether over 100 commercial banks have been involved in co-financing: this could offer a useful way of assisting Third World commercial banks to make loans to LDCs. For the most part, co-financing has been to well-established borrowers like Brazil and Argentina, and so has not made much contribution to providing access to finance to low-income countries.

Co-financing with the private sector (by bilateral donors as well as the World Bank and Regional Banks) could increase access to low-income countries in two ways; first by releasing World Bank and Regional Bank resources from other countries which may then be used in these countries; secondly, by co-financing in low-income countries, so directly contributing to their access to commercial sector finance. Co-financing requires that projects offer a harder return than in the case of concessional finance. For some very low-income countries this could prove a major obstacle. But for other countries — roughly those between the $300 and $650 income per capita — co-financing could substantially increase access to commercial finance. This is indicated by the differential access to non-concessional finance. Low-income countries on the OECD definition,[28] excluding the least developed, received 18.2 per cent of multilateral non-concessional finance in 1978 (i.e. hard term World Bank and Regional Bank finance), but they received only 4.2 per cent of private sector bank lending.[29] If these countries had received the same proportion of bank lending as of multilateral finance, they would have secured an additional $3.5 billion; alternatively if all multilateral finance had been on a 50:50 co-finance basis, the extra finance would have been $0.7 billion. One cannot assume, of course, that all co-financing will produce *additional* finance. It should, however, improve the country distribution of financial flows, and, if properly supervised, should be on better terms (lower interest, longer maturity) and involve more assistance in project identification and evaluation than ordinary commercial finance.

Very low-income countries are in a rather different position. They receive only a very small amount of multilateral non-concessional finance. The least developed[30] received 1.7 per cent of multilateral non-concessional finance in 1978, which in part reflects assessment of capacity to repay. The proportion is greater than their (negligible) share of private bank lending. But they do receive some hard finance in the form of export credits (three times as great as multilateral non-concessional finance in 1978, and on much harder terms). For very low-income countries, a switch in concessional resources towards them (made possible by co-financing in the slightly richer countries), and also greater access to non-concessional multilateral finance may have more to offer than co-financing with the private sector.

Aid-blending: at present there is a sharp distinction between 'hard' IBRD loans and IDA lending. World Bank loans carry a fairly hard interest rate (8¼ per cent in 1980), while IDA's loans are interest free, with a 0.75 per cent service charge. But the IBRD rate is substantially below rates charged by the private sector (around 11.75 per cent in 1979). A very large proportion of IDA (92 per cent in 1980) goes to low-income countries, while only 12.7 per cent of 1980 IBRD loan approvals went to low-income countries.[31] This is a much higher proportion, however, than that of the commercial sector, while the distribution within middle-income countries is much more even for World Bank loans than for private bank loans.

Re-direction of IBRD loans could make a substantial contribution, providing low-income countries with finance on better terms than export credit bank lending or co-financed loans. If low-income countries received 50 per cent of IBRD lending this would have added more than $3 billion in 1980, the amount rising as World Bank lending rises (estimated to increase by 5 per cent per annum in real terms over the next few years). Shortage of well-identified projects has limited this type of expansion. But structural adjustment loans and programme aid offer a way in which a major switch in IBRD loans could be achieved. Projects (or programme/ structural adjustment loans) that are financed with a mixture of IDA and IBRD could offer low-income countries finance on terms they can afford. IDA terms involve a significantly negative real interest rate. An interest rate of 4–5 per cent, which is what would be payable if each loan were half IDA and half IBRD, would still mean negative rates in real terms, and would seem to be within the repayment capacity of many countries. By varying the proportions of IDA/IBRD according to countries' payment capacity, World Bank assistance (and that of other multilateral agencies) could be tuned more sensitively to the needs of low-income countries.

The recycling route and the low-income countries

Any move away from the commercial routes to public routes will involve greater resource access for low-income countries. Almost certainly any public international institution — the World Bank, the Regional Banks, the new Third World Agency, etc. — would raise the proportion going to low-income countries. This in itself, apart from the other considerations discussed in Chapter Three, is a powerful reason for planning an expansion of this route at the expense of commercial routes. For non-concessional flows, the increase in access would be mainly for the richer of the low-income countries, and for middle-income countries which are currently getting rather little commercial finance. For very low-income countries, a substantial increase in access will depend on their receiving more concessional finance.

Gold as a source of finance

It has been convincingly argued[32] that LDCs have suffered a major loss in share of international reserves through the fact that they held only a small proportion of their reserves in gold during the period of the massive rise in the price of gold from $35 per ounce to $520 in March 1981. It is estimated that had they held their reserves in gold in the same proportion as the five major gold-accumulating countries, then they would have been $100 billion richer today. It is therefore suggested that they should be compensated by the profits made on the IMF's remaining gold. This − which amounts to 103 million ounces − could offer a source of finance for subsidized lending to the low-income countries, a continuation, for example, of the use of the profits on the sale of the first third of the IMF gold in the Trust Fund. The total capital gain involved would be around $50 billion.

While the justice of the case seems to be acknowledged, many people in the IMF believe that the gold is useful as an informal collateral as they start borrowing from the market. Others believe that no such collateral will be necessary.

There is a strong case that the LDCs are entitled to the profits from the IMF gold, and this could provide a significant source of finance for low-income countries.

The link

Another way of securing more resources for low-income countries is through the 'link', i.e. the allocation of a more than proportionate share of any new issue of SDRs to low-income countries. Since interest rates have been raised on SDRs to market rates, the link would no longer provide low-income countries with concessional resources (although the terms would be better than much private borrowing). But it could be accompanied by an interest subsidy so as to provide a concessional element. Even if the link does not provide additional resources, but is at the expense, for example, of bilateral aid, it would have substantial advantages in improving the country distribution of resource flows as compared with bilateral aid, as well as being virtually unconditional.

Table 5.3   Percentage distribution of external financing

	1973	1977	1980
All non-oil LDCs:			
Non-debt-creating flows, net	43.8	34.3	26.7
Official long-term capital, net	26.2	37.1	24.9
Private long-term capital, net	30.5	43.6	35.0
Other financing capital flows, net	−0.5	−14.9	13.4
Low-income LDCs:			
Non-debt-creating flows, net	39.5	37.9	36.7
Official long-term capital, net	28.9	39.7	51.0
Private long-term capital, net	34.2	3.4	1.0
Other financing capital flows, net	−2.6	20.7	10.2

Source: IMF, *World Economic Outlook,* 1980, Tables 20 and 21.

Table 5.4   Net disbursements of ODA

% of total to all LDCs:	1973	1979
OPEC	2.2	1.0
NICs	6.3	2.1
Other middle income	31.8	39.2
Low income	48.6	45.2
Unallocated	11.3	12.5

Source: Geographical Distribution of financing flows to developing countries, 1980, OECD.

Distribution of DAC bilateral ODA

% going to:	1970	1978
Middle income	44	52
Low income	47	38
Unallocated	9	10

Source: IBRD, *World Development Report*, 1980, Table 3.7.

Conclusions

Low-income countries suffered disproportionately in the 1970s and are likely to suffer disproportionately again in the 1980s, unless some radical changes are made to the system of international resource flows.

It is estimated that the real purchasing power of low-income countries' exports net of fuel imports *will be quite markedly lower in 1990 than in 1970.*[33] The problems caused by the substantial deterioration in the external environment have been compounded by an inability to secure commercial private sector commercial loans, at a time when these are becoming a much more important part of international capital flows.

These facts mean that there is now a very powerful case for using official funds to increase resources for low-income countries. A quite small increase in total aid flows could make a very significant difference to the situation of low-income countries, if all the increment went to them. A major switch in ODA so that two-thirds of the total went to low-income countries by 1985 would go a long way to meeting their needs. Other methods include co-financing with the private sector; switching IBRD and other 'hard' official loans towards low-income countries; and expanding the share of the public international sector in resource transfer, since it offers greater access to low-income countries than the commercial sector and on better terms.

Notes

1 This chapter is beset by difficulties because of differences in definition as to 'low income' among various sources: the OECD definition is countries having a per capita income of less than $450 in 1978; the IMF definition is countries having a per capita income of less than $300 in 1977 (minus India); the World Bank definition is countries having a per capita income of less than $360 in 1978. In the rest of the chapter note reference will show which source is being used. In general it is the details rather than the overall picture which is affected by the definitional changes.

2 World Bank; external finance is net of amortization and includes public and private flows. In these calculations, it excludes short-term borrowing.

3 World Bank.

4 IMF definitions: *Development Co-operation*, OECD, 1980, Table IV-9.
5 World Bank. See Table 5.1.
6 See Table 5.3.
7 IMF definition: see Table 5.4.
8 *World Development Report 1981,* Table 3.2.
9 Under the agreement between Mexico and Venezuela, 30 per cent of the cost of oil purchases in the region are returned to the purchasing countries in the form of loans at 4 per cent over 5 years, or 2 per cent over 20 years, if the credits are used to develop energy sources. The agreement means that about $0.7 billion returns to the region each year in the form of loans. *Financial Times,* 9 April 1981.
10 *World Development Report 1981,* Table 3.7.
11 IMF.
12 IMF.
13 *World Development Report, 1980,* op. cit., Table SA 1.
14 *World Development Report, 1981,* Table 2.10.
15 'Thus, without a strong policy response during the adjustment period [by ICs and OPEC], the Low case is the likelier outcome. And a number of factors, including serious political instability, major problems in capital markets or a breakdown of world economic cooperation, could bring about a much worse outcome'. *World Development Report, 1980,* op. cit., p. 6.
16 *Development Co-operation, 1980,* op. cit., pp. 103 and 130.
17 *World Development Report, 1980,* op. cit., p. 29.
18 These calculations are based on the aid figures given in *World Development Report, 1980,* op. cit.
19 See note 9 above.
20 *World Development Report, 1980,* op. cit., Table 2.4.
21 OECD definition excluding an 'unallocated' item. The OECD has made an estimate 'allocating' the 'unallocated' which raises the proportion in 1978 to 57.3 per cent. In the rest of this chapter — and in devising targets — we work in terms of the 'allocated' proportion.
22 From World Bank, see Table 5.7.
23 *World Development Report, 1980,* op. cit., p. 29.
24 Figures are for 1979.
25 1979; Turkey is another substantial recipient of US aid.
26 *Development Co-operation,* op. cit., p. 125.
27 Report by Group of Experts, Commonwealth Secretariat, op. cit., p. 97. The precise calculations of course depend on the assumptions made.

28 As noted, OECD includes countries with incomes of less than $625 per capita in 1980. In 1978 the cut-off was $450.

29 OECD, *Development Co-operation*, op. cit., Table 4–10.

30 This is a list of 30 countries (1980) internationally recognized as 'least developed'.

31 World Bank. 34 per cent of World Bank lending in 1980 went to countries with incomes below $625 (1978 dollars).

32 For a full discussion see D. Brodsky and G. Sampson, Background Paper.

33 These estimates are for the unrealistic High case. *World Development Report, 1981*, Table 3.7.

6 WHOSE CONDITIONALITY?

Introduction

The IMF imposes conditions on countries making drawings on their facilities. The conditions are more formal and more stringent for drawings on upper credit tranches. Among the special facilities, low conditionality is a feature of the Oil Facility and the Compensatory Finance Facility, while the Extended Fund Facility is characterized by high conditionality. Three-quarters of Fund finance is currently provided in conjunction with economic adjustment programmes, whereas in the 1970s the proportion was closer to a quarter.[1] The question of the legitimacy of having conditionality at all and the justification of the particular form of conditionality adopted by the Fund has long been a central issue between the Fund and its critics.[2] The issue has become more important for the 1980s than before. In the first place LDCs' need for external finance will be very great, while the capacity of the commercial sector alone to meet this need may have diminished. Moreover, heavy borrowing by some countries in the seventies has left a legacy of debt problems which leave little option other than increasing recourse to the Fund. In the second place, other sources of finance for LDCs — notably the commercial sector, but also some public financing facilities — are increasingly making their finance conditional on the country reaching prior agreement with the Fund.[3] Fund conditions are therefore becoming an important element in LDC economic management, since the total resource flows dependent on Fund approval are far in excess of the finance for which the Fund is directly responsible. For countries in crisis IMF approval may be a necessary pre-condition for securing substantial capital inflow from any source.

This chapter asks a number of questions about condition-ality: the first question is why conditionality? Is it the con-sequence of a particular institutional structure (the IMF and the World Bank dominated by developed countries) or an unavoidable feature of resource flows from surplus to deficit countries? The second question is about the nature of con-ditionality: is there just one set of conditions which are a correct response to any situation, or are there alternatives? The third question is *whose* conditionality? Is it unavoidable that conditionality should be designed by the North and imposed on the South, or does self-imposed conditionality make sense? In order to answer these questions, we look first at historical experience in relation to conditionality and adjustment.

History of conditionality

Conditionality is probably as old as loans between govern-ments. A recent study[4] describes missions to Latin America in the 1920s by Montagu and others, which required financial orthodoxy of the countries visited. In modern times, however, conditionality has come to be associated with the IMF.[5] Conditionality was not an intrinsic feature of Fund opera-tions from the beginning, but was introduced (at an early stage) largely under pressure from the United States. As Dell puts it:

> The Europeans had the best of the argument, perhaps, but it was the United States that had the resources, and it was resources that counted, especially in the aftermath of World War II . . . it was a desire to enlist the cooperation of the United States as the principal source of credit that prompted other Fund members to give way to American views on the question of conditionality rather than any conviction on their part that adoption of the United States concept of conditionality was indispensable for a sucess-fully functioning IMF.[6]

Thus although the initial articles of agreement did not con-tain any provision for conditionality, in 1952 the executive board agreed on a general statement approving conditionality.

By 1955 it was decided that the larger the drawing in relation to a member's quota the stronger the conditionality. In 1969 conditionality was incorporated into the Fund Articles of Agreements. Gold tranche drawings were made unconditional. Concern at progressive tightening of Fund policies on conditionality, and in particular the 'multiplicity of performance criteria', was expressed at a ministerial meeting of the Intergovernmental Group of 24 in September 1978. In March 1979 the Executive Board of the Fund adopted a set of guidelines on conditionality, including the requirement that the Fund should 'pay due regard to the domestic social and political objectives, the economic priorities, and the circumstances of members, including the causes of their balance of payments problems'.

The World Bank structural adjustment loans, introduced in 1980, have been associated with a new form of (World Bank) conditionality.

Historically, then, conditionality has its origin in the insistence of the then sole creditor country, which provided finance for drawings on the Fund — the US. While the Europeans — at that point the major potential borrowers from the Fund — initially opposed conditionality, their attitude changed when LDCs became the chief borrowers. Today, each of the main Western industrialized powers supports orthodox Fund conditionality. There seem to be two motives for the insistence on conditionality, which need distinguishing. First, there is the creditors' desire to ensure repayment, in the case of the Fund rapid repayment because its finance was explicitly revolving and temporary. The revolving and temporary nature of Fund finance — which despite some relaxation has continued to be a major feature of its operations — leads directly to the requirement of some rather stringent conditionality.[7] While some element of conditionality arose from the repayment requirements and would probably apply, although in different form, to some more long-term forms of finance, in addition initially the US and later other Western countries appeared to wish to impose conditions out of a form of paternalism or grandmotherliness.[8] The US wished to use the Fund to advance its vision of the world economic order. While the domination of the US has substantially diminished, domination of the Fund by the industrialized countries remains, and the desire to maintain a particular world order is still a very important feature of Fund operations.

This was quite explicit in recent negotiations with Mexico. According to a Fund memorandum:

> If this [continuous devaluation and a cumulative inflationary spiral] were to occur it would probably have effects on Mexico's commercial and financial relations with the rest of the world and provoke radical alterations in the country's economic objectives. It is therefore of critical importance to act as quickly as possible on various political fronts to reduce pressures on the exchange rate.[9]

The second motive — the grandmotherly motive — goes a long way to explaining the particular set of conditions adopted — the bias in favour of free trade, the use of price policy, private investment, and so on. This will become clear in discussion of the particular form that Fund conditionality has taken.

In practice, the two motives cannot be clearly distinguished. On the one hand, the temporary nature of Fund finance, although a constraint in the context of the way the Fund functions does not need to be taken as a constraint in the medium term. This feature — responsible for much of the nature of conditionality — could have been, or indeed could be, changed if those who govern the Fund wished to change it. Thus in one way, the temporary aspect of Fund operations can be seen as a method by which the dominating countries maintain the stringent conditionality desired. On the other hand, politicians, economists (and others) responsible for the Fund genuinely believe that the conditions imposed — e.g. the bias in favour of free trade just mentioned — are in the best interests of recipient countries.[10] Thus the paternalism or grandmotherliness is not just a question of promoting a particular US/Western vision of the world, but is genuinely seen by those responsible as promoting the best interests of recipient countries. This mixture of motives and beliefs makes it difficult to settle the debate on conditionality.

IMF conditions in practice

The conditionality associated with the use of Fund resources requires the member using those resources to undertake a programme to adjust its Balance of Payments . . . the Fund's financial assistance should be used to support the implementation of economic policies which give a substantial assurance that a viable payments position will be attained within a reasonable time.[11]

A viable balance of payments is defined as one that can be sustained 'without resort to restrictions on trade and payments'.[12]

Fund objectives include improved balance of payments and control of inflation in the context of the objectives (embodied in the Articles of Agreement) of promoting trade liberalization and 'orderly' exchange rate management.

The actual conditions in a programme are determined in the light of these objectives plus a set of beliefs − on the part of Fund officials − about economic causality.[13] For example, it is believed that inflation and balance of payments difficulties are often due to excessive credit creation, itself a function of excessive public expenditure. It is believed that balance of payments imbalances 'were often exacerbated by distortions in cost–price relations that affected the international competitive position of the economy and prevented supply from achieving its full potential'.[14] Another example of Fund beliefs is contained in the statement of the IMF Managing Director that 'two of the most effective policy instruments in less developed countries are interest rates and exchange rates'.[15]

Given these common objectives and beliefs about economic causality, it is not surprising that in practice many conditions are common to Fund Agreements in rather different countries. For example, a Fund Survey of 21 programmes 1973–5 judged that in 15 cases the deficits were due to 'excessive domestic demand'; in 11 the maintenance of an unrealistic exchange was a major source of difficulty; and in 16 cases there were price distortions. All 21 programmes contained credit ceilings; exchange rate devaluation was contained in 10; 10 contained trade liberalization clauses;

16 had clauses to prevent an increase in external debt and 16 had clauses on government pricing policies.[16] Another study[17] of the 1969–78 period found that clauses on domestic credit creation and/or budget balance were contained in around 60 per cent in 1969 rising to 95 per cent by the end of the period; setting out new or additional taxes rose from 80 to 85 per cent; required reductions in government expenditure rose from 10 to 47 per cent; prices policy for non-financial public enterprises from 5 to 75 per cent; a reduction in consumer subsidies from 0 to 60 per cent.

As these figures indicate, the degree of conditionality on these clauses has risen. But recently there has been some change in Fund conditionality. In the first place, the new Guidelines contain reference to social and political circumstances as well as economic, although this remains rather vague at the moment. Secondly, the Fund acknowledges that current problems are 'structural' and require a longer period before balance of payments viability can be restored. Thirdly, the Fund acknowledges the importance of 'supply conditions' for bringing about the necessary structural change. In practice, interpretation of supply conditions seems to be exclusively in terms of changing prices (e.g. raising interest rates, changing exchange rates, raising prices of parastatals) so as to provide incentives for the required structural changes. Thus while the purpose of the policy instruments now includes supply as well as demand, the actual use of instruments (in nature and direction) remains much the same as before. This is in keeping with the prevailing economic philosophy/beliefs in the Fund which are enormously influential in determining the content of Fund programmes.

One issue that has aroused much controversy concerns monitoring rather than conditionality itself. The Fund has used various precise macro-economic variables as monitoring devices or 'performance criteria'. These are summarized by Guitan:

> The path of the main policy variables was set in quantitative terms for sub-periods — such as quarters . . . The quantitative policy instruments and targets, which were called performance criteria, became the guideposts to

assess whether the programme was being satisfactorily implemented . . . The criteria most frequently included . . . related to the rate of expansion of credit by the central bank or banking system; the reliance of the government or the public sector on bank credit; the recourse to external short-term and medium-term foreign borrowing; and the management of external reserves.

The Fund has been prepared to moderate or stop disbursements if the country fails on these criteria, sometimes even by a small extent. One of the reasons why Jamaica was refused further second tranche credit in December 1977 was her failure to meet the agreed ceiling on the net domestic assets of the Bank of Jamaica by 2.5 per cent.[18]

World Bank conditionality: for the past few decades most World Bank (and IDA) finance has taken the form of project finance. The flow of finance has therefore been dependent, primarily, on identification and development of projects which the Bank believed would generate adequate returns. General country reviews permitted discussion about broad economic policies, but for the most part project finance was not conditional on general policy advice being taken. The small element of programme finance (4.5 per cent of total Bank/IDA commitments in 1976–80) might have given rise to greater potential macro-conditionality. But this was rarely used in any strict way. Most programme finance took the form of emergency assistance in response to natural or other disasters, and did not permit on-going policy advice since the programmes were short term. As the Bank has moved into 'soft' sectors and into financing sectoral programmes, such as water supply, certain conditions have been built into the programmes, e.g. in the case of water, provisions for charging consumers. But these conditions have been confined to policies in the particular sector being financed. Recently, however, the Bank has started to negotiate 'structural adjustment loans' in response to the economic crisis in many countries and the need for general balance of payments support rather than project aid.[19] These loans are intended to assist countries to adjust to changed economic circumstances, specifically to the worsening external financial situation following the oil price rise. They are conditional on agreement being reached about changes in economic policies aimed at achieving structural adjustment. The first loans were designed to be released in tranches subject to a review of progress.

Experience by countries negotiating structural adjustment loans to date suggests a strong element of conditionality in these loans. Progress in reaching agreement has been slow; at one stage Tanzania had succeeded in getting agreement with the IMF but had not been able to reach agreement with the World Bank. Analysis of the conditions included in the first five loans show the following elements:

(i) changes in public investment programmes involving redirection and (usually) reduction in the programmes;
(ii) changes in agricultural marketing and pricing policies;
(iii) reform of (usually increasing) public enterprise tariffs;
(iv) reform of taxation;
(v) 'rationalization' of protection (usually reduced protection and replacement of quotas by tariffs);
(vi) 'rationalizing' and increasing export incentives;
(vii) raising interest rates;
(viii) reduction/elimination of consumer price subsidies;
(ix) wage and salary control;
(x) improved management of external debt.

The conditions involved in World Bank structural adjustment loans are thus complementary to IMF conditions, with similar types of policies (reliance on price incentives, a tendency to aim for redirection of resources towards the private sector, emphasis on trade liberalization), but they aim to achieve longer-run changes and are less concerned with short-run demand management, though the programmes do contain references to the need for IMF-type demand management. In most cases countries securing structural adjustment loans are already negotiating with the IMF so that short-run adjustments are left to these negotiations. World Bank conditionality will not have the impact of that of the IMF since structural adjustment loans are likely to be small in total magnitude (rising it is estimated to 0.6–0.8 billion dollars for the financial years 1980/81)[20] and covering far fewer countries than Fund assistance. It is likely — given the overall resource constraints of the Bank — that these loans will not be additional to the Bank's other activities but mainly substitute for them.[21] They thus introduce a new element of macro-policy conditionality without adding to total resource flows.

LDC reaction to conditionality

There is considerable hostility among LDCs to Fund conditionality. This has been expressed in part in reluctance to use Fund resources. This is one explanation of the very small contribution the Fund made to the recycling process in the seventies. Between 1973 and 1975 India drew 5.5 billion rupees from the (unconditional) compensatory financing and oil facilities and the reserve and first credit tranches. But she drew only 2.9 billion rupees under the conditional facilities (upper tranche and Extend Fund Facility) as against a maximum of 24 billion rupees that could have been drawn.[22] The Indian Minister for External Affairs was quite explicit: '. . . India was faced with a very severe balance of payments problem. Government was reluctant to make additional drawings from the IMF because of the stiffer conditions attached to drawings from the IMF in the higher credit tranches.'[23]

Brazilian reluctance to use Fund facilities because of the conditionality — especially because Brazil believes the Fund would try to eliminate indexation — is well known. There are numerous other cases. From 1974 to 1976 only 10 countries drew on the Fund beyond the first credit tranche.[24]

In the case of Jamaica and Tanzania, the hostility has been more overt and explicit:

> . . . the severe suffering imposed on a developing society through IMF conditionality is endured without any real prospect of a favourable economic outcome and without an adequate foundation of social welfare provisions to mitigate the hardships experienced by the people . . . the punitive withholding of tranches of foreign exchange as a consequence of the failure to meet periodic IMF tests

condemns the defaulting country to a worsening of the
foreign-exchange situation which the IMF involvement
itself is aimed at improving. (Michael Manley.)[25]

. . . the IMF always lays down conditions for using any of its
facilities. We therefore expected that there would be certain conditions imposed should we desire to use the IMF
Extended Fund Facility. But we expected these conditions
to be non-ideological, and related to ensuring that money
lent to us is not wasted, pocketed by political leaders or
bureaucrats used to build private villas at home or abroad,
or deposited in private Swiss bank accounts . . . My Government is not prepared to give up our national endeavour
to provide primary education for every child, basic
medicines and some clean water for all our people. Cuts
may have to be made in our national expenditure, but we
will decide whether they fall on public services or private
expenditure. Nor are we prepared to deal with inflation
and shortages by relying only on monetary policy regardless of its relative effect on the poorest and the poor.
(President Nyerere.)[26]

The Arusha Initiative argues that,[27]

The IMF is not neutral because it systematically bases its
prescriptions on market ideology, giving the preponderant
role to local private enterprise and transnational investment . . . we wish to highlight our solidarity with Jamaica,
Tanzania and other countries in similar situations. Their
chosen development paths and their confrontation with
the fund deserve international backing. It is morally and
politically unacceptable that their efforts at independent
and equitable developments be blocked by the IMF.

The LDC reaction to conditionality is based on a perception of the causes of their balance of payments disequilibrium, which is different from the orthodox IMF approach.
First, the LDCs believe that their balance of payments
deficits are symptoms of structural disequilibrium, and not
primarily related to factors that can be controlled by curbing
demand and operating on market prices. Secondly, such
structural disequilibrium reflects inelasticity of import

demand, or non-availability in the short run of domestic substitutes, so that the volume of imports cannot be reduced without reducing very sharply the level of income. It also reflects inelasticity of export supplies, implying that capacities are not available where there is sustained export demand. Thirdly, such a disequilibrium can be corrected only over a long run, with policies of investment planning and institutional reform and not simply by traditional market related policies dependent on high supply elasticities in response to prices. Fourthly, a part of the payments deficits of the LDCs, is believed to be due to external factors, over which they have no control, such as deteriorating terms of trade and protectionist policies of developed countries. In the face of these considerations, the IMF conditions aimed at improving the balance of payments in the short term to ensure repayment are regarded by the LDCs as conflicting with their primary objectives of increasing output and employment and achieving desired changes in the pattern of income and asset distribution.

While LDCs have shown considerable hostility towards Fund conditionality there has been little systematic attempt to present alternative packages in negotiating. This was perhaps illustrated in the case of Jamaica, where it seemed that towards the end of his government Manley was denying the need for any substantial change — a denial which went against the face of all the evidence since all the main elements in Jamaica's external financing were drying up. The IMF package is one possible adjustment pattern; but the experience of the seventies shows that there are alternatives.

Adjustment in the seventies

This section does not aim to review the great mass of experience in the seventies,[28] but briefly to explore how far it suggests alternatives in the options that countries face.

Countries' adjustment policies in the seventies depended critically on their particular circumstances, including three features especially:

(i) the extent to which their external circumstances

deteriorated as a result of adverse terms of trade and
deteriorating export markets;

(ii) the structure of their production and consequently
their capacity to adjust through export promotion/
import substitution; and

(iii) their ability to attract commercial loans.

Middle-income LDCs, while being substantially adversely
affected by the oil-price rise, were in a potentially good
position because they had large enough manufacturing
sectors to adjust through export promotion/import substitution, and also, for the most part, were able to borrow
on the commercial market. Consequently many of them
did not need to have recourse to the IMF and some countries,
e.g. Brazil, S. Korea and Uruguay, were notably successful
in borrowing, raising their overall investment rates, and
promoting exports. Thus it is clear that for this class of
countries there was an alternative to the IMF-type package.
Despite the fact that the heavy borrowing/high investment
strategy has led to some problems (e.g. Brazil's high debt
service ratio), middle-income countries as a whole grew
faster than developed countries or low-income countries.
While export promotion played an important part, some
countries also adopted fairly tight import controls/limita-
tions (including Brazil and S. Korea). This too was a divergence from the IMF package.

Other middle-income countries which deviated from the
IMF package were less successful, using their external borrowing to maintain consumption rather than investment and
with little attempt to improve the external balance of export
promotion/import substitution. While these countries were
able to maintain incomes in the short run, rapidly rising debt
service ratios mean that medium-term prospects were less good.
Turkey is an example of a country which borrowed as a substitute for adjustment and found itself in severe difficulties at
the end of the period. Jamaica is another example of this sort
of strategy; but in her case the accompanying socialist policies
brought about international reaction (from the bauxite
companies which reduced production and exports, from
tourists who stayed away and from the commercial banks,

responsible for a capital flight) which brought forward and accentuated the external crisis.

Chile and Peru are examples of middle-income countries which adopted most of the elements of the IMF package. In each case, the package was effective in the short run in improving the balance of payments through severe deflation. After an initial period, the rate of inflation came down. But the costs in terms of political, economic and social consequences were very high. In Chile, there was a substantial decline in national income and very heavy unemployment, while low-income groups were most severely affected.[29] In Santiago, the unemployment rate rose from 3.8 per cent (1972) to 16.7 per cent (1976). GNP in 1977 was estimated to be 20 per cent below its potential.[30] In Peru, there was a sharp fall in growth of GDP (from 3.2 per cent per head 1970-5 to −2 per cent p.a. 1975-7) while investment fell by 35 per cent in real terms.[31] After some years of stagnation, exports, investment and GDP started to rise although prospects, in both countries, are uncertain and largely dependent on a sustained inflow of private capital. In Peru, the improvement in the situation was largely an extraneous development,[32] although in Chile the dynamism of nontraditional exports is widely attributed to the orthodox policy package. The political and social costs of the package remain.

An analysis[33] of Chile, Argentina, Uruguay and Brazil in the 1970s, which followed stringent stabilization policies promoted by military governments, identified the following elements: in addition to control over aggregate demand through fiscal and monetary policy, the package also included reduced size of the public sector, higher prices for public utilities, wage repression, freeing of prices, gradual elimination of import controls, devaluation, sale of public enterprises to the private sector and free market interest rates. These programmes were primarily initiated by the governments, not the international public institutions, but they include major elements commonly found in the packages of the IMF and the World Bank. According to Foxley, the general results of these programmes were persistence of inflation, prolonged economic stagnation, higher unemployment, very large reductions in real wages and a worsening of the size distribution of income (although only limited evidence is available to test this).

However, an IMF staff analysis of Fund standby programmes in an earlier period[34] found that the programmes neither increased nor reduced growth rates, that external accounts improved in three-quarters of the case but only one quarter in statistically significant terms, and that the programmes did not affect the rate of inflation.

The economies of middle-income countries, with established manufacturing sectors and an established entrepreneurial class, may in the medium to long term respond favourably to a package involving import liberalization and devaluation. Even in these countries there are major problems, both political and economic. Politically, few countries are able to pursue the package of policies consistently given their short-run social and economic costs.[35] Moreover, from an economic point of view the package requires that supply and demand should be responsive to changes in price. Although the structure of their economies is more diverse and flexible than low-income countries, for large sectors of the economies of some middle-income countries, there is still limited price responsiveness especially in the short run. In Peru, for example, 'the problem with existing export lines was not lack of competitiveness but a very fundamental supply constraint which could not be affected by short-run measures'.[36]

Low-income countries, mainly dependent on a few primary products for exports and with a small manufacturing sector, have very much more limited options. The strategy of borrowing/maintaining investment/promoting exports is normally ruled out because of limited access to commercial borrowing, a shortage of good investment projects and limited capacity to diversify exports. These countries were therefore forced to pursue deflationary policies to limit imports. In theory they should have had some choice in what was cut (as Nyerere pointed out), for example, a choice between cutting social or private consumption. They also have some freedom to determine long-run development strategy, which will affect their capacity to adjust to future crises. Because of limited access to commercial borrowing, this group of countries was more immediately faced with the need for public resources, especially from the Fund. Ironically, however, in some ways the Fund package was least geared to the needs of this group of countries.

For very low income countries, with a small manufacturing sector and almost no local entrepreneurial class, the orthodox package is likely to have negative effects on development, in the long run as well as the short. In such economies, investment in infrastructure — roads, marketing, education and so on — is essential to obtain long-run growth; if a manufacturing sector is to be developed — and the experience of middle-income countries suggests that it was the existence of a sizeable manufacturing sector, generally developed behind massive import barriers, that enabled them to adjust into exports — then low-income countries do need very substantial protection for that sector for some time. Expenditure on social services is especially important in low-income countries to build up human capital as well as to make an immediate contribution towards raising the appalling standards of health. Thus for low-income countries, any package of adjustment policies must include policies to promote infrastructural investment, social expenditure and promotion/ protection of the manufacturing sector.

Low-income countries, especially in Sub-Saharan Africa, suffered in the 1970s from a very severe deterioration of their external position. The real purchasing power of their exports net of fuel imports was reduced by nearly 50 per cent between 1970 and 1980. For such countries to combine adjustment and growth, they needed very large inflows of finance on a long-term basis, as well as appropriate adjustment policies. But what they were offered was rather little finance and on a very short-term basis. Hence deflationary policies, which tended to weaken their long-run economic potential, appeared the only feasible option. A major problem for many of these countries was the financial constraint itself. For some countries it would have been impossible to devise any package which would promote development, with the financial constraint in being.

This brief look at experience of the seventies suggests the following conclusions:

1   If the objective were only an improvement in short-term balance of payments, the IMF package may 'work' for middle-income and low-income countries through its deflationary effects in restricting imports and also sometimes as a result of attracting other capital.

2   The short-run achievements have a heavy cost in terms of reduction in GDP, in investment and in increased unemployment.

3   In the longer run (five years plus), in middle-income countries the import liberalization/devaluation package may lead to a sustained growth in exports, if accompanied by other policies to diversify and promote the capacity of the export industries.

4   For many low-income countries, especially those with small manufacturing sectors and few private entrepreneurs, the package may well impede rather than help long-run development. Cuts in social and productive investment and extensive import liberalization are likely to endanger long-run growth prospects and hinder export diversification. Additional policies towards building up infrastructure and promoting investment are essential if the Fund set of conditions is not to result in prolonged stagnation.

5   For some low-income countries, especially adversely hit by external events, it may be impossible to continue adjustment and development without a much larger (and longer-term) inflow of finance than was available in the 1970s.

6   The IMF package is not politically neutral, but involves a bias towards the private sector and against the working class.[37]

7   Middle-income countries have alternative options: they may, for example, combine borrowing from abroad, promoting investment and exports; these policies can lead to a sustained growth in incomes.

8   Countries can maintain external equilibrium and growth, while maintaining tough restrictions on imports.

9   Different social and political objectives and different

political conditions may justify different policies — for example, greater restriction of private consumption, rather than public, discouragement of foreign private investment and so on. Differences in time horizon may also justify differences in policy packages.

Conditionality: some conclusions

In the light of this brief survey of conditionality and adjustment we are in a better position to answer the questions put forward at the beginning of this chapter.

First, *why conditionality*: as we saw, historically conditionality has two elements. One is the desire of creditors to ensure repayment, which is an unavoidable aspect of any lending; for private sector lending macro-economic conditionality appears to be avoided but the cost is high interest rates, short-term maturity, and the risk of sudden withdrawal. Moreover, even in the private sector there is some 'hidden' conditionality, as argued in Chapter 2 especially when countries are in difficulties. The second element in conditionality is the desire by creditor countries to impose their own vision of the world on recipients. This is partly out of a belief that this is the only way to ensure repayment, but is not the whole explanation since there are other sets of policies which would ensure repayment. Most public lending involves this second element because of governments' responsibilities and ambitions. As we have seen, IMF style conditionality, which has influence well beyond the actual flows of finance that go directly through the IMF, largely reflects the industrialized capitalist countries' vision of the world. This vision essentially consists of the belief that market forces alone, with major impetus coming from the private sector, are sufficient to bring about adjustment and ensure the generation of foreign exchange to meet repayment obligations. By implication, institutional and basic structural reforms are not believed to be necessary, while alternative instruments (e.g. controls and licences) are regarded almost always as inferior to the price mechanism. The situation is ironic since it means that the industrialized capitalist countries' vision of the world is imparted to LDCs through IMF conditionality despite the fact that these countries are no longer the main source of finance. This is another aspect of the institutional lag we have discussed before.

This analysis of conditionality has implications for possible reforms. First, LDCs need to accept that the first kind of conditionality is unavoidable if they are to borrow substantial sums. However, the implications of the first type of conditionality (that related to repayment) very much depend on the quantity and terms of the finance in question. With a substantial increase in quantity and medium-term repayment, the repayment conditions would permit more emphasis on investment for structural adjustment and less on short-term control of demand. Secondly, with the changing location of surpluses and therefore of financial power there is much less reason why LDCs need to accept the industrialized countries' vision of the world. Only if the new surplus countries share this vision and wish to promote it does this element need to remain. However, so far while the LDCs have been very articulate about why they dislike IMF conditionality, they have not really articulated alternative packages. Yet alternative packages are necessary because the new creditor countries also wish to be sure of repayment. Therefore, lacking alternatives, it is not surprising that the new creditors have supported the old style conditionality which at minimum does seem to be successful in ensuring repayment. Thus a major policy conclusion is that if the LDCs dislike IMF type conditionality, they will have to develop alternative packages.

Alternative packages may be preferred for a number of reasons: these include differences in *objectives*, differences in *timing*, differences in *economic philosophy*, and differences in evaluation of and weight attributed to effects on the *political system*.

As far as objectives are concerned, the Fund places major emphasis on control of inflation and on a (short-term) turn around in the balance of payments. No explicit emphasis is placed on the fulfilment of basic needs or on income distribution objectives. The Fund programmes are only concerned with economic growth in so far as short-term adjustment is regarded as necessary for long-run growth. Difference in objectives was clearly a major element in the differences between Tanzania and the Fund. Because of the short-term nature of Fund finance,[38] the Fund is concerned with almost immediate improvements in the balance of payments. This unavoidably means emphasis on reductions in expenditure, which can bring about immediate improvement, as against building up productive capacity, which could bring about more long-term improvements. Countries are generally more concerned with what happens to the economy in the longer term. Differences in economic philosophy are a major cause of differences in approach. There are very major differences in opinion among economists about macro-economic policy and the control of inflation and about the responsiveness of the balance of payments to instruments such as the exchange rate as against controls. A recent Report of the United Kingdom Parliamentary Treasury and Civil Service Committee identified four distinct schools of thought on the question of the relationship between monetary policy and inflation.[39] Work by Taylor[40] has shown that under certain assumptions orthodox stabilization policies (devaluation, monetary contraction and fiscal restraint) may be both contractionary and inflationary. There is considerable debate among economists, too, about the relative efficacy of the exchange rate as against import controls.[41] The Fund tends to take the orthodox view of these matters. The major differences among economists on these matters make it likely that others may take a different view.

The Fund appears to make very little attempt to incorporate effects on the political system into its calculations or its programmes. Yet the programmes do have very significant political effects, with riots and changes of government being not infrequent consequences. One analysis of 23 devaluations between 1953 and 1966 found that in 30 per cent of the cases the government fell within one year of devaluation and in 60 per cent Ministers of Finance lost their jobs within a year.[42] In many cases, it appears to be fears about the political consequences — which if dramatic enough can wipe out all economic gains — that are the critical factor in resistance to Fund programmes.[43] A greater appreciation of the extent and importance of political factors could lead to quite a different programme from that which might be suggested by economic analysis alone.

For all these reasons, countries may be justified in desiring alternative packages from those suggested by the Fund. Moreover, alternative packages are potentially viable, i.e. could be designed which would ensure the first principle of conditionality, viz. repayment in the medium term. This is indicated by the variety of adjustment experience in the seventies. It is not being argued here that Fund packages are invariably inappropriate, as sometimes seems to be suggested, rather that to countries which differ in some of the respects described, more appropriate packages could be designed which would still meet the overriding requirements with regard to debt servicing and repayment.

Alternative packages will differ according to the circumstances of each country — political, social and economic. Thus it is not possible to identify a single alternative package. But work on recent adjustment experience suggests the following elements that might be part of alternative packages:

(i) Macro-economic management must be such that repayment is permitted. This does *not* need to mean a balanced budget, nor a particular level of credit creation, but does mean that supply and demand have to be planned at the macro-level, so as to allow sufficient resources to meet the repayment requirement.

(ii) The foreign exchange requirement for repayment needs to be met as well as the resource requirement. This requires that incentives and controls are sufficient for the resources available to be translated into foreign exchange. Hence the exchange rate, tariffs, import controls, export subsidies and other trade policies must together be sufficient to secure the desired repayment obligation.

(iii) In managing macro-economic demand and supply and the foreign balance, there are a set of alternative instruments. The orthodox package tends to make use of one set of instruments (namely control of aggregate demand via public expenditure, taxation and credit creation) and use of the exchange rate for balance of payments. Alternative packages would encompass a much wider set of instruments, selecting between them according to economic conditions and economic efficiency and social, political and economic objectives. For example, import controls and export incentives, multiple exchange rates, bilateral trade agreements all form alternatives (or supplements) to the exchange rate. On macro-economic management, increase in supply is of relevance as well as reductions in demand. Emphasis on basic needs and income distribution as objectives mean that luxury taxation and reductions in defence expenditure may be used to control demand, rather than expenditure on social services and food subsidies.

(iv) Emphasis on long-run development objectives is likely to mean that investments in infrastructure, social services and productive capacity form part of the package.

(v) Structural adjustment packages would normally include specific *sectoral* programmes to develop the capacity of key sectors to meet local demands and to export. Key sectors are likely always to include food and energy. Other priority sectors will have to be identified in particular cases.

(vi) There should be no particular prejudice against (or for) the public sector. The relative efficiency of the public as against the private sector depends on the nature of the economy (in some economies the potential of the private sector is minimal), the structure of incentives and the history of the two sectors. Relative efficiency of course is by no means the only consideration determining which sector should be responsible for which activity.

The set of provisions discussed above in no way consists of a full articulation of alternative packages. Rather it indicates the sort of areas in which alternatives would differ from the orthodox package.[44] An alternative package in any particular case requires detailed work on the conditions and prospects in that country. It is clear that LDCs do need to articulate alternatives if they are to succeed in negotiating on that basis. But it is very difficult for countries in crisis and with limited local knowledge of what the various options are to develop an alternative package. This is probably a major reason why LDCs have been rather weak in negotiating on the basis of alternatives. A major policy conclusion, therefore, is that there should be a central unit — possibly financed by the Third World directly, or by UNCTAD – whose job would be to examine the various adjustment policy options, by looking at the experience in the world as a whole and provide assistance to particular countries in difficulties, in developing alternative packages.

The central question of this chapter has been *whose conditionality*? It is clear that the nature of the conditions depend critically on who is imposing them. The IMF has been identified with a particular world view and an interest in revolving its finance in a short period. Its adjustment requirements follow from these two considerations. The LDCs, on the other hand, look upon borrowing as an instrument for structural reform, with sustained long-term growth of income and exports guaranteeing proper absorption and repayment of loans. The OPEC countries, with their temporary surpluses from the revenues from exhaustible resources, also require structural reforms and deployment of resources in diverse assets in order to generate a long-term return. In a genuine sense, their interests and those of the LDCs are similar. OPEC and the Third World together now have an opportunity to gain control over conditionality and thus to change the conditions for particular countries to self-imposed conditions, which might truly reflect 'the domestic social and political objectives, the economic priorities and the circumstances of members'.

Notes

1 Address by J. de Larosiere to Economic and Social Council of the United Nations, 3 July 1981.

2 See S. Dell, Background Paper, for the historical origin of the debate. The paper has been published as 'On Being Grandmotherly: The Evolution of IMF Conditionality', Essays in International Finance, No. 144, October 1981, Princeton.

3 Besides the commercial banks which, in a number of recent cases – e.g. Turkey, Jamaica, Sri Lanka – have made their commitment in a country conditional on Fund support, the Paris Club debt renegotiation is almost always dependent on agreement with the Fund (see C. Hardy, Background Paper). In the case of Jamaica, British Export Credit Guarantee was made conditional on the Jamaicans coming to an agreement with the Fund.

4 E. Bacha and C. Diaz Alejandro, 'Tropical Reflections on the History and Theory of International Financial Markets' in G. K. Helleiner (ed.), *For Good or Evil: Economic Theory and North-South Negotiations*, Croom Helm (forthcoming).

5 See S. Dell, Background Paper for a masterly historical survey.

6 Dell, op. cit.

7 This is the main justification used by M. Guitan, 'Fund Conditionality and the International Adjustment Process: the Early Period, 1950-70', *Finance and Development*, December 1980.

8 Dell quotes Keynes, describing the views of the US government as 'In their eyes it should have discretionary and policing powers and should exercise something of the same measure of grandmotherly influence and control over the central banks of member countries, that these central banks in turn are accustomed to exercise over the other banks within their own countries'.

9 IMF Staff internal memorandum, 22 September 1976 quoted in L. Whitehead, 'Mexico from Bust to Boom: A Political Evaluation of the 1976-1979 Stabilisation Programme' in *World Development*, November 1980.

10 See, for example, J. Williamson, 'The Economics of IMF Conditionality', paper for Refnes conference, 1980, in G. K. Helleiner (ed.), *For Good or Evil, Economic Theory and North South Relations*, Croom Helm (forthcoming).

11 Guitan, op. cit.

12 Ibid.

13 See Williamson, op. cit. for a succinct account of these beliefs, which are also illustrated in Guitan and in almost any issue of the IMF Surveys.

14 Guitan, op. cit.

15 *IMF Survey*, 21.1.1980.

16 T. Reichman, 'The Fund's Conditional Assistance and the Problems of Adjustment, 1973-75', *Finance and Development*, December 1978.

17 W. Beveridge and M. Kelly, 'Fiscal content of Financial Programmes supported by Stand-by Arrangements in the Upper-Credit Tranches, 1969-78', *IMF Staff Papers*, Vol. 27, No. 2, June 1980.

18 *Development Dialogue*, 1980, 2, p. 124.

19 See E. P. Wright, 'World Bank Lending for Structural Adjustment', *Finance and Development*, September 1980.

20 Wright, op. cit., p. 23.

21 'Structural adjustment lending will, for the most part, substitute for sector and project lending and not constitute additional flows of external assistance', ibid., p. 23.

22 S. Dell and R. Lawrence, op. cit., 1980, p. 45.
23 Statement to Parliament, 15 May 1978, quoted in Dell and Lawrence, op. cit., p. 113.
24 S. Dell, 'The International Environment for Adjustment in Developing Countries', *World Development*, November 1980.
25 Message from Michael Manley to the South-North Conference on the International Monetary System and the New International Order, quoted in *Development Dialogue*, 1980, 2, p. 5.
26 President Nyerere's New Year Message to the Diplomats accredited to Tanzania – quoted in *Development Dialogue*, op. cit., p. 7.
27 Ibid.
28 For much more in-depth analysis see Dell and Lawrence, op. cit.; S. Griffith-Jones, op. cit.; W. Cline and S. Weintraub (eds), *Economic Stabilization in Developing Countries*, Brookings, 1981; and *World Development Report 1981*, Chapter 6.
29 See A. Foxley, 'Stabilization Policies and Stagflation: The Cases of Brazil and Chile', *World Development*, November 1980.
30 Ibid., Table 2, p. 889.
31 A. Angell and R. Thorp, 'Inflation, Stabilization and Attempted Redemocratization in Peru, 1975-9', *World Development*, November 1980.
32 Ibid.
33 See A. Foxley, 'Stabilization Policies and Their Effects on Employment and Income Distribution; a Latin American Perspective', in W. Cline and S. Weintraub (eds), op. cit.
34 T. Reichmann and R. Stillson, 'Experience with Programmes of Balance of Payments Adjustment: Standby Arrangements in the Higher Credit Tranches 1963-1972', *IMF Staff Papers*, 25, June 1978.
35 See *Economic Stabilization in Latin America: Political Dimensions*, special issue of *World Development*, November 1980, edited by A. Foxley and L. Whitehead.
36 Angell and Thorp, op. cit.
37 'In both Brazil and Chile distribution was affected by the stabilization programmes and this is the result of the political model lying behind the programmes, which, in both Brazil and Chile implied the exclusion of workers and the full participation of private capitalist owners. In this sense there is not the "neutrality of policies" which the orthodox approach itself advocates', Foxley, op. cit.
38 Until recently most Fund programmes lasted just one year. Now the timing has relaxed so that three year programmes may be concluded.

39 See G. Maynard, 'Mrs. Thatcher's Economic Policy and the Treasury Committee', *The Banker*, May 1981, quoted in UNCTAD/MFD/TA/15, 'Structural Adjustment Policies'.

40 L. Taylor, 'IS/LM in the Tropics: Diagrammatics of the New Structuralist Macro Critique', in Cline and Weintraub (eds), op. cit.

41 See the work of W. Godley and F. Cripps in the *Cambridge Economic Review*.

42 See 'Currency Devaluation in Developing Countries' in R. Cooper, in *International Trade and Money*, edited by M. Connolly and A. Swoboda, Allen and Unwin, 1973.

43 This has been a major problem in Egypt, Jamaica and Ghana for example.

44 For more discussion of alternatives see 'Structural Adjustment Policies' (UNCTAD/MFD/TA/15) op. cit.

7   INTERNATIONAL CURRENCY REFORM

There is deep-seated dissatisfaction among developing countries with the present system of international payments. This was reflected in the central recommendation of the Arusha South–North Conference for 'The establishment of an international currency unit as the international means of exchange and primary reserve asset'.[1] The aim behind this proposal is to replace national currencies — notably the dollar — by an international currency because it is believed that the use of national currencies bestows power and wealth on particular developed countries and also imparts instability to the system as a whole.

Some of the main impetus for a new international currency unit has come from supporters of a *commodity-backed* currency: this was the proposal contained in the main Background Document for the Arusha Conference.[2] But others have argued for an unbacked fiat currency which might be brought about by an extension of the use of the SDR. The first part of this chapter looks at recent proposals for a commodity-backed currency. The second considers briefly how developments in the present system of SDRs might fulfil the functions required of an international currency.

A commodity-backed international currency

There are a number of variants of proposals for a commodity-backed international currency. In what follows we take the proposal put forward at Arusha as the basis of discussion. That had the following main features:
— a commodity unit would be established, consisting of a basket of primary commodities. The commodities (and weights within the basket) would be established on the basis of their importance in international trade, but only

commodities which are storable and homogeneous would be included;[3]

— a new World Central Bank would be established which would issue a new international currency unit (ICU) whose value was defined in terms of the basket of commodities; the Bank would (directly or indirectly) buy commodities in exchange for ICUs, or sell ICUs in exchange for commodities at the predetermined price; the new ICU would in effect be a 'warehouse receipt' for the bundle of commodities;

— there would be a fiduciary issue of ICUs to Central Banks, in addition to the backed issue; initially the ICU would be a deposit currency, held only by Central Banks of member countries;

— the existing system of SDRs would be incorporated into the new system, SDRs being valued in terms of commodities rather than currencies, while gold would be incorporated as one item in the bundle of commodities;[4] the Arusha document is not explicit about how other forms of reserves (notably the dollar) would be included, but the obvious intention is to replace them as an international reserve currency by the ICU.

The idea of a commodity-backed reserve currency has been supported on the following grounds:[5]

(i)   to stabilize (and improve) prices of primary commodities;
(ii) to reduce international inflation;
(iii) to stabilize (and raise) levels of world demand;
(iv) to reduce currency speculation;
(v)   to change and widen control over international reserve creation;
(vi) to change the distributional effects of international reserve creation.

Each of these arguments will be considered, as well as estimates of the costs of the scheme especially with reference to costs of storing commodities.

(i) *Price stabilization of primary commodities*

Developing countries suffer from poor, fluctuating and, over certain periods, deteriorating terms of trade for primary commodities. Individual countries tend to suffer more than the Third World as a whole since many countries are heavily dependent on just one or two commodities. Many international schemes have been devised to deal with the problems that arise: these include schemes for compensation for export shortfalls, individual international commodity agreements and the Common Fund Integrated Programme for Commodities. If a new currency made a major contribution to stabilization, this would be a very big advantage of the scheme for Third World countries, which would obviate the need for other schemes which have proved difficult to negotiate on any substantial scale.

The proposed new currency would make some contribution to raising and stabilizing terms of trade for primary products in two ways. First the Central Bank would need to accumulate some stocks of primary products in the initial years, and would thus increase the demand for these commodities, raising their price. Secondly, the scheme would stabilize the price of the bundle of primary commodities included in the basket in terms of the new currency unit.[6] When there was a tendency for the price of the bundle as a whole to fall, the Central Bank would buy primary commodities, while if there were a tendency for the price to rise, the Central Bank would sell. Although this would stabilize the price of the bundle it would not stabilize the price of individual commodities within the bundle: their price fluctuations should in general be modified, but they would not be eliminated, and in certain circumstances[7] might actually be increased.[8]

If prices of all commodities in the bundle moved together (upwards and downwards) and more or less to the same extent then any move to stabilize the price of the bundle would also contribute to stabilizing the price of individual commodities. But where prices of the bundle move in different directions — as might easily happen if gold or oil were included — stabilization of the price of the bundle could be destabilizing in terms of effects on prices of particular commodities (and incomes of particular countries).

To achieve price stabilization of particular commodities, the scheme would be faced with all the problems that have been raised in connection with the Common Fund, including the fact that the knowledge about the volume of purchases needed to achieve a target margin of stabilization is very limited – the main technical problem of the Common Fund. If very strong commodities were excluded, e.g. gold and oil, stabilization of individual commodities would be easier to achieve, but then confidence in the new currency unit would be likely to be less and its effects on stabilization of prices in the world as a whole and on the control of reserve creation would be correspondingly reduced.

To conclude, it seems that the scheme could contribute to overall price stabilization, but it would be a substantial and complex task, of the kind discussed in connection with the Common Fund, also to achieve individual commodity price stabilization. A further problem is that while the scheme would contribute towards price stabilization of primary commodities in terms of the new currency, variations in the value of the new currency in terms of national currencies and changes in the national price of manufactures could mean that it had a lesser (or even nil) effect in stabilizing the primary products/manufacturing products terms of trade.

(ii) *Reduced international inflation*

There are two mechanisms by which it might be argued that the scheme would reduce international inflation: (i) by stabilizing the price of primary commodities; and (ii) by limiting international credit creation. By stabilizing the price of a major element in world trade – the primary commodity bundle – the scheme would place a limit on world price inflation, whereas there is no such limit in a fiat money such as the dollar or SDR, whose value can fall indefinitely in terms of commodities. However, while this is true for international money and international prices valued in terms of the ICU, national prices could continue to escalate. For example, suppose there is strong trade union pressure within a DC for wage increases; such wage increases could be accommodated in national currency, and the exchange rate of the national currency and the ICU depreciated to compensate. In terms of the national currency the depreciation would

have the effect of raising prices of imports and thus introducing further national inflationary pressures. This sort of
inflationary situation could arise in each individual country.
With fixed exchange rates between national currencies and
ICUs the counter-inflationary impact would be greater, but
most national governments are not prepared – or even able,
given internal pressures – to give up the right to change their
exchange rates.[9] Fixed exchange rates do impart a less
inflationary impetus to the world economy – this is true
independently of the proposal and a combination of the
proposed commodity-backed currency, which stabilized
prices of primary products in ICUs, and fixed exchange
rates (for individual currencies or for groupings of currencies)
would, if effective, undoubtedly limit international inflation
at the cost of reduced flexibility for individual countries'
economic management.

The second way in which a new currency is supposed to
limit international inflation is by limiting 'uncontrolled
international credit creation'.[10] But it is now well established
that it is very difficult even to find any way of controlling
national credit creation by controlling the monetary base.
The problems would be far greater in international credit
creation because of the lack of any way of enforcing ratios
between the monetary base and total credit creation on an
international basis. None of the proposed schemes demon-
strate any mechanism which could eliminate, for example,
the rapid growth in the euro-dollar market. Moreover, there
is no reason why the commodity-backed scheme – which
includes a Fiduciary Issue – need differ in level of credit
creation from a non-backed form of international money.
It would differ if the Fiduciary Issue were limited to some
ratio of stored commodities. But in theory a non-backed
SDR scheme could be similarly controlled.[11] However,
a commodity backed scheme would involve some automatic
controls on the level of credit created by the scheme, whereas
the same degree of control for a non-backed scheme would
only be achieved by conscious control.

As far as inflation is concerned, the scheme as proposed is
not likely to have a marked effect. Substantial additions to
the scheme might – but these are so substantial that they

really need to be considered on their own, and indeed, both with respect to fixed exchange rates and with respect to international credit creation, could, if effective, make a contribution independently of the commodity-backed currency in combination with other types of international arrangements.

(iii) *Stabilization of world demand*

To the extent that the scheme led to a steady expansion in incomes of primary producers it might be conducive to a steady (or steadier) expansion in world demand and world output. But the proposed scheme would not necessarily lead to the desired steady expansion in income and expenditure among primary producers.

The major problem is that the scheme would stabilize the price of a bundle of commodities, but not the price of individual commodities. Fluctuations in the prices of individual commodities would result in fluctuations in the national incomes and expenditures of particular countries, and also in aggregate incomes and expenditure.[12] In addition, the real purchasing power of primary products over manufactures could fluctuate with changes in the prices of manufactured products in terms of the ICU.

Despite these qualifications, it does seem likely that a scheme which tends to improve the terms of trade for primary products and to iron out some of the fluctuations in the incomes of primary producers as a whole would tend to produce a steadier expansion of world demand. This arises from the way in which the money creation aspects of the scheme are tied to fluctuations in primary product prices and thus to world demand. A similar stabilizing effect could be achieved by a fiat international money, but it would be less automatic. However, fiat money has the advantages of less automaticity as well as its disadvantages, i.e. monetary expansion need not occur when considered inappropriate, and it can occur even if the primary product price situation does not warrant it. For example, the large oil price rise of the 1970s led to severe international deflation because of the relatively low propensity to spend among oil exporters, adjustment problems among oil importers and deficiencies in recycling mechanisms. In this situation an increase in world reserve creation (appropriately distributed) would have been an appropriate solution, not the decrease that a commodity-backed reserve scheme, which included oil as one commodity, would have involved.

It is clear that many of the objectives of the scheme — price stabilization, income stabilization — depend on the ICU being stabilized in terms of the price of manufactures as well as primary commodities. A partial solution would be to stabilize the exchange rate between the ICU and industrial currencies. To do this would involve a heavy commitment of currencies by the industrialized countries and a (collective) surrender of freedom to change their exchange rates. A critical question then would be whether the industrialized countries would be prepared to agree to this.

(iv) *Reduced international currency speculation*

International currency speculation would be reduced compared with that in the current situation where gold, the dollar and other currencies are all actual and potential reserve currencies. This would be an advantage of the proposed commodity currency, but one that is shared by any *single* international currency (e.g. non-backed SDRs). Moreover, this scheme would only have this advantage so long as it fully displaced alternative reserves, such as gold and the dollar. So long as alternatives persist speculation could continue, changing the prices of the alternatives in terms of each other and the ICU.

It is by no means clear that any proposal for an international reserve currency — be it backed by commodities or unbacked (like the substitution account) — can eliminate the diversity of forms in which *de facto* international reserves are held. So long as reserves are held in more than one form, then there remains scope for currency speculation and for consequent changes in relative prices, which may be unrelated to real factors. A new international currency, or other arrangement, can at any one time, reduce the total amount of reserves held in some form particularly subject to speculation — as is the intention of the proposed substitution account *vis-à-vis* outstanding dollar balances — and thus moderate the problem, but it cannot eliminate it. Moreover, it is obvious that this role is not confined to a commodity-backed reserve but may also be fulfilled by a fiat currency. A commodity-backed reserve may also introduce a new form of commodity speculation so that the prices of individual commodities become subject to a form of currency speculation. Thus the scheme cannot be expected to eliminate currency speculation and may not do much more in this direction than an unbacked scheme.

(v) *Widen control over international reserve creation*

The hidden agenda behind much Third World dissatisfaction is the question of control. This is quite explicit in places in the discussion about international reserve creation. It is felt that with the existing system the level of dollar reserves depends on the balance of payments of the US which can choose what level of deficit to run. The SDRs are under international control, but administered by the IMF: control remains mainly in the hands of developed countries. A central plank of the Arusha initiative is the establishment of 'Democratic management and control'.

It seems clear that the aim of achieving democratic management and control — although not easy to interpret with precision — is an important one. It is important for the world as a whole, that the world economy is not subject to massive inflation or deflation due to rather arbitrary changes which are the incidental results of various developments and over which no authority is exercising control. The oil-price rise and subsequent recycling problem illustrates the need for a world authority which helps to control the level of world credit creation and acts as a lender of the last resort.[13] From a Third World point of view, it is clearly of importance that any such authority should be democratic, in the sense that individual nations have some say on its operations and the old oligopoly of the North does not dominate the institution.

The first step towards achieving democratic management and control is to achieve *some* international control over international credit creation. While no new currency, or new authority, can, by the nature of international money, achieve complete control, since no authority can rule out the use of uncontrolled items to fulfil the functions of international money,[14] a new credit-creating institution can have some influence on what happens at the margin, and to this extent contribute towards control over total level and distribution of credit creation. But this, if achievable at all, could just as well be attained by a fiat international money as by commodity-backed money. Any new institution/currency which achieves this will only do so if it has the support of the North as well as the South. It seems likely that it will be easier to persuade the North for the need for some control over international credit creation — indeed to some extent countries are already persuaded of this — than to persuade them that the South should have a substantial say in the new institution. Indeed for some, the idea that the South should have a substantial element of control would be a decisive reason against introducing any major international control, preferring to retain *de facto* control by leaving the critical decisions in the hands of national governments of the North. Thus the objective of achieving control may be in conflict, in real negotiations, with the objective of achieving democratic control. Control itself is so important, for the South as well as the North, that it may initially be worth getting that established before pressing too hard for democratic control.

While, as argued above, an international fiat money could just as easily be controlled by the international community as an international commodity-backed money — indeed in some ways more easily — the significance of the South as producers of commodities makes it appear that, if established, a commodity-backed money would lend itself to control by the South, just as the use of dollar reserves confers some powers of control on the USA.

The exercise of control would depend upon international agreement, and cannot be related to the supply of reserve assets. If the South were the major producer of the bundle, they would make some seigniorage gains, but if they were to try to use their position as producers to exercise control, there would be severe confidence problems probably frustrating the whole exercise.

(vi) *The distributional effects of international reserve creation*

The net distributional effect depends on a number of factors: (i) what it is being compared with; (ii) how the fiduciary issue is distributed; (iii) how the costs of the scheme are financed; (iv) whether — and at what level — the new currency is interest bearing; (v) the effects on commodity prices, in general and individually; and (vi) the distribution of production of commodities.

As far as the fiduciary issue is concerned, there is no reason why the distributional effects should differ from any unbacked international reserve creation. Objections to an SDR 'link' would equally be applicable here, and if these objections could be overcome here they would presumably equally be overcome with respect to the SDR. Thus it seems reasonable to leave out any 'linked' distribution of the fiduciary issue.

Any new international currency, whether backed or un-backed, even without any 'link' would have more favourable distributional effects, as far as the Third World is concerned, than a system of gold or dollar reserves, whose seigniorage benefits are likely to be confined to a few non-Third World countries. In comparison with a system of gold and foreign exchange reserves, the distributional effects of an unlinked fiduciary issue would be favourable to the Third World. But compared with an unbacked international reserve creation, they need not be more favourable. The level of benefits arising from the distribution of a fiduciary issue depend on the level of interest rate payable. If commercial interest rates are payable, then the distributional effects become rather insignificant.

The other major distributional effect comes from a positive effect on the prices of primary commodities. Here the benefits depend on the (unknown) total effect and (unknown) distribution among commodities. But as Table 7.1 shows, the North is also of considerable significance in the production of a number of commodities, so the benefits of the support to primary prices would not be confined to countries of the South.

However, it is likely that support for the prices of primary

Table 7.1   Percentage of world exports of commodities, 1976

	(1)	(2)	(3)	(4)
No. of commodities:	27	36	18	16
% of world trade				
Developing market economies	38.0	36.9	55.3	56.0
of which				
high income	1.7	2.1	2.9	2.5
middle income	26.1	25.6	36.9	37.2
low income	7.7	7.5	11.7	12.0
Rest of the World	62.0	63.1	44.7	44.0

(1)–(4) consist of different bundles of commodities:

(1) and (2) are listed by Hart. (2) consisting of 27 commodities are those Hart defines as 'apparently well-standardized and durable in storage'.

(3) is the UNCTAD list of the Integrated Programme of Commodities.

(4) is the UNCTAD list excluding iron ore and bauxite, which Hart argues as unsuitable for inclusion.

Sources: A. G. Hart (1976), 'The case as of 1976 for International Commodity Reserve Currency', *Weltwirtschaftliches Archiv*, No. 112; UN Trade Statistics.

commodities will help the Third World as a whole as *net* exporters of primary commodities, and be paid for by the North, as a whole, as *net* importers of commodities. From this point of view, the commodity-backed reserve scheme will involve significant distributional benefits for the Third World, as a whole, as would a large-scale Common Fund. But, as often pointed out in criticism of the Common Fund, the distributional effects within the Third World may not favour the poorest countries or the poorest people.[15]

Costs of a commodity-backed international currency[16]

The major palpable direct cost is that of storing commodities necessary for the new institution to stabilize prices. The costs depend on what level of stocks would be involved, and the extent to which these might act as a substitute for existing national (public and private) stockpiles, rather than being a net addition, as well as estimates of the costs of storage. The costs to the new institution would depend on how far they had to store commodities directly and how far the existence of the scheme encouraged or substituted for private stock holding. Some believe that private operators could undertake the whole stock-holding operation required. Estimates of costs vary from $4.5 billion to $12–20 billion at 1966 prices and volumes.[17] Since then the total value of exports of food and raw materials has increased over four-fold, and costs at 1980 prices may therefore be expected to have increased by as much, giving a range of storage costs of $18 billion to $48–80 billion. These costs are considerably greater than cost estimates for the buffer stocks involved in the Common Fund. One estimate put these at $2.5 billion for eleven commodities, and $12.5 billion for 13 commodities, including wheat and rice.[18] However, a substantially larger number of commodities are involved in the commodity reserve currency.

The advantages of a commodity reserve scheme compared with an unbacked international currency

The SDR – an unbacked international currency – is now an accepted part of the international reserve and payments system. There would have to be significant gains to be made for switching to a backed-currency to persuade authorities to change and to justify the complex political bargaining and negotiation involved. If the same gains could be made from changes in the SDR system, these would be easier to attain.

As we have already noted, many of the benefits claimed for a commodity reserve currency would also be effected by reforms in the (unbacked) SDRs. An SDR system could contribute to controlling the total supply of international money, and could be used to operate countercyclically (and more sensitively) than a commodity scheme. If SDRs replaced other reserve currencies (as proposed with the substitution account) they could reduce currency speculation as effectively as a commodity-backed money, while they would not encourage speculation in commodities for monetary reasons. Potentially, the SDR system could be associated with more 'democratic control', but in practice this is less likely than with a commodity money. The distributional effects of the issue of SDRs could be designed to be equivalent to those of a commodity money, but a commodity reserve currency would automatically confer benefits on the Third World (through raising the price of primary commodities) which would only be achieved by a conscious allocation policy in an SDR system.

The major differences between a commodity-backed reserve currency and an unbacked reserve currency lie in three areas: *one* that some of the effects would be *automatic* with a commodity-backed currency, which would be subject to conscious decision in the case of SDRs. This is true with respect to its countercyclical effects; and also with respect to some of its distributional effects. But given that in any practical version of the scheme, many of the decisions would have, *de facto*, to be discretionary, the significance of this element for good or ill may be exaggerated. Moreover, as Williamson puts it with respect to a gold standard 'The trouble with this argument [that which favours automaticity] is that it assumes that government would obey a self-denying ordinance committing them to a gold standard but that they would not obey a self-denying ordinance on deliberate liquidity creation'.[19]

The *second* group of advantages of a commodity-backed reserve currency concerns the effects on commodity prices. To the extent that the scheme stabilized commodity prices in relation to manufacturing prices, this would confer important benefits on the Third World and the world as a whole, which is in no way achieved by a fiat reserve system. This aspect of the scheme closely resembles the Third World conception of a large-scale Common Fund. The almost total failure of the Third World to negotiate a Common Fund for both technical and political reasons suggests the likelihood of equal failure with respect to this scheme. Indeed current North hostility towards substantive commodity price stabilization proposals could be such as to endanger the scheme as a whole.

It has been pointed out that many of the advantages of a commodity-backed currency could accrue to a fiat type international money. While this is so theoretically experience suggests very considerable difficulties in getting a fiat money widely accepted internationally. The SDR is the first real attempt to introduce an international fiat money, but so far it has made only very limited inroads into the international monetary field; national currencies and gold remain dominant. The SDR was introduced in 1970. Since then 17.4 million have been issued. SDRs accounted for 3.6 per cent of international reserves excluding gold at the end of 1980.[20] SDRs remain a central bankers money and are not accepted directly as means of international payment for goods and services. Recently interest rates have been raised on SDRs – making them closer to credit than money – in an attempt to make them acceptable internationally. Some people believe that without any backing a fiat money will never acquire sufficient acceptability to make it the main international currency. This is the *third* area in which commodity-backed currency has an advantage over fiat money. If this last argument were accepted, it would be very powerful since a fiat money would then appear to be a will-o'-the-wisp. However, there has not really been a serious attempt to make the SDR more widely acceptable so it seems too soon to write it off. Moreover, the commodity-backed currency would also meet severe obstacles – as already discussed – before it could be put into effect.

Taking the third argument as the major reason for supporting commodity backing suggests taking a rather different approach to a commodity-backed money than that discussed above.[21]

The 'basket of commodities' approach was justified as being necessary to stabilize the price of commodities and demand – these being the prime aims of the new currency. But suppose the prime aim of commodity backing is to make the international currency acceptable. In that case what is required is the availability of a stock of commodities to back the currency, in rather the same way that in the early days of banking pawnbrokers had a stock of goods that justified the issuing notes – without any particular predetermined relationship between the note issue and the items that formed the backing. In effect such a loose relationship could be achieved by some institutional tie-up between commodity stocks and the issue of international money: even without any precise predetermined price between the currency and commodities, the knowledge that there was commodity backing, and that the ICUs could be exchanged for commodities,[22] should give credibility to the currency as the goods at the pawnshop did for early note issues. This approach to commodity-backed money rather turns the question upside down: in the basket version, the point of the ICU relationship was to increase the value of commodities; in this version the point of the commodity backing is to give value to the ICUs. This is not just a logical change but also a practical one, in that the first step towards such a system is the development of some internationally owned and controlled stocks of commodities (or callable commodities); the issue of ICUs comes second. The commodity-backed ICUs are therefore likely to be a natural development following from the successful introduction of a Common Fund/ Integrated Programme for Commodities, rather than being a natural development of the present system of SDRs. But since it is obvious that these developments are far from being immediately acceptable or likely, it is worth pursuing reform of the present SDR system to see whether it could become an acceptable international money without commodity backing.

Reform of the SDR: toward a fiat international currency

Discussion above suggests that the major functions required of an international currency include controlling the total supply of money; countercyclical operation; reduction in currency speculation; democratic control; and improved distribution. At the moment the system of SDRs is making only very limited contribution to any of these aims. In order to meet these aims some major changes would be required. For the last two (democratic control and improved distribution) there are no major technical problems involved; the changes required are political. For the first three the problems are both technical and political.

Substitution: to control the total supply of international money, and eliminate or substantially reduce international speculation the SDR would have to substitute for the use of existing reserves of national currencies (notably the dollar) and gold. Various proposals have been put forward for a substitution account — these are directed at substitution for the use of national currencies rather than gold, but could be extended to gold.[23] Proposals for substitution have met political obstacles — their nature depending on the circumstances when the proposals were made and the details of the proposals. For example, when the proposals appear to be a device for supporting the dollar, they tend to be opposed by other developed countries and by developing countries. Conversely the Americans are not anxious to support a system which involves them in heavy long-run repayments in order to amortize their balances and prohibits them from paying for future deficits by running up further balances. Negotiations on a substitution account have broken down on these issues and on the shares of the cost of the proposed schemes between different parties. There are therefore very serious political problems impeding progress. But there are also technical problems about whether it is possible to replace national currencies (or gold) if traders continue to find these desirable trading and reserve currencies. While they could be replaced in national reserves, by government decision, this would not mean that they were replaced in private use. If widely used privately, governments would be under considerable pressure to include them in official reserves which are needed to support private transactions.

It is generally agreed that a voluntary substitution account would not achieve very much beyond being the first step towards a compulsory system. It is much more difficult to reach agreement about a compulsory system. If a compulsory system were instituted, in which governments agreed to substitute SDRs for their reserves of gold and national currencies, this would be a first step towards international control of international liquidity, but it would not be sufficient to secure effective control over real international liquidity (as against official reserves).

Developing countries have opposed the substitution account in the past on the grounds that — as put forward — it would be unlikely to hurt their immediate interests: for example, the 1972 UNCTAD Report concludes: 'Although, in terms of broad policy considerations, developing countries stand to gain from a strengthening of the SDR mechanism, their interests could be adversely affected, perhaps substantially, by the consolidation holdings. The principal reason for this is that higher interest rates on SDRs would be required if SDRs were to become a viable substitute for reserve currencies'.[24]

Developing countries could benefit from a substitution account because some system of substitution is an essential first step towards international control over the level of official reserves, which in turn is a prerequisite for more democratic control. In the long run developing countries as a whole are likely to gain from a system which is in the conscious control of the international community, rather than the outcome of uncoordinated economic forces, although some of the semi-industrialized countries who have done very well from borrowing on the euro-dollar market may prefer an 'uncontrolled' situation. Some of the disadvantages of a substitution account for LDCs, such as higher interest rates on SDRs, are occurring anyway, without a substitution account. Potentially there are a variety of ways in which a bias against LDCs in a new system could be offset, or more than offset, some of which could be incorporated into a substitution account. For example, any interest differential between interest received by a substitution account fund on national currency reserves and interest paid on SDRs could be directed towards the LDCs.[25] The 'link' offers another more direct way in which LDCs could be compensated. Even without a link, SDR allocation offers more to LDCs than other forms of reserve creation have offered (e.g. gold or dollars). It would therefore seem worthwhile for LDCs to concentrate on securing a substitution account SDR system that is in their interests.

The 'link' giving LDCs a large share of new issues of SDRs should be supported as an element in any extension of SDRs as an international currency. The benefits of the link have been diminished as a result of the increase in interest rates payable on SDRs. But these interest rates remain below the rates LDCs would have to pay for commercial borrowing. This, together with certain access, means that the link still offers LDCs benefits, which could be increased if interest rate differentials were offered to low-income countries. Even without a link, the ordinary issue of SDRs tends to give LDCs a greater share than other additions to world reserves.

In aggregate international liquidity has increased fast in the 1970s, especially as a result of the increase in the gold price. Yet developing countries have not shared proportionately in this rise, because of the smaller element of gold in their reserves.[26] Although for developing countries as a whole there was some rise in the ratio of reserves to imports in the 1970s, a number suffered a deterioration. At the end of 1978, 30 of the 93 countries for which data is available had reserves of less than two months imports.[27] There is a strong case for additional SDRs for LDCs so as to increase their reserves and also to substitute unconditional finance for conditional finance. One estimate suggests that non-oil LDCs need an additional 6 billion SDRs p.a.[28] This could be achieved with or without a 'link', depending on the size of the general increase in SDRs.

Other ways of strengthening the SDRs[29]

The *Programme of Action* adopted by Finance Ministers of the Group of Seventy-seven in Belgrade in 1979 declared that:

> Arrangements should be made for the creation of international liquidity through truly collective international action in line with the requirements of an expanding world economy, and the special needs of developing countries, and with such safeguards as would ensure that the total supply and distribution of international liquidity is not unduly influenced by the balance of payments position of any country or group of countries. The SDR should become the principle reserve asset of the system.[30]

Taking this — which is consistent with the major functions for international currency outlined above — as the ultimate objective, various short-term measures have been identified which might strengthen the SDR.[31] Minor changes were suggested in valuation and in improving the liquidity of SDRs by extending the freedom, speed and anonymity of transactions. A more substantive (and also controversial) change concerns the use of SDRs for private transactions. The denomination of transactions in SDRs, to reduce risks incurred by denominating in national currencies, may be helpful (as noted earlier in relation to recycling and financial assets), but will do little to extend the acceptability of SDRs as a reserve asset. On the other hand, if private holdings in SDRs were permitted, then SDRs could be used as a trading currency. This would increase the attractiveness of SDRs as money: indeed, SDRs cannot function as money in the way that for example the dollar does without such an extension of their use. If the dollar and other national currencies are to be displaced as forms of international liquidity, then the SDR would have to replace them in trading. Even the extension of SDR denomination of transactions is likely to be limited so long as obligations are incurred in national currencies. But if the SDR does become a trading currency, with private holdings permitted, then the Fund (or whichever central body is responsible) will lose control over the total amount in the system, since private banks will be able to create SDR balances, just as they can create dollar balances.

A central dilemma about the role of the SDR, or any international money, is identified in this debate. On the one hand, by keeping it as 'official' money the role of the SDR will tend to remain peripheral and other international assets will continue to function as international money. On the other hand, if the SDR does displace other assets in international trading and international finance, control over this form of international credit creation will be diluted. This is one of the central contradictions which arise in any monetary system, national or international. Complete and effective control over the creation of credit can never be achieved because if one asset is controlled, then other substitutes develop if the need arises. None the less, displacement of national currencies by an international currency would improve control and would extend it from a few countries towards international control. From this point of view, the use of SDRs as a trading currency should be encouraged.

Conclusions

Potentially, reforms of the SDR system could achieve many of the changes required. Technically and politically, it would appear less cumbersome to get reform this way, than through instituting a commodity-backed system. Only if commodity backing were the one way to achieve acceptability of international money would it be essential. The debate on this question is a very old one; for national currencies commodity backing is no longer required. At the national level, however, the political authority guarantees the integrity of the currency. At the international level similar international political backing is required. Otherwise the currency will lack credibility and acceptability.

One general point needs to be made: one country or group of countries cannot decide what another country or group of countries will accept as means of payment. There has to be agreement. The South, therefore, is not in a position to determine the means of payment acceptable in payment to the North. For this reason, whatever the merits or demerits of a particular proposal, the final outcome has to be a matter of negotiation, with the more powerful party (in this case the North) having the major say.

Notes

1 'The Arusha Initiative', *Development Dialogue*, 1980-2.
2 'The International Monetary System and the New International Order', Main Document for the South–North Conference, Arusha, 1980.
3 The requirement of homogeneity, strictly interpreted, could narrow the potential candidates for the bundle considerably; for example, even such apparently homogeneous commodities as tea or coffee include different varieties and grades. In order to avoid narrowing the bundle too much on grounds of non-homogeneity, the Central Bank would have to allow for a variety of grades within each commodity. This would create severe administrative problems.
4 The inclusion of gold could create problems since its price may well move out of line with the prices of other commodities in the bundle; yet if excluded (or retained as a separate currency as proposed in the Hart–Kaldor–Tinbergen version — see A. G. Hart, N. Kaldor, J. Tinbergen, 'The Case for an International Commodity

Reserve Currency', UNCTAD, 1964) confidence problems would arise between the use of gold and that of the new ICU.

5 The Arusha Background paper summarizes the arguments thus: 'A commodity-backed SDR would be able to address the three problems that are hindering the viability and proper functioning of the international economy, namely, inadequate growth of output and employment, persistent rise in prices and instability of primary exports.'

6 Within the margin of buying and selling prices of perhaps 5 per cent.

7 See P. Tinios, 'Survey of Proposals for an International Commodity Reserve Standard', mimeo, Oxford, 1980, p. 22. What happened to the price of individual commodities would depend partly on how far the proportions of different commodities included in the basket were permitted to vary in the short run. Variability in proportion would help stabilize the price of individual commodities. Commodities outside the bundle (e.g. perishables like bananas) would obviously not be stabilized by the scheme.

8 L. Spaventa, 'Comments on the Long-term Proposals for Restructuring the International Monetary System', *Development Dialogue*, 1980-2. Spaventa argues that stabilization would harm the *weaker* commodities, because if the price of the 'strong' commodities, e.g. oil or gold, rose, the Central Bank could only stabilize the bundle as a whole by securing falls in the prices of the weaker commodities, since the Bank would not have the resources to reduce the price of the strong commodities. This effect would only occur in extreme form if the Central Bank were permitted to vary proportions in which it buys and sells individual commodities and thus secure aggregate stabilization of the bundle by operating in the markets of the individual commodities. If the Bank has to buy and sell in fixed proportion bundles, the effect would be modified. In the Hart–Kaldor–Tinbergen scheme, commodities whose prices rise sharply are to be excluded from the bundle to avoid this effect.

9 Keynes argued against a fixed exchange rate commodity standard on the grounds that, like the Gold Standard, it 'imposed [national] price levels from without . . . Commodity standards which try to impose [wage policies] from without will break down just as surely as the rigid gold standard', J. M. Keynes (1943), 'The Objectives of International Price Stability', *Economic Journal*.

10 'Arusha Initiative', op. cit.

11 Indeed the 'Arusha Initiative' statement was referring to a controlled unbacked international currency.

12 This effect would be especially likely to the extent that the strong

commodities tend to have their prices raised while the prices of the weak commodities fall, since countries selling strong commodities tend to have a low propensity to consume relative to countries producing weak commodities.

13   See also Chapters Two and Eight.

14   This is the fundamental problem of control over national money supply as well.

15   See, for example, W. Cline (ed.), *Policy Alternatives for a New International Economic Order*, 1979, New York.

16   See Tinios, op. cit. (pp. 29–34) for a fuller discussion.

17   The low estimate is that of A. G. Hart in 'The Case For and Against and International Commodity-Reserve Currency', *Oxford Economic Papers*, 1966 – he estimates the operating cost at 3½ per cent of the value of turnover. The high estimates are those of H. G. Grubel, who takes costs to be 6 per cent of turnover in 'The Case Against an International Commodity Reserve Currency', *Oxford Economic Papers*, 1965; as a chief proponent Hart's estimates are likely to be low, while as an opponent Grubel's estimates probably exaggerate costs, so we may take their estimates as giving a range of costs in 1966 prices.

18   See Cline, op. cit.

19   J. Williamson, 'Survey of International Liquidity', *Economic Journal*, 1973.

20   As a percentage of international reserves *including* gold at market prices, SDRs were 2.1 per cent of reserves in the middle of 1980. (See UNCTAD/MFD/TA111, 'Measures to Strengthen the SDR', March 1981.)

21   We owe this point to discussions with Sidney Dell.

22   In practice some criteria for determining the exchange rate between ICUs and commodities would have to be laid down.

23   See G. Bird, 'Reserve Currency Consolidation and International Monetary Reform', *World Development* (forthcoming); 'The consolidation of Currency Balances and Developing Countries', UNCTAD/FIN/4, July 1972; and 'Implications for Developing Countries of Current Proposals for a Substitution Account', Report to the Group of Twenty-Four, prepared by V. B. Kadam, UNDP/UNCTAD project INT/75/015, UNCTAD/MRD/TA/1, August 1979.

24   UNCTAD, 1972, op. cit.

25   These and other proposals for using the substitution account to direct resources towards LDCs are discussed in Bird, op. cit.

26   See D. Brodsky and G. Sampson, 'Gold, Special Drawing Rights and Developing Countries', *Trade and Development*, 2, 1980.

27 See 'Measures to Strengthen the SDRs', op. cit.
28 Ibid.
29 These are discussed in 'Measures to Strengthen the SDRs', op. cit.
30 *Outline for a Program of Action on International Monetary Reform*, Group of Twenty-Four, 1979.
31 In 'Measures to Strengthen the SDRs', op. cit.

8 A WORLD VIEW: THE CASE FOR A WORLD DEVELOPMENT COUNCIL

This chapter explores the case for a *world* institution which would take a global view of expenditure and resource transfers in relation to the requirements of global development, levels of output and employment and reduction in disparities in incomes. Such an institution should be capable of taking appropriate action in the light of this global view. The need for such an institution has been alluded to in previous chapters. Here we briefly draw the arguments together.

The case for a global institution of this kind rests on the following hypotheses:

(i) that at present, economic decisions with major effects on the world economy are taken in a near-autonomous way by nation states and private financial institutions;

(ii) that the combined effects of these decisions may be severely to restrain economic growth and development of individual states and of the world as a whole;

(iii) that despite the existence of some institutions which are nominally global, in practice they rarely take a global view and are mainly concerned with sectional interests. The way they function makes them powerless to take the sort of action which would be necessary to have a significant effect at global level.

The exact form and constitution of this global institution will have to be worked out in much greater detail. Special studies may be needed on the different aspects of its functioning. Considerable negotiations will be required by the international community to establish such an institution. The case for an effective world economic planning institution is based on a felt need and fashioned after an idealistic belief that the world would be a much more rational place

if activities which have consequences for all were coordinated
in the interests of all. It is based on belief in planning, not
in the sense of a monolithic, over-centralized strait-jacket,
but as a method of pursuing objectives with interrelated
instruments of policy in an efficient manner. How far this
proposal will be acceptable will depend upon the wisdom
and the will of the different actors, especially nation states,
to accept restraints on autonomy – in some areas, to achieve
optimal results in the relevant fields.

The events of the 1970s – specifically world reaction to the
oil-price rise – highlighted deficiencies in world economic
management. Faced with the escalation in oil prices and
the prospects of huge deficits, most developed countries
reacted by deflation (curtailing expenditure/raising taxes),
so slowing down growth in output, increasing unemployment
and (paradoxically) reducing the incentive to save energy.
The net effect, as shown in Chapter Two, was that developed
countries soon eliminated their balance of payment deficits.
Despite the reduced markets for primary products and
manufactures that this implied, the better placed LDCs
(middle-income) were able to maintain growth by borrowing
heavily from the private banking sector. The extent to which
this was possible depended on the individual decisions of
less than a dozen 'lead' banks, which took these decisions in
the light of their desire for profits and assessment of country
risks and prospects. They might have lent much more (and
to different countries) or much less – in either case with
major implications for the prospects for particular countries
and for the world economy.

The net effects of the crisis and reaction to it therefore
depended mainly on two sets of decisions:

(i) on the decisions of ICs not to permit massive deficits
in their balance of payments (and correspondingly
deficits in their budgets), for which they could have
found finance; and

(ii) the decisions by private international banks about their
lending to LDCs.

The first set of decisions was taken by IC governments
for two rather different types of reason: first, because for

political (and other) reasons they believed this was the best policy to counter inflation; secondly, because they feared the consequences on their national standing, creditworthiness and exchange rate of 'going-it-alone' in permitting sustained large deficits.

Neither of the two sets of decisions depended on or was motivated by – even in part – concern for the *world economy* (i.e. the aggregate of world demand), or for the prospects for LDCs economies, except in so far as these were seen to have immediate consequences for the national economies in question or for individual banks. The prosperity of the world economy, which clearly affects the prosperity of individual nations, was not an explicit consideration, but rather the outcome of these uncoordinated national and private decisions. Two recent analyses come to similar conclusions:

> What happens to individual countries affects the international economy as a whole, and vice-versa. A higher level of lending might help to create a more favourable environment in which borrowers were more creditworthy than they would be with more limited debt. The evaluation of risk on a country by country approach could lead to a less desirable outcome than centralized decisions that take such interdependence into account. (A. Fishlow, 'Latin American External Debt: Problem of Solution', mimeo, Yale, 1981.)

and:

> ... if the world economic system had been actively and sensibly managed there would have been no need for, or benefit from, any general recession. (*Cambridge Economic Policy Review*, December 1980.)

The oil crisis illustrated the lacuna in world economic management, but the lack of international coordination or concern for world economic prosperity much predates that situation. Long before the oil crisis, the absence of world countercyclical mechanisms had been apparent, as had the absence of any institution for ensuring an adequate flow of resources to LDCs. The devastating effect on LDCs (and world demand) of fluctuations in primary producer prices had led to the demand for an Integrated Programme for Commodities. It was also a major motive behind the proposal for a commodity-backed reserve currency, which, as described in the last chapter, was intended to be a major automatic counter-cyclical mechanism.

Two functions are required of an institution designed to promote world economic management: an *analytic* function; and an *action oriented* function.

The analytic function would consist of analysis of world economic and development problems at a high level and on a sustained basis.[1] In so far as possible, the analysis would make use of all sorts of analytic techniques, without prejudice, and would not reflect just one school of thought or 'vision'.[2]

The action oriented function would promote and sometimes directly undertake actions identified in the analysis stage. These actions would include action to be undertaken by existing (or new) international institutions and promotion of national actions in the desired directions.

The two functions could be separated: there is an urgent need for sustained analysis of world problems to lay the ground for national and international action. While perhaps the overriding need is for an institution capable of taking appropriate action, if this proved impossible to achieve for political reasons, there would still be an important role for an institution whose main functions were analytic.

There are institutions which operate at a world level and might be thought to provide the required institutional basis for global economic analysis and management. These include the World Bank and the IMF, and, at a more political level, the Development Committee of the World Bank and the Economic and Social Council of the United Nations. But none of these bodies properly fulfils either analytic or action-oriented functions.

The World Bank and the IMF undertake periodic world economic surveys (as do other institutions, e.g. the OECD). The World Bank also analyses particular issues in more depth. The issues tend to be selected on a somewhat *ad hoc* way, while the 'vision' in both general economic analysis and discussion of particular issues is somewhat narrow, mainly confined to a conventional Western developed country approach.

As far as action is concerned, their activities tend to be largely confined to dealing with countries on a national level. The World Bank's lending programme is constrained by its capital subscriptions and gearing ratio. Its advice to individual countries is given on a country-by-country basis, taking world economic trends as a given background to this advice. Moreover the World Bank no longer advises major ICs, many of which individually have a substantial influence over the world economy. The World Bank's project approach makes it ill-suited to take short-term action on resource transfers in the light of the needs of the world economy.

The IMF has so far only contributed a small amount to world resource transfers from North to South (3.1 per cent of total flows 1973–80). It regards this finance as being short term in nature, to finance countries' trade deficits while they take measures to adjust. The IMF only works with deficit countries; its aim in those countries is to achieve a 'viable' balance, which is defined as a balance of payments situation that is sustainable in the medium term without recourse to IMF finance. It seldom persuades the surplus countries to adjust, so that the burden of adjustment is born by deficit countries. Moreover, it does not take a world view of the appropriate level of surpluses and deficits (or import restrictions). Hence, in its country activities, the IMF too is essentially operating within *a given world economy*, and not trying to change it. For example each deficit is treated separately and no view is taken as to whether LDCs as a whole (or ICs as a whole) should be permitted or encouraged to finance near permanent balance of payments deficits, given the state of the world economy. In practice, IMF activities *do* change the world economy – probably in a rather deflationary direction – but this is the outcome of individual country programmes rather than the overt intention. Neither countercyclical objectives nor those of long-term balance in the world economy are explicit elements in decisions on resource transfer.

The Development Committee of the World Bank is, in theory, a body more suited to produce action at a world

level. But it meets briefly and has no permanent secretariat
to provide the required sustained and in-depth analysis. In
practice it is difficult to trace any action to its activities. The
Economic and Social Council of the United Nations has
also made little contribution to sustained analysis of world
economic problems or to relevant action. It provides a useful
forum for discussions, but not much more.

The Brandt Commission came nearest to providing analysis
of world economic problems. But because it tried to cover
everything within a short period it failed to do sufficient
work on many of the issues, especially on obstacles to the
actions it identified. Moreover, it was a one-off event. We
are arguing here in a way for a continuous Brandt Commission, as far as analysis is concerned.

The net effect of the way economic decisions are made in
the world has been very deflationary in recent years for
developed countries as calculations by the Cambridge Economic Group illustrate.

Table 8.1

	% Increase p.a. in per capita spending		Assumed Target	Projection
	1964–73	1973–8	1979–85	1979–85
USA	3.2	2.0	2.5	0.6
West Germany	4.0	1.2	3.0	1.1
Japan	8.4	1.4	4.0	3.8
Other Developed	2.8	1.3	3.0	1.3
World			2.7	1.2

Source: Cambridge Economic Policy Review, December 1980. Tables 1.3
and 2.9.

There has been a marked slow-down in growth among the
developed countries. LDCs also suffered a slow-down in
growth of real income, especially marked among low-income
countries. The Cambridge Economic Policy Group figures contrast 'target' figures (roughly those in which unemployment

remains stable) with projected figures. As Table 8.1 shows, for the world as a whole projections of growth in per capita spending with realistic financial adjustment are for 1.2 per cent growth in per capita spending, that is less than half the target level, indicating continued substantial world deflation.

What might be done

If the world economy continues to be the victim of rather random and uncoordinated decisions, prospects look very poor. Some serendipitous occurrence might rescue it. But otherwise world economic activity, and specifically development prospects of LDCs, will be constrained not by real resource constraints but by the absence of economic planning and suitable financial mechanisms at a world level. What is needed is for some world body with the function and power to make a significant contribution to world economic management.

A world economic planning body which could be called a *World Development Council* should initially act in an advisory capacity. Its task would be to analyse global trends in demand and supply at an aggregate level and in relation to specific sectors (e.g. energy). It would examine major social and economic problems emerging from these trends and make recommendations to national governments and to international institutions in the light of its analysis. The World Development Council would not itself be a financing agency, but should be able to coordinate and influence the international financing agencies. It would thus provide some link between the short-term concerns of the IMF and the longer-term concerns of the World Bank. It would also assist in guiding and coordinating other emerging global institutions, such as those discussed earlier in this book. A global economic planning body would identify gaps or defects in existing institutions, examine the consistency of national policies in terms of global objectives and formulate feasible international programmes.

One possibility is that the World Development Council should be part of the United Nations, set up as a parallel body to the Security Council, perhaps as a development of

ECOSOC. World economic development would seem to justify as much attention as world security. The advantage of this would be that it would give the body status and also power so long as the major powers retained a right of veto, as on the Security Council. The disadvantage is that the body would then be subject to all the political pressures normal in a UN institution, and might be rendered rather ineffective. As an alternative possibility, the Council might be conceived as a primarily advisory body with an independent status, but having jurisdiction to examine those activities of international institutions and national governments which have global implications.

The World Development Council would consider many of the problems discussed earlier in this book, as well as other problems, outside the realm of finance. The full scope of its operations would evolve over time: it would consider, for example, the level and distribution of world liquidity; the level and distribution of financial flows; world energy prospects for the poorest countries and the poorest people; the problem of world inflation; harmonization of national stabilization policies; the problem of fluctuating commodity prices and trends in the terms of trade; remedies for structural disequilibrium among LDCs; international trade, structural adjustment and protection at a world level.

In many of these areas there are institutional gaps, some of which have been identified in this study. For example, on financial flows there is a need for some Keynesian 'lender of the last resort' which can ensure adequate levels of lending. At least initially the Council would act in an advisory capacity and would not directly meet any gaps identified, but rather help other institutions to do so. If these gaps persisted, then there might be a case for the Council setting up subsidiary bodies to fulfil the various functions.

Looking at the real world and the past experience in international bureaucracies one can see some problems about the proposed institution. For example:

(i) One World Development Council might be too *monolithic*. The force of this criticism would be less in so far as the body retained a purely advisory role, but if it gradually acquired more direct financial and economic powers it would be necessary to devise procedures for decentralization. However, there would continue to be a large number of independent decision-making bodies at national and international level, just as there are at the level of security, so the charge of monolithiticity may not be an important one.

(ii) The question of *control*. Developing countries are anxious to get a 'democratically'-controlled institution.[3] Interpreted as one country one vote, this would mean control by developing countries. But it is unlikely in such a situation that the institution would secure any financial power. If controlled by the ICs, the institution might do rather little, as ICs do not appear to see the need for such an institution. If OPEC were persuaded of the need for such an institution, they could supply much of the financial support. A one-third; one-third; one-third formula (DCs, OPEC, LDCs) might offer a good starting arrangement. There need be no single control formula: control could depend on function. But it is important that however the institution is controlled it is not too politicized so that its decisions depend mainly on economic and development criteria.

(iii) The question of *finance*. In its advisory capacity there would be no need for finance. On the other hand, if it identifies major financial gaps there would be a need for financial commitment. It is likely that the institution itself would do little directly, but would identify needs and pass on any financing function to other institutions (e.g. new recycling mechanisms, as discussed in earlier chapters, the World Bank and Regional Banks, the Fund and so on). It would not then need finance itself but these other institutions would. The World Development Council would be in a good position to assess and make recommendations on sources of finance.

The major obstacles to world economic management are undoubtedly political rather than institutional. If the significant international decision-makers — notably the major public institutions and industrialized countries' governments — are not prepared to coordinate their economic policies, then an institutional framework by itself may achieve nothing. The failure of existing institutions in terms of global economic management could be interpreted as proving that the major problem is one of political will rather than of institutions.

While recognizing the importance of this point, we believe a global institution could still make some contribution. Existing institutions are deficient; provided with an appropriate framework, appropriate action will be easier and political problems more readily overcome. Moreover, the 'prisoners dilemma' holds in the realm of international action, so that each nation might be made better off individually with appropriate international machinery.

Political problems are likely to postpone (perhaps indefinitely) any action here. For this reason, it may be easier to get the 'analytic' function accepted initially, than the action-oriented function.

Conclusion

Many of the earlier chapters have pointed in the same direction; that the world as a whole, and LDCs in particular, suffer greatly from the absence of any world economic management. This is true with respect to world economic cycles and commodity prices, to adjustments to major world events such as the oil-price rise, to the recycling of financial surpluses, and to the question of the level and distribution of international liquidity. Existing 'world' institutions do not operate at a world level in the way required. Hence a new world institution (or changes in existing institutions) is required to act in an advisory and coordinatory way in all these areas, and to ensure that uncoordinated decisions do not result in low levels of activity and maldistribution of world resources — from many points of view, a second-best outcome.

Notes

1 See G. K. Helleiner, 'The One World of Economics: Towards Global Economic Analysis', mimeo, 1981 (for *Essays in Honour of Lloyd Reynolds*, ed. G. Ranis).
2 See discussion of 'vision' in Chapter Six.
3 See 'Arusha Initiative'.

9   SOUTH–SOUTH MONETARY COOPERATION

All of the topics considered so far have involved North and South. The South on its own is not in a position to put the changes discussed into effect: for example, a world institution or an international currency can only be effective with the active support of the North. But recently the North has shown itself very reluctant to make any real progress in North–South negotiations. Hence it may be unrealistic to expect very much change which requires Northern support. But there are many areas in which the South can act on its own. Some of these areas involve cooperative action by OPEC and oil-importing LDCs; others are LDC ventures, where OPEC support is obviously desirable, as part of the South, but OPEC finance is not essential. This chapter considers a range of issues in which South–South monetary cooperation could produce major benefits.

The various arrangements cover three types of situation: first, financial recycling from OPEC to LDCs; secondly, arrangements to facilitate LDC trade in general, including South–North trade; and thirdly, arrangements to promote South–South trade.

1. Recycling from OPEC to LDCs

This question has been extensively discussed in earlier chapters, so little will be added here. The need for new institutions and new financial instruments for recycling was argued in Chapters Two and Three. One recycling route involves the direct transfer of funds from OPEC to LDCs, either through the commercial sector or through Third World public institutions. In the past this route only accounted for a very small proportion of the total transfer of funds. Most went through the ICs mainly via the commercial sector (IC banks and IC bond markets), and to a lesser extent through international financial institutions. There appear to be two reasons for the small amount of direct OPEC–LDC transfers. One is that ICs appeared to offer financial security to OPEC investors; secondly (and associated), there was a lack of institutions, either private or public for direct recycling. To some extent the institutional gap is less now with the development of Third World commercial banks, but these are still incapable of recycling more than a small proportion of the funds.[1] In addition, some joint ventures between OPEC and other Third World countries include very large financial transfers. For example, Singapore and Kuwait have set up the International Petroleum Centre which may lead to a project of $½ billion.[2] There remains an institutional gap for Third World public agencies for recycling. The proposed Third World Development Agency[3] could make a major contribution to direct recycling. Another contribution could come from the expansion of the Regional Development Banks, with direct borrowing from OPEC countries. The Inter-American Development Bank has proposed to act 'as a broker to channel more surplus oil wealth from the financial markets into large energy and industrial projects in Latin America'.[4] As evolved at the moment, the proposal is that the Bank will identify projects, evaluate them and then find finance. The Regional Banks could also expand their own direct lending if they raised their capital subscriptions or changed their gearing ratios.

Direct recycling (i.e. without channelling the funds through ICs) would improve the terms of LDC borrowing, which tend to be raised by the indirect route taken; it would also increase both OPEC and LDC independence from ICs. The 'security' argument for using the IC route lost much of its force with the freezing of Iranian assets, while in recent years rapid inflation in ICs has reduced the effective financial returns. New financial mechanisms (for example, SDR denomination) discussed in Chapter Four could increase the security of direct recycling. One possible measure would be to provide a cover for exchange risk, which, by reducing risk, could reduce the real return paid by LDCs.

2. Export credit refinance and guarantee facilities

In any reform of the international financial structure designed to improve the financial strength of LDCs high priority must be given to schemes to facilitate increased export earnings. In the ultimate analysis it is export earnings which determine LDCs' ability to sustain a rapid growth in income by raising their capacity to pay for imports and to service debt. In 1979 almost 80 per cent of the imports of the developing countries were financed by export earnings.[5]

In view of the slow growth of world demand for most primary products, growth of exports of LDCs depends on diversification towards manufactures. In general, both income and price elasticity of demand is higher for manufactures than for primary products. The success of LDC efforts to increase manufactured exports depends on their ability to succeed in a highly competitive world market. One important element in international competition is the terms of credit on which exports can be offered. Even where the products of a developing country are competitive in quality and their prices are reasonable, LDCs may not be able to expand their exports unless they can match the credit terms offered by their competitors.

Although the bulk of international trade transactions, particularly of LDCs, still takes place on a cash basis or with credits of less than 90 days, the amount of exports financed with longer-term credits has been increasing fairly rapidly in recent years. For exports of capital equipment and of complete plants and projects, long-term credits, extending often beyond five to ten years, have become quite common methods of finance, while an increasing proportion of exports of engineering and durable consumer products is being financed by medium-term credits of one to five years. Although short-term credits or cash are the basis of trade for most exports of light manufactures and raw materials, even in these cases medium-term credit is sometimes offered.

The developed countries offer extensive export credit on a short-, medium- and long-term basis, with guarantees and insurance provided by the government: in many cases there are elements of subsidies in the guarantees provided.[6]

It may be particularly important for LDC exporters to match these terms where they are trying to break into established markets. This applies to trade between South and North but especially to South–South trade, since LDC importers rely heavily on export credit for finance. Export credit facilities in the South are much weaker than those in the major industrialized countries. It is estimated that less than 10 per cent of LDC trade is covered by export credit.[7] One estimate for LDCs suggests that gross disbursement requirements for export credits in 1980 may be $3 billion per annum.[8]

Several LDCs have instituted national arrangements for providing postshipment credit to the domestic exporter in terms of local currency. With these arrangements, an exporting firm can enter into a contract with a foreign importer offering him competitive credit terms and then secure credit from the national credit corporations in domestic currency. Although the problems of the individual exporter are solved through this device, the basic problem for the country of postponement of receipt of foreign exchange remains. This is often compounded by the fact that the execution of the export contract requires imports of component parts and raw materials for which no concomitant credit terms are available, and the exporter needs foreign exchange for these imports. When a national institution takes over the burden of providing export credit in foreign exchange to the foreign buyer, it helps the individual exporter to carry on business unhampered by the requirements of raising foreign exchange finance; it also makes it easier for the LDC to secure refinance on these export credits in the international market and thus to avoid the deferment of the receipt of foreign exchange. The creditworthiness of the exporter generally determines the availability of refinance in the international capital market. A few LDC exporting units do have high credit ratings in the financial markets of the world, but, in general, exporting firms from the less developed countries suffer from not being backed by internationally reputable financial institutions and therefore do not have access to rediscounting facilities in the international capital market, at least at a reasonable cost.

There are two ways by which international arrangements could solve the problems of refinancing of export credits provided by less developed countries. First, international facilities could be set up directly to refinance export credits offered by less developed countries, either for all exports of manufactures or engineering products or for some selected exports, and made either to all destinations or to restricted destinations (for example, to developing countries only). Secondly, international arrangements could be worked out for a facility to guarantee the export credit provided by the less developed countries. Such an international guarantee should enable the exporting country to obtain refinance on the export bills or notes by discounting them with an international financial institution. Unlike the facility for direct refinancing, where the international community would have to put up funds to refinance export credits, the money for refinance of export credits guaranteed by an international facility would come from the international capital market and therefore might be additional to whatever the international community chooses to provide developing countries through official aid and loans.

If such an international facility provides guarantees but not insurance cover, these guarantees would normally be with recourse to the central bank of the exporting country, or any other nominated agency. If there is a default in the payment of the export credit, because of failure by the exporter or for any other reason, the international bank which has provided refinance for the export credit would be immediately reimbursed by the guarantee facility, which in its turn would recover the amount from the exporting country's central bank. The only risk of loss that the international guarantee facility would undertake is that of the exporting country's central bank refusing to reimburse the export credit which has been refinanced.

If the international facility also provides insurance cover, then it will have to bear more substantial risks of possible capital loss, depending on the number of co-insurers and the type of risk for which cover is provided. In that case, the portfolio of export credits would need to be diversified to minimize the average risk. The capital requirement for setting up such a facility would be larger than would be necessary for establishing a pure guarantee facility. Still, it may not be right to rule out the option of insurance cover altogether. If there is an insurance cover by an international facility the acceptability of LDC export credit instruments in the international capital market would improve significantly, thereby reducing the cost of refinance of such credit.

Once the international community agrees to set up a guarantee facility along the lines suggested above, it should not be difficult to work out the *modus operandi* of such a facility, its objectives, and source of funds. There would need to be agreement regarding the types of credits which would be supported, the period of credit, the type of transactions and products to be covered, whether there should be ceilings on the volumes of credits provided by any particular country or offered to any particular buyer, and arrangements to deal with the situation that arises if recourse to reimbursement by a particular central bank fails. There would also have to be some agreement regarding the amount of paid-in and callable capital, as well as the source of such funds and contributions of the different members. It is estimated that callable capital of $1 to $1.5 billion would be sufficient for the first five years of operation. This would involve paid-up capital of $200 million to $300 million.[9] Although it would help financially if the developed countries made some capital contribution, this is not a necessary feature of the scheme which could be financed by the South alone. OPEC backing would greatly add to the credibility and effectiveness of the institution.

3. Arrangements to promote South–South trade

There is a strong general case for promoting South–South trade. In addition to this general case, there is a special case to be made at this juncture, given the poor prospects for trade with the North and the likelihood of very large payments deficits, which countries are going to find very hard to finance.

Historic colonial North–South ties left a trading pattern which was heavily North–South in orientation. All the trading infrastructure – transport, finance, culture and tastes – had been developed on North–South lines. Thus it is impossible to say that existing patterns of trade (which are mainly North–South with 75 per cent of Southern exports going to the North) are the natural ones or reflect comparative advantage. What they reflect is the historic heritage. This historic heritage has been reinforced by new post (or neo-) colonial ties such as tied aid and multinational investment which tends to involve North–South trading relationships. There is a case for building up the infrastructure for South–South trade simply from the point of view of righting this historic bias. One part of this infrastructure is finance; South monetary arrangements would provide the finance, encouraging the provision of other elements of infrastructure, notably transport. But independently of the question of historic and current biases in trading arrangements, there is a positive case to be made for South–South trade. Trade between countries of the South is likely to be in more appropriate products and use more appropriate technology than trade between North and South. Thus for manufactured exports, both capital goods and consumer goods tend to be simpler and less expensive when they are produced in the South.[10] Given the prevalence of low incomes and the low level of investible resources per head in most Third World countries, simpler and less expensive capital and consumer goods from other Third World countries may help to fulfil some needs more effectively than more expensive and sophisticated goods from the North.[11] Such products often require less advanced, less sophisticated and less capital-intensive technology and methods of production. In addition, the case for greater self-reliance within the South becomes increasingly persuasive, as some of the disadvantages of excessive dependence on the North become apparent.[12] The movement for TCDC[13] is a reflection of the desire for greater cooperation among the South and a greater degree of self-reliance.

In the present world economic situation expansion of trade within the South appears to offer an alternative to the rather poor prospects for South–North trade. In the 1970s the South as a whole maintained its growth rate significantly better than the North, and this may recur in the 1980s. The

most rapidly growing countries (described as the Newly
Industrializing Countries) in the South offer expanding
markets as well as supplies of goods and services. For any
given level of trade with the North, and for any given overall
trade deficit with the North, a more rapid expansion in trade
within the South would permit higher income and higher
employment. Given the limits on expansion of trade with
the North, imposed by trade restrictions in the North and
the problem of financing huge prospective deficits with the
North, an expansion in South–South trade may offer possibilities for expanding trade, income and employment, without
any diversion of trade with the North. Of course, this would
only be the case if there were goods and services which
different countries in the South wished to buy and sell to
each other. It has sometimes been suggested that there are
narrow limits to the expansion of South–South trade because
all countries in the South are producing the same goods
(simple consumer goods) and there is therefore very limited
potential for trade. But with the diversity in development
patterns in the South this situation does not hold. Many of
the NICs produce a great variety of quite complex capital
and intermediate goods as well as consumer goods and are
able to supply a considerable range of technical services.[14]
While the less developed countries in the South are currently
specializing in producing simple consumer goods they can
supply these goods and a range of primary products which
the newly industrialized developing countries need. That
there is scope for expansion of trade within the South is
indicated by the rapid rate of expansion which did take
place in the 1970s, despite the obstacles to trade expansion.
In the 1970s while small in absolute terms this was the most
expansionary element in world trade, as shown in Table 9.1.
The rate of increase of Southern exports to all areas is reduced
substantially if fuel is excluded, but the reduction is less for
South–South trade than for South–North trade, and South–
South trade remains the most expansionary element in
non-fuel trade.

Between 1970 and 1977 the South accounted for a growing proportion of its imports in all the major categories of
trade with the exception of raw materials, as Table 9.2 shows.

Table 9.1   Expansion of world trade, current values ($b.)

Market economies	1970	1977	% increase 1970–77
1. Total exports of market economies	266.5	961.3	361
2. North–North	68.1	200.6	295
3. North–South	41.9	172.9	413
4. South–North	40.9	205.1	502
5. South–South	11.1	67.1	605

Source: UN Year Book of International Trade Statistics, 1978, ST/ESA/ STAT/ser 6/27, Special Table C.

Table 9.2   Imports from South countries as a proportion of total South imports, %

Trade category	1970	1977
Total imports	21.9	27.9
Food	33.3	35.5
Raw materials	53.9	42.7
Fuels	81.1	93.2
Chemicals	5.2	5.5
Machinery	1.8	6.0
Other manufactures	11.7	20.0

Source: as Table 9.1

Apart from fuel — which expanded fast in value terms because of the price rise — major expansion was recorded in machinery and other manufactures. These items (especially machinery) started from a very small base. None the less their growth is a significant pointer to the potential for growth in trade in manufactures among developing countries.

The expansion of trade between developing countries that has followed customs union and payments arrangements[15] also shows the potential for intra-South trade. Among five groups of countries that have had effective integration schemes since the early 1960s, there has been a considerably faster expansion of intra-group trade than of total trade. For the five groups as a whole, intra-group exports rose from 7.2 per cent (1960) to 15.4 per cent (1978).[16] This upward trend occurred within each group.

It is not proposed here that South–South trade could substitute for a large part of North–South trade, but rather that it could expand quite substantially at the margin. Growth of trade among LDCs need not be at the cost of their trade with developed countries, but in addition to it, particularly at a time when there are severe restraints – as a result of deflation and import restrictions – on the growth of trade with developed countries.

Singh concludes a survey of industrial prospects for Third World countries, with similar emphasis on the need to expand Third World trade.[17] He finds that 'In general, the major constraint on future industrial development in the market economies of the Third World is likely to be the rate of growth of demand rather than the supply side factors'; secondly, '. . . in the long term, accelerated industrialization in the Third World requires a relatively much faster expansion of internal demand, individually and collectively, in these cases than has been the case hitherto'.

There are of course many obstacles to South–South trade besides finance and many different schemes which would facilitate such trade; for example, changes in tariff arrangements and transport facilities. There is no suggestion that financial arrangements on their own would be sufficient. However, effective financial arrangements encourage changes in other elements because they increase the incentive and reduce the risks of closer trading ties.

In the past there have been a large number of attempts to foster closer Third World ties, in the form of customs unions of various kinds and also joint monetary arrangements. A few have been successful but many have broken down, generally in the face of political dissension among the partners.[18] But almost all these agreements have been *regional*: there has been very little attempt to introduce new arrangements inter-regionally or for the Third World as a whole. A GATT protocol was instituted in 1973 for trade preferences between developing countries. There were 16 signatories, covering the main geographic areas. But while trade in the commodities for which concessions were negotiated has increased substantially it remains a very small part of the total trade of the participating countries. An Arusha Ministerial meeting of the Group of 77 (1979) endorsed guidelines for the negotiation of wider reaching and more comprehensive trade preferences among Third World countries. Such measures were to 'be linked to measures for financing the expansion of inter-developing country trade, including where necessary, cooperation in monetary matters'.[19]

The desirability of global Third World arrangements on trade and finance is now accepted. But it might be thought that if regional arrangements have broken down for political reasons, the prospect for inter-regional Third World arrangements must be very poor. Whether this is so or not depends on the nature of the arrangements. Most customs unions have required rather close cooperation and have involved a number of joint schemes, for example, for infra-structure and joint services. The details of the schemes have affected significant vested interests in the individual countries, the need for on-going cooperation and agreement, for example, with respect to running the joint services, has given daily opportunity for dissension and breakdown. If a general Third World scheme is to have any chance of success it must avoid those features which have led to the breakdown of regional schemes, i.e. avoid the need for on-going day-to-day cooperation, or for negotiations immediately affecting significant internal interests. The proposals considered below should be free from many of the pressures which have led to collapse of regional agreements; they require once-and-for-all agreement on the details of the scheme, but after that will operate independently of particular countries.

Clearing Union: The simplest form of payments arrangements among developing countries would be the formation of a clearing union. The idea behind it is that if developing countries could trade among themselves without having to use a hard currency of a developed country, this would permit rapid growth in trade. Within a clearing union, day-to-day transactions would be recorded in a central office and, at agreed intervals, the accumulated debits and credits would be multilaterally offset against each other, leaving only net balances to be settled. The simplest form of clearing union would provide for the settlement of the net balances in convertible currencies, and the agreed interval would be short, not exceeding three months. The participants in a clearing agreement would agree to provide only a minimum amount of interim short-term credit, just enough to permit periodic settlement.

A Payments Union: A payments union generally builds upon a clearing arrangement; participants agree to provide medium-term balance of payments credit to each other, thus extending the small amount of interim credit available within a clearing union. A payments union would have a broader scope of operation than simple clearing arrangements. By agreeing to provide medium-term credit to finance imbalances in their mutual trade, the participant countries would provide a more economical method of payment for their mutual trade transactions, as in the case of a clearing union, and would also allow each other more time to make the necessary balance of payments adjustments.

There are a number of ways in which payments arrangements could stimulate growth of trade among LDCs; first, by promoting greater multilateralization in the method of payments. Where clearing arrangements are formed among countries which previously had bilateral payments arrangements giving rise to inconvertible balances, the establishment of a clearing union would obviously promote greater multilateralism and greater efficiency in method of payment. The European Payments Union is often quoted as an example of successful evolution of multilateral intra-European trade from a network of bilateral payments arrangements. It is sometimes argued that since most of the trade of the developing countries today is settled in convertible currency and not within a framework of bilateral payments arrangements, the formation of a clearing union among them would not make any contribution to the multilateralization of payments. But the fact that payments are effected in convertible currency should not be taken automatically as an index of multilateralism in trade transactions among developing countries. Since most developing countries suffer from balance of payments constraints and inadequate reserves, they all follow stringent exchange control measures, in the context of which multilateralism merely means that it is just as difficult to obtain foreign exchange release for one currency as for another. But with a clearing union, currencies of member countries would be much more easily convertible and exchange licences for imports from member countries should be freely obtainable so long as the credit line is not exhausted. A clearing union would also involve a substantial economy in the use of foreign exchange reserves as working balances for invoicing and financing trade transactions with each other.

The benefits of payments arrangements to the participant countries do not depend upon the formation of a customs union among them or the dismantling of all tariff walls or quantitative restrictions among these countries. Even when such payments arrangements are not accompanied by other forms of economic integration or trade liberalization, the volume of trade is likely to expand, as relaxation of financing arrangements permits an expansion of trade to exploit even small differences in the comparative cost advantages between them.[20] If such arrangements are accompanied by liberalization of trade among member countries, the stimulus to growth of trade would be much more substantial. The existence of a Payments Union is likely to encourage such trade liberalization, by providing the finance.

There are a number of possible variations in the actual form of payments union. Credit may be automatic or discretionary; the net deficit countries' receipt of credit may be conditional while the net surplus countries' credit commitments may be unconditional; the net imbalances may be financed entirely by the net surplus countries' credits to the union or partly by such credits and partly by convertible currencies to be drawn from the payments union reserve fund; the ceilings on credit commitments or debit entitlements of different countries may be determined according to a number of different criteria including the wealth and income position of the different countries as well as their global balance of payments; net deficits beyond the ceiling may be financed by convertible currencies or by additional discretionary credit arrangement; and, finally, the period of credit may be fixed, after which the credits have to be liquidated in convertible currency, or they may be indefinite, where repayment is expected to occur as a result of the reversal of the credit position of the participating country with respect to other members of the union. If the settlement of the net imbalances were made entirely through credits of the net surplus countries, the payments union would require only a small amount of working capital to conduct day-to-day operations. However, if a part of the settlement has to be in convertible currency or the credits were not self-liquidating but eventually had to be settled in convertible currency or another Payments Union is whether the schemes amounts of convertible currency for these purposes. Accordingly, proposals have been made to require contribution to the Union of convertible currencies by member countries (and possibly also by some non-participant developed countries or international organizations).

Rediscounting of the net surplus position of creditor countries in the international capital market would be one way of economizing on the use of foreign exchange, and of reducing problems arising from persistent imbalances. The mechanism would be similar to refinancing of export credits.

A South currency: the proposal for a South currency[21] really amounts to a variant of a Payments Union among developing countries — indeed it would work best in the context of such a payments union. The proposal is for developing countries to issue a certain amount of new South currency to each participant country and to agree to accept this currency as part payment for goods and services traded among themselves. The proposal could form part of a clearing union — in which case the currency would only be used for net balances. But it could be used without such a clearing union. This would greatly reduce administrative requirements since it would do away with the administrative problems involved in a clearing union, viz. the recording of all transactions among the countries concerned. But at the same time it would have the major advantage of a clearing union, since the hard currency element in financing transactions among members would be reduced. To the extent that these South monetary arrangements are intended to cover all (or as much as agrees) of the South, ranging geographically over the whole world, a clearing union could involve insurmountable administrative problems, leading to delays which could obviate its major objectives of encouraging trade amongst LDCs by easing payments.

The South currency would increase the purchasing power of each member country over the goods and services of every other member. It would be equivalent to unconditional credit for the purchase of goods and services of members, and in this respect is identical to one variant of a Payments Union which extends credit. Countries which run down their balances would pay interest, while countries which accumulate balances would receive interest.

There is one major problem in any Payments Union which provides credit which also applies to this scheme. While such schemes work very well if every member remains broadly in balance, in terms of payments, with every other member, accumulating South currency in some years and running balances down in others, it is quite unrealistic to assume that this is the probable situation. In fact some countries are likely to be in persistent surplus with the other members, others in persistent deficit. In the South currency scheme this would mean some members would accumulate large amounts of South currency while others used them up. In the more conventional credit-type scheme it would mean that some countries use all their drawing rights with the Union, while others are in continuous credit. There are obviously problems about such a situation. Once it has developed, the trade creating aspects of the scheme would simply come to a halt. Moreover, countries may be unwilling to join the scheme if they believe they are likely to have to give substantial credits, particularly if their general balance of payments situation is poor and they need the hard currency they might otherwise have earned. To some extent the situation may be self-righting, since surplus countries would have an incentive to buy goods and services from other members of the Union, while deficit countries would have an incentive to divert exports towards members of the Union to pay for their drawings. But to make the scheme viable it may be necessary to have more stringent repayment conditions. There are a variety of possibilities. First, as with other types of debt, a time limit may be placed on accumulated debts, while creditor countries would similarly have a time limit placed on accumulated credits. The central union would enforce these time limits using receipts from debtor countries to repay creditor countries. An alternative (or supplementary) provision would be for interest rates to rise as countries ran down or accumulated balances over a long period. In the South currency scheme, the proportion of payment received in South currency for trade with other member countries could rise as the total accumulated balances rose, until after some agreed level, the country no longer accepted South currency as payment. This would reduce the cost to creditor countries and increase the incentive for deficit countries to correct their trade balance with these countries.

One important question is the determination of the exchange rate of LDC national currencies with a South currency. If they are fixed, as derived from their rate of exchange with the $ or other basket of international currencies, then the currency would function as a clearing arrangement together with some credit facilities. If the external exchange rate of the currency is fixed independently of any Northern currency, with flexible rates according to demand and supply for the South currency by each country, some of the problems of imbalances within the South would be solved. The rate of exchange between the South currency and Northern currencies would then be the outcome of the market process; the result would be that exchange rates of Southern countries as a whole would tend to rise or fall jointly *vis-à-vis* Northern currencies. A general South devaluation against the North would tend to encourage each South country to import more from each other.[22]

While it is obvious that any scheme would involve some costs for some countries, it would also offer gains in terms of extending markets and facilitating trade liberalization among members. This could be particularly important at a time when trade restraints are likely to become severe. Major exporters of manufactures would be likely to gain access to South markets on preferential terms. In return they would give credit on their exports, but only to the extent that this is not offset by imports of raw materials (and manufactures) from other South countries. Less developed countries — whose potential for exporting manufactures is much less — would gain in receiving credit for their imports of manufactures from other South countries. While the gains from such a scheme would be likely to be greater the greater the number of countries joining, no country need join if they think the net consequences would be deleterious, and members could leave, without imperilling the scheme as a whole. This is a major advantage of a scheme which aims to cover the South as a whole, as against smaller regional Unions. For the latter, the decision of one member with respect to joining or leaving can be enough to make or break the schemes.

A South Payments Union would not be a substitute for regional arrangements, but rather a supplement. Regional arrangements — because they are conducted between much fewer and more homogeneous countries — may involve a greater variety of arrangements than would be included in the global arrangements considered here. For example, regional arrangements normally involve agreements on tariffs and trade restrictions among members, often various joint services and sometimes joint negotiation on a range of issues with the outside world. All these features can make a major contribution to regional welfare, permitting greater specialization and exploitation of economies of scale, and increasing the bargaining power of the region as against the outside world. A South Payments Union would not conflict with such arrangements and could provide support for them.

One issue that would need to be decided for either a South currency or other Payments Union is whether the schemes should involve backing of hard currencies provided by contributions by members (and possibly others). Backing both strengthens and weakens these schemes. It strengthens them to the extent that it provides the central organization with hard currency which it may use for a variety of purposes: for example, it could use the convertible currencies to repay countries which have accumulated excessive credits, or as a guarantee against the rediscounting of these credits on the international market. Interest on convertible currency reserves would help meet the operating costs of the organization.

The problems about convertible currency backing are two: first, it involves a potentially costly contribution on the part of members; secondly, use of the backing, while strengthening the scheme in the short run, might endanger it in the long run since if the central organization ran out of convertible currencies, as it might well, then confidence in the scheme as a whole might collapse, whereas without any backing the arrangements would have to stand on their own right from the start.

Reserve Centre or Reserve Fund: proposals for a reserve centre, in which participant members pool part of their reserves of convertible currencies, could be an aspect of a Payments Union arrangement, or could be pursued independently.

The pooling of reserves is a first step towards joint management of reserves. This should enable developing countries as a whole to manage with a lower level of reserves in relation to imports. It would also assist some countries – particularly the smaller ones – in management of the reserves, which can be a source of considerable difficulty in a world of floating exchange rates and variable interest rates.[23] However, joint management of reserves requires a very substantial degree of cooperation among countries and confidence in the management of the Fund, which may well prove difficult to secure.

A reserve centre could operate like a Payments Union with members being permitted to draw upon the reserves according to their payments deficits with other members. Alternatively, drawing rights may be determined according to the global balance of payments deficits of members. The establishment of a multilateral reserve centre of this type would be similar to establishing another IMF-type organization. Such a centre could supplement the functions of the IMF, in relation to general balance of payments problems of members, while giving special assistance for schemes which promote trade among members.

General shortage of convertible currencies among LDCs could make members unwilling or unable to contribute to such a centre,[24] but OPEC contributions could greatly enhance the potential resources of the institution, making it a very worthwhile use of reserves for member countries. The establishment of a supplementary LDC financed and controlled Monetary Fund would greatly increase LDCs' ability to put into effect 'alternative conditionality'[25] and would generally lessen the LDC dependence on the North.

Conclusions

Negotiations on the New International Economic Order have made it very obvious that the South cannot expect any significant concessions from the North. The current political situation in some countries of the North and the general economic climate suggest that the North is unlikely to exert an expansionary influence on the South for the next few years, perhaps even the next decade or more. It follows then, that from many points of view, the South will need to rely largely on changes it can make itself, to 'pull itself up by its bootstraps'. Quite a number of the changes suggested in earlier chapters are likely to come to nothing because they require a significant degree of cooperation from the North. This chapter has been concerned with initiatives the South can take for itself. The position of OPEC – as part of the South but also as a major financial power – greatly increases the possibilities for South action on its own. But while most of the changes considered in this chapter would be made much easier by OPEC commitment and support, for the most part they could be viable, on some scale, if the non-oil LDCs were to take action on their own. All of the changes require a quite substantial amount of cooperation among countries of the South. If that is not forthcoming then these schemes will rapidly founder. The rhetoric of politicians and thinkers from the South suggests that such cooperation would be forthcoming were viable schemes available. But so far very little action has followed that rhetoric. Whether or not action will occur depends partly on whether the schemes would actually harm particular countries in the South.

Although a wide range of schemes have been covered, it has only been possible to sketch their implications. Detailed study and negotiation would be needed if any of these schemes were to be adopted. It is the conviction of this study that many of the schemes offer major potential gains to the countries of the South. The first step needed is to get a South conference of politicians and administrators to decide, in principle, on the need for new schemes and the main directions to be followed. Detailed study and negotiation can then follow.

Notes

1 This was the unanimous view of a group of commercial bankers from the Third World that we consulted.
2 *Financial Times*, 16 April 1981.
3 See Chapter Three.
4 See *Financial Times*, 27 March 1981, 'IADB plans to route oil funds to Latin America'.
5 *World Development Report 1980*, Table 8.
6 See 'Export Credit Facilities: an International Comparison', *Midland Bank Review*, Autumn 1980.
7 See Expert Group on Export Credits, Document DB/B/552, June 1975.
8 A. Sengupta, 'The Structure of International Finance and the Less Developed Economies', mimeo, 1979.
9 A. Sengupta, op. cit., p. 18.
10 See, for example, D. Lecraw, 'Direct Investment by Firms from Less Developed Countries', *Oxford Economic Papers*, 1977.
11 This is not to argue that Third World countries *only* need rather simple and cheap goods; but rather that such goods have an important function. In some areas there is an indubitable need for sophisticated North style products.
12 See M. ul Haq, 'Beyond the Slogan of South–South Cooperation', *World Development*, 8, 1980.
13 Technical Cooperation among Developing Countries.
14 See S. Lall, 'Developing Countries as Exporters of Technology', in *Developing Countries in the International Economy*, Macmillan, 1981.
15 See, for example, L. N. Willmore, 'Free Trade in Manufactures Among Developing Countries: the Central American Experience', *Economic Development and Cultural Change*, 1972.
16 The five groups are: the Latin American Association for Integration, the Central American Common Market, the Caribbean Community and Common Market, the Central African Customs and Economic Union and the West African Customs and Economic Union and the West African Economic Community. See 'Economic Cooperation Among Developing Countries', mimeo, 1980.

17 A. Singh, 'Industrialisation in the Third World, De-industrialisation in Advanced Countries and the Structure of the World Economy', mimeo, Cambridge, 1980.

18 See TD/B/AC 19/R 6. 'A Study of Monetary Cooperation among Developing Countries', by J. Gonzalez del Valle.

19 See 'Economic Cooperation among Developing Countries', op. cit.

20 This argument has been elaborated by J. Vanek: 'Payments Union among the Less Developed Countries and Their Economic Integration', in *Journal of Common Market Studies*, Vol. II, December 1966, pp. 107-91. D. Schydlowsky also built upon this argument in his report to UNCTAD, 'A Payments Union for Underdeveloped Countries', DD/B/AC.3/R.29, June 1966.

21 See F. Stewart and M. Stewart, 'A New Currency for Trade Among Developing Countries', *Trade and Development*, UNCTAD, 1981.

22 Joint devaluation has been suggested as a means of encouraging South–South trade, but in the absence of a South currency this is difficult to make effective.

23 See G. K. Helleiner, 'The Impact of the Exchange Rate System on the Developing Countries', UNDP/UNCTAD Project INT/75/015, September 1980; and M. J. Stewart, 'Floating Exchange Rates in the 1970s, and their impact on the World Economy', Commonwealth Secretariat, FMM (80) 9, August 1980.

24 Total non-oil LDC reserves of gold and foreign currency were SDR 97.7 billion at end 1979 or 35.2 per cent of 1979 imports. OPEC reserves were SDR 65.5 billion.

25 See Chapter Six.

The analysis in this Report suggests that the international financial system will — without major reforms — severely constrain world demand and employment, with particular deleterious effects on poor countries in the Third World. The study has identified a number of changes to improve the situation.

The major aims behind these changes are: to improve the recycling process from surplus to deficit countries, thus permitting a higher level of world demand and a greater expansion in investment and incomes in the Third World; secondly, to improve the situation of the poorest countries, which did worst in the 1970s; thirdly, to improve world economic management, leaving less to an uncoordinated combination of events; fourthly, to increase Third World and OPEC participation in world economic management; fifthly, to facilitate South–South trade and financial flows.

In analysing possible reforms, the aim has been to identify changes which appear to be acceptable to the major participants of the system. No time was spent on proposals involving, for example, a massive increase in aid, as this would seem too unlikely to be realistic. Where reforms are in the immediate and obvious interests of all relevant parties, it is likely that they will already have been put into effect. But there are areas where proposals seem widely acceptable *a priori*, but still have not been introduced. One reason for this is an institutional lag (and a lag in ideas) which accompanies major economic and political changes. In the case of the international financial system, the change in financial power that has occurred with the formation of OPEC has involved such a lag. Similarly, political independence, the formation of the Group of 77 and the failure of the NIEO negotiations, are together events calling for new ideas and institutions. Another reason is that there are many conflicts of interest involved and reforms very often are in the interests of some groups in some countries but not that of others, or some countries but not others. The reforms identified in this book fall into each of these categories.

The main actors involved are the North, the oil-importing South and OPEC. None of these groups are homogeneous, and differences within them are a major obstacle to reform. Possibly we have neglected the lack of homogeneity too much, leading to an unrealistic set of proposals. But while we recognize that differences (e.g. between the middle-income and lower-income LDCs) may prevent some changes occurring, overemphasis on differences can lead to complete inaction. Some of the changes that we have identified require joint action by all three groups, some by just one or two of the groups, some may be feasible with action by a subset of countries. For the most part, the changes are mutually consistent and action may occur in one area without threatening (or requiring) action elsewhere.

We would put most emphasis on those actions we have identified that the South (OPEC and LDCs, or just LDCs) can take by itself. We do so for two reasons; first, because the North has appeared reluctant to act in recent years, so relying on action by the North may mean postponing all action. This is especially true given the new US administration's attitude to the South and to economic affairs. Secondly, because in general we find the South's attitude to international reform has consisted too much of asking the North to take actions and too little in exploring and negotiating change it can take itself.

Possible areas for reform

(i) *Recycling*: our analysis of the past and of likely prospects with current institutions suggests the need for expansion of the activities of existing public institutions – the World Bank, the Regional Banks and the IMF – *and* for new institutions. These changes are required to increase the total amount of recycling and to improve its distribution. Of the many possible new institutions, we recommend the creation of a Third World Agency, a development of the ideas that have been put forward by the governments of Algeria and Venezuela. Such an agency would be financed directly by OPEC and would lend funds to the Third World. It could make a major contribution to a number of objectives — it would involve direct recycling from OPEC to oil-importing LDCs, increasing Third World control over financial institutions as well as making a major contribution to the general recycling problem. Current limitations on the expansion of the World Bank make such a change especially urgent. The veto on proposals for new institutions in which the industrialized countries participate, which is being exercised by the US at the moment (e.g. in relation to the proposed energy affiliate of the World Bank), means that any action needs to bypass the ICs, involving direct relationships between OPEC and the LDCs. Expansion of the Regional Banks and the proposed Third World Agency both meet this requirement.

(ii) *Financial mechanisms*: in practice, despite apparent problems, those LDCs that have been able to borrow in the past decade have done so on generally good terms. The major defect was limited access to commercial borrowing for many countries, and general uncertainty as to whether, with rising debt ratios, countries that had borrowed in the past would be able to continue to do so on good terms. Proposals for SDR denomination of loans are designed to reduce uncertainties for lenders and borrowers and therefore to increase the flow of funds at a time of fluctuating exchange rates. We think lenders and borrowers should give careful consideration to this proposal, but we do not believe it will make a major difference to the flow of funds. The proposal for an indexed bond is designed to allow long-term borrowing at a time of high and fluctuating inflation. Such a bond is likely to permit long-term borrowing, so reducing 'rollover' requirements, but at the probable price of raising the cost of borrowing. So long as borrowing countries are finding their 'rollover' financing manageable, they should be hesitant about introducing an indexed bond. An indexed bond would not help the countries in acute short-term difficulties which is when 'rollover' does become a major problem. There may come a time when lenders insist on some indexation, or borrowers find their financial problems resulting from short-term maturities intolerable. In either of these cases, the indexed bond would be a useful financial mechanism. But we do not think it is the situation at the moment.

Whatever new institutional arrangements are made, the commercial sector will continue to play a very substantial role in moving money around the world. In many ways this is in the interests of borrowing countries since the large number of private financial institutions increase their options. But from a development point of view, it is important to improve the distribution of commercial lending between countries. An international guarantee facility financed by members and/or by outside sources could make a contribution to improving the distribution of private sector finance. It is recommended that such a facility should be instituted.

(iii) *Low-income countries*: the proposals described above for new institutions and new financial mechanisms are likely primarily to improve borrowing facilities among middle-income LDCs. For the most part, the poorest countries cannot afford to pay commercial terms. They need aid directly or in the form of subsidies on loans to improve their position. The total sums involved are not large: an additional $4 billion p.a. would do much to meet their needs. About half of this is for the extra costs of imported energy. Additional aid from OPEC would be appropriate to meet this cost. This would amount to about 38 per cent of aid (1979), and 1.7 per cent of the 1980 OPEC current account surplus. The other half is to offset the indirect effects of recession and higher prices among industrialized countries. The OECD countries would only need to increase their total aid flows by 8 per cent (1980 values) to achieve this.

It is proposed that there should be a substantial redirection of aid towards the poorest countries, with a target of 2/3 of total aid to be distributed to low-income countries by 1985. If this target were achieved it would increase their receipts by $4 billion (1980 values), making a substantial contribution to their needs. Any given amount of aid can be 'stretched' in the short run by using the aid as interest subsidies or by co-financing of aid with loans on hard terms. We propose that the use of these mechanisms should be extended. A new guarantee facility discussed above — which should improve access of middle-income countries to 'hard' finance — provides additional justification for the proposed redirection of aid.

The capital gains associated with the IMF's stock of gold provide an important potential source of finance for low-income countries. We believe that the principle that the LDCs are entitled to this sum should be acknowledged, but more study is needed on the best way of using this large but once-and-for-all source of finance.

(iv) *Conditionality*: a major element behind the imposition of conditionality is creditors' desire for repayment. If LDCs wish to borrow they will have to meet the requirements for credible repayment. But, in addition, creditors tend to use their position to try and impose their own vision of the world on debtor countries. This occurs quite explicitly through the IMF. If alternative sources of finance are available or if they can gain more influence over existing sources, then borrowing countries need not accept this second element in conditionality.

OPEC funds provide an opportunity to search for alternative conditionality. So far the Third World has done very little about presenting alternatives, tending to reject (or accept) IMF conditions without seeking alternatives. We propose that a body should be established to identify alternative packages and to advise countries when in difficulties and negotiating for loans.

(v) *International currency*: our analysis of the proposal for a commodity-backed international currency suggests that — as at present suggested — it is very complex administratively, requires unlikely support from the ICs, and may not meet its major objectives. We therefore think that reforms in the unbacked international currency — the SDRs — should be pursued to meet some of the objectives of the proposed commodity-backed currency, in particular to extend international control over international reserve creation, improve distribution, and reduce speculation. If IC support for commodity reserves and commodity price stabilization eventually materializes, then a link could be established between the commodity reserve institution and the issue of international currency, leading to a form of informal backing for the international currency. Reforms of the SDR system include substituting SDRs for existing international reserves and improving the distribution of SDRs. With any extension of the use of SDRs (as in a substitution account) the desirability and importance of 'the link' (i.e. giving LDCs a large share in the SDR issue) is increased. But the benefits of such a link have been reduced by the market interest now payable on SDRs.

(vi) *World Economic Management*: there is a vacuum in world economic management, while decisions which are taken individually have significant repercussions on world economic prospects and the prospects for developing countries. This central vacuum has sometimes led to highly undesirable outcomes, such as the deflation of the 1930s, and the stagflation of today, a high degree of instability in commodity prices and inadequate levels of world demand, employment, trade and finance. The apparent 'world' institutions, such as the IMF and the World Bank, in reality operate primarily at a national level. There is a need for a world economic institution to assess world economic developments, and identify action required on the international level of demand and financial flows, international liquidity and national policies. We propose the establishment of a *World Development Council*, initially to be an advisory body on questions of international economic management.

(vii) *South–South financial cooperation*: with one major exception, the reforms identified above require the active support of the North as well as the South, and may therefore flounder on Northern inaction. The one exception was the proposal for a Third World Agency. There are a considerable number of other areas where the South can act on its own. These include the development of a joint export credit guarantee facility, and a variety of Payments Union type institutions. A Payments Union, which could be associated with the issue of a South international currency, would facilitate South–South trade. With some pooling of reserves it could also form a sort of South IMF able to give short-term balance of payments assistance to members, with its own (South) conditionality. The development of South monetary arrangements should be given high priority by the

Third World in order to give some reality to the concept of 'self-reliance' as well as to promote South–South trade and ease payments problems.

Conclusion

Despite much talk about the way the existing financial institutions are biased against the South and the need for more South–South cooperation, very little that is both concrete and realistic has been put on the international negotiating agenda. It is our belief that there are many proposals that would assist in offsetting the bias against the South, help development and contribute to South–South cooperation. The aim of this study has been to identify and analyse such proposals. It is common knowledge that many of these proposals are now sufficiently well worked out for serious negotiations to begin. Since North–South negotiation has produced no substantive results, the South should itself attempt to institute its own Bretton Woods.

ARTICLES CONTRIBUTED TOWARDS THE FINAL REPORT ON INTERNATIONAL FINANCIAL COOPERATION

Abdelkader Sid Ahmed – The Role of the New OPEC Development Agency*

Dragoslav Avramovic – Open Issues in International Finance*

David A. Bodsky & Gary P. Sampson – Gold, SDRs and Developing Countries

David A. Brodsky & Gary P. Sampson – A Gold Account for Development: Objectives and Rebuttals*

David A. Brodsky & Gary P. Sampson – Current National Valuations of Reserves Asset Gold – Some Additional Notes

Sidney Dell – On Being Grandmotherly

Chandra Hardy – The Rescheduling of LDC Debt. A Study of Debt Renegotiations 1956–1980

G. K. Helleiner – Foreign Exchange Risk and the Recycling Problem

Dr Lal Jayawardena – The 'Massive Transfer' of Resources to Developing Countries*

Vijay Joshi – Development Finance in the Nineteen Eighties*

Vijay Joshi – A Note on Development Finance in the Eighties

Robert Mabro – OPEC Surplus Fund*

Arjun Sengupta – Non-Alignment and the Restructuring of the World Economy

Frances Stewart – The Role of the Commercial Sector in the Recycling Process

Frances Stewart – The New International Currency

Frances Stewart & Michael Stewart – A New Currency for Trade Among Developing Countries

Michael Stewart – Massive Transfers of Resources: Mechanisms and Institutions*

John Williamson – The Why and How of Funding LDC Debt*

* The full text of these articles will appear in Volume 2

Index

Adjustment policies, in 1970s, 121–7; stabilization programmes of military governments, 123

African Development Bank, 57, 58

Aid, 40, 41–2; contributions as percentage of GNP, 41; for low-income countries, 98; generating resource flows, 102; need to increase to low-income countries, 100, 101; OPEC's view of sources, 66; proportion to low-income countries, 99; *see also* OPEC Fund for International Development; Official Development Assistance (ODA)

Arab Bank for Economic Development in Africa, 57, 58

Arab Banking Corporation, 68

Arlabank, 68

Arusha South–North Conference, 137

Asian Development Bank, 57, 58

Assets, financial, denominated in SDRs, 82; indexation, 75–81; protection against exchange rate fluctuations, 81–3

Balance of payments, adjustments for oil surpluses, 10–11; divergence in views of IMF and LDCs, 120; related to IMF borrowings, 50–1, 52; use of IMF assistance, 115

Banks, caution over future recycling role, 31–2; of LDCs and OPEC, 68–9; regional, 57–9; stability related to country indebtedness, 25–8; World Central Bank proposed, 138

Banque Arabe Internationale d'Investissement, 68

Bond issues, for indexation of OPEC assets, 75–6; from LDCs, 32–3; indexed to lengthen maturities, 78; of a Third World Development Agency, 63; 'OPEC Development Bonds', 53; possibility of indexation increasing borrowing costs, 80

Brandt Commission, analytical function, 166; proposal for World Development Fund, 59–61

Bretton Woods system, 2

Clearing union, 181–2

Co-financing with private and commercial sectors, 102–3

Commercial sector, conditions of lending, 22–4; developmental effects of loans, 24–5; distribution of lending in 1970s, 19–22; future flows of resources, 42–9; importance of role in 1980s, 30, 196; increasing resource transfer effects of aid, 102; loan guarantee facility, 84; not involved in World Development Fund, 60; unsatisfactory aspects, 49

Commodities, price stabilization, 138–40; influence on international inflation, 140; stabilizing world demand, 142–3

Commodity units, 137; *see also* International currency: commodity-backed

Common Fund Integrated Programme for Commodities, 139

Compensatory Finance Facility, conditionality, 111

Conditionality, attached to guarantee scheme, 86; capitalist countries' views passed on to LDCs, 127–8; history, 112–14; IMF conditions, 115–19; LDC reaction, 119–21; motives for imposition, 113–14; need for alternatives to, 197; of commercial lending, 22–4; reasons for, 127; variations between

profits to LDCs, 106; guarantee mechanism, 83; new packages for LDC needs, 128; political effects of programmes, 129; practical effects of conditionality, 115–19; proposals for expanded role, 50–3; recent developments in operation, 51; summary of effects of package on LDCs, 126–7; use of performance criteria, 116–17

International Monetary System (IMS), dissatisfaction with, 1

Investment in LDCs, 12

Less developed countries (LDCs), adjustment policies in 1970s, 121–7; advantages from indexation scheme, 77; advantages of public routes for recycling, 105; alternative external finance requirements in 1980s, 39; arrangements to promote South–South trade, 176–89; banking sector, 68–9; colonial North–South trade pattern, 176–7; defining 'sufficient' finance, 45–6; exchange rates for a South currency, 186; external finance for low-income countries, 93, 98–9; financial requirements affected by ICs' economic policies, 47; growing political power, 4; import capacity and economic performance, 21; increasing proportion of imports, 178–9; indexation of loans, 75; 77–81; major sources of finance, 12–14; need for global trade and finance arrangements, 181; need for programme finance, 56, 61; need to formulate new IMF packages for, 128; outlook for low-income countries in 1980s, 196–7; political breakdown of economic cooperative schemes, 180; political repercussions of IMF packages, 129; possible limitation on borrowing in 1980s, 31; problems of commodity price fluctuations, 138–9; problems of IMF package for low-income countries, 124–5; problems of very-low-income countries, 104; product-sharing with OPEC, 64–5; pros and cons of distribution account, 153; reaction to

conditionality, 119–21; recycling of OPEC surpluses to, 171–2; short maturity loans to, 22; slow growth in 1970s, 93; South–South monetary cooperation, 171–90, 198–9; structural adjustments, 46, related to IMF loans, 50–1, 52; switch to manufactures from primary products, 173; Third World Development Agency, 62–7, 172

Loans affected by debt servicing ratio, 33; by bond issue, 32–3; countries with payment arrears, 26; defaulting on repayments, 55; falling share of low-income countries, 93; from commercial sector in 1970s, 19–22; guarantee facility, 84; inflation as an aid to debtors, 79; LDCs' alternative requirements in 1980s, 69–71; lengthening maturities, 78; net long-term, 12, 13–14, 15; of a Third World Development Agency, 66; problems of low-income countries, 96; repayment related to terms of trade movements, 80–1; World Bank and IDA compared, 104–5

London Inter-Bank Offer Rate (LIBOR), 22

Mexican Proposal, 54

Newly-industrialized countries (NICs), ability to raise loan finance, 79

Official Development Assistance (ODA), 41; political reasons for some aid payments, 100–1; related to World Development Fund contribution, 60; share of low-income countries, 94

Oil Facility, conditionality, 111

Oil-price rises, creating unique situation, 9; deflationary effects, 142–3; effect of 1979–80 increase, 162; effect on low-income countries, 94–5; indexation, 75

Organization for Economic Cooperation and Development (OECD), and DAC proposal for resource flows, 54–5; ODA contributions, 41

Organization of Petroleum Exporting

HOMEFALL

HOMEFALL

THE LAST LEGION: BOOK 4

CHRIS BUNCH

orbit

www.orbitbooks.net

ORBIT

First published in the United States in 2001 by Roc,
Penguin Group (USA) Inc.
First published in Great Britain in 2007 by Orbit
Reprinted 2008

A CIP catalogue record for this book
is available from the British Library.

ISBN 978-1-84149-629-0

Typest in Garamond by M Rules
Printed and bound in Great Britain by
Mackays of Chatham plc

Orbit
An imprint of
Lirrle, Brown Book Group
100 Vicoria Embankment
London EC4Y 0DY

An Hachette Livre UK Company
www.hachettelivre.co.uk

www.orbitbooks.net

For
Warren Lapine
and
Angela Kessler

Thanks to Ringling Bros and
Barnum & Bailey Circus for their help . . .
and minor apologies to Bertolt Brecht.

— CRB

ONE

There were ten of them, wearing dappled camouflaged uniforms, heavily armed. They were dirty, and smelled like the jungle they'd been living in for the past four days.

Now, they crouched in meter-deep muck at the edge of a swamp, and watched the security patrol move past. The patrol's heatscanners were blocked by the insulated fabric the ten wore, and no one in her right mind would dream anyone would hide out in the reeking swampy goo.

The man on point looked at the team's leader, pointed to half a dozen bubble shelters a hundred yards away, drew a question mark in the air. The woman in charge nodded. The point man held up one finger . . . one sentry? The woman in charge shook her head — two. She pointed, and the point man saw the second, moving stealthily behind the first.

She motioned two others forward, tapped her combat knife. One smiled tightly, drew his blade, and crept forward, his partner behind him . . .

Haut Njangu Yoshitaro picked up his mug of tea, sipped, grimaced at the tepid mixture, then turned back to the holo.

'The problem, boss,' he said, 'is that they've got anti-aircraft here . . . here . . . and I'll bet more missiles right under that finger of land that looks so frigging inviting for an LZ.

'I don't see any way to honk our Griersons into this LZ over here, either, so we could make a decent attack.'

Caud Garvin Jaansma, Commanding Officer, Second Regiment, Strike Force Angara, studied the projection, spun it, spun it again.

'Howsabout we whack 'em with a wave or so of Shrikes on the finger, then put in the combat vehicles through the mess?'

'No can do,' Njangu, his Executive Officer, said. 'We've got Nan Company right here . . . Rast Company backing them up, too close in to chance a blue-on-blue friendly casualty.'

Garvin Jaansma was every centimeter a soldier – tall, muscular, blond-haired, blue-eyed, square-jawed. Everyone agreed he made a perfect recruiting poster. Everyone except Jaansma, which might have been part of his charm. Few people knew the devious mind concealed beneath his straight-arrow appearance.

But almost everyone agreed Njangu Yoshitaro was exactly what he looked like – sneaky and dangerous. Slender, dark-skinned, black-haired, he'd come from the depths of a slum world, forced into the military by a hanging judge.

'Shit,' Garvin muttered. 'Whose dumb-ass idea was it to put our grunts right on top of the baddies?'

'Uh . . . yours.'

'Shit twice. I guess we can't tolerate friendly fire from our own artillery, can we?'

'Not after yesterday,' Njangu said. 'And all the *aksai* are tied up working for Brigade. Look. Try this. We take a flight of Zhukovs up high . . . above Shadow range, then have 'em come straight down toward—'

He broke off, hearing a soft grunt, as of someone being sapped.

'Aw hell,' he said, moving swiftly across the bubble toward his combat harness. He'd barely touched the butt of his pistol when the bug shield was ripped aside, and three dirty men and a woman jumped into the shelter.

He tried for the gun anyway, and two blasters chattered. Njangu grunted, looked at the bloody mess of his chest, fell on his face, and lay still.

Garvin had his blaster up, and the woman in charge of the team shot him in the face. He went backward through the holo, sending the projector to the ground.

'All right,' *Cent* Monique Lir said briskly. 'Spread out and take care of the rest of the command group until you get killed. Don't get taken prisoner . . . interrogation is a righteous pain in the ass.'

Her Intelligence and Reconnaissance troops went back out, and the sound of blasters thumping came.

Lir sat down in a camp chair, put her feet up on another.

'Nice dying, boss. The new ones love a little realism.'

Garvin sat up, wiped sticky red dye off his face.

'Thanks. How the hell'd you get through the lines?'

'Just looked for the shittiest part of the world and started crawling,' Lir said.

Njangu got to his feet and looked at his uniform distastefully.

'I hope to hell this crap washes out.'

'Guaranteed,' Lir said. 'Now, if you'll excuse me, I've got to go finish wiping out your headquarters.'

She left the bubble.

'Fitzgerald is gonna rip my lungs out for getting killed,' Garvin said.

'I think she's likely to have her own worries,' Njangu said. 'Last time I got a sitrep, she was up to her ass in cliffs and Aggressors.'

He went to an unmarked cooler, opened it, and took out two beers.

'I guess since we're officially dead, we can have one, eh?'

'Why not?' Garvin said, drinking deeply. 'This was about an abortion of a war game, wasn't it?'

'Only goes to show first that a brigade attacking an entrenched brigade takes it up the old koondingie,' Njangu said. 'Just like in the books.

'Not to mention that well-trained thugs like I&R can always pull a sneaking number on crunchies like we're in charge of.'

'As if I ever doubted that,' Garvin said. He took another swallow of beer. 'You know, it was a lot more fun when *we* got to play Aggressor and do dirty deeds dirt cheap and ruin other people's plans, wasn't it?'

'Maybe,' Njangu said. 'But when the blaster rounds got real, we also got killed a lot, remember? Which also was real, remember? That was one reason we decided to get ambitious and move upward in the chain of command, like good little heroes.

'More money in that, too.'

'But it sure is duller'n shit in peacetime,' Garvin said.

'Shut up,' Njangu suggested. 'Death comes knocking too early in the morning anyway.

'Let's see if we can't wrap this whole mess into one untidy ball, pull the troops out, and go looking for a shower and a drink.'

'After,' Garvin said gloomily, 'we get our asses chewed for losing.'

*

'Ouch,' Garvin said, rubbing imaginary wounds. 'I keep forgetting that one reason you get promoted to high command is an ability with words. I wish *Caud* Fitzgerald had done the critique instead of *Dant* Angara.'

It was late the next afternoon before the Legion's CO had finished his after-game commentary and the troops had been bathed, fed, and turned loose for a deserved two-day pass.

'I bleed, I moan, I sorrow,' Njangu said. 'What did he say about me? "Ineptly planned, carelessly executed, stupidly ended"?'

'I got worse, nanner,' Garvin said. '"Incorrect intelligence, failure to control staff, assumption of a degree of intelligence, deservedly assassinated, generally lazy staff and field work that can only be ascribed to the torpid assumption that peacetime exercises aren't important."'

'The Man *can* talk some shit,' Njangu said, absently returning the salute of an *Aspirant* trotting at the head of his platoon as they went up the steps into the Camp Mahan Officers' Club. 'What time's Jasith coming over for you?'

'Eighteen-thirty or so. She said I wasn't supposed to let you get me too drunk.'

''At's funny,' Njangu said. 'That's the same thing Maev said about you.'

'Great minds, in the same track,' Garvin said. 'Like sewers.' He wriggled. 'Sure feels nice to be clean again.'

'Gettin' soft, boss,' Njangu said. 'You ain't much of a field troopie if a mere day or three without a 'fresher gets to you. And you wanted to be out slitherin' through *giptel* doots with Lir? Getting old, grandpa. What are you, almost twenty-six? That's a year up on me.'

'Maybe I am turning into a candy ass,' Garvin said. 'Unlike you younger goons. Hey. Look.'

He pointed across the cavernous club to a table in the rear, where a very large, prematurely balding man in a flight suit sat, morosely staring at an almost-empty pitcher of beer.

'What's our Ben brooding about?' Njangu said. 'He can't be too broke to drink. We just got paid a week ago.'

'Dunno,' Garvin said. He went to the bar, got two pitchers and two glasses, and he and Njangu went to *Cent* Ben Dill's table.

'Oo looks unhappy,' Njangu cooed. 'Did oo faw down getting out of oo's *aksai* and dent oo's ickle nose?'

'Worse,' Dill said. 'Far, far worse. Mrs. Dill's favorite son got killed today.'

'Big frigging deal,' Njangu said. 'So did we.'

'No, I don't mean playing some stupid war game,' Dill scowled. 'I mean killed killed.'

Garvin reached over and poked the pilot.

'You seem pretty solid for a ghost.'

'I don't mean killed killed killed,' Ben said. 'Just killed killed.'

'I'm getting confused,' Garvin said.

'Here,' Njangu said. 'Drink beer and tell Aunt Yoshitaro all.'

'Can't do it,' Dill said. 'What's your clearance?'

'Crypto Quex,' both officers said smugly. 'There ain't no higher,' Njangu added.

'Oh yeh?' Dill growled. 'What about HOMEFALL?'

Jaansma and Yoshitaro looked at each other blankly.

'Ho-ho,' Dill said. 'If you ain't heard of it, you ain't got clearance enough, and I can't talk to you.'

'I surely understand your caution,' Njangu said. 'Being here in a nest of spies and all.'

'Come on,' Garvin said. 'Security's important.'

'Only for other people,' Njangu said. 'Now, let us do

a little intel analysis while we sit here and work on the beer we just put on Mr. Dill's tab.

'First, we should be aware that, since I've been demoted from my former lofty position as one of *Dant* Angara's intelligence sorts, the quality of Two Section has slipped astoundingly.

'This means that my replacements have slid into the easy grip of giving a certain operation a code name that suggests what it's about.

'We might suspicion that . . .' and Njangu reflexively lowered his voice, looked to make sure the tables around them were empty, '. . . HOMEFALL might just happen to have something to do with the Force starting to investigate why our ever-so-beloved Confederation has vanished and left us out on the far frontiers with a tear in our eye, our dick in our hand, and a hole in our pants.'

Dill covered his flinch. 'Jeez,' he said, 'you're getting as wordy as Jaansma.'

'There probably has been a certain cross-cultural leveling flow,' Njangu admitted.

'More like I've been able to drag him up to our level,' Garvin said. 'Njangu's doing a good job of guessing, since all of the hot-rod pilots have been detached for a special assignment . . . people like you and Alikhan and Boursier, for instance. And if you get killed killed, but not killed killed killed, maybe you're running pilotless craft out into the wild black yonder.

'But I don't think we ought to get specific if you want to tell us any details.'

Dill nodded. 'Let's just say I stuck my dick out where it shouldn't've been and got it shortened by about forty centimeters, leaving me with only a ninety-centimeter stub.'

The Confederation was a centuries-old federation,

sometimes authoritarian enough to be called an Empire, scattering across several galaxies. One of its Strike Forces, the Legion, had been assigned to the mineral-rich Cumbre system, which sat on the edges of 'civilization,' with the alien, hostile Musth 'beyond' and the aggressive systems of Larix and Kura 'behind' them.

Garvin and Njangu had been raw recruits on the last transport from the Confederation's capital world of Centrum to support Cumbre, barely escaping a high-jacking by Larix and Kura to make it to D-Cumbre.

And then all communications, all transport, ended.

The Force, now isolated, fought first a civil war against the 'Raum, worker-terrorists of Cumbre; then against the Musth; and, not much over an E-year past, a brutal campaign against Larix and Kura.

Now there was peace. But sooner or later everyone knew the Legion, as it was unofficially known, would have to go looking for the Confederation, or its remnants.

And so, very quietly, Force scientists had built drones, with realtime controllers on D-Cumbre 'flying' them. The commands to the ship bounced from satellite to satellite as the drone jumped from hyperspace navigation point to nav point, making them ideal for taking a peek at places elsewhere.

'I think we can figure out what happened,' Njangu said. 'You were out playing with your drone, and some-body or something blew you off. Sorry about that.'

'At least we're not sending manned ships out,' Garvin said.

'Still, it's damned unsettling, getting killed,' Dill said, drinking straight from a pitcher until it was dry, ignor-ing Garvin's protests. 'Shuddup. If I'm buying, it's my beer, so I can drink it if I want.

'Right?'

He glared at Garvin, who nodded hastily. Ben Dill was, thankfully, a cheerful sort of prime mover. Mostly. The problem was that no one in the Force was precisely sure what set his temper off, since it seemed to vary from day to day and mood to mood.

Jaansma waved at a bartender for another round.

'You know,' Njangu said thoughtfully, 'maybe it's time I put my finely tuned mind to considering things.'

'What sort of things?' Dill said, accepting one of the three new pitchers.

'Oh,' Njangu said, 'like how you got so ugly.'

Dill was about to respond when he saw a nightmare entering the club. It was over two meters tall, with many-banded coarse fur in various shades of yellowish brown. It had a small head, on a very long neck, that peered constantly about.

The creature walked upright on large rear legs, and its front legs were clawed. It had a small tail and wore a weapons harness in the Confederation colors of blue and white.

'Hey, Alikhan,' Dill bellowed to the Musth mercenary pilot. 'Get your fuzzy butt over here and help me deal with a couple of line slime!'

The alien made his way to their table.

'Whassamatter?' Dill asked. 'You don't look happy.'

He was one of the few who claimed he could decipher Musth expressions.

'I cannot say,' Alikhan said. He, unlike most Musth, who had trouble with sibilants, spoke excellent Common Speech. 'But if I were where I was not, I would not be here with you.'

'Aw,' Ben Dill said. 'Order up some of your stinky

meat and get wasted with us. The whole lot of us have gotten killed.'

'Yes,' Njangu Yoshitaro said thoughtfully. 'Time and past time for me to be thinking about this whole Confederation mess.'

TWO

Jasith Mellusin considered Garvin Jaansma's skinned nose, and giggled.

'I told you that you've got to be born on D-Cumbre, or maybe some other world with a lot of water, before you can wave-ride.'

'Nonsense,' Garvin said, eyeing his equally battered chest. 'I merely need guidance. You never told me you can fall out of a wave.'

'Because I never knew anyone who did it before,' Jasith said.

Jasith Mellusin, at twenty-three, was one of the richest women in the Cumbre system, controlling Mellusin Mining and its many ancillary corporations that her grandfather and father had built. She and Garvin had been lovers, ex-lovers, then came together again during the Musth occupation of D-Cumbre.

'I'll just lie here and sunburn a while,' Garvin groaned, 'then rise up and fight again. Hand me that glass, if you would.'

Jasith reached under the umbrella's shade, passing the tumbler sitting atop the small portable bar to him. He gurgled down alcohol. Behind them, on the deserted beach, was Jasith's lim. Beyond, large waves smashed down slithered up the black sands.

'Ah. I may live.' He stretched. 'You know, you're doing an extraordinary job of making me forget that tomorrow's a duty day.'

'My intent,' Jasith purred. 'Speaking of which—'

She broke off.

'Maybe you want to put your pants back on, and give me that towel. I hear music.'

'Naah. You're cracking up.' But Garvin obeyed, as two figures hove down the slope toward them. One was Njangu Yoshitaro, the other Maev Stiofan, recently rescued from Larissan service, now the head of *Dant* Angara's bodyguards.

She was turning a handle on a brightly painted box, and Yoshitaro carried a cooler in one hand, something in wrapping paper in the other.

'Ah-yut-dut-dut-dut-dut-dah-doo,' Njangu sang as they approached. 'We bring gifts of great import, O fearless leader.'

'How the hell did you find us?' Garvin demanded. 'Thisyere beach is private property, and we didn't tell anyone where we were going.'

'Ah,' Yoshitaro said, looking mysterious. 'Have you not learned by now I know everything?'

'Hey, Jasith,' Maev said. 'This is all his idea, and I don't have a clue what he's got in mind.'

'As usual with these two,' Jasith said. 'Pull up a towel and have a drink.'

'Did I say to stop playing?' Njangu said as he opened his cooler and took out two beers.

Maev obediently began turning the crank, and more tinny music floated out.

'What in God's tattooed butt is that?' Garvin demanded.

'Hah,' Njangu said. 'And here you claim to be a circus master.'

'Ringmaster,' Garvin corrected, looking closer at the box. 'I'll be dipped,' he said. 'It's a music box. And it's playing, uh, the "Elephant Song."'

'Actually, "March of the Elephants,"' Njangu said. 'Maev found it in some antiquey store, which gave me the idea. Here.' He passed the parcel across.

'It's not my birthday,' Garvin said suspiciously.

'Nope,' Njangu agreed. 'Merely my sub-tile way of leading you into yet another of my brilliant schemes.'

Garvin tore paper off. Inside was a disk, and on the disk was a tiny figure of a man wearing clothing several sizes too big for him; a dancer standing on the back of a quadruped, another woman wearing tights, and in the center a man in very old-fashioned formal wear. It was made of plas, and the paint or anodizing had worn off here and there.

'I had to get the motor replaced before it'd work,' Njangu said. 'Hit that button, there.'

Garvin did, and the clown in the baggy clothes pranced about, the horse ran around the ring while its rider did a handstand, the woman in tights tumbled back and forth around the ring, and the formally dressed man held out his hands here and there.

'Well, I shall be damned,' Garvin said softly. His eyes filled.

'What is it?' Jasith asked.

'It's the center ring of a circus,' Jaansma said. 'A circus from a very, very long time ago. Thank you, Njangu.'

'You see how well my plan's working,' Yoshitaro said. 'Almost got him blubbing like a babe. Softened the idiot up, I have.'

Garvin turned the device off.

'This is quite a buildup.'

'This is quite a plan,' Njangu agreed.

'First, consider what we've been doing wrong. Back

when we were expecting trouble with ol' Protector Redruth, we went and sent a snoopy shit out to see what was whuppin', right? And, thanks to that late and unlamented spy, they wuz lurkin' on us, and we got our butt buzz-sawed, right?

'Now, and ladies, I'll expect you to plug your li'l bitty ears and not listen to what I'm saying, we're now engaged in a certain enterprise, being sneaky once more, and what's happening?'

'You mean those drones we've been losing?' Maev said. 'You're not supposed to know anything about Operation HOMEFALL.'

Njangu raised several eyelids.

'Neither are you, you common bodyguard.'

'Surely am,' Maev said smugly. 'Who do you think *Dant* Angara uses for his couriers? I got a HOMEFALL clearance about a month ago.'

'And never told me?'

'You, my dear, don't have a need to know.'

'Zeus on a poop deck,' Njangu said. 'You see, Jasith, m'dear, why you're best staying well away from the military? Corrupts even the most loving relationship with its insistence on dirty, dark secrets.'

'I know,' Jasith agreed. 'That's why I felt so bad about not telling Garvin here about the Legion contracting to have its drones built by Mellusin Yards.'

Both men stared at each other.

'Thank any species of gods we don't believe in there aren't any spies about anymore,' Garvin said finally. 'This goddamned society leaks like . . . like a noncom with bladder problems.'

'How can we have spies if we don't even know who the frigging villains are yet?' Njangu asked reasonably, drained his beer, got another from the cooler.

'Having been thoroughly sidetracked, I might as well stay that way. Jasith, my love, my darling, my bestest friend's delight, could I borrow a ship from you?'

'What sort?'

'Something big and clunky. Some power to it. Interstellar, of course. Doesn't have to be too fast or maneuverable.'

'What shape are you going to bring it back in?'

'Damfino,' Njangu said. 'Maybe perfect. Maybe in a collection of brown paper bags. Maybe not at all, although if that happens, you won't be able to rack my heinie, since I plan on being aboard it.'

Jasith grinned.

'I think I've got what you need.

'I happen to have a certain clunker in the yards right now. Commissioned right after the war. Designed to carry and deploy, without a dock, mining machinery . . . I mean *big* mining machinery, like self-contained drilling units, even full mills . . . D- to E-Cumbre and to the outworlds for exploration. It's huge, almost three kilometers long, and gives ugly a hard way to go. Best description I could have is it looks like the universe's biggest nose cone, with landing-support fins that nobody built the rest of the ship for. Lotsa bulges and extrusions. Since it was to be the ultimate pig, and a good tax write-off, we went ahead and put stardrive in it.

'You could fit a whole handful of patrol ships, plus maybe a couple-four *aksai* in it. Takes a smallish crew to run . . . I don't remember just how many . . . and has living space that can be configured as dorms, cubicles, or even single bedrooms. It'll sleep fifteen hundred or more . . . in comfort and happily, since nobody wants to be around a smelly, angry miner.

'The holds can be sectioned, and, since we sometimes

tote delicate stuff around, there's triply redundant anti-grav,' she added. 'I'll lease the *Heavy Hauler VI* to the Force for, oh, ten credits a year, being the sentimental patriotic sort that I am.'

'Step one is now accomplished,' Njangu announced. 'By the way, I admire the romantic names you Mellusins give your spaceships.'

'You want to tell me what some lardpig of a spaceship has got to do with a circus?' Garvin asked.

'Why, we'll need a lardpig to haul our circus around in.'

'*Our* circus?' Garvin said.

'What a very thick young *caud* you be, *Caud* Jaansma,' Njangu said. 'What do you think I've been hinting broadly about? And aren't you the one who's always been nattering on, whenever you get drunk and maudlin, about giving all this up and running away and joining the circus, like the ones your family used to run?'

'Mmmh.' Garvin considered.

'What we do,' Njangu went on, getting more enthusiastic, 'is we put together a troupe . . . I went and looked that word up . . . made up of Forcemen, and then we go out, hiding in plain sight, doing a show here, a show there, and all the time we're working our way closer to, maybe the Capella system and Centrum.

'We don't have to be very good, just not visibly anyone interested in anything other than a quick credit.

'We'd best put in some crooked games,' he said thoughtfully. 'First, nobody'd expect a Confed soldier to be crooked; second, that could be some good coinage for our retirement.

'When we get an eyeful and an earful on what's happening out there in the great beyond, we slide on back home, report, and let *Dant* Angara figure out what to do next. But at least we get an idea of what's out there . . . besides blackness and nothing.'

Maev nodded understanding, coming from another system herself. Jasith, who'd known nothing but Cumbre her entire life, shrugged.

'Interesting,' Garvin said after being silent for a while. 'Very interesting.'

'You want to go for it?' Njangu asked.

'Some of it,' Garvin said, pretending utter casualness. 'I've got a few ideas of my own, you know.'

'The last time you tried some of them, you damned near got yourself executed, remember?' Njangu said. 'I'm the brains of this operation, right?'

Maev started laughing. 'If that's true, boy are you two clowns in trouble.'

'Clowns,' Garvin said, a bit dreamily. 'I've always dreamed of having a center ring full of clowns, so many when they shivaree nobody'll be able to make me out.

'You'll make a good clown, Njangu.'

'Me? Uh-uh. I'm gonna be the guy who goes in front, getting the people ready.'

'Boss hostler? Dunno if you've got the talent,' Garvin said, mock-seriously.

'Wait a minute,' Jasith said. 'You two are talking about going out, running around, and having fun.'

'Oh no,' Njangu said piously. 'Lotsa big risks out there. We're laughing, ho-ho, in the face of danger.'

'Fine,' Jasith said. 'Change one. You want my ship, you're taking me with you.'

'Huh?' Garvin said.

'You're always the ones having adventures,' Jasith said. 'No more.'

'What sort of slot would you want?' he said.

'Are you going to have dancing girls?'

'Sure,' Garvin said. 'What's a good circus without a little bit of sex around the edges. Most respectable, of course,' he added hastily.

'And with me along, it'll be doubly so,' Jasith said firmly.

'I have learned,' Garvin said to Njangu, 'never to argue with Mellusin when she gets that tone of voice to her voice.'

''Kay,' Njangu said. 'She goes. That'll keep you straight. Plus she can run payroll and the books, being the business yoink she is.'

'And I'll take care of you,' Maev said. 'Since you said something about recruiting from the Force.'

Njangu grinned and kissed her.

'If *Dant* Angara turns you loose, why not?'

'Lions and horses and maybe even bears,' Garvin said, lost in his vision.

'Yeh,' Njangu said. 'Sure. Just where on Cumbre are you gonna find any of them?'

Garvin smiled mysteriously, then came to his feet. 'Come on. Let's go tell Angara about your latest craziness.'

Dant Grig Angara, the Legion's Commander, stared at the small holo of the *Heavy Hauler VI* as it went through its paces — extruding ramps, opening huge ports, its decks changing — without seeing it.

'My parents took me to a circus once, when I was a kid,' he said slowly. 'And the prettiest lady in the world, who wore white tights, gave me some candy that was like a pink cloud when you bit into it.'

'You see?' Garvin said to Njangu. 'Everybody loves a circus. Cotton candy for all.'

Angara brought himself back.

'An interesting idea,' he mused. 'Of course you'd punt out without leaving any tracks so you could be followed back to Cumbre.'

'Of course, sir.'

'And we could hold a Field Day for the Force, and you could pick any athletes you want.'

'Actually,' Njangu said, 'we could do it for the whole system, since we don't have to worry about this having any kind of security hold.'

Angara made a face. 'I don't know if I agree. I don't like everybody knowing our business. But maybe you're right.'

'If you want to have a mass tryout, sir,' Garvin said, 'that's fine. But our first stop . . . unless you order otherwise . . . will be at one of the circus worlds.'

'Circus worlds?' Angara said, a note of incredulity to his voice.

'Yessir. I know of three. Circus people have to have a place to get away from the flatties . . . the crowd. Even in olden times there were circus towns where the troupers and their animals would go in the off-season.

'That's where they recruit people, practice new tricks, change jobs, catch up on the gossip.'

'What will that give you?'

'Animal acts,' Garvin said. 'Trapeze artists. Flash.'

'How will you pay for that?' Angara asked. 'It's peace-time, and PlanGov is getting a little tight with the budget. I don't want to have to stand up and say, "fine, ladies, gentlemen, we're going to put on a show you'll never see."'

'Mellusin Mining has already agreed to fund us,' Garvin said. 'Plus I&R's got a ton of money in a discretionary fund that was given us by Mellusin back during the Musth war.'

'I am getting very fond of this idea,' *Cent* Erik Penwyth, one of Angara's aides said. He was a member of Cumbre's elite, the Rentiers, and ex-member of the elite I&R Company, sometimes considered the most handsome man in the Force.

'And we'd love to have you,' Garvin said. 'Maybe as advance man.'

'Hey,' Njangu said. 'I thought that was my slot.'

'Not a chance,' Garvin said. 'I wasn't kidding when I said I want clowns. Plus,' he added thoughtfully, 'I want somebody close at hand for security.'

'Oh. Oh,' Njangu said in a mollified tone. 'That's different.'

'Which brings up another problem,' Angara said. 'This little mission is going to strip the Force clean of some of its best troops. I've got to assume worst case, and you'll have problems. I agree this mission is important – but I don't want it accomplished with the loss of some fine soldiers a long way from home.'

Garvin inclined his head in agreement. 'First, I plan on bringing everyone back. Second is that some of what I'll call best may not be on your roster.'

'A good point,' Angara agreed after a bit of thought. 'I&R troops don't always make the best line soldiers. I assume you'll be taking a lot of them with you.'

'With your permission, sir,' Garvin said. 'Since we're at peace, that'll give them something to keep out of trouble.'

'Bigger trouble generally does,' Angara said. 'So you'll collect a team . . . a troupe, you called it, and start gathering intelligence. Let's for the sake of argument, and to keep one small measure of security of things, call the operation HOMEFALL, like another, similar one we have running presently. That should thoroughly confuse the issue.

'But back to the matter at hand. What happens if or when, you run into trouble?'

'We'll have the ship armed to the eyebrows,' Garvin said. 'With all the goodies out of sight. I'll take some *aksai*, some of the Nana-class patrol boats we took back from Redruth's mob.'

'Won't that appear suspicious?'

'If the Confederation has fallen apart,' Garvin said, 'which seems a little more than logical, considering the drones I know nothing about that have been getting disappeared lately, I'd assume anybody going anywhere off their own homeworlds goes armed these days.'

''Kay,' Angara agreed. 'Probably right on that one.'

'By the way, we're going to rename the *Hauler*, for good luck,' Garvin said. 'It'll be *Big Bertha*.'

'*Damned* romantic,' Penwyth said sarcastically.

'Named after the biggest circus of them all,' Garvin said. 'Way back on Earth. Ringling Brothers and Bailey and Barnum.'

'Whatever you want,' Angara said.

'There is one other thing I'd like, sir,' Garvin said diffidently. 'This whole situation might get a little . . . tense. And I'm just a young trooper. Shouldn't we find some diplomat to go with us? Just to make sure we don't make any mistakes. Soldiers have a, well—'

'Tendency to pull triggers when in question or in doubt,' Angara finished.

'Well . . . yessir.'

Angara considered for a moment. 'Not a bad idea, *Caud*. There's only one problem. I can't think of any politico in this system who qualifies as any kind of subtle peacemaker or -keeper. Cumbre's history over the past few years doesn't exactly suggest any names to me. Do you have any candidates?'

Garvin shook his head, looked at Njangu.

'Other than me,' Yoshitaro said, 'sorry, files are empty.'

'So I'm afraid,' Angara said, 'you'll have to play things as best they appear to you. How far do you want to go?'

'As far as I can get, sir,' Garvin said firmly. 'Hopefully, all the way to the heart of the Confederation to Centrum itself.'

THREE

'At the moment,' *Caud* Fitzgerald said to Garvin, 'you are not one of my favorite Regimental Commanders.'

'No, ma'am.'

'And you, *Haut* Yoshitaro, are on the same shit list.'

'Yes, ma'am,' Njangu said. Both Jaansma and Yoshitaro stood at rigid attention in front of their Brigade Commander.

'Once again, I've got to remind both of you. This Force has something called a chain of command. That means when you two thugs have an idea, it is supposed to go to me, then, and only then, assuming I approve up the chain of command to *Dant* Angara.

'Instead, I find I'm losing both of you to go haring out into the unknown as if you were both still with I&R . . . and the scheme was your idea in the first place.'

'Sorry, *Caud*,' Garvin tried. 'I forgot.'

'Old habits die hard,' Njangu hurried.

'It's a pity that *Dant* Angara doesn't approve of some field punishments other armies used, such as crucifixion.'

Garvin looked into the woman's hard eyes, not sure if she was joking, and said nothing.

'Very well,' Fitzgerald said. 'Since Angara's already approved, there's nothing I can do but rail at you.

'Don't fail ... or, if you do, come back dead. Otherwise, I might have to remember this conversation when it's time for your next fitness reports.

'Now get your asses out of here ... and, incidentally, the best of luck.'

Ben Dill shambled into Garvin's office, something just bigger than a cubicle, with an inspiring view of the Second Regiment's motor pool. He managed a salute, didn't wait for Jaansma to return it, and sat down.

''Kay,' he growled. 'First, I'll listen to you tell me why I can't go on this wildhair trip of yours, then I'll tell you why I'm going.'

'Save it, Ben,' Garvin advised. 'You're already on the roster.'

Dill blinked. 'Howcum I don't have to threaten you, like usual?'

'I need a good pilot,' Garvin said, 'but I'll take you. We're bringing along three *aksai*, plus a hangar queen for spare parts, and I understand you know which end of those evil-flying bastards goes first.'

'I am only the best *aksai* pilot in the cosmos, including any Musth that might think, just 'cause he invented those evil pigs, he's better than me.'

'Which is why I put you down, right after Alikhan and Boursier.'

'Alikhan, 'kay,' Dill said. 'But Boursier? I can fly circles around her butt without power.'

'I just wanted to wait to see how long it took you to show up,' Garvin said, suppressing a grin. 'You want to know your other slot?

'We'll need a strongman.'

'You mean, like in the holos, stripped to the waist all

oiled up, with big ol' iron rings on my arms to show off my perfect physique?'

'Plus a corset to hold in your gut.'

'Damn,' Dill said, oblivious. 'I get to show off.'

'Within reason.'

'Hey,' the big man said, 'I got a great idea. Since you're taking Alikhan already, and nobody needs to know he speaks Common Speech, you could use him—'

'As an exhibit,' Garvin interrupted. 'Meet Man's Deadliest Foe . . . See Him in an Orgy of Decayed Flesh . . . a Cannibal Fiend from a Nightmare Beyond the Stars. And anybody who comes close to his cage will talk freely, not knowing he's got big ears on 'em.'

'Aw shit,' Dill said. 'You went and beat me to it.'

'Always,' Garvin said.

Dill chortled. 'It'll be worth the price of admission just seeing him in a cage.'

'Only when the gilly-galloos are around.'

''At'll be enough. I'll bring . . . what're they . . . nut-peas to throw at him.'

'I suppose,' Njangu said, 'all this is in the noble tradition of I&R volunteering for everything.' His hand swept out, indicated the company formation in front of him. 'Is there anybody missing?'

'Nossir,' *Cent* Monique Lir said briskly. 'Other than one man in hospital who won't be discharged before takeoff time.'

''Kay,' Njangu said, then raised his voice. 'I'm proud of all you sneaky mud-eaters for courage and general stupidity.

'Now, my flyer mentioned specific talents. Anybody who's got one of them, stay in formation. The rest of you who're just looking for some cheap adventure like I am fall out and go back to your barracks.'

He waited, and, grudgingly, people began slinking away, until only about sixty of the 130-plus unit remained.

"Kay,' Njangu said. 'Now, we'll start screening.'

He eyed the men and women.

'Striker Fleam . . . what are you planning to add to things? Besides your general surly attitude, I mean.'

The hard-faced Striker, who always refused promotion but was one of the best field soldiers in I&R, which meant the entire Force, grinned thinly.

'Knots, sir.'

'Beg pardon.'

'I can tie any knot known. One-handed, off-handed, upside down, in my sleep, on a drunk.'

'A knot-tier,' Njangu said, beginning to enjoy this, 'wasn't on the list.'

'Nossir,' Fleam agreed. 'But I checked around, and went and looked up circuses, and all of them talk about ropes and lines and pulleys and shit like that.'

"Kay,' Njangu said. 'You're aboard. What about you, *Cent* Lir?'

'I've been a dancer with an opera company.'

"Kay. We'll need somebody to ramrod the dance troupe. What about you, *Alt* Montagna?'

'Swimming, sir. High diving too. And I thought I could learn trapeze, since I'm not a bad climber.'

'Have either of you thought about what's going to happen to I&R with both the Company Commander and Exec away?'

'Already taken care of, sir,' Lir said briskly. 'We'll vet Lav Huran up to take over as CO, give him a temp commission that'll go to permanent if we don't come back, Abana Calafo as XO, also with a temporary rank. Already approved by *Caud* Jaansma.'

'Mmmh.' Njangu turned serious. Of course the

incredibly competent Lir would be welcome, although he hadn't heard of her opera experience.

Darod Montagna was another story. Garvin, in spite of his ongoing affair with Jasith Mellusin, had more than a casual interest in the young black-haired sniper/officer. Njangu had caught them kissing when both were drunk during the war with Larix/Kura, but didn't think much further had happened.

It would've been trouble if it had, except Montagna had gotten herself commissioned during the war, so the traditional ban on enlisted/officer relationships wasn't there.

But still . . . Njangu remembered two things. First, that Jasith was going on the expedition and, second and more important, he wasn't Garvin's keeper.

"Kay,' he grudged. 'Now, let's sort the rest of you fools out.'

'Send him in,' Garvin said. He leaned back in his chair. It had been a very long week, vetting volunteers, listening to the lies of commanders trying to fob off the lame and lazy on him, and to the screeches of other COs who were losing their best. And now this.

Dr. Danfin Froude was one of Cumbre's most respected mathematicians, though his talents led into most areas of applied science. In addition, in spite of his over-sixty years, the rumpled small man was a daredevil and had accompanied the Force on several hazardous missions, getting a reputation for complete fearlessness. During the Larix/Kura war, he'd fallen in love hard with one of the Forcewomen, not uncommon when romance comes late in life. She'd been killed, and Froude's world seemed to have ended. He was still there for the Force for any desired analysis, but he was a bit distant, as if a part of him had died with Ho Kang.

The door came open, and Garvin jumped. The man standing in front of him wore exaggerated stage makeup, the saddest man in the world, with a peculiarly obnoxious long nose. His pants sagged, his shoes were holed, and ridiculously oversize, his vest tattered as much as his archaic hat.

'Hello, Garvin,' Froude said. 'You're looking very well.' He snuffled. 'I'm not.' He began taking a large handkerchief from a sleeve, and more and more material came out, until he was holding something the size of a bedsheet. There was a flutter in its midst, and a *stobor*, one of the two-legged snakes peculiar to D-Cumbre slithered out, landed on Garvin's desk, hissed, and fled into the outer office.

'Oh, sorry, Garvin,' Froude said, still in the same monotone. A tear dripped from one eye, and he wiped it away. When the handkerchief was gone, his long nose had changed into a red rubber ball. He scratched it, took it off, bounced it against a wall, shrugged.

'I don't guess you're going to let me come with you, are you?'

'You learned all this in two days?'

Froude nodded, and his pants fell down.

'You know there's no way I'd refuse a Willie the Weeper,' Garvin said.

Froude snuffled, picked up his pants.

'You're not just saying that to try to make me smile, now are you?'

He lifted his hat, and some species of flying object scrawked and flapped away.

'You're aboard, you're aboard,' Garvin said, starting to laugh. 'Now get the hell out before you produce some carnivore out of your pants.'

'Thank you, sir, thank you, thank you,' Froude said,

still in the monotone, bowing and scraping. 'But I have one more boon, a small favor, just a little service, since Ann Heiser is off getting married to Jon Hedley, and wants to stay home for a while, which means I won't have anyone to bounce my ideas off of.'

Garvin noticed the way Froude's face twisted when he said 'married,' but said nothing.

Froude went to the door, opened it.

Garvin looked suspiciously at the completely undistinguished man who hunched into his office. He was short, a bit over a meter and a half tall, wearing battered clothes that the poorest of poor clerks might disdain.

'This is my colleague, Jabish Ristori,' Froude said.

Ristori extended a hand. Garvin reached to take it, and Ristori did a backflip, landing on his feet. He held out his hand again, and as Garvin stepped forward, the man cartwheeled against the wall, then, somehow, up onto Garvin's desk, and against the other wall, once more came down with a graceful bounce, and solemnly shook Garvin's hand.

'Pleased to meetcha, meetcha, meetcha,' and Ristori turned another flip to show his pleasure.

'Professor Jabish Ristori,' Froude said. 'Nice enough guy, a colleague of mine for years, even if he does belong to one of those fields that can hardly be called a discipline.'

'Socisocisocisociology,' Ristori said, doing a handstand, then lifting one hand off the ground.

'Jabish became curious ten years ago about wandering entertainers, and determined to learn their tricks,' Froude went on.

'And I never, ever, ever went back to the univee,' Ristori said with an infectious giggle. 'Dull, dry, dry, dull.'

He pushed off from the ground and landed on his feet.

'Welcome to the circus,' Garvin said. 'We can always use a tumbler.'

'A tumbler, bumbler, stumbler,' Ristori said. 'Here. I believe this is yours.'

He gave Garvin back the identity card that, until a few seconds ago, had been clipped to Jaansma's shirt pocket.

'How'd you . . . oh. Sorry,' Garvin said. 'I should know, never wise up the mark.'

'And this is yours,' Ristori said, giving Garvin back his watch ring. 'And this.' It was Garvin's wallet, which had been most secure in his buttoned rear pocket.

'But you never got within a meter of me!' Garvin blurted.

'I didn't, did I?' Ristori said, in a deep voice full of ominous significance. 'If I had, I might have all your credits, which you'll find in your left front pocket.'

'You two,' Garvin said, knowing without checking, the money would somehow be there. 'Out. Report to Njangu and draw your gear.

'And try to leave him with his pants.'

The tall man in greasy coveralls slid out from underneath a Zhukov Aerial Combat Vehicle. He held an unpowered torque wrench about as long as his arm.

Njangu saluted him smartly as he got to his feet.

Mil Taf Liskeard returned the salute, after noting the wings on Yoshitaro's chest.

'Didn't think you flyboys would even recognize my existence these days,' he said bitterly.

Njangu didn't respond to that, but said, 'Sir, I'd like to speak to you privately.'

Liskeard looked across at the two mechanics, who were visibly not paying the slightest attention.

'In that grease trap that passes for my office, then.'

Njangu followed him inside, closed the door.

'All right. What do you want, Yoshitaro? Aren't you too busy putting together your latest scheme to be wasting time on a grounded old fart who broke under fire?'

'I want you, sir, as one of the pilots on that scheme.'

'Bad joke,' Liskeard said shortly. 'I say again my last. I broke, remember? I had Angara ground me. Or hadn't you heard? I couldn't take killing people.'

'I know,' Yoshitaro said. 'But I still want you. To fly that Big Ugly Flopper we're going out in. I looked your record up, sir. You had more than two thousand hours in converted civilian transports before you transferred to Griersons. And we're very, very short on people who've got experience moving hogs of steel about.'

'I did do that for a while,' Liskeard said. 'I should have known my limits and kept pushing those BUFs around the sky.

'But that's not the point. I couldn't take it, busting other transports apart like the ones I flew, like gutting fish, and turned my wings in. Angara said he'd make sure I never flew anything military again, and would have my ass out of the Force as soon as he got around to it.

'I guess he forgot about me down here in this motor pool,' Liskeard went on. 'And I'll be damned if I know why I didn't remind him.'

He rubbed his forehead, leaving a greasy smear.

'No, Yoshitaro. You've got something else in mind than rehabilitating a coward. Am I supposed to be the Judas Goat on this new operation? I hear you're famous for nasty little tricks like that.'

'I want you,' and Njangu paused, trying to hold back his temper, trying to hold to his purpose. But the words didn't come easy, 'for personal reasons. A month or so after you . . . grounded yourself, I got in the center of somebody's sights and they dropped a barrage on me. And I broke, too.'

'But you came back. Obviously, or you'd be under that Zhukov with me, looking for grease points.'

'Yeh,' Njangu said. 'I did. Maybe because I was too cowardly to tell somebody who saw me go down that I was shattered, that I couldn't keep on keeping on.'

Liskeard's manner changed. He eyed Njangu.

'So this is a kind of rehabilitation. You're willing to take a chance on me again?'

'We're not going out in *Big Bertha* to shoot at people,' Njangu said. 'We're going out to have a look around and get our asses back here to report.'

'That doesn't mean I'll be able to hold together if things get sticky.'

'Then I'll yank your ass off the controls and break it myself for real. Sir.' Njangu growled, his fingers unconsciously curling into a strike hand.

Liskeard saw his hands, then started laughing, very hard.

'Does Angara know you're trying to recruit me?'

'He does,' Njangu said. 'And he growled something about I better be sure I'm right.'

Liskeard looked surprised. 'That's the last thing I'd expect that hard-ass old bastard to say.'

He took a deep breath.

'Yoshitaro, I'll put the wings back on for you. And if I snap again . . . you won't have to take care of me. I'll do it myself.

'And . . . thanks. I owe you. Very, very large.'

Njangu, never happy with sentiment, came to attention, saluted, and turned. Over his shoulder he said:

'Then get over to *Big Bertha* — she comes out of the yards in two hours — and start learning what a pig she is to fly. Sir.'

'You're sure that dance is authentic?' Garvin asked doubtfully.

Dec Running Bear, resplendent in breechclout, a rawhide necklace of long teeth, face paint, and a feather sticking sideways out of his braided hair, grinned.

'Just as my mother's mother's mother taught me. Or, if the people I'm dancing for start lookin' like they think I'm shitting them, my father's father's father's father. Hell, I'll tell 'em next performance I'm gonna put bone spikes through my tits, hang in the air, and yodel for the ancient Sun Dance.'

'I dunno,' Garvin said, 'still skeptical.

'Look, sir. I could really use some action. I'm bored cross-cocked doing nothing but fly *Dant* Angara around. Great Spirit on a bicycle, I actually found myself wanting a little shooting last week.'

Running Bear absently rubbed a scarred arm. He was one of the few living holders of the Confederation Cross, gained in what he called 'one ee-holay mad moment.'

'So I dance some, tell some stories . . . those are for real from back when, maybe even back to Earth . . . my gran taught me . . . smoke a peace pipe, sing some chants, look like a dangerous warrior.

'Isn't that a good way to meet women? Sir?'

'Doesn't sound that bad,' Garvin said. 'Plus we can always use another certified crazy besides Ben Dill. And you can fly.'

'Anything short of a Zhukov, right through the eye of a goddamned needle, sir.'

'Well, we're pissing off *Dant* Angara bad enough

already, taking his best. Might as well grab his chauffeur as well,' Garvin decided.

'Might be fun,' Erik Penwyth drawled. 'Wandering out there, a day in front of you folks, seeing who and what can be taken advantage of.'

'Just don't get cute on me,' Njangu promised. 'Remember, you're in the job I wanted.'

'Would you stop whining?' Garvin said. 'Clown master you are, and clown master you remain. Pass the goddamned bottle, would you?'

Njangu pushed it across, just as a tap came on the door.

'Enter,' he said.

The door opened, and a woman wearing hospital whites came in.

'Well, I'll be goto,' Garvin said. '*Alt* Mahim. Siddown, Doc. I thought we'd detached you to medical school.'

She sat, on the edge of one of Garvin's chairs.

'I am . . . was, sir. Until three days ago, when the term finished. I took a long leave.'

'Uh-oh,' Njangu said meaningfully. 'The sy-reen call of excitement.'

'Come on, Jil,' Garvin said. 'First, knock off the "sir." Or have you forgotten I&R tradition, such as it is?'

'Noss . . . no, boss. I came to see if you need a good medico aboard.'

'Damme,' Penwyth said. 'What is it about the old I&R crew? You try to put them in place where they just might not get killed, learn how to do valuable things like deliver babies and do brain surgery that'll give them a slot on the outside, and they come roarin' back to the cannon's mouth, every time.'

'I won't even try to argue with you,' Garvin said. 'Hell

yes, we need a good combat medic. Here. Pour yourself a drink.'

'Not right now, boss,' Mahim said, getting to her feet. 'I've got to go steal what medpak supplies I'll need. But thanks.'

She saluted, was gone.

Penwyth shook his head.

'We'll never learn, will we?'

Garvin got out of his lifter, started up the long steps to the Mellusin mansion, Hillcrest. He was at the door when he heard a loud crash. He opened the door, heard an obscenity, then another crash.

'Assholes!' Jasith shouted.

There was another smash.

Garvin went carefully toward the sound of the destruction. It was in the remnants of the kitchen.

Jasith Mellusin was glaring at a smashed communicator. Then she went back to the serving cabinet, selected a platter, and threw it the length of the dining room.

'Shitheads!'

She picked up a plate in each hand.

'Uh . . . I'm home, dear,' Garvin said.

She looked at him angrily, threw both plates at the wall.

'Sons of bitches!'

'Since you're talking plural,' Garvin said, 'I can hope you're not sonsabitchin' me.'

'Not you!'

'Then can I kiss you?'

Jasith pursed lips. Garvin strode through the ruins of most of their dinner service, kissed her. After a bit, they broke apart.

'That's a little better,' Jasith admitted. 'Not that it makes me want to stop cursing.'

Garvin lifted an eyebrow.

'My goddamned Board of Directors, my twice-god-damned stockholders, my three-times-screwed executives!'

'Pretty comprehensive list.'

'Don't stay so calm, Garvin! They just told me I can't go with you!'

'But . . . you're Mellusin Mining, I mean, the only one,' he said bewilderedly. 'You can do what you want, can't you?'

'No,' she said, starting to steam once again. 'Not if it affects the price of the stock, or the confidence of the stockholders if their chief executive happens to be out-system, maybe even in danger and God forbid I go and get killed. The entire goddamned board went and voted they'd resign if I go out with you. Said I didn't have any regard for my own company if I'd go do something dangerous that I didn't have to, that was the job of proper soldiers, not immature little girls like they seem to think I still am!

'Fughpigs!'

A very large crystal dessert tray Garvin had rather liked skimmed across the room and disintegrated in rainbow shards.

'Oh,' Garvin said.

'You want to throw something?'

'Uh . . . no.'

She gave him a suspicious look.

'Aren't you sorry I'm not going?'

'Of course, sure I am,' Garvin said hastily. 'So don't go and lob anything my way. Honest, Jasith.'

'Dammit, dammit, dammit,' she said, and started crying.

Garvin, cautiously, put his arms around her again.

'Why don't they ever let me have any fun?' Jasith said into the hollow of his shoulder.

'I always thought,' Garvin said, 'the really rich were free.'

'Nobody's free, dammit,' Jasith said. 'Except maybe the dead.'

'What do you think?' Maev said, raising her voice to a singsong, 'Candy, lifts, chewies, balloons, candy, lifts, chewies, balloons, a prize in every box.'

'I think,' Njangu said, eyeing her very scanty costume, 'nobody's gonna be looking at your goodies. At least not the ones in that tray.'

'Sure they will,' Maev said. 'Little children love me.'

'Then what's this about selling lifts?'

'Nothing addictive,' Maev said. 'A mild mood-enhancer. With about an eight hundred percent profit.

'And if they are ogling m' boobs, that's fine, too. They'll never notice . . .'

And her hand moved under the tray slung around her neck, came out with a smallish, large-barreled projectile weapon.

'. . . this. Guaranteed I can put two of these slugs between somebody's eyes at fifteen meters. For less lethal response . . .'

Again, her hand went under the tray, came out with a squat cylinder.

'. . . blindspray. Give you convulsions for half an hour, vomiting for an hour, can't see squat for two hours.'

'That's if somebody tries to get friendly?'

'Other than you,' Maev said. 'Or somebody really, really rich.' She took off her tray.

'Now, I need a drink. This security operation is sweaty work.'

'Already made for you, m'love,' Njangu said. 'Over on the sideboard.'

It wasn't financially convenient, but Njangu had kept the lease on the apartment across the bay from Camp Mahan, on the outskirts of D-Cumbre's capital of Leggett, as a convenient way of getting away from uniforms when the military made him want to howl at the moons.

'Pity about poor Jasith,' Maev said.

'What? I haven't heard squat.'

Maev told him about the near revolt by the officers of Mellusin Mining.

'So she's out, sulking like a fiend.'

'Uh-oh,' Njangu said inadvertently, thinking of Darod Montagna.

'What?'

'Nothing,' Njangu said hastily.

'You're holding back.'

'I surely am.'

'How terribly interesting,' Darod Montagna said. 'Poor Miss Mellusin, forced to stay home and count all her money and not go play with us.'

'Dammit,' Monique Lir told her XO, 'I hope you're going to be a good girl.'

'I'm going to be a *very* good girl,' Darod said in her most sultry voice. 'I'm going to be the best girl that man's ever seen.'

'Uh-oh,' Lir said.

Finally Stage One – planning; Stage Two – logistics and personnel; and Stage Three, operations, were finished. There were almost 150 men and women picked all volunteers, including a few civilians who'd managed to penetrate the fairly tight security screen *Dant* Angara had imposed after all.

They filed into *Big Bertha* and found their assigned compartments. The old soldiers made old jokes that hadn't been that funny the first time around, the new women and men wondered why they had tight lumps in their guts instead of pride.

Garvin Jaansma kissed Jasith Mellusin.

'You better come back,' she said fiercely, then looked away.

'I'll go with what she said,' Angara said. 'But with an addition. Bring me back *something*, Garvin.' There was a flash of desperation in his eyes. 'Dammit, we can't keep on as we have, not knowing anything!'

'I'll come back,' Garvin promised. 'With the hot skinny, boss.'

He saluted Angara, kissed Jasith again, and went up *Big Berdta*'s ramp. It slid shut, and a speaker blatted: 'All personnel. All personnel on ramps. Clear ramps for takeoff. Clear ramps for takeoff. Three minute warning. Clear ramps.'

'Come on,' Angara said, taking Jasith's arm.

She followed him back into the terminal, went to a window.

The ground trembled, and *Big Bertha*'s antigravs lifted her clear of the ground. Her secondary drive cut in, and the behemoth crawled upward, became graceful, and vanished into the stratosphere and space.

Jasith stood there, watching emptiness for a long time.

FOUR

Njangu and Garvin had given themselves more tactical options than just hiding in plain sight if – or, more realistically, when – problems developed.

'I am getting very damned tired of being ambushed every time we come out of hyperspace,' Yoshitaro had said, looking pointedly at the three *aksai* pilots. 'Which is why I'm going to use your young asses as bait . . . or anyway, some kind of warning system. I just hope you won't slow down and get dead bringing us the word.'

The *aksai* was the prime fighting ship of the Musth during the war with Cumbre. Now, with peace looming on all sides and trade flourishing with Man, the *aksai* were being built for the Force, somewhat modified for human pilotage. It was a flying wing, C-shaped, about twenty-five meters from horn to horn with one, two, or three fighting compartments, capsules, mounted on the concave forward edge of the wing, weapons either encapsulated or just hung below the wing. It was impossibly fast and, as Ben Dill said, 'harder to fly than a whore on roller skates.'

Jacqueline Boursier, the self-described 'shit-hot pilot,' tried to put together a fund to hire an athletic prostitute, buy some old-fashioned roller skates, and lock Ben Dill in a gymnasium with her to see what happened. She had no takers.

In-atmosphere, the *aksai* would stall handily and snaproll into the ground if flying speed wasn't kept up, and transitioning between the standard antigravity lift system to secondary and then stardrives took a most delicate touch.

Out-atmosphere, its instant acceleration and speed were as likely to stuff its pilot into something unpleasantly solid as punt her to the fringes of the system before reaction time could take over.

But those who could fly the ships invariably fell in love with them. They were possibly the most acrobatic craft ever built, with the possible exception of Dawnage propeller ships.

The procedure Garvin and Njangu had come up with to keep from being mousetrapped was complicatedly simple: *Big Bertha* would set a hyperspace jump to the desired navigational point. However, the navigational instruments were set with a pause feature, rather than the usual, automatic reemergence into N-space.

Hanging in something beyond nothingness, the mother ship would launch an *aksai*. The *aksai* would enter real space and make a preliminary recon for bad guys, surprises, or flower-tossing maidens. It would pass the word back to *Big Bertha*, which could take appropriate measures.

If the system was hostile, the ship would wait as long as she could for the *aksai* to rejoin her. If the mother ship had to flee, the *aksai* was to make a hyperspace jump, to a predetermined nav point, and Mayday in all directions, hoping for rescue before the air ran out.

But this was an option none of the three *aksai* pilots believed would ever happen.

After all, they were *all* shit-hot, not just Boursier . . .

*

The inship annunciator burped sedately. The synth-voice Garvin hadn't gotten around to replacing, which, unfortunately, 'cast into all compartments, announced 'Aksai section . . . aksai section . . . ready pilot, report to the bridge.'

The man, woman, and alien cut for high card, and Alikhan obeyed the summons, round ears cocked in excitement.

The bridge of *Big Bertha* was as unusual as the rest of the bulbous starship: a self-contained pod at the 'top' of the cargo/passenger spaces, with the forward edge, monitors looking like ports, protruding from the hull a bit. Flanking the large bridge area were communication and navigation compartments and, at the rear of the pod, a secondary command center with observation ports looking 'down' into the hull's huge cargo spaces.

It would make, Garvin thought, a dandy place for a circus master to crack the whip from. Or possibly, if they kicked out a few of the windows, some sort of high-wire or other flier act.

Alikhan got his briefing, and went along a sealed catwalk through an airlock to the 'top' of the ship, where three of the state-of-the-ten-year-old-art Nana boats and the four *aksai* hung, like so many bats in a huge barn.

He wedged himself rear legs first into the *aksai*'s pod on his belly, then closed the clear canopy. He turned power on, checked controls, touched sensors, read the displays on his canopy as the main and secondary drives came alive, then announced he was ready to launch.

'This is Command,' Garvin told him. 'Your coordinates and flight pattern have been fed into your computer. Launch at will.'

A hatch above him slid back, and a steel arm lifted the *aksai* clear of *Big Bertha*. Alikhan watched readouts blink on his canopy, trying to convince himself that the blur of

N-space around him wasn't vaguely nauseating, certainly not for a combat-experienced Musth.

Gravity spun, vanished, and he was beyond the ship's grav field. Alikhan considered what Garvin had told him about the system he was to enter — three worlds, settled over two hundred E-years ago, no data on government, military, peacefulness. It'd been chosen for the first system to enter because it was distant from the nav points 'close' to Larix and Kura, and hence, Garvin assumed, hadn't been slandered by Redruth, and, hopefully, wouldn't be that hostile to an intruder.

Alikhan touched a sensor, and the *aksai* dropped out of hyperspace, the swirl around him becoming stars and not-too-distant planets. He went at full drive toward the second planet, reportedly the first colonized, searching all common bands for 'casts.

Within an E-hour, he sent a com back into hyperspace to *Big Bertha*: no hostiles. Safe to enter. Request assistance, nonemergency.

The big ship obeyed, and the two patrol craft, Chaka in command of the flight, were launched, shot toward the homing signal on Alikhan's *aksai*. Behind them came *Big Bertha*.

Dill was riding shotgun on one of the patrol ships.

'What's the problem, little friend?' he asked on a standard voice channel as the two ships closed.

'Your data, to use a phrase of yours, sucketh goats, whatever a goat is.'

A louder signal boomed from *Big Bertha*: 'Scout One, this is Command. Give details. Over.' Garvin didn't sound thrilled at the relaxed com procedure.

'Command, Scout One,' Alikhan 'cast. 'Details are: There is nothing here, and it appears there never was. No cities, no buildings, no humans. Over.'

And so it was. None of the three planets that were supposedly colonized, all within the habitability range, showed any sign of settlement or abandonment.

'This makes no goddamned sense,' Njangu snarled. 'Howinhell could the Confederation punt some people out with their little shovels and picks and tents . . . I assume they did that, unless this whole goddamned scheme was some bureaucrat's fiddle to steal something large . . . and then not check on them, not follow up, not send the occasional goddamned checkup team . . . for two hundred goddamned years?'

Garvin shook his head.

'It makes me goddamned wonder,' Njangu raved on, 'just how much of our goddamned Empire was a goddamned phony. Maybe the whole goddamned thing was some kind of a shadow play.'

'That makes little sense,' Danfin Froude said mildly.

'Then give me some explanation that does. Goddamit!'

Froude held his palms up, helplessly.

''Kay,' Garvin decided. 'Forget it. We'll pull the recon elements back and try again.

'I don't like this,' he finished. 'I don't like things that don't have explanations.'

Froude looked at him.

'In another life, you could have been a scientist.'

'The hell,' Garvin said. 'In another life, I'm going to be a frigging boulder on a beach somewhere, with nothing to do but watch pretty naked women and slowly turn into sand.

'Get ready for another jump.'

Garvin had made one major break with naval tradition. The *Big Bertha* had a club, but it was for all ranks, not just officers. Njangu had agreed with this, since both of them found a noncommissioned officers' club far livelier than anything for upper ranks.

As to the old military policy that these restrictions gave rankers a place to relax and discuss their problems without being around the enlisted sorts, Garvin's answer was short and sweet: 'Let those who want to play footsie or whine do it in their own compartments.'

He'd found a corner with a beer, and was still wondering about that colony that evidently never had been, when he saw Darod Montagna, mug in hand.

'Greetings, boss,' she said. 'Are you in deep thought, or can I join you?'

'Grab a chair,' Garvin said. 'Njangu should be here in a mo, so obviously it's not deep.'

She sat, sipped at her beer.

'Thanks for letting me go on this little detail.'

'So far, no thanks . . . or blame . . . needed,' he said.

They sat in comfortable silence for a few minutes. Garvin realized he didn't feel any particular need to be entertaining or even companionable, somewhat like the peacefulness he felt around Njangu.

He saw his XO enter the rather crowded compartment, make his way toward them.

'I guess I better scoot,' Darod said. 'Deep, dark secrets and all that.'

She got up, just as *Big Bertha* twitched a little, making another jump, and fell into his lap.

'Bastard!' she swore, picking herself up. 'I'll never get used to going out of N-space.'

Garvin just smiled, thinking how she felt rather nice against him.

'Who does?' Njangu said, taking her seat. 'And I'm gonna rip a strip off our damned watch officer, who's supposed to notify us before we hippety-hop in or out of the wild black yonder out yonder.'

'Oh ... maybe I should have said something,' Montagna said. 'The PA system's down ... one of the techs is trying to get rid of that old lady in the system.'

As she spoke, the overhead speaker crackled into life: 'Time to next jump ... three ship-hours.' It was still the weird synthesized voice they were all growing to hate.

'I love technology,' Njangu said. 'Let's take an ax to the system and put in voice tubes like the first starships had. Or uniformed messengers. Or signal starships had. Or uniformed messengers. Or signal flags.'

'Good night, sirs,' Darod said, and left. Njangu watched her leave.

'Not hard on the eyes at all,' he said.

'Not at all,' Garvin said, pretending casual notice.

'Did she have anything in particular to talk about ... being nosy?'

'Other'n what a nosy sort you are,' Garvin said, 'nothing much.'

'Careful, Garvin,' Njangu said.

'Careful about what?'

Njangu waited a moment. 'Careful that you don't spill your beer in your lap. Sir.'

'Mother Mary on a bender,' Garvin said softly, staring into the screen.

'Yeh,' Njangu said. 'Evidently *somebody* didn't have any qualms about going nuke.'

The planet below it, like the twin moons that were supposed to be fortified, was nothing but desolation. A counter roared radioactivity at them.

'Any 'casts?' Garvin asked the com officer.

'There's a lot of clutter from the craters, sir,' the man reported. 'We've blanked all that come from obvious bomb sources . . . and there's nothing left. We thought for a minute we were getting some sort of code from one of the moons, but it's pure random noise.

'Nothing else, sir.'

Njangu scratched his chin.

'The whole goddamned system gone,' he mused. 'The book said it had a population of five billion.'

He shuddered a little. 'Guess there's things worse than Empire, huh?'

'Maybe,' Garvin said. 'Unless the Confederation was the one who decided to break policy first. Watch officer!'

'Sir!'

'Take us the hell out of here. Next possibility.'

'I've got a question,' Maev asked.

'I've got an answer,' Njangu said, yawning. 'Your head is very comfortable on my chest, by the bye.'

'I got that notion,' Stiofan said, 'that you and Garvin had the idea, at one time, of deserting, the first time you hit a world where there'd be some kind of main chance.'

'Ah, but that was in the sinful days of our yout',' he said. 'Before we became aware of the stellar virtues of serving the Confederation forever and ever or at least until somebody shoots our asses off.'

'I don't suppose this whole thing' — and she made a circle in the semidarkness with her hand — 'is some elaborate con to get you two to somewhere profitable, at which point you'll exit stage left.'

'I'll be a son,' Njangu said, sitting up abruptly. 'You know, I never even *thought* of that possibility. What a dummy.'

Maev also sat up.

'I'm afraid,' she said. 'You actually sound like you were telling the truth. If I can't tell . . .'

'I *was* telling the truth,' Yoshitaro said with an injured tone. 'I hardly ever lie, and never ever to the woman wot I adore.'

''Kay,' Maev said briskly. 'But assuming you're not lying . . . which is a big assumption . . . let's say we run across somewhere like a nice Eden in our travels, where there's connable marks left and right, and nobody has ever heard of a truth scan. What then?'

'What an *interestin'* possibility,' Njangu said. 'Naah. Anything like that would've been kicked over in the early days after the Confederation did whatever it did to itself. All those wonderful little sheepies would be shorn bare by now.

'Besides,' and he sounded serious, 'even if we found such a hog heaven, I've got to assume that there's wolves out there in the darkness, to really screw my analogy up. So we'd sit there makin' credits up the yinger, and sooner or later, probably sooner, given my luck, some baddies with lotsandlots of guns would swoop.

'No, Maev my love, I'm afeared you've cast your lot with an honest dullard. At least for the moment.'

'What, the lot, or the dullard?' she asked.

'Probably both. Now, if you'd be good enough to hand me that knotted cord again, I might find the energy for one more round before my engine runs out, since it's evidently the raw, nekkid trut', honesty, and loyalty of a Confeddie ossifer is wot powers me to new heights.'

The next system was still inhabited.

Dill brought his *aksai* out of hyperspace, and his sensors were already buzing. His briefing had said there were supposed to be four inhabited worlds in this system,

called in the star catalogs R897Q33, with an archaic des-
ignation of 2345554, and a system name of Carroll.

Three . . . no, five ships were homing on him, two of
them sweeping the com bands for a frequency this
unknown ship would be on.

He obliged them by opening on the standard
Confederation emergency frequency:

'Unknown ships, unknown ships, this is the
Scoutship, uh, *Dill*,' as he realized nobody ever got
around to naming any of the *aksai*, and he wasn't interested in being One, Two, or Three.

Another com beeped, announcing the arrival of a
patrol boat from *Big Bertha*, then Boursier in another
aksai.

'Scoutship *Dill*, this is the destroyer *Lopat*,' came a
return com. 'Be advised you have entered into
Confederation space.'

Dill's eyes widened, and he broadcast a second message to *Big Bertha*.

A secondary screen that had been added before *Big
Bertha* left Cumbre started scrolling:

JANE'S ID positive . . . three ships positive ID . . .
Confederation *Diaz*-class . . . the borderline obso-
lescence at time of final Confederation revision this
file . . .

Dill ignored the weapons and crew entry.

Sumbeech, sumbeech, we're home, we're home, he thought
gleefully, ignoring the sarcastic part of his mind that
asked what and where the hell home was, anyway.

He started to ID himself correctly, stopped, remembering belatedly that anyone could say he was
Confederation.

'This is *Dill*,' he said. 'Understood your last, that we are in Confederation space. Extreme approval on this side.'

Another, larger ship blinked into existence.

The ever-watchful *Jane's* told him it was a completely obsolete light cruiser, Daant-class, probably *Quiroga*.

'This is Fleet Commander von Hayn,' was the com. 'We do not recognize your ship class at all for leading two ships. No linkage shown to Confederation. Third ship identified as standard-manufacture planetary patrol craft. Explain. Over.'

'This is the *Dill*,' Ben said. 'My ship is locally built, and you have correctly ID'd the patrol ship. Over.'

'Neither of you look long-range capable,' the grating voice said. 'Suspect you are outrunners of larger ships. Give system of origin at once.'

'Uh . . . Erwhon,' Dill said, wishing to hell Garvin was here, or maybe Froude. 'And we do have other ships in hyperspace, waiting assessment of the situation.'

'That system you named is unknown to us.'

'We were just being colonized when we fell out of contact with the Confederation. I guess nobody sent the proper bulletins around. What happened to our Empire, anyway?' Dill couldn't hold back the question.

There was a long time of dead air.

'This is Fleet Commander von Hayn,' the voice came reluctantly. 'We are not in contact with the Homeworlds, but have sustained order through our own devices for some years, maintaining peace and the rule of law and order.'

'As have we,' Dill said. 'And now we're trying to reestablish contact.'

Again, a long silence, and Dill was about to rebroadcast.

'We have communicated with our superiors,' von Hayn's voice came. 'Permission to enter the Carroll system is denied. Be advised a full launch of our fleet has been made, and any other ships appearing in normal space will be treated as enemy and fire will be opened on them immediately.

'Again, you are refused entry. Leave this system at once, or face immediate attack.'

'You paranoid old poop,' Dill muttered to himself, not knowing age or sex of the fleet commander, and opened his mike.

'Von Hayn, this is the *Dill*. We come in peace, I say again, meaning no harm, but wishing only supplies . . . and you rotten bug diddler!'

The *Quiroga* had just launched a pair of missiles at the *aksai*.

Ben wanted desperately to make a counterstrike, but remembered his orders and fled back into hyperspace, even as the patrol ship disappeared with him.

He locked aboard *Big Bertha*, and steamed for the bridge.

Garvin, Froude, and Njangu were waiting.

'Thor with an anvil up his ass, but those bastards were unfriendly,' he snapped.

'We know,' Froude said. 'Remember, we were monitoring all 'casts.'

'Well what the hell are we going to do?' Dill asked.

'We're going to make another jump, far, far away from here,' Garvin said. 'Listen. Here's a couple of selections the patrol boat's com picked up. Both came from the homeworld.'

He touched a key.

A harsh voice grated:

'Meal hours for all Zed-, Extang-, and Hald-class

citizens have been changed by point-one-five tics. Be advised the grace period for change will be four shifts, then penalties may be assessed. Further—'

Static, then a woman's voice said:

'Due to compliance with voluntary work output, issuance of rapture tabs are authorized for the following districts: Alf, Mass—'

'Oy yoy,' Ben Dill said. 'They tells you when you can eat, get your head ruined. How much you want to bet they let you know when it's 'kay to screw?'

'I don't think we need to trouble ourselves with these people,' Froude said. 'At least, not until we're prepared to come back in force and discuss this system of peace, law, and order.'

The three *aksai* pilots sat in their ready room, waiting for either mess call or another alert.

'I'm starting to think,' Ben Dill mused, 'this universe might not be that friendly a place.'

'When was it ever?' Boursier asked. 'Or weren't you paying attention in Astronomy One?'

'I don't mean black holes and wormholes and ghosties and goblins and that,' Dill said. 'I'm talking about people.

'Not to mention we ain't found squat beside ruination.'

'Do not despair,' Alikhan said. 'For I remember the tale of a great Musth warrior who was once lost in a trackless forest. But he kept on looking, trying different trails, different signals. His belief was 'seek a thousand tracks, and one of them will lead to home.'

Dill looked at the alien thoughtfully.

'Be damned. I didn't think you Musth ever said anything reassuring.'

'Neither did I,' Boursier said. 'How long did it take this warrior to reach his home?'

'He never made it,' Alikhan said. 'They found those words scratched on the outside of a tree, next to which he had starved.'

FIVE

Salamonsky

'Take it in closer, Ben,' Garvin said, his voice showing no emotion.

'Yessir,' Dill said, and dived into Salamonsky's atmosphere.

Garvin turned away from the projection.

'What sort of lousy bastard would attack a circus world?' he asked no one in particular. 'We never did anything to anyone . . . gave them something to laugh at, something to wonder about, sent home with stars in their eyes and a smile on their lips.'

The enlisted woman on one of the radars turned. 'You ever hear of some people called Jews, sir?'

Garvin looked at her, then away.

Dill was coming in fast a thousand kilometers below — even at his height above land, there was perceptible ground rush.

'Captain Liskeard,' Garvin said, 'bring it in-atmosphere. We'll have a look, maybe get some idea of who the bad guys could have been. Put two patrol boats out now for top cover.'

'Sir.'

'As soon as we're below the stratosphere, launch the other *aksai* and the patrol boat. Keep them sweeping, looking for trouble.'

Njangu came up to him.

'You got a crawly feeling?'

'Not necessarily,' Garvin said. 'I'm probably just hoping there's something to shoot at, no more.'

Dill flared the *aksai* two hundred meters above the landing field he'd targeted. Small carpet bombs had knocked the tower askew and set fire to hangars and admin buildings. Then strafers must have come in to finish the job. There were remnants of ships scattered around the field, some that would have been modern, others beyond-belief rust buckets that transported small dog-and-pony acts or even sideshows around the region. All of them had been anodized in the most garish colors that were now just beginning to flake.

'I'd guess,' Njangu said, 'whoever hit them came in less than an E-year ago. There's still cables dangling, looks like some rope that's not rotted hanging from that drive stand, and that old hovercraft cushion's still inflated.'

The image on-screen changed as Dill's *aksai* banked over the port's small city. It sprawled for some kilometers, and was mostly separate houses of wildly varying styles and sizes.

'I wonder,' Garvin said absently, 'if any of those houses belonged to any little people. I remember, when I was a kid, going to one family, and everything was built to scale, and they were smaller than I was, so for the first time I felt like a giant.

'All of them but their daughter,' he went on. 'She was, oh, maybe thirteen, and as pretty as I'd ever seen. I fell in love with her . . . but of course she didn't know nine-year-olds existed.'

The city's business center was a cratered ruin.

'I hope they fought back,' Garvin said 'It would've been—'

The watch communications officer came into the bridge.

'Sir. We're getting a transmission, in Common, on a Confederation guard channel. Shall I pipe it through?'

'Now,' Garvin ordered. 'And get DF finding out where it's coming from.'

The transmission quality was wavery, and the woman's voice was flat, tired, as if she'd done the 'cast a thousand thousand times:

'Unknown ship . . . our detectors picked up a disturbance entering atmosphere . . . unknown ship . . . we are refugees in hiding after our world was looted . . . we're only a handful of survivors . . . oh Allah, be a ship, not another damned meteorite. Please.'

The emotion stopped, and once more the woman said her plea.

Garvin was reaching for the mike, when Njangu caught his arm.

'Let her run on for a minute. It won't hurt.'

'Why?'

'It might not be a bad idea . . . once we find out where she's 'casting from, to drop a drone down before *Big Bertha* wallows over there, don't you think? Since I'm the only me I've got, I'd like to take precautions.'

Garvin's lip thinned, then he caught himself.

'You're right. Sorry.'

Njangu ordered one of the patrol ships to launch a drone in-atmosphere. Moments later, the direction finders had a location for the plea for help.

'Nap of the earth,' Njangu ordered the drone's pilot on the patrol ship. 'I want a realtime normal-vision transmit, and metal detection patched to me.'

'Sir.'

A tech moved a screen down, and it lit up, showing the drone's point of view, approaching the ground.

Njangu told Dill what was going on, ordered him and the other ships to low altitudes.

The drone was flashing over wooded hills, then a lake, a small valley, then more woods.

'That was where she DF'ed from. Nothing to see,' Liskeard said. 'The poor scared bastards must be hiding.'

'Look at *that* display, sir,' a technician said.

Garvin looked as well . . . and saw high-zigging lines.

'Nothing but brushes and woodses down there,' Njangu said. 'And a lot of hidden metal. Like ships under camou nets maybe?'

'Shit!' somebody in the control room swore as ragged black smoke dotted the sky on-screen.

'Most poor scared bastards don't have antiaircraft guns . . . or use 'em on rescuers,' Liskeard said wryly.

'No,' Garvin said. 'No, they don't. Commo, give me an all-channels.'

'Sir. You're on.'

'All *Bertha* elements. Target Acquisition on our main screen. Indicators show hidden ships . . . and we got fire. Suspect cannon, not missiles. Nana elements, to ten thousand meters, stand off two kilometers. Goddard launch on command.

'*Aksai*, stay clear until we open things up a little, then we'll send you . . . cancel that for the moment.'

Garvin hadn't needed the technician's warning. He'd seen a ship lift through trees below.

'Nana Flight . . . take him out.'

'Sir,' *Alt* Rad Draf said. 'Two, do you have that ship?'

'Affirm . . .'

'I'm firing. Two shadows . . . on command . . . FIRE!'

The meter-long Shadow antiship missiles spat from their pods.

'We have a counterlaunch and countermeasures in effect,' Draf's ECM officer reported. 'Divert one . . . two . . . hit! Hit!'

The seething ball of flame that'd been a small starship spun back toward the ground.

'Nanas . . . proceed with Goddard launch!' Garvin ordered.

'On my command,' Draf said, still calm-voiced. 'All elements . . . target from flagship . . . one Goddard per Nana . . . FIRE!'

The Goddards were heavy shipkillers, six meters long, sixty centimeters in diameter, with a five hundred-km range. They drove toward the valley at full speed.

AA guns on the ground yammered up, but struck wide.

All four targeted within fifteen meters of each other, and the ground roiled, bucked, and net covering guns and two more ships on the ground burst into flames. Secondary explosions sent flame waves boiling into the air.

'*Aksai*,' Garvin said, 'if there's anything left to kill . . . go on in.'

The fighting ships dived down, swept the small valley. Boursier's chainguns yammered once, again.

'Half a dozen men . . . with guns,' she reported. 'No more.'

'That's it,' Garvin said. 'All *Bertha* elements . . . recover.'

He looked again at the screen showing the destroyed valley, then at Njangu.

'Hope none of the people they captured were down there,' Yoshitaro said.

Garvin flushed.

'Goddammit, if they were . . . they were leading us into a trap!'

'True,' Njangu said. 'Sorry. Boss.'

Garvin's face returned to normal.

'No. My turn for the apology. This one got to me a little.'

'Forget it,' Njangu said. 'I suppose you've got another place to look for your elephants.'

'I do. Two more, if it comes to that,' Garvin said. 'But number three is halfway to hell and gone.'

'Then . . . unless you want to land, and sift some ashes trying to figure out where those raiders came from, and do a few paybacks . . . I guess we should depart this fair clime.'

'Yeh,' Garvin said heavily. 'There's nothing for us . . . or anyone else . . . here.'

Two of the next seven nav points were in inhabited systems. Scouting *aksai* reported those worlds were settled, primarily agricultural and, from detected emissions, were obviously out of contact with the Confederation, slowly working their way back down the energy ladder.

Boursier reported, in rather shocked tones, the second system was even using some nuclear power.

'Obviously,' Njangu said, 'there's no point in stopping for help when somebody's worse off than we are.'

'Nope,' Garvin agreed. 'Besides, the next jump will be Grimaldi, full of fun, laughter, and life.

'I bleeding well hope.'

SIX

Langnes 4567/Grimaldi

'This is Grimaldi Control,' a woman said. 'Link to Channel five-five-four-point-eight-seven ... you are cleared to land. You will descend vertically from present position, then take course Nan Eleven, as indicated on your Standard Instrument Screen for approximately twenty-two, that is two-two, kilometers. We have clear weather, so you should have visual contact with Joey Field at that point. Use Beam Eleven Teng to guide you to your landing spot.'

The voice paused, then said: 'Be advised we are a peaceful world, and are welcoming you.

'If, however, you have other intentions, also be advised you are being tracked by various weapons systems we do not want to use. Over.'

'This is *Big Bertha*,' Liskeard said into a mike. 'We are just what we claim to be ... understand Course Nan Eleven for two-two kilometers, use standard Beam Eleven Teng and visual flight regulations to land on field. Monitoring Channel five-five-four-point-eight-seven. Over.'

'Assuming you know what the name of your ship

means,' the voice said, 'welcome home. Grimaldi Control, clear.'

Njangu glanced at Garvin, swore that the other man had tears in his eyes. He wondered what would be a home to him, one day, wondered not for the first time if there was one. Sure as hell not the corrupt sewer of Ross 248 that he'd been born on.

'Sir,' Liskeard said, 'we're bringing it in. Do you want to do the benediction?'

Garvin jolted back to the bridge of the ship.

'Yeh. Yeh, sorry.' He took a microphone.

'This is Gaffer Jaansma.' He'd decided to start using the title before they entered the Grimaldi system, figuring it was time to get the troops used to it.

'From here on out, all of you who aren't civilians are now. For the love of Harriet's Crucifixion, don't go around in step or counting cadence.

'You've all been briefed on who we are . . . more or less amateur circus buffs who've fallen into money, and are trying to give peace a chance by making people happy and laughing, and maybe are curious about whatever happened to the Confederation.

'You don't have to look moronic when you say that. The people we'll encounter will already think you're a skid short of an even landing for looking for what is obviously big trouble.

'From here on out, things should get interesting.'

He keyed the mike off and looked at Njangu, grinning broadly.

'*Damn*, but this is gonna be fun.'

Garvin might have been awash in sentiment, but that didn't make him altogether a fool. The two *aksai* followed within *Big Bertha*'s radar shadow until the

behemoth landed, then orbited closely overhead. The
Nana boats were ready for an instant launch, and certain
unobtrusive compartments, normally kept sealed, were
now open and their 35mm chainguns, firing depleted
uranium rounds at 6000rpm, and the smallish one meter
long Shrikes, which could be launched at anything and
guided by anyone, were ready.

But nothing warlike happened, and so Garvin, and an
assemblage of his more impressive people, from Ben Dill
to Njangu to Monique Lir went down the wide gangway
after the lock opened.

Waiting were a dozen or more lifters, some circus-col-
ored, others nondescript, two loudly claiming the holo
stations they had been dispatched by.

About forty men and women waited, most as excited
as Garvin. They were also somewhat unusual in appearance, Lir noticed. Three.had elaborate tattoos showing on
their bare arms, one was almost as big as Ben Dill,
another woman had a rather remarkable beard, and two,
including one journoh with a holo recorder, were
midgets.

One woman, distinguished-looking, very long-haired,
wearing tanned, fringed leathers, came forward.

'We welcome *Big Bertha*,' she said formally. 'I hope
you will find what you're seeking here on Grimaldi. I am
Agar-Robertes, and people have given me the title of
Gaffer, one of several on this world. That's an ancient
term that means—'

'I know what it means,' Garvin said. 'I'm Gaffer
Jaansma.'

The woman lifted her eyebrows.

'Of *the* Jaansmas?'

'I am Garvin,' Garvin said. 'My mother was Clyte, my
father Frahnk, my uncle Hahrl. Before that—'

'Stop,' the woman said. 'You've been kicking sawdust longer than any of us.'

Garvin inclined his head.

'Son of a bitch,' Njangu managed sotto voce to Dill. 'The bastard's for real about this circus stuff!'

'That is quite a ship you own,' Agar-Robertes said looking up at the looming behemoth. 'Might I ask your cargo?'

'We have little at present,' Garvin said. 'Which is why we came to Grimaldi. We intend to build a circus and seek women, men, nonhumans, animals.'

'Then the time has come round again,' Agar-Robertes said reverently amid a babble from the other men and women of Grimaldi. 'When it is safe for circuses, it is safe for all.'

Garvin made a face.

'I wish I could say you're right. We've had encounters since we left our native worlds to suggest the time is not here, not yet.'

'Still,' Agar-Robertes said. 'It might be a beginning.

'And you won't lack for prospective troupers. We're so stricken we've gone beyond entertaining each other.' She lowered her voice. 'Some of us have even been forced to take flatty *jobs*!'

The people of Grimaldi took the Cumbrians to their hearts and homes. The *Big Bertha* was given a parking slot on a corner of the field, the *aksai* and other ships moved into revetments for maintenance, and the circus itself sprawled out around the ship.

The tent was set up, the midway a long fat finger in front of the main tent, and the other 'tents' — the mess tent, the clown tent, all actually prefab shelters — around it.

Some of the crew and troupers decided they could do without living aboard unless they had to, and made arrangements with the locals. Garvin didn't care, as long as everyone was present for his work shift.

It would also be good, he knew, for the Cumbrians to experience another culture than the one they'd been born into . . . and the Grimaldians were a bit unusual.

Some of the population, including the original settlers, were circus workers, as many of them strongbacks, clerical, or computer sorts as freaks and performers. Others were retirees, vacationers who'd been trapped when the Confederation collapsed, circus fans or settlers who seemed to have chosen Grimaldi with a dart and a star chart.

All shared a common belief in individual freedom, although, as one put it, 'Yer rights end at my nose.'

Seemingly incongruously, almost all desperately missed the Confederation. But one explained to Njangu, 'It's best to have some kind of law and order. Makes travel easier, and keeps you from getting mugged after you've run your con and are trying to get out of town with the snide.'

Njangu was starting to understand what Garvin had missed for so many years . . . but still hadn't the foggiest why Jaansma was still with the military.

Nor why he was, either.

'What in the name of God's holiest dildo is *that*?' Njangu asked suspiciously, staring at the huge pile of off-white heavy cloth, leather reinforcements, iron eyes, and heavy line.

'It's a tent,' Garvin said. 'A real tent.'

'Which you use for what?'

'We're going to be the best damned circus ever . . .

or, anyway, the best one still flitting around this galaxy,' Garvin said. 'So, when we can, we'll set up under canvas.'

'Why? We've got a perfectly good ship that unfolds like one of those paper sculptures . . . ory . . . eerie . . . you know. Sushimi. All safe and warm, and nice lanes to the cages and quarters.'

'Because nothing smells more like a circus than canvas,' Garvin said. 'And roasting groundnuts and popcorn and . . . and elephant shit.'

'I'll be sure to tell Jasith your favorite smells,' Njangu said. 'It'll thrill her no end and probably spark a new line of perfumes from the Mellusin empire.'

Not that Njangu was very successful in maintaining his own usual superciliousness.

Maev came around a corner, and found him buried in a mass of little people, some dwarves, most perfect scale replicas of 'normal' humans.

They were shouting something about contract scale, and he was trying to argue, with a rather beatific look on his face.

Maev crept back round her corner and never mentioned it to Yoshitaro.

'We've got a serious problem,' Garvin said. 'Siddown, have a drink, and help me out.'

'A better invite has seldom been spoke,' Njangu said, and sat down in front of Jaansma's desk. He pulled the bottle over, poured into a glass, drank.

'Whoo. What's that? Exhaust wash?'

'Close,' Garvin said. 'Triple-run alcohol our fearless, peerless engine department came up with. Try another hit. It grows on you.'

'Yeh,' Njangu said. 'Like fungus.' But he obeyed.
'Now, what's the problem?'

'Every circus has got to have a theme that everything
sort of centers around, from the pretty women in the
spec . . . that's the spectacle, the pageant that opens
things . . . to the blowoff. The costumes should be
designed sorta around that theme.'

'Mmmh.' Njangu considered.

'It sort of helps if it's kind of wallowy and sentimental.'

'Oh. Easy, then. Refill me,' Yoshitaro said.

Garvin obeyed.

'This shit does improve with usage,' Njangu admitted. 'But I still think it'd be best injected, so your throat
doesn't have to take all the damage.

'You want a theme . . . you got a theme. Even fits in
with our tippy-top secret mission. Call it, oh, Many
Worlds Together.

'You can hit that ol' tocsin of the Confederation and
how we all miss it, put people in any kinda costume you
want . . . even look to see if there's ever been any nudist
worlds . . . and go from there.'

'Why Njangu Yoshitaro,' Garvin said. 'Sometimes I
suspect you of genius. Intelligence, even.'

'Took you long enough.'

'Uh, boss, what's going on?' Darod Montagna asked
Njangu. They were outside *Big Bertha*, and a high, circular fence had been put up, using one of the ship's fins
for a base. Inside the fence were Garvin and Ben Dill.

'Our fearless leader is about to negotiate for a bear.'

'A what?'

'Some kind of ancient animal . . . supposedly goes all
the way back to Earth,' Njangu said. 'I looked the

creature up, and it was listed as a fine animal who left everybody alone, but if you messed with it, it messed back on an all-out basis. Garvin thinks he's got to have one.'

'Why? What do they do? Or is eating people going to be a sideshow?'

'If they're well trained, Garvin told me,' Njangu explained, 'a bear will ride two-wheelers, dance, do a little tumbling . . . just about anything a rather stupid man can be taught.'

'Why do we need one?'

'Because,' Njangu said, 'a circus just . . .'

And Montagna finished the now shopworn phrase:

'. . . isn't a circus without a bear. Or a bunch of tumblers. Or whatever else the gaffer comes up with.'

'So, anyway,' Njangu went on, 'it turns out there's this nuthead back in the hills who raises real bears. Agar-Robertes suggested we buy a couple of robot bears, but not our Garvin. He's gotta have the real thing.

'Look. This has got to be the bear-breeder.'

The lifter wandering toward the field looked as if it had been crashed on a weekly basis for some time. In the open back was a large cage, holding a very large, very dark brown, furry animal with very large claws and teeth.

'Yeets,' Darod said. 'Scares me just looking at him. Anybody bring a blaster?'

'Garvin said the trainer told him the bear was as gentle as a baby.'

The animal in the back roared so loudly the cage bars rattled.

'What kind of baby?' she wondered aloud.

'Nobody said.'

The lifter grounded, and a rather hairy man got out. He greeted Garvin, introduced himself as Eneas, and limped to the back of the cage.

'This 'ere's Li'l Doni,' he said. 'Cutest li'l thing I ever did see. Got two more back t' th' ranch just like her, if you want real star power.'

Njangu was holding back a snicker.

'Star power?' he muttered.

'You said she was gentle,' Garvin said, eyeing a ragged scar down the trainer's arm.

''At was her mother's doin',' Eneas said. 'On'y thing Doni's ever did t' me was break m' leg, an' that was my fault. Mostly.

'Here. Lemme let 'er out, you c'n see for yourself.'

Garvin was seeing for himself that Li'l Doni was not only in a cage, but had chains around her upper legs. Eneas opened the cage, and Doni rolled out, snarling, came to her feet, and snapped both chains.

She growled, took a swipe at Eneas, who sensibly dived under the lifter.

Doni saw Ben Dill, and charged after him. Dill followed Eneas. That left Garvin, and Doni went for him. There wasn't room enough under the lift for three, and so Garvin climbed, later swearing he levitated, to the top of the cage.

Doni, in command of the theater, snarled three times around the lift, considered a side window, and smashed it casually.

Njangu was laughing so hard he had to hold himself up against the ship's fin.

Li'l Doni spotted Yoshitaro, and, roaring rampage, charged the fence. She banged off it once, then went up and over it as if it was a ladder.

Njangu Yoshitaro went up *Big Bertha*'s fin as if it also were a ladder.

Darod Montagna found business back inside the ship, closing the lock behind her.

Eventually Eneas came out from under his lift, found more chains, and Li'l Doni vanished from the circus's life.

Three days later, Njangu invoiced for the lease of two robot bears. He insisted on naming one of them Li'l Doni.

The music conductor was named Raf Aterton, and Njangu swore he had to be the reincarnation of at least six generals and two dictators. He was silver-haired, slender, severe in countenance, and brooked no argument from any of the forty musicians the circus had taken on. His voice sounded soft, but somehow carried from one end of the spaceport to the other.

'All of you will now listen very closely. You've got sheet music in front of you. The piece is the "Confederation Peace March". You will learn it until you can play it in your sleep, as some of you have been functioning already, I've noticed.

'This is the most important part of being on the show. The "Peace March" is the sign of trouble. Fire. The cats on a rampage. A big clem, a catastrophe.

'When it's played, all the muscle on the show will start looking to solve the problem, however they can. If we're under canvas, all the animals will get out, right then, as will the kinkers.

'The talent is priceless, and you, my ham-fingered men and women are not. So after everyone's altered, you'll join the roustabouts in solving the problem.'

'Question, sir,' a synthesizer toggler asked. 'What if we're in the ship and something happens?'

'Hit the tune, then get out of the ship. Or follow orders if Gaffer Jaansma's around.'

'And if we're in space?'

'Now that,' Aterton mused, 'could be a bit of a poser.'

*

The woman spun lazily twice high above the net, as a man released the trapeze, and twisted across the open air. Their catcher extended long tentacles, caught them both, sent them flying higher into the air, then had them once more and they were back at their perch.

"Kay,' Ben Dill said. 'Half the troupe's human or looks it, anyway. What species are those octopot-lookin' types?'

'They call themselves *ra'felan*,' Garvin said. 'The troupe master says they've got about the same intelligence as a low-normal human.'

'Interestin',' Erik Penwyth drawled. 'With half a dozen legs to punch buttons with, and no particular intelligence, we ought to recruit 'em as pilots.'

'Watchit,' Dill warned.

The *ra'felan* had rather tubular bodies, with tentacles dangling at paired intervals. Their eyes bulged ominously from the center body.

'Can they talk?' Dill asked.

'If spoken to politely,' Garvin said.

'*Both* you bastards are being cute today,' Dill complained.

'I assume you signed them,' Penwyth said, ignoring Dill.

The *ra'felan* swung back and forth on his trapeze three times, then jumped straight up, toward a rope that crossed between the two high poles. He . . . or she, or it, for Garvin never found out their sexes, if any, went tentacle over tentacle on the rope across to the other pole, then hooked a trapeze, swung once, and somersaulted down, spinning, into the net.

'Damned straight I did,' Garvin said fervently.

'You should've been here a couple of minutes ago, when they were throwing ten people around like they were paper aircraft.'

'If they were real fishies,' Dill said, 'y' think they'd be working for scale? See, now I'm getting to your level.'

'I say again my last about pilots,' Penwyth said. 'Except p'raps, I was overly kindly about their intelligence being low-normal.'

'Hit it, maestro, it's doors, and the crowd's a turnaway,' Garvin shouted. He was resplendent in white formal wear of ancient times, including a tall white hat, black boots, and a black whip.

Aterton obeyed, and music boomed through the hold, and Garvin touched his throat mike.

'Men, women, children of all ages . . . Welcome, welcome, welcome, to the Circus of Galactic Delights. I'm your host for the show. Now, what we'll have first . . .'

Half a dozen clowns tumbled into view, began assaulting Garvin in various ways, some trying to drench him with water, others to push him over a kneeling clown, still others throwing rotten vegetables. But all missed, and he drove them away with his whip.

'Sorry, sorry, but we've got these strange ones who're completely out of control with us . . .' Garvin lowered his voice, cut out of his spiel. 'When we get a full complement, we'll have carpet clowns working the stands. Next will come the spec, with all kinds of women on lifts, on horses, on elephants if we get elephants, the candy butchers working the stands, the cats coming through . . .

'Maestro, sorry to put you through this, but we'll need bits for each act as they enter.'

'Of course,' Aterton said haughtily. 'I, at least, know my business and am hardly a first-of-Mayer.'

Garvin made a face, decided to let it pass.

'Then, after the spec goes out the back door of the

tent, or the hold, or the amphitheater . . . I don't have the
foggiest where we'll be playing . . . then we'll have the
first act, which'll be something I haven't decided on,
maybe some flyers, maybe have some little people working the ground, maybe some pongers, 'though I haven't
seen nearly enough acrobats.'

He seemed quite at home amid the confusion.

'Earth cats?' Garvin asked.

'At one time,' the chubby, rather prissy man with a
moustache said, a bit mournfully. 'Since then, they've
apparently mutated . . . and the perihelion of the species
are with Doctor Emton's Phantastic Felines, Who'll
Make You Wonder If You're Really Superior and Dazzle
You. A Fine Act for the Whole Family.'

Garvin looked skeptically at the six lean but well-
brushed animals sitting on his desk. They regarded him
with equal dispassion.

'Ticonderoga,' Emton said. 'Insect. On picture. Catch
it for him.'

He pointed at Garvin, but made no other move.

A cat leapt suddenly from the desk up to the mounted
holo of Jasith, caught a bug, bit once, and dropped it
daintily in Garvin's lap.

'Interesting,' Garvin said. 'But more suitable for a
sideshow. Which we aren't.'

'Pyramid,' Emton said, and three cats moved
together, two more jumped on their backs, and the third
completed the figure.

'Play ball,' he said, taking a small red ball from his
pocket, and tossing it at them. The pyramid disassembled, the cats formed a ring, and began passing it back
and forth.

'Hmm,' Garvin said. 'We will have projection screens

so the audience can see what's going on . . . maybe something with the clowns?'

'Clowns,' Emton said, and the six cats stood on their paws, walked about, then sprang cartwheels.

'I'm afraid not,' Garvin said.

'Oh. Oh. Very well,' Emton said, and got up. His cats sprang back into the two carriers he'd brought in.

'Oh . . . one other thing . . . I, uh, understand that tryouts are welcome at your dukey?'

'Certainly,' Garvin said, and noted a slight look of desperation about the man. It must've been his imagination, but it seemed the cats had the same expression. 'We're happy to feed you. And your animals.'

'Well . . . thank you for your time, anyway,' Emton said as he fastened the carrier closers.

Garvin, feeling every bit a saphead, said, 'Hang on a second. Can I ask you a personal question?'

Emton's expression was a bit frosty, but he said, 'You may.'

'Can I ask what your last performance was?'

Emton looked wistful.

'Last time we were on a show . . . just one going back and forth, a mud show really, more to keep from getting rusty . . . actually, was, well, almost an E-year ago.'

Garvin nodded.

'I said something about clowns. Do you have any objection to working with them?'

'Of course not,' Emton said eagerly.

'Perhaps I'm not seeing your act's full potential, or maybe you could use some new material,' Garvin said. 'I'll buzz our Professor Ristori to meet you at the main lock in, oh, thirty minutes or so.' He hastily added, seeing Emton's expression, 'Sorry, an hour. Time enough for you and your troupe to get fed at the cook tent.'

'Thank you,' Emton said eagerly. 'I promise, you won't be sorry.'

'I'm sure I won't,' Garvin said, thinking that Jasith wouldn't mind spending a little of what had been her money this way.

Besides, the creatures might be useful somehow.

Clowns and more clowns inundated *Big Bertha* until Garvin had more than thirty signed up. He made Ristori clown master, gave Njangu other duties.

'All right, all right, break,' Garvin shouted. The robot bears' handler looked sheepish, and the aerialists over-head went back to their pedestal boards.

'People, we're trying to hit some kind of rhythm here. Let's take it back, to where the bears just come on.'

'This much better,' the *ra'felan* told Monique Lir. 'Used to be, was real rope nets. If a human not land right . . . on back of neck . . . could get hurt. Break leg. Maybe bounce out and no catcher. Bad, very bad.'

The circus 'net' was composed of a series of antigrav projectors, all pointed up and inward, now set up in the tent's center ring. Anyone falling from a trapeze above would be slowed, then stopped two meters above the ground. The net also had the advantage of being almost invisible. Only a small blur could be seen from the pro-jector mouths, so the audience could get the thrill of thinking the performers were chancing death every time they went aloft.

The being rolled an eye at Lir.

'Why you want to learn iron-jaw act?'

'Why not?'

The *ra'felan* reached up with a tentacle and pulled down the rope with the metal bit at its end.

'Good. You put in mouth, just clamp teeth. Hold firm. Now, we pull off ground. Just little.

'You see how easy? Human jaw strong. Now, we teach how to spin, turn, maybe . . . you look like strong woman . . . do kicks and things.'

Njangu eyed the animals skeptically. They looked at him with interest. Not to maybe mention hunger.

There were a round dozen of them, identified by their trainer as lions, tigers, leopards, and panthers.

'You know,' he said, 'I'd be a lot happier, a whole lot happier, if the bars were between me and your friends.'

'Ah, there's nothing to worry about,' the tall handsome man with the scarred face said.

Njangu remembered Garvin telling him once, when they thought they were about to die, why he'd ended up joining the Force – the circus he'd been ringmaster for had turned out to be crook, and the locals had realized the hustles and started a riot. Jaansma saw someone about to torch the horses' enclosure, went, as he said, 'a little ape shit,' and turned the big cats loose on the crowd

'Yeh,' he said doubtfully.

'Not that the diddlies'll ever realize how tame m'pussies are,' the slanger – trainer – said. He cracked a big whip, and instantly the inside of the huge enclosure, a huge birdcage almost twenty meters in diameter, was furry chaos, as cats roared, screamed, clawed at the air, sprang from stand to stand, and the trainer was firing blanks from an old-fashioned pistol into the air as he tossed rings through the air, and the animals plummeted through them.

Then all was still again.

The trainer, who said his name was Sir Douglas, grinned, his scar standing out against his near-ebony complexion. 'See what I mean?'

'Maybe,' Njangu said. 'Uh . . . where'd you get the scar, if you don't mind my asking?'

'Muldoon . . . that's the leopard over there . . . gets moody first thing in the mornings. And I was being a little pushy.' He gestured. 'Accidents do happen, don't they.'

'They do,' Njangu said, moving toward the cage door. 'By the way, what do these fine friends of yours eat?'

'Meat,' Sir Douglas said with a ferocious grin. 'As much as I'll let 'em have.'

'Have they figured out yet, that *we're* meat?'

'No,' the trainer said. 'But they're working on it.'

Njangu noticed Garvin's habits were changing. Now he would sleep all day, waking at nightfall for a light meal, then doing business all night long, breaking frequently to visit various acts around the ship. At dawn, he'd have a big meal and half a bottle of wine, and retire.

Njangu caught him eyeing Darod Montagna, but so far nothing had happened.

So far.

Besides, Njangu had other business to take care of, with two Intelligence Section assistants. He was interviewing, as subtly and thoroughly as he could, everyone who joined the circus about where they'd come from, what they knew of the collapse, and their own personal travels.

A problem was that circus people don't especially like to get personal. They were reluctant to say where they came from, but would say 'I was with the Zymecas,' or 'I came from Butler and Daughter.'

Njangu, so far, was amassing confusion. Some worlds or sectors seemed to have made a decision to declare their independence from the Confederation. Nobody seemed to know what happened to the Confederation officials assigned to those areas.

Other worlds, Njangu found, seemed to have lost contact. Their freightliners went out and didn't come back, ordered cargoes never materialized, troops were never replaced, and so forth.

A few troupers had specific stories – of expecting an act or a relative to arrive, and no ship ever appeared in their skies, or contracts had been signed, but the transport never showed up.

There didn't seem to be any single crash, just a series of crumblings.

Njangu had no theories whatsoever.

'Great gods playing feetball,' Dill said. 'They're goddamned enormous!'

'Nobody really realizes how big an elephant is until they get close to one for the first time,' Garvin said. 'Isn't that right?'

'We would not know,' one of the slim brown-skinned men said.

The other man nodded. 'We have been around our friends since . . . since we were born.'

One of the men was named Sunya Thanon, the other Phraphas Phanon. They had sixteen elephants, all named, plus two babies, no more than an E-year old, Imp and Loti.

'Do you wish us to display our friends' skills?'

'Not necessary,' Garvin said. 'I watched the holo you sent me. You are more than welcome."

'Good,' Sunya said. 'Feeding our friends on our small

budget becomes wearisome.' He, like Phraphas, spoke careful, unaccented Common as if he were more familiar with another language.

'But we must caution you.' Phraphas said. 'We are searching for a place, and if, in our travels, we find a way to reach it, we must insist on being allowed to leave the show instantly.'

'I suppose that can be arranged,' Garvin said cautiously. 'And that place is?'

'Have you ever heard of a planet named Coando?' Sunya asked.

'No,' Garvin said. 'Not that it means much, for I'm not an astrogator.'

The two looked disappointed.

'We do not know its location either,' Phraphas said. 'But we heard of it once, and determined we must make it our life's work to go there with our friends'

'Why is it so special?' Dill asked.

'The legend is,' Phraphas said, 'that men of our culture left ancient Earth . . . with the elephants they had always worked together with . . . to make their home on a planet that was jungled, hot, like the land they came from.

'But here, no one would hunt their friends for their skins, for the ivory of their tusks, or . . . or just for the monstrous pleasure in killing something bigger than they were.

'The tale is, they found such a world, and named it Coando, and, as they developed this world, being careful to keep it as it was, as their homeland had been before it was despoiled, and then sent expeditions back to Earth, to bring wild elephants to join them.

'That, the tale goes, is why elephants are so rare with only the friends of the circus, who choose to work with us, and some others around what was the Confederation.

'That is the world we seek, the world we have been seeking, as our parents did before us, and their parents before them.'

Dill thought of saying the obvious, then realized he wasn't that much of an asshole. He and Garvin exchanged looks.

'I assume,' Garvin asked, 'that you've asked since you've been here on Grimaldi?'

'Asked, and consulted star charts,' Sunya said. 'But without success.'

'That's all right,' Dill said, surprising both Garvin and himself. 'Coando's out there . . . and we'll find it or, anyway, find where it is. Maybe when . . . if . . . we reach Centrum, we can see if the old Confederation master records still exist.'

Sunya looked at his partner.

'You see? I knew we had luck when we first saw this ship approach from the skies.'

Garvin and Dill turned the beasts and their handlers over to Lir, started back for the ship.

'Anybody ever tell you that you're a sentimental slob?' Garvin asked.

'And, of course, you're not?' Dill asked.

Garvin and Montagna watched the horses pour through the hoops and around the ring like milk, liquid grace, while two long-haired women and an impressively moustached man with equally long hair sat, rolled, tumbled on their mounts' backs as if they were standing still.

'I am going to learn to do that,' Montagna said firmly. 'No matter how hard it is.'

'You'll do fine,' Garvin said absently. She smiled at him, reflexively moved a bit closer. They caught themselves, and stepped back.

The man, Rudy Kwiek, leapt from the back of one, did a double roll in midair, and landed in front of the pair.

'Are my vrai not wonderful?'

'They are,' Garvin agreed. 'What's the gaff?'

Kwiek looked injured.

'There is no gaff. My horses, my vrai, are from a very special, very sleek family, bred only by a few Rom on isolated worlds, and almost never allowed to be seen in public.

'And I have the best of the breed, an attraction so special and so highly trained your circus should not only count itself lucky to have the chance to sign us, but it will double, nay triple your bunce.'

'Yeh,' Garvin said flatly.

'Maybe,' Montagna said, 'you wouldn't mind having one of your horses lift a foot?'

'Ah,' Kwiek said. 'The lady is not only beautiful, but bright.'

'No,' Montagna said. 'I just thought I saw metal gleam when your horse jumped that stand.'

'Ah once more,' Kwiek sald. 'I must work with the animal. I must confess that I have made my poor horses' task a bit easier.'

'What?' Garvin asked with a grin. 'A little antigrav unit in each shoe?'

Kwiek bowed.

'I can see I will have no secrets with you, Gaffer. Perhaps we should adjourn to your office and taste a bit of the raki I have brought with me, and discuss in what manner my wives and I shall be able to work together.'

Garvin nodded.

'Sorry about that dinner invite in town, Darod. It's going to be a hard night's bargaining.'

*

'I am not going to sit on that beast,' the young woman stormed.

'And why not, my temperamental little one?' the circus's choreographer, a tiny and somewhat effete man named Knox said. 'We've been promised they do not eat people.'

'I won't, because . . . because they've got hairy little spikes all over them, and I don't want my bottom to be a pincushion.'

Monique Lir, standing near the hull's gangway, muttered to Garvin: 'They're all like that. All goddamned thirty of those goddamned showgirls. They won't do this, they won't do that, they don't care what their contracts say, their room's too hot, it's too cold, it's too close to the horses, it's too . . . aargh. Boss, please. Give me all thirty of them for a week, and I promise, those that're left won't be doing any more of this frigging sniveling.'

'Now, now,' Garvin soothed, hiding a grin. 'We must allow for artistic temperament.'

'Temperament my left tit,' Lir snarled. 'All they're supposed to do is wave their pretty little asses about, smile like they've got an idea what day it is, and be frigging foils for the clowns.'

'Speaking of which,' Garvin said.

'Now, Adele,' Knox said, still calm. 'I really don't want to put pressure on you . . . but if you won't take that assignment, I'll have to find you another.'

'Anything!' the blonde stormed. 'Anything but that!'

'Heh . . . heh . . . heh . . . anything?' and suddenly Professor Ristori slunk into view, wearing a long black raincoat and hat. 'We have, ho-ho, we have, a little sketch . . .' and extended one leg, with a baggy pair of pants on it. He pulled on the other leg, and the pants leg was revealed as no more than the cuffs, and a pair of suspenders going upward.

'A sketch, a sketch,' he said, 'most funny, perhaps a little adult, a little adult, a little adult for our younger sort, where you and I are wedded, wedded forever, for eternal bliss.

'I roll you onstage, in a wedding bed, and then, after I make my ablutions, abluting, abluting, then I climb into bed with you, singing, and we embrace. Then you discover, somehow, in the bed with us, are two, perhaps three of my friends ... little people ... who I've invited—'

'Stop,' Adele shrilled. 'No more. All right, Knox. I'll ride your dinged elephant!'

'You see,' Garvin told Lir. 'There's more than one way to skin a showgirl.'

The three men threw things at the woman, Qi Fen Tan – chairs, a small table, and she caught them stacked them atop each other askew, her hands a blur. Then one man, Jiang Yuan Fong, gave a second leg up, and he spun up through the air, to the top of the stack, balancing easily.

The second man went up as well.

Then a very small child, Jia Yin Fong, toddled toward the man, and she, too, went spinning up to the top of the pile, and, from nowhere, produced a dozen sticks and began juggling them.

The thrower nodded, and the acrobats disassembled.

'You, of course, are more than welcome,' Garvin said through the dying traces of a raki hangover.

'Good,' the man, Fong, said. 'For we have heard that you will be attempting to reach Centrum, and from there it should be easy for my family and cousins to continue our journey.'

'To where?' Garvin asked. 'We already have some people who are hitching with us.'

Fong looked sad. 'Yes. I know who you mean, and I fear their planet is no more than a dream, although I hope otherwise.

'Our journey is to a quite real place. We are returning to Earth, to our native land called China, as, in the end, all Chinese will do.

'We have been, through a dozen generations, through the galaxy, and now it is time to return home to our village of Tai Sheng and rebuild our souls.'

Garvin shook hands with the man, wondered if Ken Fong, back on Cumbre, was any kind of relation, then went back toward his office for a soothing beer and to contemplate the many reasons his troupe had . . . or claimed to have . . . for joining him.

They were almost crewed up, and rehearsing twice a day. Garvin had set their lift date, and tempers were getting short.

The big cats snarled at anyone who came within range of their cages, including their handler, Sir Douglas. The elephants were cranky, and their occasional screeches echoed through the transport. Acrobatic partners snapped at each other, aerialists bit their lips, and roustabouts met behind the ship to settle their differences.

Only a few of the experienced hands were pleased. This was the way it always went before a show was ready to roll . . . and if all had been peaceful and happy, they would've known they were in for trouble.

Garvin picked up the rifle, aimed carefully, and pulled the trigger. The ancient projectile weapon cracked, and the target was motionless.

'Try again, try again, can't win the doll for your lady without you take another chance,' the talker chanted.

'The problem with you, Sopi,' Njangu said, 'is that you think everybody is too dumb to count.'

The fat, cheery-looking man tried to look angry, failed, settled on offended.

'Howinhell can you think I'm not a bon homy?' he demanded, his voice high, squeaky.

'For openers, the barrel of that rifle's been tweaked so hard it shoots sideways,' he said.

'Same thing with your wheel of fortune,' Garvin joined in. 'I could see the magnets, and watch the talker's foot kick switches. And we won't even think about your roulette wheel, which barely turns.'

'Now, 'at's not good,' Sopi Midt agreed. 'Have to get them side curtains lowered some.'

'And the ball throw was weighted,' Garvin went on. 'The bottles in the ring toss were too close together, so nothing could land right.'

'But whadja think of the jill show?'

'That won't fly at all,' Garvin said. 'First we've got our showgirls already. And I know sex sells . . . but we're not trying to get in trouble.'

'I don't get in trouble,' Midt said. 'We always play things right up to the wire, and make sure the rozzer's been tipped so there's no arrests.

'Play to the community standards, maybe a meter or so beyond, and you'll never ever, or hardly ever anyway, get in trouble,' he said piously.

'You do have a problem,' Garvin agreed with Njangu. 'You're too quick to go chasing after the credit.

'But I've got a problem, too. I need a midway, I want to be on the road yesterday, and you've got twelve booths, not including the girlie show, and you're not trying to shove freaks at me, although I wouldn't mind a good giant or two.'

'Know where I can get 'em, have 'em here by morning,' Midt said.

'Shut up for a minute,' Garvin said. 'Try this for a proposition. Instead of the cut being sixty-forty, like you suggested, let's try seventy-thirty.'

'Why're you willing to screw yourself?' Midt asked suspiciously.

''Cause I want a straight show . . . or, anyway, fairly straight. I want you to go through, fix the graft so it isn't too bad a rape, and we have a deal.

'The other condition is you deal straight with me, all the way. Or I'll leave your fat ass, and your crew, in the middle of whatever fix you'll have caused, on whatever miserable world of flatties it happens on.'

Midt considered.

'Damn,' he said. 'If there was any other show goin' . . . I'm not sure I'm real good at bein' honest.'

'Then you'd best start learning,' Njangu said, finding all this very funny.

Midt stuck out a paw.

''Kay. Hard bargaining. But I'll take the deal.'

'Then you better get to work, straightening some gun barrels and unwiring your graft,' Garvin said curtly, and started back for the ship.

'We sure have a crew,' Njangu said. 'Crooked sideshows, gypsies, aliens, elephants, and killer cats.'

'I know,' Garvin said happily. 'It really is starting to feel like a circus. And, like you said, back in Cumbre, nobody's gonna think a rooty-tootin' spy mission of heroes is also running some games that are somewhat on the diddly.'

*

It was dress rehearsal.

Garvin, in spite of his romantic lust to do his first show under canvas, had been sensible and performed in *Big Bertha*'s main hold.

He would use exactly the same dimensions whether they were inship or outship: bleachers were set up on either side of the rectangular area, almost half a kilometer in length. The bleachers could be adjusted depending on the crowd they drew, so Circus Jaansma would never look poorly attended.

The horse track ran from the troupers' entrance around the performing area, then back out the entrance on the other side.

Garvin, ever the traditionalist, would run three rings, each about twenty-five meters in diameter. They could be spaced closer or farther apart, depending, again, on the size of the crowd. The crowd came in through the main cargo airlock, whose secondary portal could be stowed on a breathable world.

Overhead was the maze of lines and guy wires for the aerialists, and, high above them was the rear of the command capsule.

Outside the ship was the midway, and at lock's entrance there were spielers, still working on their ballyhoos, drawing the crowd inside.

Garvin had invited anyone on Grimaldi who wanted to attend. The bleachers were full and extra seats, called cattle guards, had been set in front of the general admission seats.

Then it began, and the clowns attacked the pompous ringmaster, and Garvin whipped them away, just as the aerialists, like clouds of satin, dangled by strange monsters, filled the skies.

There were elephants, more clowns, acrobats, big cats,

even a finicky man with real Earth cats, constantly harassed by the clowns.

The horses came and went, and more clowns, and the children were starting to yawn, and then it was the blowoff, and the candy butchers swarmed the stands.

'Not bad,' Garvin grudged.

'Not bad at all,' Njangu agreed. He laughed. 'I guess it's time to go to war.'

'Sir,' Liskeard said. 'All compartments report ready to lift, we have hull integrity, no problems reported.'

'Then, Mr. Liskeard,' Garvin said 'we're trouping!'

Liskeard grinned, touched controls, and *Big Bertha* lifted clear of Grimaldi and waddled toward the stars.

SEVEN

N-space

Garvin could have gone straight for Centrum, but he knew better. Njangu's digging indicated that whatever had happened to the Confederation now looked like it had happened in chunks, rather than a total implosion/explosion from the center.

He felt if he went straight for the heart of the matter, he'd most likely get his head rolled, and thought it wiser to skirt the fringes . . . actually well into the heart of the Confederation . . . gathering intelligence before going for broke.

His goal was the multiple systems of Tiborg. That hadn't been his original target, back on Cumbre, but he hadn't planned on having to go all the way to Grimaldi to gather his troupe, either. Tiborg had been one of the secondary options he'd chosen, because a Confederation fiche, fairly classified, said the sector could be 'interesting in its approach to diplomacy.'

'Which means,' Garvin had said, 'they're royal pains in the ass . . . or were, anyway, to the Confederation, I'd guess. Well worth talking to.'

'Yeh. Right,' Njangu said. 'This is the old "enemy of

my friend could be worth knowing" routine. It's generally been my experience that somebody who's a good
enemy is an all-around pain in the ass to everyone who
comes in contact with him.

'But you're the brave leader and all.'

Big Bertha jumped through five systems, four inhabited, without landing or contacting the locals. Penwyth,
Lir, Dill, and Froude went to Yoshita – Garvin having
refused to see them, taking advantage of the old military
law that an absence of response always means no and go
away – to request *Big Bertha* make landings.

'That'll give the planets' peoples *something*,' Penwyth
said 'The mere assurance that there's folks out there, concerned about the Confederation.'

'Touching,' Njangu said, not quite sneering. 'Truly
touching. Especially you, Ben, being one of the peti-
tioners, being a hardened killer of the ether. There are . . .
were . . . how many planets in the Confederation at last
count? A hundred thousand? A million? Don't you think
we might grow old gracefully on such a charming errand
of mercy, rather than doing what the hell we're out here
for in the first place?'

Penwyth and Dill might've said more, but Froude recognized that Yoshitaro was right. They didn't have time
to waste. Lir knew, after the time with him in I&R,
better than to argue when the boss got a certain coldness
to him.

Njangu asked Monique to stay behind after the
others.

'Getting soft?' he asked, and there wasn't a trace of
sarcasm in his voice.

She took it as meant, thought for a bit.

'No, boss. I don't think so.'

'Good,' he said. 'We've got soft hearts enough and I

suspect this operation will get sticky before we belly up to the bar at the Shelburne again.'

Tiborg

'Boursier One, this is Tiborg Alpha Delta Control,' crackled in Boursier's headphones. 'You are cleared to land at field, using Channel three-four-three for instrument approach, or under visual flight conditions once in-atmosphere under pilot's discretion. Over.'

'This is Boursier One,' Jacqueline Boursier said into her mike – Dill had started something by using his own name for a call sign. 'Roger your instructions on Channel three-four-three. Be advised I am forerunner of Transport *Big Bertha*, who will be entering your system shortly.'

There was a pause.

'Boursier One, this is Control. You should be advised we have patrol ships out . . . but your transport name is certainly disarming.'

Boursier, fairly close to being humorless, opened her mike. 'Roger your last. We intend no harm. We are a circus ship.'

'Say again your last?'

'Circus,' Boursier said. 'As in entertainment.'

A long pause.

'This is Control. I looked the word up. My superior says proceed as before.'

'Roger . . . thank you, Control. Switching channels.' Boursier touched a sensor, signaled *Big Bertha*.

A few minutes later, one of the patrol ships dropped into normal space. Garvin Jaansma was aboard it.

'Boursier One, this is Jaansma,' he said. 'No problems?'

'None that I can see.'

'Then let's be hung for sheepsies . . . go on down and see what's happening, Boursier One.'

'Roger. Switching frequencies.' Again, Boursier touched a sensor.

'Tiborg Alpha Delta Control, this is Boursier One. Proceeding to landing. Other two ships will follow me.'

The Nana boat went back into hyperspace, and then it returned, followed by *Big Bertha*, and they closed on the planet below.

'Interesting,' Garvin said to no one in particular. 'Supposedly these systems are democratic, but they've all got names like some soldier named them. Alpha Delta whatever my left nostril!'

'Or else the people only think they've got democracy,' a tech murmured.

'That too.'

'Purpose of your visit?' the customs officer asked briskly.

'To entertain your people . . . and maybe make a few credits,' Garvin said.

The customs officer looked up at *Big Bertha* looming over her, then smiled.

'You know, you're the first person I've ever cleared who wasn't from one of the Tiborg systems. You . . . and your people . . . are truly welcome.'

'Ladies and gentlemen, children of all ages, citizens of our Confederation, welcome to Circus Jaansma,' Garvin called, and cracked his whip sharply.

The main cargo area of *Big Bertha* was about half-full of people. Garvin had decided for their first real performance, and the first night on an unknown world, it would be safer to keep things close at hand and pitch the tent later.

'We bring you wonders from beyond the stars, from old Earth, from worlds unknown to man, with strange aliens, monsters, deadly beasts, death-defying acrobats high above you, to chill and amaze—'

At this point, the clowns attacked Garvin, as planned. He flailed and whipped them off, the clowns stumbling into each other, their every scheme foiled by idiocy; then one shrieked warning, and pointed off.

Through a portal Alikhan loomed, growling, snarling, 'guarded' by Ben Dill, wearing a pair of tights and iron rings about his biceps.

There were screams, especially from the children. Perhaps there were a few adults who knew what a Musth was, but none of them could know whether or not he was friendly.

Behind Alikhan streamed the circus – tumbling acrobats, the aerialists pirouetting on lifters, the cats in their cages, the elephants, the horses, Darod Montagna proudly if a little shakily standing on one of them, and the show began.

They played day-on, day-off for the next four days, honing the routines.

Njangu wasn't around much – he was again scouting libraries for data on the Confederation, looking for possible info sources, but without that much success.

Tiborg had been mostly out of contact with the Confederation for more than ten years, longer than Cumbre. Researching back through the holos of the time, it seemed the break-off hadn't been of much concern.

He wondered what the word 'mostly' meant, decided to look further, even though he got the idea the people of Tiborg were perfectly happy to be left alone, content to let the Universe roll on by.

He made some attempts to size up the local military, found, in common with many worlds, curiosity wasn't encouraged. He did discover there was an Armed Forces Club in the capital, and considered if there might be something there.

Running Bear paced back and forth, stepping carefully, chanting as he did, moving steadily down the sawdust around the three main rings.

It was coming back to him, he thought, wishing he'd had a grandfather or father he was sure actually had remembered the rituals.

He only half believed in racial memory, but was trying desperately under the face paint and body paint.

He tried to remember a time before the whites, when his people ruled the plains of a distant world, warrior lords of the prairies.

He came back, realized there was a small girl staring solemnly at him, who'd come out of her seat in the stands.

'Are you real?' she asked.

'Nope,' Running Bear said. 'I'm a ghost. A ghost dancer.'

'Oh. What are you doing?' she asked.

'A rain dance of my people,' Running Bear intoned, trying to keep from laughing.

'Oh.' The little girl nodded, started back for her seat, then turned back.

'It's a good dance,' she said. 'It just started raining when we got here.'

Running Bear grunted like a good AmerInd should; felt, inside, a tiny ripple of fear for messing about in the territory of the gods.

*

'We certainly seem,' Ristori said to Froude, 'to have arrived in interesting times. I assume you've noted there's a campaign going on for Planetary Premier?'

'I've seen something on a holo,' Froude said. 'Unfortunately, I was trying to learn that damned forward roll you think my old bones are capable of.'

'Shame, Doctor,' Ristori said. 'Wolves should always attend on the doings of the sheep. Otherwise, they might miss the hiring of a new and dangerous shepherd. Or a flock of sheepdogs.'

'I'm worse than that,' Froude confessed. 'I don't even know how the damned system works.'

'Most simple, simple, simple,' Ristori said, reverting to his chosen clamor. 'Sorry. You have a supposedly freely elected Premier and Vice Premier, plus their various appointed secretaries. They, in turn, help rule all of Tiborg's twenty-odd worlds through four systems.'

'Interesting device,' Froude said. 'Sounds like it might be fairly representative.'

'Perhaps,' Ristori said doubtfully. 'However, I also noted there are some thirty members of what's known as a Directorate. There's very little on the holos about them, but they seem to be former planetary politicians, who, and I am quoting here, advise the Premiers, bringing their years of experience to bear.'

'Mmmh,' Froude said. 'How much real power do they have?'

'No one says, which suggests a lot.'

'Indeed. So the Premiers are puppets, then.'

'In a manner of speaking . . . except that it seems to me that one of them who's properly cooperative and understanding will have his name set down as a potential Director.'

'Ah, humans,' Froude said. 'We do come up with strange ways of doing things.'

'Especially this election here on Delta. It would seem that the government is a shade on the corrupt side, and has held power for some eight years. Gaming, whoring . . . whatever. Delta seems wide-open, which we haven't seen, not having gone downtown nearly enough, for other citizens of Tiborg to find this an exciting place to vacation.

'But now there's a young reformer named Dorn Fili who's a candidate for Premier, swearing he's going to throw the rascals out, bring honesty, truth, and justice to government, rule hands-on and such. He's very pretty, according to the holos I've seen.'

'Ah?'

'The interesting thing that I've discovered,' Ristori said, 'is that Mr. Fili's father was Premier some years back, thrown out of office by outraged reformers.'

'Oh.'

'Precisely. Let's tear the old crooks away from the trough so new crooks can have their turn to come in and fatten.'

'You know,' Garvin said contentedly, 'I could get into this habit of making money.'

'You mean we're actually in profits?' Njangu said.

'Well, if you ignore the initial outlay from Jasith . . . and the cost of the ship . . . we're making credits hand over fist.'

'Always easy to show a profit if you blow off the overhead,' Njangu said. 'That's why being a thief attracted me so much.

'Speaking of which, I've got the angle on this Armed Forces Club thing. It's got a big building near the center of the capital, provides rooms for its members, has a bar, meeting halls, some kind of museum serves meals . . . I'd guess the usual private club menu of gray vegetables and boiled meat.

'However, they're very proud of their charities.'

'Ah-hah.'

'Exackle,' Njangu said. 'I'm gonna roll Penwyth in, and say the circus would be delighted to sail some Annie Oakleys . . . that's the term, right, for freebies? . . . for their gimpy kids or something.'

'Which'll give us what?'

'Which'll give us maybe a temporary membership for Erik.'

'Which'll give us . . . besides having to listen to Penwyth whine about the food . . . what?'

'Soldiers love other soldiers,' Njangu explained carefully. 'They really suck up to bigger militaries.'

'I wouldn't know,' Garvin said. 'Never having been around a bigger one . . . but maybe you would, given your fondness for the late Larissan military.'

'Screw off,' Njangu said. 'So, assuming there might've been some kind of contact beyond this break-off ten years gone, we might be able to pick up some data of interest about the Confeds and what happened.

'Maybe.'

'Thin, my little brownish brother. Very thin indeed,' Garvin said. 'But I agree. We should—'

There was a tap at the cabin door.

'It's open,' Garvin said, and the door slid open and one of the gangway sentries stood there. With him was a handsome man in his early thirties and a heavyset, satisfied-looking companion in his late middle age. Both men wore business wear that Njangu, even though he knew nothing of the planetary style, decided looked expensive.

The younger man was very handsome, in a rugged sort of way, his face open, exuding confidence and trust.

Njangu decided that he hated him.

'Good evening, gents,' the middle-aged man said. 'I'd like you to meet Dorn Fili, soon to be Premier of Delta, and possibly we can discuss some matters of mutual benefice.'

'Now, now,' Fili said with a smile, 'we've yet to win the election, Sam'l.'

'We have the people behind us, Dorn,' the older man said. 'They're tired of corruption and dirt in public office.'

'I hope so,' Fili said. 'But we don't have to campaign in front of these people, who we hope will do us some good. My friend here, is Sam'l Brek. He's advising me, which he's been doing since I was born, and before that was one of my father's most trusted men.'

'Thank you,' Brek said.

'You said we might do you some good,' Garvin said carefully. 'In what way?'

'I'll explain . . . may I sit down?' Fili said. Garvin waved him to a chair – the cabin was crowded with more than two people in it. Brek stood against the wall, looking interested at whatever idea Fili was going to propose, as if he'd never heard it before.

Njangu watched both men very carefully.

'As Sam'l said, I'm running for Premier,' Fili went on. 'I'm fortunate enough to have been left quite a bit of credits by my family, which I've dedicated to defeating the machine that's been holding Delta back for eight years now.

'I'm doing what used to be referred to as a full press, hitting the Constitutionalists high, low, here, and there.

'One of the means I'd like to use is your circus, which

I was lucky enough to see tonight. What a show! What an amazing show!'

'Thank you,' Garvin said.

'I would like to put your resources to work on my team, for which you'll be well paid during the campaign, and, if I'm elected, you and your team would be considered good friends.'

'Thank you for your offer,' Garvin said. 'Unfortunately, we're not wealthy, and can't afford to volunteer to help anyone.'

'Plus we're outsiders,' Njangu put in. 'I've never noticed folks are real fond of strangers coming in and helping them with their business.'

'I think you misunderstand me,' Fili said, frowning, his expression echoed by Brek. 'I don't want you to starve in my service . . . nor to be widely known for helping me.'

'What I need, I pay for. I'd guess, for instance, that your performance tonight probably grossed about thirty thousand credits.'

Garvin covered his surprise. In fact, that was only seven thousand credits below the actual gate.

'I would want to hire your entire show for two, perhaps three, benefits, for which I'd pay fifty thousand per show.'

Both Garvin and Njangu looked very interested.

'Plus there are certain charities and good works I support, such as crusades against crippling diseases, against birth defects, and such, and I would want to hire certain of your specialists, perhaps the elephants and perhaps the horses to perform outside hospitals three or four times in the next few weeks.'

'How would this be tied in with your campaign?' Njangu said skeptically. 'The elephants will carry banners in their trunks?'

'Nothing so crass,' Brek broke in. 'The posters would

merely mention that your circus is performing under the auspices of one or another of Dorn's committees. We'd leave it to the voters to make the obvious association.'

Garvin considered. He could see no problems, and it would certainly be good for some of the acts to get away and work on their own.

'We wouldn't be able to cut any of our people free on show days,' he said.

'Of course not,' Fili said heartily. 'And we'll provide volunteer workers for anything you might need beyond your normal functions.'

'Security, for instance,' Brek said.

Garvin looked at Njangu, who moved his head microscopically up and down.

'I think something could well be arranged,' Jaansma said.

Fili was on his feet.

'Good, good. That's wonderful news. And you'll never regret your decision, and I'm sure you'll enjoy being part of my campaign.'

There was more glad-handing, exchange of com numbers for the working out of the details, and Fili and Brek left.

'Free money,' Garvin gloated, cackling, rubbing his hands together in his most miserly imitation.

'Looks like,' Njangu agreed. 'I just wish I liked Fili.'

'What's the matter with him?'

'Handsome bastards always grate on my spine.'

'Then why're you my friend?' Garvin asked blandly.

Njangu snorted. 'Maybe because you take instruction well.'

Njangu and Maev rolled out of bed, pistols in hand to the scream of sirens and the synthed voice:

'Emergency! Emergency! In the . . . cat area. In the . . . cat area!'

Njangu found time for a pair of pants, Maev for a robe, and they went out of their cabin, pelted down the corridors and two companionways into the hold, others behind them.

They pushed past a throng into the cat compartment, into horror.

Muldoon the leopard crouched, growling, over a bloody, torn body. Against one cage wall lay Sir Douglas, moaning, barely conscious.

'What the hell?' Njangu snapped.

A tiny acrobat answered: 'I . . . I heard commotion, opened the door, just as Sir Douglas arrived. That black monster had this man down, and the cage door was ajar.

'Other cats were coming out of their sleeping cage. Sir Douglas went into the main cage . . . he didn't even have his whip . . . slammed it closed behind him.

'One of the striped cats got behind him, and he was shouting for it to get back. The animal got scared and hit him . . . I think more by accident than anything else . . .' and the woman started crying.

'Who's the man?' Njangu demanded.

No one knew. Njangu thought of shooting Muldoon, but with his small pistol didn't know if he'd do more than make the leopard angrier.

Garvin, bare naked, ran into the compartment, caught the situation up.

'Get blasters,' he ordered. 'We'll have to kill the cat.'

'Not yet,' someone said. It was Alikhan, and behind him was Ben Dill, carrying a meter-long bar of steel as thick as his forearm. 'Let me try to get the animal away.'

Garvin shook his head, realized Alikhan's intent and jumped for him, but was too late as Alikhan opened the cage, went inside. Dill knocked Jaansma out of the way and went after him, muttering, 'Goddamned fool of a dumb-ass frigging alien bastard!'

Muldoon growled a warning, but Alikhan paid no mind, moving toward the animal steadily, calmly, waving his arms. Muldoon crouched, about to spring, and Dill braced for the charge. Then the leopard, evidently, caught the alien's scent.

He growled once more, slid back from his barely moving victim, then scampered into his sleeping area.

The other cats, still half-asleep, also scented the alien and sulkily went back into their own quarters.

Alikhan banged shut the doors between the cages.

'Now,' he started, but the main cage entrance was already open, and Jil Mahim was kneeling over the man, medikit at her side.

'Hell if I know who he is . . . phew, he's been drinking a storm,' she said. 'Some fool drunk maybe who hid out when the show broke up and wanted to play with the kitties.'

Someone shouted, 'I've got a medic flight on the way.'

'Good,' Mahim said, her fingers moving easily through her kit, punching a trach tube through the man's ruined throat, feeling the man's pulse, hitting him with three painkillers and an anticoagulant, tapping blood substitute into a vein. 'Get one of the stretchers from the corridor.' Crewmen ran to obey.

The moaning man was taken out of the cage, just as Sir Douglas stumbled to his feet, shaking his head.

'I did not see who hit me,' he said. 'Was it that bad Muldoon?'

'One of the tigers,' someone said.

'I was careless,' Sir Douglas said. 'I thought they were my calm friends. I should have allowed for the excitement.'

'Not you,' someone cracked, 'but that idiot on the stretcher.'

'Who,' Mahim said, 'is probably going to live, and father many idiots. There's no justice.'

'All right, everyone,' Garvin said. 'The excitement's over.'

'Uh, boss,' Njangu said, trying not to laugh. 'Maybe you want to be the first to leave?'

Garvin looked down at himself, realized his nakedness, and reddened, especially when he saw Darod Montagna eyeing him thoughtfully.

'Not bad at all,' she murmured, and Jaansma fled for his quarters.

'Ain't that the thing about circus life,' Njangu said. 'Never a dull moment.'

'You wished?' Phraphas Phanon asked Sir Douglas.

'I was wondering if you have any interest in expanding your gaff,' the animal trainer said.

'We are always interested in the new,' Sunya Thanon said. 'What do you have in mind?'

'Combining my Deadly Dangerous Beasts with your Monsters of the Midway.'

'Ah,' Phanon said. 'Your large cats and our friends. An interesting thought.'

'I don't know if you've ever worked with cats,' Sir Douglas said. 'I've never done anything with elephants. If their hides aren't as thick as they look, we could maybe use pads.'

'What sort of tricks would you have in mind?'

'Oh, leaping from one elephant to another,' Sir Douglas said, a bit vaguely. 'Posing next to them.'

'Hmm,' Phanon said. 'Perhaps we could come up with something more spectacular.'

*

Njangu stood at the side of the mess line in the compartment known as the cook tent. Running Bear, plate laden, came past him.

'Better grub than some we've known,' he said.

'Careful,' Njangu warned.

'I meant, in some of the circuses we've trouped in,' the AmerInd said innocently, went on, found a seat.

The conversation was a buzz of various languages, some translated into Common, others between men and women from the same planet. Garvin sat at the head of one table, chattering away like one of the Earth monkeys he despised.

It felt happy, Njangu decided. Maybe like a family. *And how would you know what a family really is*, he thought wryly. *No. Maybe I do. Maybe the Force. And isn't that a helluva thought?*

'You wished to see me?' Garvin said. He was sweating gently, having just come out of the ring on the break, the clowns cavorting to keep the crowd's interest.

The man waiting for him was elderly, every man's beloved grandfather, richly and conservatively dressed. 'I did indeed.'

'Perhaps my office, though we'll have to hurry, since I'm back on in half an hour,' Jaansma suggested.

'Perhaps so, Gaffer Jaansma,' the man said. He had a gentle yet firm voice, and followed Garvin through the managed chaos of backstage. Garvin saw Njangu, made a slight gesture.

In Garvin's office, the man declined a drink, sat down.

'If you don't mind . . . I think my mind's as spry as ever, but these bones thank you for a bit of relaxation.

'I'll only take a minute of your time. I'm Director Fen

Bertl, by the way, and happened to be here on Delta on business to do with Dorn Fili's campaign.

'First, let me say how much I'm enjoying your show. Fantastic. You're certainly right when you say it's for children of all ages, for it certainly took me back to much younger days, when we were all innocent.' He smiled beatifically.

'I thought the very least I could do in return is offer a bit of advice, although I'm certainly aware of what most people think of unsolicited suggestions.'

'Sir, I'm always willing to listen to any suggestions,' Garvin said truthfully. 'I keep an open door, and always have.'

'Many people say they do just that, but don't really mean it. If you do, I'm most impressed. Perhaps you were in the military once?'

'No, no,' Garvin said. 'I've been circus all my life.'

Bertl nodded.

'My advice has to do with your involvement with the Fili campaign. No, don't look angry or upset that I've learned about it. There are very few secrets to a Director, particularly one who's decided to back Dorn, just as I backed his father years ago.

'My advice is this: People love to wallow in their vices for a time, then loudly want redemption. This is the crest Dorn Fili is riding, hopefully to the highest office, as his father did, who also had the intellect to realize when to back off his crusade.

'Something you should be aware of is that elections throughout the Tiborg system are, shall we say, most freewheeling, particularly when there appears to be a radical change in the direction of government proposed.

'Our elections can get bloody, I'm ashamed to admit.'

'All I agreed was to do a few shows for Fili,' Garvin said. 'For hire, not as a believing volunteer.'

'Unfortunately the opposition frequently takes small things like that and magnifies them out of all import-ance. This is one reason I think they will lose the election, for they've lost the sense of perspective all of us in politics must maintain. Because of this, it's now the turn of the loyal opposition to take office.'

'You have, if you'll forgive me, for I'm hardly inter-ested in politics,' Garvin said, 'quite a system. First, it's Set A, then Set B, then Set A again. Aren't you worried that the people are, sooner or later, going to ask for a real change?'

'No,' Bertl said calmly. 'No, my romantic friend, I'm not. Our system has worked well for almost five hundred years, in spite of Confederation meddling . . . not for an honest election, I assure you, but because they wanted Set C, their own handpicked fellows, to take office.

'Besides, we have certain . . . control measures to keep matters from getting out of hand in an emergency.

'My own personal belief is that we absolutely should have real free elections one of these years, when the time is right and the populace is sufficiently educated and mature for such an event.

'But until then . . . matters should stay as they are.' He got up. 'To return to the reason for my visit, I thought I should tell you, as, perhaps, thanks for your job of entertaining me . . . and the people of Delta . . . that you may have made a mistake, no matter how well paid you'll be for your services.'

'I don't see any way to undo my agreement,' Garvin said.

'Neither do I,' Bertl admitted, 'since you're more than evidently an honest man. I, on the other hand, would cheerfully find a way to loudly abrogate the agreement. But you are what you are. At least I thought I might give you the chance to be on your guard.

'As I said, all I can offer is a bit of a warning.'

He smiled in a most fatherly manner, bowed, and was gone.

Garvin waited a minute, and Njangu came into his office.

'Not an election this year, nor next year, but by gum your grandchildren will be happy as snot,' Njangu snarled. 'Why is it shitheels like that never think it's the right time for the people to have squat in the way of power?'

'I dunno,' Garvin said. 'And howcum there's wars?'

'What makes me worry,' Njangu said, 'are these emergency measures. Like martial law, maybe, which we surely don't want to get caught up in.'

Garvin poured drinks from a decanter, gave one to Njangu, shot his own back.

'I'm starting to wonder if we might have made a slight error,' he said quietly.

Director Fen Bertl got into his lim.

'Back to our ship,' he ordered, and the lifter silently came off the ground.

'Well, sir?' his supposed driver asked.

'An interesting young man. Most subtle for his years. He only looked twice at where I assume some sort of pickup was hidden in the wall spaces,' Bertl said.

'A very nice young man, who's playing politics and has men looking for data on the Confederation.

'I think it might be wise to find out a bit more about him and his circus.'

*

'I know our cooks are the best recyclers in the universe,' Darod Montagna said. 'But it sure is nice to get out and eat something that isn't seasoned with what used to be your own sweat.'

'How genteel. How ladylike. How guaranteed to spoil my appetite,' Garvin said. He poured what remained of the bottle of wine between their glasses, and, unobtrusively, the busboy was there to take it away and the sommelier to provide another.

'Oh, I'm just so sorry,' Darod said, staring pointedly at the bony remains of a fish on Garvin's well-polished plate.

'I kept eating just for politeness,' he explained.

'I thought I'd never get another chance at that dinner you promised,' Montagna said.

'I'm always a man of my word,' Garvin said. 'Sometimes the word is just a tiddly slow.'

He looked around the restaurant. It was quite a place, a polished wooden ocean ship that had somehow been transported to the lake near the field *Big Bertha* was parked on. Its waiters wore white gloves, liquids were served in real crystal, and there were actual tablecloths.

'It is nice to get out,' he said. 'I was starting to think everything smelled like elephant.'

'Speaking of being indelicate,' Darod said. She put a hand on Garvin's, and he let it stay there. 'I was most impressed by your command presence the other morning.'

Garvin held back laughter. 'You just said that to make me blush.'

'Oh no,' Darod said. 'I already saw you blush, and I must say you do a very thorough job of it.'

She giggled.

*

Garvin yawned as he took the lifter off from the lot beside the moored restaurant ship.

'And so back to grim reality.'

'I guess so,' Darod said, then pointed. 'Not yet . . . unless we have to. See that point, way up there? And there's two . . . no, three moons out. Can you land up there?'

'With a bottle of that wine in me, I could land on the head of a pin and dance.'

'Just put us down on the big rock,' Darod said. 'Dancing might be for later.'

Garvin brought it in skillfully, surprising himself, and set it down.

They sat in silence for a few minutes, contentedly looking at the moons, the silver lake below, the lights of the ship.

'For some reason,' Garvin said, a bit surprised that his voice was a bit hoarse, 'I feel like kissing you.'

'That can be arranged,' Darod said, turning to him, and her mouth opened under his.

Some time later, her formal dress slid down about her waist, she found herself in the lifter's huge rear seat, looking up at Garvin.

'Perhaps you'd lift your hips?' Garvin said.

She obeyed.

'You'll notice,' she said, 'no underwear, meaning I was hoping something like this or maybe just this was going to happen.' Then she gasped.

'I hope you know what you think you're doing,' was Monique Lir's only comment when Darod Montagna bleared into her compartment the next morning just after dawn.

'*You* hope,' was Darod's only reply.

*

'Well, well, well,' Njangu said, pushing the holo screen to Garvin. 'Guess who's a man of his word, a worthy candidate for public office.'

Garvin ignored the pics, scanned the readout Candidate for Premier Dorn Flli was pleased to announce that Circus Jaansma had joined his campaign, at least so to speak, for they'd be doing benefits and charitable appearances for various worthy causes.

'So much for letting the voters make the correct assumptions,' Njangu said.

'Problem?'

'Flip the page,' Njangu suggested, 'and read the top two stories.'

Garvin did. One was of a bombing by 'unknown terrorists' of one of Fili's campaign headquarters, the other was the savage beating of three of his precinct walkers.

'Not good,' Garvin said. 'I think, between that moron wandering loose inside *Big Bertha* who wanted to play with our pussies . . . he is, by the way, indeed going to live, unfortunately, as Jil predicted . . . and this, we better start being a little more concerned about security. Ideas?'

'Yeh,' Njangu said. 'Pull everybody in I&R who's not a kinker onto security. Double the gangway guards . . . no, triple 'em. Put a roving patrol out around the ship.

'Cancel your idea of putting up that smelly tent for the show. Only let the midway outside the ship, and keep roving patrols through it. If Sopi loses a few of his crooked grafters, that's tough titty for him.

'Have either an *aksai* or Nana boat ready to launch on short notice if they try a heavy hit.

'From now on nobody goes into town or anywhere alone, and if there's enough of them going to make a target, they'll have to have a security tail gunner.

'Other than that,' he finished, 'it's just lovely life as usual.'

That night, there was a bit of a clem on the midway, set up just outside *Big Bertha*, and all but two of the gangway sentries were drawn into it, to Njangu's later wrath.

Then those two guards were distracted by four happy drunks who wanted to serenade them.

No one noticed the unobtrusive figure slip up to one of the ship's fins, take a chest-size centimeter-thick pad, anodized to exactly match the ship's skin color, from his coat, and hold it against *Big Bertha*. The epoxy bonded the pad to the ship's fin instantly, and the man went away, as anonymously as he'd come.

Monique Lir muttered obscenities as she tracked the dozen squealing women through the shopping district. She swore this had been either Garvin or Njangu's idea of a joke.

Guarding the showgirls indeed. As if anyone . . . other than a brain surgeon studying vacuums or a lech who didn't believe in conversation would bother any of them, on their promised shopping expedition into the capital

If someone had told Monique the only reason she went unnoticed was because of the brazen display of the showgirls, she would've most likely spat in their eye, or perhaps broken an arm or two.

As it was, she concentrated on her duty, eyes moving back and forth constantly behind very dark wraparounds, watching for anything, one hand on the grip of the heavy blaster hanging from a sling under her very stylish, very useful, long coat.

The dozen had just stopped to admire the holos swaying through the air outside a boutique when Monique saw the man, small, shabbily dressed, dash from a recess, saw the gun in his hand come up, and fire once.

Lir heard a woman scream in agony, but pald no mind to whoever was hit. She shed the coat, had her blaster up, safety off.

The man spun, about to run, and saw Lir and her gun.

'Stop!' she shouted. 'Freeze!' knowing assassins must be taken alive.

But the man's gun was lifting, aiming, and she pulled the trigger.

The bolt took the man in the middle of the chest, spinning him back across a concrete bench.

The crowds were screaming, running, women and men going flat, and there were alarms howling.

Lir paid no mind, quickly went through the corpse's pouch, took everything, then was up and running, leaving the blaster across the body.

'Thanks,' Njangu said, shutting off the com and turning to Garvin. 'The showgirl . . . her name was Chapu, by the way . . . just died.'

'Bastards,' Garvin said, sorting through the contents of the shooter's pouch.

The com buzzed again, and Njangu took it, spoke briefly.

'That was Fili,' he said. 'Expressing his sympathies, even though he's sure it had nothing to do with politics or him, just some mental case.'

'Yeh,' Garvin said, flatly.

Njangu picked up the com, told the ship's com center to hold all outside calls, but log them, joined Garvin in examining the meager contents of the pouch.

'Too much money,' he murmured. 'Nice crisp credit

bills, nonconsecutive numbers. A for-hire job. Ho. What's this. A com number?

'Maybe his bosses forgot to shake him before he went out, eh?'

He went back to the com, told the center to connect him with that number.

'It's NG,' he reported, said into the mike, 'try the old code of adding one or subtracting one number.' He waited. 'Nothing connects going down one. Try up one.' Again, he waited, then swiftly broke contact. 'Here we go. Add one number, and we just happen to get a voice that says "Constitutionalist District Four Maya speaking."'

'Sloppy, sloppy work.'

'Yeh,' Garvin said.

'You know,' Njangu said, 'in a properly run democracy, that wouldn't be anything more than minor evidence.'

'Which is why I'm damned glad I'm not running a democracy,' Garvin said grimly.

EIGHT

'Sorry to hear about your casualty,' the slender man with the carefully trimmed moustache said to Erik Penwyth. He wore an expensive but somewhat shabby civilian suit like a uniform.

'We circus people don't think like you soldiers,' Erik drawled. 'We don't take what I suppose you call calculated risk into account. P'raps we should, though,' he softened his response, burying his flash of anger. 'Considering some of the risks taken.'

'But I gather the woman who that madman shot was no more than a decoration,' the man said. 'Hardly someone who gets in a cage with monsters.'

'I guess we all die, sooner or later,' Erik said. 'Here. Stand you a drink?'

'Thanks,' the man said, and motioned to the human barkeep. 'Whiskey. And a glass of charged water.'

Penwyth nodded to the bartender to refill his brandy and ginger, although he was still getting used to the local brandy, better than anything native to Cumbre, and the mix, far gingerier than expected.

The man took his drink, lifted it to Erik.

'As we used to say . . . here's to a nice, neat war, with quick promotions.'

Erik smiled, drank.

'Although,' the man said, 'none of us in the Club have ever seen a real war.'

The Armed Forces Club's walls were decorated with old weaponry, regimental banners, holos of stiff men looking proud.

'Just riots, a few raiders, every now and then a district or a world deciding it can go on its own and needs reminding about the proper order of things,' the man said. 'Oh, by the way, I'm Kuprin Freron. Retired *T'ousan*, last duty assignment with the General Staff.'

'Erik Penwyth. I'm one of the publicity hounds.'

'I know,' the man said, started to go on, changed the subject. 'What will your people do about the tragedy?'

'What *should* we do?' Penwyth said carefully. 'The killer was some lunatic who killed our trouper, then got shot down by an unknown civilian. That's what your holos say, anyway.'

Freron raised an eyebrow. 'I wonder about that quote unknown civilian end quote. We have very stringent gun laws here on Delta . . . although it certainly never seems to stop a criminal or one of our political thugs from arming himself with anything he wishes for his villainy.'

'Crooks everywhere generally don't worry about breaking small laws,' Penwyth said. 'But I still don't understand what you're saying.'

'I just thought that you offworlders might have your own . . . resources . . . when trouble happens, which is good, since I doubt if our authorities will do anything about searching for the people everyone knows are behind this bloodshed.'

'Perhaps we do,' Penwyth said. 'If so, they've never told me about anything like that. By the way, you said you know me, but I don't remember us having met.'

'We haven't,' Jabish said. 'I heard about your show, and the largesse your circus has extended to some of the charities the Club supports.' He glanced to either side, saw no one was close, dropped his voice. 'I've also heard that you've been inquiring about the Confederation.'

'Surely,' Penwyth said, alarms going off. 'We're loyal citizens . . . although it's certainly been a long time since we've been able to show our loyalty. Traveling people like order. And, speaking personally, I'm most curious how something that huge can vanish, seemingly overnight.'

'Soldiers also like order,' Freron said. 'You know, I was lucky enough to do an intelligence course on Centrum itself a long time ago.

'And one of my jobs on the Staff, before the damned politicians decided there was more profit going our own way, was liasing with the Confederation attachés.'

'Interesting,' Erik said.

'I thought so at the time,' Freron said. 'And think so now, as I'm considering writing my memoirs.

'Because I kept thorough records. *Very* thorough records of everything I encountered dealing with the Confederation. But right now, it seems that no one is terribly interested in these anecdotes of the past.'

'I always was, as a kid,' Erik lied. 'Somehow adults always had better things to talk about than us lads did.' He wondered where the word 'lads' had come from, decided that was the kind of word Freron would use. 'But you said something about keeping records?'

'I did, and I suppose that was illegal, then, since a lot of the Confederation material I have was fairly classified then.

'Now it's just dusty fiches, although some might find it interesting.'

'Such as?' Penwyth said, wishing to hell he had a bug

detector in his pocket to see if Freron was Tiborg coun-
terintelligence, trolling.

'Oh . . . historians, perhaps. People who're making the
Confederation a subject of study, for whatever reasons.
People who're well funded, since my pension hardly
extends as far as I'd like.'

'*T'ousan* Freron,' Erik said, waving to the bartender.
'You interest me greatly. Perhaps we should find a table
and discuss this matter.'

'Call me Kuprin.'

Garvin was rather pleased that about half of his circus
quietly came up and asked if he was going to do something about Chapu's murder, and if so, could they help.

He was, but he only needed nineteen, all chosen from
I&R. They boarded one of the circus lifters in the late
afternoon and flew into the capital, landing very quietly,
on the roof of a building overlooking Constitutionalist
District Four headquarters. High above, two *aksai* were
flying cover, Dill and Alikhan as pilots.

Four soldiers, the best Shrike gunners in the Force,
their modified missiles hidden in innocuous-looking
cases, plus their gun guards, went down from the roof
and found firing positions in alcoves and alleys.

Six others, lugging Squad Support Weapons, the
tripod-mounted blasters, and their assistant gunners
went to firing locations near the three entrances to the
precinct building, under Lir's direction.

Then they waited, ducking into cover anytime any of
the planetary police lifters came past.

Garvin and Njangu had chosen to land just after
normal quitting time.

'That'll let the innocent, which means the smallscale
sorts, get out before the fun starts,' Garvin had said.

'What, just to be cynical, about the secretary whose boss ordered her to work late?' Njangu said.

Garvin looked at him coldly.

'Sorry,' Yoshitaro said. 'I didn't mean to throw shit in the game.'

It was just dusk, and about a third of the windows across the way were still lit when Garvin opened the com to his troops.

'Shrike element . . . fire as instructed.'

Two of the missiles were aimed at the fourth story of the five-story building, the other two at its midsection.

Launchers whooshed, and the missiles arrived before their sound. The explosions sent shock waves across the capital, shattering windows for blocks. The building rocked, and its façade cracked, fell toward the street, forcing one SSW team to run.

Flames flickered from three floors of the building.

There were screams, shouts, and men and women ran downstairs into the street.

'SSW, clear to fire.'

Perhaps politics on Delta was a young man's occupation, but Garvin doubted it. He'd given orders for the SSW teams to pick out anyone middle-aged, anyone who looked expensive, and especially anyone who looked like a Constitutionalist goon.

A police lifter rounded a corner, and a gunner put a burst into its engine. It bounced off a parked lifter, crashed. The cops piled out and, no fools against auto-blasters, ran like hell.

Dill's voice came into one of Garvin's earpieces.

'Boss. Time to scoot. I've got some things that look like fire engines and maybe some military lifters in the air headed yours.'

Garvin thumbed to the *aksai* channel.

'We're pulling out. Stay in the air until we're gone, then go on home.' Then, without waiting for acknowledgment, he went to the grunt channel.

''Kay, troops. We're gone.'

The women and men cascaded back up the stairs to the roof, piled in the lifter as Njangu took it up a few centimeters, dancing against the rooftop, then at full power down an avenue, below the roofs, and away.

In minutes, they were back at the field and *Big Bertha*.

'Any idea on casualties?' Montagna asked, a bit angry for not having been chosen, as they landed.

'Not nearly enough, whatever it was,' Lir said harshly.

Garvin swallowed half a liter of sport drink.

'All right, friends,' he told Liskeard, Lir, and Yoshitaro. 'That's evened things up a little. Now, recall anybody that's in the city back home, get the troops to start packing and the midway struck aboard. We'll be gone by midnight, and Tiborg Alpha Delta can find its own path to hell.'

'Hang on a second, boss,' Njangu said. 'Could you maybe gimme a moment of solitude?'

Garvin hesitated, then nodded. The others filed out.

'We just got a spanner up our asses, I think, as far as beating feet,' Njangu said. 'Erik just wandered back, a little buzzed, with something interesting.'

Yoshitaro told him about Penwyth's evening with Freron, the retired staff officer. Garvin started to open another sport drink, curled his nose.

'This calls for alcohol.'

''Deed it do,' Njangu agreed, found two beers in Garvin's cooler, and opened them.

Garvin drank mightily.

'Why do I ever consider putting anything healthy

inside me,' he wondered, 'when the evil stuff tastes so much better? 'Kay. So we've got somebody with . . . maybe . . . some good intel, high-level or fairly high anyway, on the Confederation. Ten years old, though.'

'Older than ours, but surely at a higher level than anything the Force has, isn't it?' Njangu said.

Garvin nodded.

'But that'll also mean we'll still be targets for those assholes,' he said.

'Which set?'

'Does it matter?' Garvin said. 'A Constitutionalist bolt'll do you just as dead as one from . . . what's our boy's party . . . the Social Democrats, right?'

The com buzzed, and Njangu fielded it, listened, hung up.

'Speaking of which,' he said, 'we've got our pet candidate, ol' Dorn the Mouth and his aide pounding on the gangway. Shall we let 'em in?'

'Why not?' Garvin said, draining the beer and tossing it into the cycler. 'I don't guess we can just up our hooks and scamper, now can we?'

'Not until we find out if this guy we're suborning is honest and subornable, or some kind of goddamned counteragent,' Njangu said. 'Though I'm not much more fond of the idea of hanging around than you are.'

There was a knock at the door, Garvin touched the sensor, and a wide-eyed Dorn Fili, flanked by Brek, hurried in.

'Great gods,' Fili said. 'You people are dangerous!'

'I beg your pardon?'

'Dangerous and careful,' Brek said. 'I suppose you haven't heard about somebody blowing up a Constitutionalist headquarters an hour or so ago.'

''Fraid not,' Garvin said. 'We've been concentrating on

our own right now, and getting ready for poor Chapu's funeral.'

'They're saying over a hundred and twenty-five Constitutionalist workers were killed, and the attackers used rockets and fully automatic blasters, like the army has,' Fili said. 'I've heard of ten for one . . . but . . .' He let his voice trail off.

'Sounds like,' Njangu said to Garvin, 'there must've been some kind of industrial explosion, hmm?'

'Is that it?' Garvin asked innocently.

'This evening we were discussing whether or not we'd lose you,' Brek said, 'which we could easily understand, and were wondering if we could convince you to stay if we provided some of the security elements of our party.'

'Your circus has added a new note to the campaign,' Fili said. 'Adding holo bits of your various benefits has raised viewership on what otherwise might be considered nothing but political natterings, and we'd hate to have you leave before the victory celebration.'

'We're not leaving yet,' Garvin said. 'We made a deal, and we'll hold to it.'

'Good, good,' Fili said heartily. 'Especially the final rally for our party workers. That'll give them a huge morale boost for the last week of the campaign.'

'And, as I've said,' Brek added, 'you'll have full security cooperation from us.'

'We'll use you,' Njangu said. 'Outside the ship. No outsider with guns inside. Period.'

'You're certainly confident enough about being able to defend yourselves . . . and my workers . . .' Fili said doubtfully.

'We are,' Njangu said. 'Especially since if everyone's thinking that unfortunate accident had anything to do with us, that should calm the waters.'

'Don't be too sure,' Brek said. 'The Constitutionalists have been in office for a while, and they'll take some convincing to change their ways.'

Garvin remembered what Director Bertl had said about their having lost a sense of proportion . . . and then about the possible trail, so far the best they'd come across, toward Cumbre.

'No,' he said again. 'We're staying. Although there'll have to be a discussion about our fees.'

'Migods,' Darod Montagna said weakly, 'you certainly get passionate after action.'

She unwound her legs from Garvin's thighs, and he rolled on his side.

'Do I?' he said, running a thumbnail down her breasts and across her stomach.

She drew in her breath sharply.

'Can I say something? And then I've got a question.'

'Talk.'

'I won't be able to unless you stop kissing my nipples,' she said. 'First, is something I want you to know, that I'm not going to think that what we're doing has anything to do with anything other than what we're doing, 'kay?'

'Odin's birdhouse, but I'm glad you went and joined the army, so you could learn to express yourself clearly,' Garvin said.

'You know what I mean,' Darod said. 'Now, let me change the subject before you turn on the lights and see that I can blush better'n you.

'What're we going to do about these idiots here?'

'Nothing,' Garvin said. 'Finish our contract and go on our way.'

'I don't know what you and Njangu have got running . . . it's none of my business. But I think it blows *giptels* for the people of Delta to have nothing better than these two parties, who seem to pass the looting back and forth.'

'I figure it's pretty much the people's business to change things when they want,' Garvin said. 'Soldiers trying to play God end up getting themselves all screwed up.'

'Even if, say, Lir and I just happened to build this thingie that just happens to go bang? And we just happen to plant it in the capital building for next inauguration, which is a known time and date, and it's easy to set up a thingie with a long det fuse? And just when the old scum are giving things over to this Fili and his new scum, there's a real loud bang? Wouldn't that help?'

'You're forgetting about the Directors, who seem to be the power behind the throne,' Garvin said. 'And I really sound like I know squat from politics, don't I?'

'We could figure *something* out and get them, too,' Montagna said stubbornly.

'First one bang, then another, then we'll have to find a third bomb . . . like I said, here we'd go, playing holy redeemer,' Garvin said.

'Garvin, I'm trying to think, and while that feels good, especially there, I'll . . .'

'You'll what?' Garvin said muffledly.

'Try not to make as much noise coming this time,' Darod said, and moaned.

'We may have erred,' Director Bertl told his aide. 'All that little transmitter does is tell us about the ship's location.

'I would like to have better data about people as . . .

immediate . . . as these circus people. They seem much more than happy wanderers from a distant planet.'

'I wondered about that as well,' the aide said. 'And have something . . . or, rather, someone, ready to go.'

'As usual, you anticipate my thinking,' Bertl purred.

'Now, here's the hot setup,' Njangu told the assembled women and men. 'The Social Democrats, who we shouldn't have gotten in bed with in the first place, but it's too late to cry over spilt drugs, are giving us security out the gump stump.

'I've seen their assembled legions, and they're about what you'd expect from a bunch of politicos — mostly big apes with glowers and hair growing out of their ears. If they've got any smooth suckers, they're keeping them around the throne.

'But that's fine with us,' he said, winking at Maev, in the front row. 'Let them swirl about and attract any baddies' attention.

'You pros, you shooters, are going to stay invisible.

'Until the shit comes down,' he said, his good humor vanishing. 'Then we obliterate the bastards.'

'Here,' Garvin said, handing Njangu a tiny button.

'You shouldn't have. What is it?'

'Something that'll tell me of your every doing, your every nefarious move.'

'Mmmph.'

'Everybody who's a shaker, aboard, including me, gets one.'

'You're anticipating more trouble?'

'Maybe . . . or maybe I'm just trying to cover my ass in all directions,' Garvin said.

'But that's my job.'

'That's what cross-training is for.'

'I'm not sure I like anyone knowing where I am,' Njangu complained.

'Tough.'

'Where am I supposed to wear this?' Njangu inquired.

'In a pocket. Glued in your frigging navel. Up your ass for all I care.'

'These fiches here are very interesting,' Freron told Penwyth, standing in the middle of his apartment, which, if an ex-military sort hadn't fussed about it every once in a while, would've been a motherless clutter. Instead, it was a well-categorized mess.

'Ah?'

'This was one of my pet projects. I was ordered to begin it when I attended that intelligence course, as I've told you, and after that I added to the file.

'It is, I think, absolutely current as of ten years ago.'

Penwyth waited.

'It is the listing, I think very close to complete, of all mechanical warning and security devices that the Confederation posted around Centrum, the three other habitable worlds in the Capella system, and all nav points approaching it.

'Also, there's a listing of where the Confederation guard points were around Capella. I should think that would interest any historian.'

Penwyth noted Freron put ostentatious verbal quote marks around the word 'historian.'

'A historian, no doubt, would be interested. What would you be asking for your material?'

'My asking . . . and selling price is one hundred and fifty thousand credits.'

Penwyth covered a minor choke.

'I think that's reasonable,' Freron said, sounding a bit injured. 'Not only for the historian, but conceivably for someone concerned about current affairs. All of these mechanical devices were built on a single world, and they were self-modifying.

'It should be simple for someone to visit that manufacturing world, perhaps institute a relationship with the builders of these devices, and be given the program for the auto-upgrades, wouldn't it?'

Penwyth scratched his nose, had another snifter of the brandy he'd brought with him.

'You have an interesting mind, Kuprin. I'm amazed you didn't reach a higher rank than *T'ousan.*'

Freron smiled, a little bitterly.

'In those days, I was a bit more interested in gaming than was healthy. Star rank in Tiborg is given only to those who have no flaws. Visible ones, at any rate.

'Another thing a historian of the final days of the Confederation might value is this complete map of Centrum itself, focusing on the various military installations.

'That would be on the market for . . . oh, I don't know. Another hundred thousand credits.

'Or, perhaps, if I encountered a well-to-do collector, I might release the map and the data on the security systems for two hundred thousand.

'As long as we're thinking large,' he went on, 'I'd be happy to donate my entire collection of material on the Confederation for, oh, half a million.'

'What does the son of a bitch think we are, kagillionaires?' Garvin complained.

'I don't guess he knows about Jasith, now does he?' Njangu said.

'Sharrup,' Garvin said. 'Erik, can we bargain?'

'Don't think so, boss,' Erik said, enjoying Jaansma's reaction. 'He had a certain air of firmness to him. Oh yeh. He's also a cagey bastard. The fiches he was waving about are only partial files. The rest is nice and secure in a deposit box in a largish bank, whose name he wouldn't give out.'

'Why that duplicitous bastard!' Garvin snarled. 'What does he think we are? Burglars?'

'Untrusting sort,' Njangu agreed. 'And I was just about to ask Erik for the floor plan of his flat. Oh well.'

'At least,' Garvin said, 'I had the sense to jack our price way up to Fili and company.'

He put his head in his hands.

'First we got a circus in the middle of politics, which my family would disown me for doing, then we've got an antiquated traitor with too high a price tag . . . nobody knows the troubles I've seen.'

'Cheer up,' Njangu said unsympathetically. 'You know it's bound to get worse.'

Kekri Katun didn't have a voice so much as a purr Garvin thought. She was also the loveliest creature he'd ever seen, from her platinum hair, which seemed natural, to her perfect face, smooth skin, generous bust, and waist that was improbably thin.

He wondered how many credits and plastic surgeons had been spent making her what she was.

'Oh yes,' she said. 'I've been trained as a tumbler and acrobat for half my life . . . and I do believe in staying in shape.'

Without effort, she fell sideways, out of her chair, onto one arm, and hoisted herself up into a one-hand stand. Her light tan dress slid over her thighs, and Garvin thought, alarmed, that she might not be wearing anything under it.

'Now I could tell a funny story, recite a poem, sing a song from right here,' she said. 'I know a lot of songs, for I was on the road with a small troupe for five years.'

Very slowly, she put another hand down, opened her legs into a Y, did a pushup, then sprang up, landing on her feet, not a hair out of place, not a breath louder than normal.

'I also, since I understand you people of the circus work at other things besides your main talents, am an excellent bookkeeper, office manager, and, if it's needed, can do poses as well.'

'Poses?'

'That's something the clubs of Delta like,' she explained. 'Especially the older gentlemen, who won't admit they'd like to see a woman just take off her clothes.'

She touched fasteners, and the dress fell away. She *wasn't* wearing underclothes.

Garvin's mouth was very dry.

Katun struck a pose.

'This is Director Randulf, one of our heroines, as she appeared on her wedding night.'

'Uh . . .'

'This is *T'ousan* Merrist, when she fled the rebels. I know several dozen more.'

'Uh . . . yes. Very interesting,' Garvin said. 'You can put your clothes back on. We don't do anything like that.'

'Oh. I thought, coming up past the attractions outside—'

'That's called the midway.'

'The midway, and I saw all those banners with ladies not wearing much of anything . . .'

'That's Sopi Midt's operation,' Garvin said. 'He believes in going for the lowest common denominator and, by the way, he isn't ashamed to cheat a little. All of the girls in his shows never get down to their underwear.

'At least they better not, or I'll slaughter him.'

'And what's the matter with a little nudity? Especially among friends?' Katun said, sliding back into her dress, and half smiling at him, lips parted.

Garvin chose to change the subject.

'We're hiring all the time,' he said. 'Right now, we need a showgirl. And I'm sure the acrobats and the show-girls would be interested in your . . . talents.'

'I saw that murder on the holos. Poor girl.'

'But the problem is, we might not be coming back this way for a while.'

Katun shrugged.

'My father was a salesman with a big territory, and I really don't remember my mother. I'm used to being on the road.' Again she smiled her sultry smile. 'And I've never been offworld. Besides, for a girl like me, there's always a way to get back home.

'Or I can find a new one.'

'Uh . . . right . . . your com number's here on the application,' Garvin said. 'I'll . . . we'll be in touch within a day or so.'

Kekri Katun got up, slunk to the door, turned back, and looked at him.

'I think performing . . . with you . . . with your circus . . . is just about the most exciting idea I've ever known,' she breathed, and the compartment door slid closed behind her.

'Phew,' Garvin muttered, went for a beer, decided he needed something stronger and got out the brandy decanter. The door slid open again, and he jumped.

'Phew indeed,' Njangu said. 'She keeps herself nicely shaved, doesn't she?'

He found and opened a beer.

'So what are we going to do about her?'

'I'm just the security man,' Njangu grinned. 'Of course, you're going to hire her.'

'Why of course?'

'Because it's always good to have a spy right under your eyes.' Njangu snickered. 'Or thighs as the case may be.'

'Aren't we being a little hard on her? What's this spy business?'

'Not as hard as she'd like it to be,' Njangu said. 'Come on, Garvin. Get your head out of your crotch and back in gear. Women like her don't blow in your ear . . . or mine, either . . . because they think we're the best-hung items since the elephants.'

Garvin slumped down in his chair.

'Yeh. You're right. I was being dumb. You got any idea who she might be reporting to?'

'I could make a guess,' Njangu said. 'Since she didn't object to offplaneting, that'd suggest to me she's working for somebody with longer-range views than either Fili or who's that guy running for the Constitutionalists.'

'And the folks who've got long-range views would be—'

'The Directors?'

'Perzackly.'

'So why shouldn't we just tell her the position's filled?'

'Because they'll try again . . . whoever they are . . . maybe buying one of our roustabouts, maybe filtering another agent in,' Njangu explained. 'If they already haven't. We've had twenty-three people quit — all citizens, naturally, who decided they like Tiborg so far, and added, uh, about thirty of the locals. Not counting ol' Cooin' Kekri.'

'Hire her, then . . . oh yeh, do you have a tendency to talk in your sleep?'

'Not as far as I know.'

'Then turn her into our agent. Screw her black-and-blue, and get her singing our tune.'

'Or else I can pop a shot in her pretty little ass, and have her singing like a buzzard, telling us everything including what, specifically, that Director Bertl wants, and never realize it when she wakes up. Remember how they screened us when we joined the Force?'

'Yeh.'

'The first way's a lot more fun, by the way.'

'Uh . . .'

'I'll never tell Jasith,' Njangu said. 'And there's surely no other reason for you not to sacrifice your virtue for the Force, now is there?'

He smiled, evilly.

Garvin glowered, realized that he must know about Darod, probably the whole damned circus knew.

'She signs on,' Njangu said, 'and I'll have all her gear shaken, and make sure if she's got a com it won't work very well . . . and whatever she transmits goes straight into my security trap.'

'Come on, Garvin. Where's your fighting spirit? And weren't you the guy who was bragging, back in Grimaldi, what with all the midgets and freaks and Chinese acrobats, that this was starting to feel a lot like a real circus?'

'Circuses don't generally have spies,' Garvin said feebly.

'Then be innovative! Start a new tradition! You owe it to yourself!

'Besides, think of ol' Randulf on her wedding night.'

'It's all done with lights,' the little boy insisted.

'Of course,' Jiang Fong agreed.

'And . . . and mirrors,' the boy said.

'How clever,' Fong said. 'You must have a closer look.'

He picked the boy up from his lift and tossed him, spinning, shrieking, up to his wife, Qi Tan, balancing on her hands three meters in the air on a weaving forked pole. She caught him with her feet, tumbled him about, tickling him with a finger until he stopped screaming and started laughing, then tossed him from one hand to another as she swayed, then dropped him back down to Gang.

Gang set him breathless, back in his lift, and Jia Yin, just a meter high, walked up to him, balancing a tray with four bowls, another tray with glasses atop that, four other clear trays with tiny budvases and flowers in them, and, on top of everything, a huge vase almost as big as she held on her chin.

'Lights and mirrors, you said,' she piped. 'Would you like me to jump, and all these glasses will land in your lap? You and your liftchair will be very wet.'

'No, no,' the boy protested.

'But I am going to do it anyway,' and she jumped, and glassware cascaded, but somehow was caught, juggled, hurled back into the air and, in somewhat reversed order, balanced again.

The boy watched, fascinated.

'I wish I could juggle,' he said in a low voice.

Jia Yin heard him, leaned closer, still without spilling anything.

'After the show,' she promised, 'I will show you how easy it is.'

'Even for somebody who can't walk, like me?'

'Especially for someone like you, 'cause you'll pay closer attention.'

A thousand meters above the hospital, a Nana-class patrol ship orbited.

'All units,' *Haut* Chaka, who'd taken a three-rank reduction in rank to go with the circus, 'I've got me a good possible. Illuminating him . . . now!'

The other Nana boat and two *aksai* watched screens and the laser indicator flashing across them.

'He's been circling the hospital since we got here,' Chaka went on. 'No ID, no big journoh markings, so I put a viewer on him. Zoomed on in, and what we've got is a lim full of gunnies. One of the stupid bastards even waved his blaster or whatever it is around a little, enough for me to see. Over.'

'All Safety elements,' Njangu said into his com. 'This is Safety Leader. Suspect he's gonna go strafin' when this breaks up. Try for us, and if he gets some of the ankle biters we're being nice to, that won't matter.

'We'll take him out now. Lir . . . hit him. Gently. You *aksai* hot rods, track him. I want more than just a handful of dead punks. *Big Bertha*, get the third *aksai* in the air and homing on the other birds.'

Mikes clicked assent.

Below, hidden behind a clump of brush, Lir checked the sights on her Shrike launcher, set the missile's fuse to proximity detonate, turned the homing device off, aimed well off the lim, and fired.

The Shrike exploded twenty meters from the goon-wagon, and it spun, almost pinwheeled, then the pilot gave it full power, gunning away in panic.

'Tracking,' Chaka said, and the *aksai* followed at altitude, above the clouds.

The lim sped around the city, on north, to a spattering of islands.

'It's coming in for a landing,' Chaka said, and swept the area ahead first with radar, then with infrared.

'Looks like there's something down there,' he reported. 'Maybe a nice little landing field.'

All three of the *aksai* were orbiting below the Nana boat.

'This is Boursier One. I've got a visual flash through the clouds. It's a field, with, oh, ten or twelve lifters. A couple of them looked like they were armored, or anyway set up for some kind of police or military use.'

'This is Safety Six,' Njangu 'cast. 'Arm 'em up troops. I'd like a nice clean billiard table down there. Take out all buildings and anybody you happen to want to shoot at. Clear.'

The *aksai* inverted, and dived, pilots' fingers/claws blurring across sensors as the attack ships shot downward.

Boursier, firing lead, toggled half a dozen Shrikes.

The missiles blasted across the field as Dill and Alikhan swept in low, chainguns roaring. Lifters exploded, and one of the three hangars burst into flames.

Men ran out, across the field, toward the safety of the jungle or water. Few made it.

Boursier came back in, a solid wave of shells sweeping the field, and the last scattered small antipersonnel firebombs from two hundred meters.

Chaka brought his patrol ship down low and slow, thought two lifters were insufficiently damaged, donated a pair of Shrikes to the cause, then climbed.

'I don't see anything left to break, Safety elements. Let's go on home.'

*

Both Garvin and Njangu thought it was very interesting that there were no holo reports of the destruction of the airport.

'I guess it's not in anybody's best interests,' Njangu said.

'Which says something about this whole damned power structure, doesn't it?' Garvin said, a bit disgustedly. 'I should've given Darod and Lir the go-ahead.'

'To do what?'

'Never mind.'

'Men are nothing but hard dicks and no brains!' Darod Montagna stormed to Monique Lir.

'So what else is new?' Lir said, grinning. 'And what has the boss done to piss you off this time?'

'I just saw him walking outside the ship with that . . . that popsy he went and hired!'

'Isn't he entitled to walk anywhere with anybody he wants?'

'Not with her!'

'Hoboy,' Lir said. 'Darod, my young former Executive Officer, you are getting, like they say, your tit in a wringer. If you're all jealous that he's just walking with this Katun, what are you going to do when we get back to Cumbre, and you've got to realize he's sleeping with Jasith Mellusin?'

'That's different! She was ahead of me in line! She outranks me!'

'Hoboy twice,' Lir said.

'This Circus Jaansma has certainly paid for itself,' Dorn Fili said. 'I know the big rally night after this will get our workers to pour in their last bit of energy. Not to mention how it'll look on the holos.'

'The offworlders *have* done well for us,' Sam'l Brek agreed. 'But we're getting close to election day, and I keep thinking of all those credits we're giving them, and how I'd like to have them for a last-minute blitzkrieg.'

'Use the after-campaign funds we've got set aside for our supporters,' Fili said.

'I could do that,' Brek agreed. 'But that would leave our friends a bit angry. If only we had a way to recoup some of that circus money . . . mmh.

'You know, I think I've got the beginnings of an idea.'

'Could it get back to us?' Fili asked.

'Very doubtful, at least if I set it up right, with the correct people.'

'Don't tell me any more,' Fili said. 'Just do it.'

'Something interesting,' Njangu told Garvin. 'We did a thorough shake on your bimbolina's gear, and guess what we found?'

'A nifty little sender?'

'Nawp.'

'A serious interstellar com?'

'Nawp.'

'What did you get?'

'Nothing . . . except that your Kekri Katun has too much in the way of cosmetics, and interesting taste in lingerie.'

'Nothing?' Garvin said, a bit incredulously. 'What does that mean? She isn't a spy?'

'Don't get your hopes up,' Njangu advised. 'It just means that she's been trained a little better than I thought.'

Penwyth passed the com across to Freron, who heard the automated teller say he now had somewhere over half a million credits to his account.

Freron smiled pleasantly, took keys from his pocket, and gave them to Erik.

'The box is nine-eight-five-four, at the Military Banking Institute. It's quite large, so you might think of taking a confrere with you.' He gave the address, added that no one would bother anyone carrying the keys.

Penwyth went to the apartment door, opened it, and gave the keys, and where they were to be used, to Ben Dill. Two hulking roustabouts were behind him.

'Now,' Penwyth said, coming back and sitting down, 'we'll just wait here until my friend Ben says he's back at the ship safely.'

Freron sighed.

'I suppose, in this dirty business, no one trusts anyone else.'

'I trust you implicitly, Kuprin,' Erik drawled. 'I'd just like to hear a couple more stories about how it was, serving in a planetary force under the Confederation before I leave.'

'Everybody's on an Annie Oakley tonight,' Garvin told Sopi Midt. 'All political sorts, so don't rape them too badly.'

'Hadn't a thought of it. Naw,' Midt said, 'I'm lyin'. Always hated those bastards who think, 'cause they know which end of a ballot box to stuff, they're somethin' special.

'Still can't figure why you let them put us in their pocket.'

Garvin made a face. 'Maybe I was worried about the gate, this first time out for real. Sure as blazes not something I'd be doing over again.'

'Ah well,' Midt sympathized. 'So far, outside of that poor showgirl, nothing's gone awry. I'll tell you, I'm glad we've got their buckos doing security. My people've taken a dozen or more guns off floppies in the midway.'

'Any idea who they were working for?' Garvin asked.

'Di'n't ask. Somebody with a gun on my midway who ain't workin' for me is nothin' but trouble, so we disarmed them, give 'em a thick ear, sent 'em on their way.'

Midt leaned closer to Garvin.

'Got a suggestion, Gaffer, if you don't mind. Are you plannin' to stick around until election day?'

'I don't know,' Garvin said. 'I'm inclined to think not a chance.'

'Good. Good: Very good,' Sopi approved. ''Cause the minute the tab's taken, one side'll be thinkin' about revenge, believing we somehow turned the tide, and the other'll be trying to get out of paying us.'

'I've had the Social Democrats pay in front.'

''At's good,' Midt approved. 'Guess you *are* your father's kid.'

By dusk, the Social Democrats were thronging in from across the planet, and several ships had come in from other planets in the system. Garvin, looking out from the nose of *Big Bertha*, dimly hearing the band in the great hold below, was thankful for the outer screen of Fili's security people. This crowd, which promised to be a solid turnaway, was burying the ducat grabbers and circus security.

He looked at himself in a mirror, adjusted his white top hat, curled his whip under his arm, and, the picture of youthful dignity, went to the lift taking him to the center ring.

Overhead, several acrobats were tossing each other around, the *ra'felan* catching them. He saw Lir among them, doing a spinning twist, almost missing her catcher, and being swung back up to the trapeze.

The man was tall, skeletal, with short hair and neat beard. He wore a shirt blazoned FILI FOR PREMIER, as did most of the other entrants. The shirt was too large for him, which helped hide the gun and shoulder stock in his belt. That wasn't intended for the task he'd hired on for, but to ensure his own escape amid the hoped-for debacle.

There was a metal detector at the gangway, but there was a press around it, and it was easy for the man to side-step the device and enter the ship's hold with the happy throng.

Phraphas Phanon hadn't exaggerated when he said he might be able to come up with something more spectacular than Sir Douglas could envision.

After much rehearsal, they had a number.

A lion menaced Imp, one of the babies. Imp didn't see the trunk that took him around the waist, lifted him to safety on the top of another elephant. The lion reared, roaring.

On a howdah on a third bull, Sir Douglas cracked a whip, as two tigers leapt onto the howdah with him. His pistol cracked, and they cowered back, jumped to the back of another elephant, just as three bulls reared, paws together, and a fourth lifted Imp to safety as other cats darted around the center ring.

The audience was agape in amazement.

And that was just the opening.

Njangu Yoshitaro was prowling the midway, looking for any signs of trouble, when it found him.

He'd ducked behind a wheel of fortune stand, intending to cut back to *Big Bertha* through the back, avoiding the crowd.

Njangu had only a moment to notice a woman had followed him, turning to see what she wanted. The anesthetic dart snapped into his neck before he could draw his gun.

Two men followed the woman, carrying a long canvas roll that looked as if it belonged somewhere in the circus.

Njangu was rolled into the middle of it, and the men picked it up, and, moving without haste, went back down the rear of the midway, into the parking area, and slid the roll into a lifter.

Seconds later, the three were aboard and the lifter was airborne, heading for the capital.

NINE

'Welcome, welcome, Social Democrats of all ages,' Garvin chanted, 'to the finest show in the galaxy. We've got clowns and bears and lions and tigers and beautiful women, and men stronger than oxen . . . all brought to you by the good graces of Dorn Fili.'

The crowd cheered, and Garvin snapped his whip twice. As the clowns mobbed him, he tried to concentrate on the routine, but kept thinking that now, with Penwyth back with the loot from Freron . . . or what he hoped was loot, awaiting analysis . . . they could pull in their horns and get away from this mess.

'Unroll him,' the woman ordered, and one of the two men in the lifter obeyed. He turned on a small sensor, ran it around Njangu's neck, held it in front of his open mouth.

'Sleepin' like a babe,' he reported. 'Vital signs just fine.'

'He'd better be,' the woman said. 'The man said alive only. And that there'd be paybacks if we screwed up and killed him.'

'Who is he?'

The woman shrugged. 'One of the offworld mucketies.'

'So why'd these guys want him grabbed?'

'Hell if I know,' the woman said. 'Blackmail, I guess.'

You got any idea who we're working for?'

'Yeh,' the woman said. 'That's why I went double on the price. Political types. The ones who're doing the campaign right now.'

'But that don't make sense,' the man behind the controls of the lim complained. 'I thought this *auzlan* circus was hired out by them.'

'Nothin' nobody does in politics *ever* makes sense,' the man crouched over Njangu's unconscious body said. 'How long we gotta be nannyin' him?'

'There'll be somebody come get him as soon as we get to the dropoff point.'

'With the other half of our credits, I hope.'

'You think I'm some kind of virgin?' the woman growled.

'Groundnuts, popcorn, candy as soft as your dreams, poppers, everything for the young and old,' Maev chanted, moving through the stands, eyes constantly moving.

An old man waved a bill at her, and she pitched him a bag of nuts, and bill and change went back and forth down the line.

There were other butchers working the crowd – a few real candy salesmen, more security.

The bear operator turned as the thin man entered his tiny booth, near one of the entrances. He had time to gape before the man's blade went into his heart. The other operator had been waylaid earlier on the midway, his body dragged out of sight.

The man pushed the body under the console, examined the sensors. He'd come to the circus for eight nights running, watching only the robots, spending his days learning how to operate remote machinery.

This setup, he decided, pulling on the helmet that gave him perspective through the 'bear's' eyes, wasn't that different from what he learned. He would have no trouble carrying out his mission.

He touched sensors, and a small screen showed him the two bears in their unnecessary cage, just offstage. One, then another, stirred as he moved the controls.

One stood, waved its arms, walked back and forth.

The man was ready.

Danfin Froude, in his Kelly makeup, looked longingly at Kekri Katun, who smiled. He came closer and, expression filled with the world's woes, started to take her hand, did a pratfall, rolled back to his feet.

Katun didn't notice Ristori, who tumbled into view from nowhere, came up from behind, leering ostentatiously, eyebrows waggling insanely.

He started to touch her bottom, and she spun, caught him by his collar . . . actually the harness under his ragged clothes . . . and tossed him high up into the safety gravs.

Froude, looking even more unhappy, was slouched on the bench. Katun went to him, sat beside him, started stroking his hand.

Ristori sank down through the layered antigravs, crept back up on the pair.

This time, Froude moved first, grabbed Ristori, and they had a knockdown battle, hitting each other with fists, padded clubs, a huge ball, anything that came to hand.

Around them other clowns were bedeviling, and being bedeviled, by the other showgirls.

Kekri saw Ben Dill trot past, in his muscleman's outfit, considered him speculatively, then saw Garvin looking at her from center ring. She slowly, deliberately, smiled at him, and licked her finger. Garvin looked hastily away, and Katun laughed to herself.

These were nice people, she thought. But they weren't very efficient. Her control had said she would be searched, and so she'd taken nothing aboard *Big Bertha*. She'd used dusting powder, sprinkled here and there, as a giveaway, and found marks that confirmed her baggage had been searched.

This night she'd gone into the midway, as she'd been instructed, and been given a small, compact case by a man who approached her and whispered the code words she'd been given.

The case held a small, powerful com, capable of insystem communication. She wasn't sure how useful it would be, but assumed she would be signaled at a certain time by the pickup team she'd been promised would be trailing the ship, and given instructions on what she was to report on, besides any information about the circus's intent and mission she would be able to get from Garvin. There had to be a secret intention, since innocents would hardly have searched her gear.

Kekri Katun turned that part of her mind off, concentrated on cartwheeling and cheering for her champion, Froude.

At last Ristori was down, and Froude, after jumping up and down on his chest, picked up the tall woman, aided by a dropper he had hidden under his baggy coat, and carried her off in his arms, to cheers from the audience.

On the bridge of *Big Bertha*, a technician glanced at a screen, reacted. One of the tiny locators was moving steadily away, almost off the screen.

He bent over its controls, started tracking the locator, called for the watch officer.

'Have an ID on that?' the woman asked.

The tech keyed a sensor.

'Yes, ma'am. Yoshitaro.'

'Allat in a supporter! I better let the boss know . . . assuming that sneaky bastard isn't doing something nobody's supposed to know about.'

The officer went to another tech, had him key the emergency com that fed into Garvin's tiny earpiece.

'Can he lift it? No one has ever been able to press a thousand kilos, and Mighty Ben is going to attempt it here, now, for your amazement,' the talker brayed. 'Let's cheer for him, wish for him, put all our energies behind Dill the Human Powerhouse.'

Dill, wearing pink leotards, a half shirt, and chrome rings around his biceps, leaned over, took a breath, made sure the droppers hidden inside the enormous weights were on, then heaved. He got a couple of centimeters off the ground before the weights smashed down. Again he tried, and again, the crowd moaning in sympathy.

At last, every muscle bulging, he heaved the weights aloft, staggered back and forth, then, turning the droppers off, got out from under.

The weights crashed down, and the noise from this side ring buried the yips from the risley act in center ring.

Dill was about to bow, move into the finale of his act, when his earpiece burped, said, 'Post. Emergency!'

The talker gaped as Dill jumped out of the ring and went, at a dead run, toward one of the corridors into the ship, then he recovered and began improvising another spiel on the acrobats in the center ring bouncing each other about on their feet.

Other select I&R people suddenly quit their tasks or performance around the circus and went after Dill.

Security people throughout the ship stood by, waiting to find out what was going on.

Darod Montagna concentrated on staying on the back of her horses as the animals poured out of the ring, to thundering applause, wondering what the hell was happening.

She reflexively waved to the bear operator in his booth, a nice one who'd helped her curry some of the horses, a bit surprised to see him with his helmeted head in the open instead of glued to the screen in his booth. She was momentarily puzzled she got no return greeting, but guessed he was concentrating on the bears' turn, which came next.

'And now, the man who's brought you all here, the man of the hour, the week, the year, Dorn Fili, soon to be your next Premier,' Garvin shouted, and the workers in the stands were on their feet, cheering. He suddenly froze and cocked his head, eyes going wide as the transmission about Njangu came in.

Fili, beaming, waved to his campaign workers, let the cheers build.

The thin man touched sensors, and the robot that Njangu had named Li'l Doni got up, pulled his cage open, and ambled through the entrance, then dropped to his four paws, and started toward the center ring where Garvin and Fili stood.

*

'My friends,' Fili said, and his voice rolled around the hold, 'and you are my friends. Tonight we're celebrating, maybe some say a bit in advance, but I say . . .'

High above, swinging back and forth, waiting for the acrobats' second turn, Lir yawned, then saw the robot bear, moving at a run toward Garvin and the politician.

Something wasn't right, and Lir was cursing that she couldn't hide a gun in her skimpy tights. She dropped off the perch, fell, tucking, toward the safety gravs below, knowing she was far too late.

A little girl was looking through Maev's tray, trying to decide what she wanted, when Maev saw Li'l Doni.

'Here, kid,' she said, pulling the tray's sling off her neck. 'Take everything and have fun.'

Gun in hand, she hurried back to the aisle, and ran down it, toward the circus floor.

'. . . a little premature, but I'm confident that we'll see victory, only a week distant, and—'

The bear was ten meters away when Garvin, about to bow away and head for the emergency post, saw him. It came to its feet and shambled toward Fili, arms open for a crushing embrace.

Garvin's hand slid into his coat, came out with a small pistol. He shot Li'l Doni twice in the head to no effect, then tackled the bear from the side, knocking it down.

Raf Aterton, the music director, heard the beginning screams and shots, cursed and grabbed a trumpet from a musician, and blasted into 'Peace March.'

The other musicians goggled for an instant, then got it, and the ragged music swelled.

And everywhere on the ship the women and men of the circus went to full alert.

Li'l Doni rolled to its feet and went for Fili, who ran for a trapeze mast, found climbing rings, started up. Then Doni had him in its paws, and was pulling him down. Fili was screaming, and there were roustabouts there, with benches, poles, smashing at the robot.

Maev was behind the bears' operators' booth, pistol out. She snapshot, blowing most of the bear operator's helmet and head off.

The skeletal man convulsed, fell dead.

Li'l Doni went suddenly limp and fell, almost on one of the roustabouts, and Fili dropped on top of him.

Garvin checked the robot, saw no signs of activity, pulled Fili to his feet, and made sure the politician's throat mike was still live.

'Keep talking,' he shouted. 'Keep them calm. We don't need a panic.'

Fili, eyes wide, opened his mouth, then closed it, then opened it again, nothing coming out.

Erik Penwyth, dragging on a white formal jacket over the dark pants he'd worn to Freron's apartment, ran into the hold, clipping a mike to his throat.

'Clowns, clowns, clowns, we've got 'em, and we don't want them,' he shouted.

Behind him ran every clown in the circus, and behind them the tumblers. The clowns ran the length of the ring, then back, peeling off into the stands, the tumblers end-over-ending along the ring banks.

The audience was trying to see what had happened, if Fili was hurt, and finally his voice came back.

'Everything's . . . fine,' he said, his voice somewhat squeaky, then steadying. 'That was a little stunt that didn't work out right . . . I guess I should've known I'm not cut out for the circus, but look at my friends around me, who are.'

His laughter sounded almost real, and the crowd settled back a little. A clown lifter zoomed toward Fili, and he was buried in joeys as two men muscled the Li'l Doni's 'corpse' into it, lifted away. Another lifter was bundling the corpse of the thin man into it, unnoticed.

'Clowns,' Penwyth said, as Aterton batted his baton and the 'Peace March' died away. 'I promised 'em, you got 'em. Take one or two home with you, please. Next we've got the high-wire artists, and artists they are, braver women and men than I surely am.'

A flyer launched herself out, was passed by another, and a *ra'felan* at each pole caught them, spun them, sent them back the way they came.

Lir, climbing up, grabbed a trapeze, and started swinging, each time higher, pulling herself into a bird's nest, and the show was back to normal.

'I have them,' Boursier reported, her *aksai* banking high above the capital's center. 'Landing on the roof of a high-rise. Looks like an apartment building. They're carrying a bundle, and there's somebody waiting for them.

'They're inside. The guard's still on the roof, though.'

'Maintain patrol,' came the orders. 'There's a civvie lifter on the way with the alert team in it, blue-white, open top, who'll get close and case things.'

The ship's compartment was packed with I&R troops.

'All right,' Garvin said. 'We'll keep this short. Somebody . . . I don't know if it's the same somebody who tried to ice Fili or not . . . has just grabbed Njangu. We've got a location, will have details in a moment, and we're going after him, right now.'

He looked around the room.

'For starters I want you, Ben, Monique, not you, Alikhan . . . no, wait, I do want you on this, Jil — we might need a medic.' He hesitated, seeing Darod's eyes on him, didn't want to, but knew better:

'You, Montagna, you're in. And me. As for—'

A speaker crackled.

'Boss, I've got that lifter with the alert team patched through.'

'Go ahead.'

The lifter went noisily down the street, well below roofline. Faces stared out from the apartment building as the drunks inside yahooed and toasted anyone in sight.

'Got Njangu,' one of the drunks, part of the normal standby I&R team, in the lifter reported. 'Or his locator, anyway. The building's sixty stories high, he's down five from the top. Stationary, so I'd guess that's where they want him to stay for a while.'

'Received,' *Big Berlha*'s com center sent back. 'Take it up to five-zero, stand by for further orders. Chaka, if anyone from outside tries to interfere, take them out. Repeat, anyone.'

The mike clicked twice, and the lifter climbed away toward the orbiting Nana boat.

''Kay,' Garvin said. 'He's close to the top of the building, and there's a sentry. We'll have to land on the roof, take that guard out, plus anyone who's with him, and then—'

'Excuse me,' a polite voice said, and Garvin wondered who the hell let Jiang Yuan Fong, a civilian, into the compartment.

'I've been listening, and if Mr. Yoshitaro is being held in a high-rise, as that transmission indicates, and you evidently plan to rescue him, rather than possibly alert that sentry on the roof, would it not be wiser to make the initial entry through, perhaps, one of the windows on the side of the building with someone who has certain acrobatic skills? Such as me, and perhaps one of the *ra'felan*?'

Garvin thought for an instant, then nodded.

'Good. Have you ever used a gun, Mr. Fong?'

'A few times I have found it necessary to defend my family, so yes.'

'Fine. Somebody issue him a blaster, and somebody grab the nearest octopus. We'll deploy from one of our cargo lifters. Let's move!'

The last elephant trumpeted out the Back Door, and the lights came up.

'All out and over,' Penwyth shouted, 'and it's a wonderful evening, and we've never had a better audience.'

The band was playing for the blowoff, and all the remaining butchers were working the crowd hard.

A little girl's mother stopped an usher.

'Excuse?'

'Yeh,' the man said, then remembered his manners. 'Sorry, I meant yes, ma'am?'

'One of your salesmen left Mara with her entire tray of sweetmeats, and told her to take whatever she wanted. But we can't do that, and the woman never came back.

'What am I supposed to do?'

'Why,' the usher said, 'you've just been gifted with the entire tray.' He forced a smile down at the girl. 'Remember our circus always.'

'Oh, thank you,' the woman said. 'You're wonderful, all of you. I hope nobody was hurt in that accident.'

'No, ma'am,' the usher said. 'Everyone's fine.'

The girl, eyes wider than any *ra'felan's*, was borne away, and the security man, one hand close to the gun under his jacket, went back to watching the crowd.

The cargo lifter's hatch was open, and the team climbed inside. The huge *ra'felan* swung in easily, found a seat next to Alikhan. The alien wore the Musth combat harness.

Garvin, buckling his fighting belt on, climbed in front.

'Haul it on out,' he ordered, and Running Bear nodded. The hatches closed, the upper hatch on *Big Bertha* opened, and the lifter sped toward the capital.

'The game might be getting interesting,' Chaka reported. 'Another lifter, this one a posh sort of lim, came in on the roof, and the same guard greeted them.

'Two people out, went inside.'

Garvin turned down the lift's speaker.

'You heard what the man said. That's got to be either an interrogation team, or else they're pickup for Njangu. So we'll have to get in quick.'

'Three minutes out,' Running Bear said.

*

The cargo lifter orbited the high building below.

'Kay,' Chaka reported. 'Stand by for transmit of what I've got on the building to your screen.'

'Got it,' Garvin said.

'Two lifters on the roof. Two drivers per vehicle, plus the sentry. Our man's in the fourth apartment in – there's a gap between units you can make out from here.'

''Kay.'

'Your plan, sir?'

Garvin saw, on one side of the building, through heavy glass that ran the height of the structure, emergency stairs.

'You stand by and take out the lifters and their crew when I give you the word. We'll go in from the side, a story high so any noise we make doesn't carry.'

'Yessir.'

Garvin leaned over to Running Bear.

'Can you put it right next to that wall with the emergency exit, fifty-sixth floor, with our doors open?'

'One-handed,' Running Bear said, 'picking my nose. Depending on the updrafts.'

'Use both hands, and take us in naw.'

The AmerInd nodded, and the lifter dropped to a hover, its doors clamshelling up.

Garvin took a small tube from his belt pack, tore it open, and unrolled it. It was a thin, small, flat, shaped charge, about fifteen centimeters on a die.

'Mr. Fong, can you get across to that window and hang there long enough to stick this right in the middle of that window? It's self-adhesive.'

'I can do that.'

Garvin gave hasty orders as the lifter closed on the building, rocking as the rising night currents sent it swaying.

'Closer,' Garvin said, and Running Bear, teeth gnawing lower lip, obeyed.

Fong braced on the lifter's hatch sill.

'Now!'

Fong sailed across, landed on the tiny window ledge, slipped, knelt, had a hold with his free hand, and was steady. The patch went on the window center. Fong looked over his shoulder at the lifter, readied, and pushed off.

He missed the lifter, but a tentacle was waiting and swooped him back aboard.

'Do not tell my wife that happened,' he said, taking a deep breath. 'I need more rehearsal time, it is evident.'

Garvin, breathing harder than the acrobat, touched the charge's detonator, and it blew with a muffled thud. Glass cascaded in a silver shower down toward the street.

'Go!' Garvin ordered the *ra'felan*. The alien swung out; keeping a firm hold on the lifter, he had the shattered window ledge in two others, a sentient grapnel, then reached with his other two legs for the team members, passing them into the stairwell.

Dill and Alikhan, not waiting for the full team, went down one flight. The door was locked, but only for an instant as Dill grabbed the knob and tore it away. He muttered, fingers inside the slot, then the door came open.

By then, the others were around him, and they went down the corridor.

'Still out,' the distinguished-looking man in the gray coat said. Njangu Yoshitaro lay on the lavish apartment's couch, eyes closed, breathing easily, a gentle smile on his face.

'He'll be waking up any second,' the woman who headed the kidnap team said. 'I know my dosages. We do this for a living, you know, and corpses don't generally pay ransoms.'

'We'll wait until he comes to, if you don't mind.' He took a thick leather envelope from under his arm. Guns were in his, and his companion's, hand.

The woman's two partners moved to the side, their hands motionless, but near their pockets.

'You can count the money while we wait,' the distinguished man said.

'We'll do that,' the woman said. 'And you can put the artillery away. We're not people who go back on—'

The outer door crashed open, and horror was in the room, a furred monster bigger than a man, head sweeping back and forth, eyes red, a strange-looking pistol in one hand. It fired, and a huge bullet took the distinguished man in the center of his chest, blowing a head-size hole in it, the edges around the hole moving as strange gray insects swarmed, eating, in the wound.

Behind the monster came a woman wearing tights, a blaster in her arms. She fired, and the man's companion spun, went down. She fired again, and the woman's head was missing.

One of her partners turned to run, but there was nowhere to go, and a huge, balding man, growling rage, had him by the back of his clothes and hurled him against the wall, headfirst. There was a crack, and he fell, lay still.

The last man in the kidnap team had his hands up, babbling surrender. Garvin shot him twice in the chest.

Explosions crashed from above as Chaka strafed the lifters on the roof.

Mahim knelt over Njangu, felt for a pulse as other

members of the team started rapidly searching the corpses and room.

'He's alive. I'd guess—'

Njangu's eyes came up.

'Of course I'm alive,' he said in a furry voice, then looked about, yawning.

'What kind of a party are we having, anyway?'

TEN

Garvin took Darod aside as they got out of the lifter. Dill and Alikhan carried the stretcher with Njangu on it, Mahim beside it, toward *Big Bertha*'s dispensary.

He'd spent much of the flight going through the documents taken from the distinguished man and his companion's corpses.

'You said something once that you and Lir had an idea of a fiendish thingie that'd deal with matters in a rather drastic manner. Were you pulling my chain?'

'I don't kid about things like that,' Montagna said indignantly. 'Lir is the one who looked everything up, with my help. I think this whole frigging planet needs a little demolition.'

'That guy who looked like he was the boss of this little caper just happened to have a membership card in the Social Democrat party.'

'Nice world, like I said,' Darod said, trying to pretend she wasn't shocked. 'The guys who hire us try to screw us. Very nifty.'

'Yeh,' Garvin said. 'You also said something about knowing where to plant said fiendish thingie and the precise date it should come to life.'

'Certainly. A piece of cake.'

'Go to it. I've had enough of these idiots. Now and forever more.'

By dawn, the midway was broken down, and all of the circus's gear was loaded.

Big Bertha sat on the landing pad all that day, locks sealed, making no response to any com. All three *aksai* orbited ominously overhead, diving close to the two holo lifters that tried approaching.

At midnight, a small lifter came out of the ship, and flew at speed, nap of the earth, below any radar horizon, toward the capital.

It hovered for an instant over a great white building on a hill, and two women in black, with heavy packs, rappelled down to the roof of one of the buildings. They pried open a window and vanished inside.

An hour later, they came back out, and the lifter came in for a pickup, flashed back to *Big Bertha*.

The watchmen on the grounds of the Civic Palace never noticed a thing.

An hour before dawn, without clearance or notifying port authorities, *Big Bertha* lifted clear of the ground and left the Tiborg system forever.

ELEVEN

Cayle/Cayle IV

The Cayle system, once a prime Confederation ship-builder, felt to Garvin like an abandoned factory.

Three of the outer worlds were supposed to be mines for Cayle IV, the most habitable and the shipyard center, but *Big Bertha* detected activity on only one, and that slight.

Cayle IV was a gray world, Garvin thought, corrected himself: gray-green.

Great forests climbed snowy mountains, and the valleys were green, welcoming, in a wintry way. Most of the cities, gray stonework, were located along the planet's wide rivers.

Landing fields on the planet were lined with finished or half-completed star craft of various Confederation types, some flecked with rust in spite of anticorrosion coating.

Njangu found some ancient lines coming as *Big Bertha* closed on the planet, didn't remember where he'd heard or read them, nor the poet's name:

'*My mother took me to the cities while I lay*
Inside her. And the coldness of the forests

Will be with me till my dying day.'

'What're you muttering?' Garvin asked.
'Poetry.'
'Didn't sound like it rhymed,' Garvin said suspiciously. 'Couldn't be very good.'
'Probably not.'

Big Bertha made three orbits around Cayle IV, broadcasting, on all open and approved frequencies, circus music, the roaring of the big cats, the trumpeting of elephants, and the ballyhooing of talkers, until only the deaf and reclusive didn't know that the circus was in town.

The Nana boats swept over the main thoroughfares of the major cities, scattering broadsides in all directions. Garvin cheerfully took complaint coms from city officials, promising to pay any fines levied for pollution, preferably in free passes.

Aksai compounded the felony, to the greater rage of politicians and the glee of children, low-flying the cities with long banners that, as the day turned into night across the planet, self-illuminated, flashing:

LIONS!! BEARS!! TIGERS!! ELEPHANTS!! EARTH
HORSES!! BEAUTIFUL LADIES!! STRANGE
ALIENS!! ACROBATS!! STRONGMEN!! CLOWNS!!
DEATH-DEFYING FEATS!!

Announcing their intentions on the last circumnavigation, *Big Bertha* orbited the capital city of Pendu three times, then, on secondary drive, slowly flew to the nearby field and settled in for a landing.

Crowds swarmed in, and spotlights caught the monstrous ship as it grounded.

Civilian lifts overflew the ship, to Captain Liskeard's mutterings.

The main lock's ramp slid out, and clowns and little people tumbled out. Garvin, in white formal, accompanied by Kekri Katun, wearing a white outfit that cast flashing, multicolored lights and covered no more than absolutely necessary, came out to meet the hastily assembled dignitaries, including the planet's ruler, *Graav* Ganeel, a mournful-looking middle-aged man with a bit of a belly. Garvin thought it interesting the head honcho himself would appear, suggesting just how much interstellar travel was current these days. Njangu, on the other hand, noted Ganeel showed up with only one aide and one driver/bodyguard. Either he wasn't an autocrat, or else everything was a lot more under control than Tiborg.

Everyone welcomed everyone, and Garvin said how thrilled they all were, and they would make sure this was an event for the ages.

Before dawn, Erik Penwyth had rented a huge open area on Pendu's outskirts and the heavy lifters, carrying canvas, the midway booths and the flying squadron, shuttled back and forth, and roustabouts set to.

Early risers – lot lice – began gathering, and if it was a school day – Garvin had forgotten to check – officials would have been frothing at the mouth. If, of course, they weren't lining the streets together with what seemed to be every kid on Cayle, as lifters swept back and forth, proclaiming the Parade Is Imminent.

It was.

Animals in their lifter cages, elephants on foot, horses prancing, with Montagna, Kwiek, and his pair of wives, not to mention a scattering of midgets, clowns afoot, in lifters, in strange, old-fashioned wheeled vehicles, tossing candy as they went, Aterton's band in a pair of lifters, Dill the strongman, the showgirls posing, acrobats rolling, tumbling amid the procession, and Garvin in front, standing in an open black lim, face utterly blissful.

In the backseat was Njangu, and, crouched out of sight, two marksmen – just in case.

They reached the lot without incident, as the tents were being guyed out.

Garvin stepped out of the lim as it grounded, bowed to the flatties watching, in some awe, and sniffed.

'I love the smell of canvas in the morning,' he said happily.

The circus was, indeed, in town.

By late afternoon the circus was sold out for a week, with more ticket orders avalanching in.

'It appears as if there's nothing much to do around these parts,' Njangu said, looking at numbers flash across screens in the 'red wagon,' actually a compartment aboard *Big Bertha*, but 'wagon' was traditionally the name for a circus's money center.

Sopi Midt grinned. 'It looks that way, indeed. Look at all that alfalfa roll in. Damn, but I wish Jaansma would let me run my games wide open. I could really show the gilly-galloos a good time.

'Do you know how rich we'd be?.' He looked hopefully at Yoshitaro.

'Sorry, Sopi,' Njangu said. 'Into each life some honesty must fall.'

'And now, our aerialists of acclaim, known galaxywide, flyers and their strange alien companions, who train secretly on dark worlds far from Man's reign,' Garvin intoned. The band played, and the flyers soared across the roof of the tent, *ra'felan* catching them, and the trapeze artists and cloud-swingers went back and forth as holo images flashed here and there just above the crowd.

Garvin bowed, himself off to spray his throat, wishing he didn't get as excited as all those kids in the hastily erected cattle-guard seats in front of the general admission bleachers. A little calmness would be easier on his vocal cords.

Darod was waiting for him outside the center ring.

'Better stick around, Garvin,' she said, handing him a jug of energy drink. 'Monique's trying a new one, and it's gonna be radical. If it flies, she's gonna want an intro next time.'

'How dangerous?'

'A lot more than it looks,' Darod said.

'Wonderful.' He knew there was no stopping Lir, however. He drank deeply from the jug, put his arm around Montagna, who snuggled closer.

The band segued into a *galop*, as Monique trotted into the center ring. Fleam grabbed a line that ran down from fifty meters up the center pole, another worker sledge-smashed an iron stake into the ground, and two others pulled the rope taut, hitched it to the pole.

Aterton waved the band to silence, except for a snare drum's snarl, and the tent lights went down as a pinspot picked out Lir.

'I wish she'd told me she was planning something,' Garvin whispered. 'I do like to be kept up on things.'

'She didn't want to bother anybody until she'd got it down,' Darod said.

'I love this,' Garvin said, a bit grimly. 'She's outside the damned safety grabbers. What's she got in mind, anyway?'

Monique answered his questions by picking up a long balance pole and starting up the angled rope, gripping with her toes through the slippers she wore.

Garvin found his lips were getting dry, drank again.

The pole flailed, and Lir wavered, then caught her balance, continued on, getting closer and closer to the center pole. Then she was a meter away, bounced twice, flipped the pole away, and backflipped clear of the rope.

The crowd shrieked, and then a long tentacle swept down, and one of the *ra'felan* had her, flung her toward the top of the tent, and another alien caught her, and pitched her to a catcher whose bar was at the top of its swing, Lir spinning knees up in a ball, as she went.

Monique had the catcher by the hands, let go, flipped again, had the catcher once more, and was safely on the bar.

Garvin realized he hadn't been breathing for a while. He sucked in air.

'That,' he said, 'is some trick. But I wish she'd told me about it so I could spiel it.'

Or, he thought, *break her lovely little goddamned thumbs for considering it*.

'As I said, she didn't want to make a big thing out of it if it went awry,' Darod said.

'Supposing it had,' Garvin asked, not really wanting to know. 'What would she have done? Quietly eaten sawdust?'

'If you look over there, back of the bandstand, next to where the bear handlers are supposed to be, if we ever get them trained,' Darod pointed, 'she's got a man with an antigrav projector.

'She thought he'd have time to get her lined up before she hit.'

'*Thought*,' Garvin snarled. ''Kay. We got a star turn

here. But we're gonna put in the safety gravs before she does that one again. Hide 'em under one of the elephant stands maybe. But I am not going to have me a flattened flyer, period. No more "I think it'll work."

'And you can tell her from me that's an order. She's still in the goddamned Legion. And I still outrank her sorry ass. You might want to remind her of that.'

Garvin was strolling the midway quite happily early the next morning. Let Njangu worry about security, he had decided. It did everybody good to get out of that damned ship and its recycled air. So the canvas smelled a little stuffy — that'd wear off in a week.

He passed the cat cages. Muldoon, the killer leopard, was lying on his back, playfully pawing at some kind of flying insect two meters over his head.

Montagna, who'd spent the night in Garvin's arms, was earnestly working on some new routine with two horses, while Ristori had a dozen clowns sweating, trying to fit into a barrel that logically would only take one.

He rounded a corner, and saw a medium-size man with a potbelly scratching Loti, the baby elephant with a stick, and deep in conversation with Phraphas Phanon, one of the elephant handlers, while Sunya Thanon had six others in a corral, crumbing them up with a bucket of soap and a long-handled brush. Garvin, as he approached, recognized the tubby man as *Graav* Ganeel, Cayle's ruler.

He wasn't sure how to greet the man, settling for a quick bob of the head.

'No, no,' Ganeel said. 'I'm the one who should be kowtowing. Fascinating, listening to my friend Phraphas talk about the world he's seeking, this Coando. Unfortunately, it's not one I've heard of.

'I will, however, talk to some of our savants, and see if they can help.'

'Speaking of help,' Garvin said, 'I would like to ask a favor of Your Highness. I suppose that's the correct title.'

'It is, if you wish,' Ganeel said, looking a bit alarmed. 'You've got to remember I'm a constitutional monarch, only the third in succession, and really don't have much authority.

'So if you want someone executed, or put in an iron maiden, whatever they were, you'll have to go through Parliament.'

Garvin, assuming he was making a joke, laughed, then cut it short seeing Ganeel's serious expression.

'No, no,' he said, 'nothing like that.'

'If you'll excuse me,' Phraphas said, 'I go to help my partner wash our friends.' He bustled away, clearly not wanting to hear gaffer's business.

Jaansma and Garvin strolled away.

'The favor I need,' Ganeel said, 'is your help with our navigational files. I would like for our tour to finish on Centrum.'

'Ambitious,' Ganeel said, sounding impressed.

'Perhaps,' Ganeel said. 'But I . . . and the rest of my troupe . . . would like to find out what happened, why our worlds are out of contact with the Confederation.'

'You, too,' Ganeel said. 'Have you seen our thriving starship "industry," for want of a weaker word? And all the ships contracted for by the Confederation, but never picked up or paid for.'

'I've seen them,' Garvin said. 'Why haven't you sent salesmen out looking for new customers?'

'Our contracts were almost always with the Confederation,' Ganeel said. 'We've sent a few ships out, with but one returning from an outer system, and that one reported chaos, with no one having the Confederation credits to do business with us.'

'That's pretty much what we've found,' Garvin said. 'And we'd like to do what we can to maybe start opening communications again.'

'A circus?' Ganeel said, with a bit of incredulity. 'Admirable, but isn't that a bit romantic?'

'When I said "we,"' Garvin explained, 'I meant some of the worlds we come from, or have visited. If people knew what had happened, why the sudden collapse, perhaps there's something that could be done to prevent a total interregnum.'

'I can explain one part of the fall,' Ganeel said, 'being a bit of a historian before my father died early and gave me the throne.

'The collapse didn't happen as quickly as most think. Rather, the Confederation was held up long past its time by force of arms . . . the remarkably efficient military the Empire had . . . plus the fact many planetary governments could lay off their problems on the distant Confederation.

'But the final, real reason was that all too many of the Confederation's citizens wanted the Confederation to be there, even while they were unwilling to participate in its government, reluctant to pay taxes or provide service. Because they imagined it was immortal, the Confederation was able to stumble on for years, decades, perhaps a century even, a walking corpse.

'And then, one day, something happened, and the corpse stumbled over a twig and fell.'

'What?' Garvin asked.

'I wish I knew,' Ganeel said. 'Because then, as you suggest, it might be possible to reanimate the body.'

He shrugged. 'I do not know. I simply do not know.'

They admired the Chinese acrobats for a moment, walked on.

'I don't either,' Garvin said. 'Which is what I'm trying to end. I want to find out what happened. Which is why I need a favor of you.'

'You may ask.'

'I've found out that Cayle provided many of the security apparati of the Confederation.'

'We did,' Ganeel said reluctantly.

'If the Confederation has collapsed, some of those machines and posts may be still manned and dangerous, or roboticized and even more deadly. I would like to borrow . . . or purchase if I must . . . your files, so I can access these machines and convince them I'm friendly when, or rather if, we're able to reach the Capella system.'

'They were highly classified,' Ganeel said.

'They were. Ten years or more gone.'

Ganeel looked vaguely frightened.

'I don't know,' he said, then brightened. 'But in any event, I wouldn't be able to provide them, since those data were not state secrets, but rather held by the manufacturer.

'That would be Berta Industries,' he said. 'Some say,' and he faked a laugh, 'that, at their peak, they were the real rulers of Cayle. Perhaps so, perhaps no.'

'Would you be willing,' Garvin asked, 'to forward my request, perhaps with your approval, to whoever heads Berta Industries? In return, if I reach Centrum, I'll happily provide you with what I've found out, as I return.'

'Berta Industries,' Ganeel said, and a look of mild fright crossed his face, then he firmed his lips.

'Yes,' he said. 'Yes, I'll do that. *That* woman can't kill me, after all.'

Garvin noted the emphasis. Ganeel changed the subject, asked why there were no primates – other than human. Garvin explained that he'd always hated the smelly, flea-bitten, dangerous apes that seemed to echo all the worst habits of man.

'Indeed,' Ganeel said. 'I've always been interested in them, although I admit I've seen nothing but holos. The last Earth monkey died almost four hundred years ago in our zoo, and somehow was never replaced.'

'Look at this,' Monique stormed, pointing to a boxed poem on the inside page of a holo.

> *'There's a legend about*
> *That her legs, arms, hands*
> *Are wrought iron*
> *Like we build ships from*
> *She's a woman of miracles*
> *Of strength and skill*
> *Our Monique, our Monique.'*

'Damn,' Ben Dill chortled, 'it surely is nice to be around someone famous.'

'Famous my left tit,' Lir growled. 'You show up tonight, and see what kind of famous I am.'

Ben did.

One entire stand, directly in front of center ring where Monique did her rope walk, was packed with women, all cheering for Lir.

Monique tried to ignore them, couldn't, especially when Garvin made her do a curtain call directly in front of those women. Dill saw that many of them were dressed in fashions more characteristic of the men of Cayle.

He thought the matter exceedingly funny, suggested

that Lir should start associating with her fan club more.

Monique told him, quite explicitly and obscenely, to shut his yap.

'I don't see why you're taking that attitude,' Njangu said reasonably. 'Look at it this way. You always had admirers who were men, right? Now you've just doubled the available talent who want to kookookachoo you under the chin.'

Monique growled incoherently, climbed high into the big top, and worked out her discomfort doing endless planges, swinging over and over, one hand and wrist in a loop.

'I could stand a beer,' Maev said. She and Njangu had gone into Pendu with a couple of quartermasters on a larder-restocking run.

'As well as not,' Yoshitaro agreed. 'They'll be haggling over flour prices for another two hours in there. 'Sides, investigating them barrooms is a big part of our exciting life as intelligence operatives, right?'

Two blocks down, they found a store that, from its signs, would sell something in bottles.

From the midday sun they went in, blinking into the darkness inside. Maev's eyes adjusted first.

'Uh-oh.'

Then Njangu could see.

'Indeed uh-oh.'

There were only two or three men of the thirty or so people in the bar. The women all wore costumes, various changes on ancient schoolgirl uniforms.

And all of them were smiling their most inviting best.

'I think,' Njangu said, backing toward the door, 'I just found out what a slab of meat feels like when Sir Douglas tosses it into the cats' cage.'

'Strange planet, this,' Darod managed.

'Yeh,' Njangu agreed, breathing a sigh of relief as they went back outside. 'Looks 'kay on the outside, but . . .'

'Maybe a little strange?' Maev suggested. 'Or do all men have the secret desire to boff kids?'

'Not one of my kinks,' Njangu said. 'Maybe it's something peculiar to Cayle. Look. There's a bar with tables outside. That'll give us running room in case we mess up again.'

Njangu inquired, found out from a local they'd just wandered into the Rot District, one of the larger ones in Pendu. 'Anything, I mean anything, can be found there,' the Caylean said enthusiastically. 'Or, since you seem interested, you can also com and they'll come to you.

'Some of us were wondering why your circus hasn't offered such entertainment.'

'Uh . . . 'cause we're shy folks,' Njangu managed.

The pair of midgets caught Darod as she came off the hidden antigravs and spun her up just as her horse trotted by.

The band changed tempo, and the horse began dancing, quick little steps in time to the music.

The faces in the seats beyond were blurred as she concentrated on keeping balance and moving with the animal. She felt the world, whatever was going on with Garvin, swirl away, and let herself be lost in the moment.

YOU AND A COMPANION ARE INVITED TO DINNER AND, ON THE FOLLOWING DAY A TOUR OF HER ESTATE AND WORKS BY LADY LIBNAH BERTA, SIX DAYS HENCE. TRANSPORTATION WILL BE PROVIDED. REPLY COM 34532

*

'*Graav* Ganeel came through. So I abase myself, and beg access to her records, right?' Garvin asked.

'Exactly,' Njangu said. 'About time we got some real Intel work out of you, instead of you just prancing about in your formal and snapping that stupid whip.'

'I guess Darod'll be thrilled,' Garvin said.

'Uh, no,' Njangu said. 'I want you to take Kekri Katun.'

'Why?'

'We shook her once,' Njangu said, 'and found *giptel* shit. I want to do it again, and have her out of the picture long enough to do a thorough job,' Njangu said.

'You aren't making my life any easier,' Garvin said.

'If that's true,' Yoshitaro said, 'why are you smiling? Masochism?'

'Guess that's what it must be,' Garvin said.

'I am never going out on this stupid planet again without a bodyguard,' Monique Lir snarled. 'Two bodyguards. Both hairy and male.'

'Why?' Darod asked. 'What happened?'

'I accept an invitation to be interviewed by this journoh, or anyway I thought she was a journoh. Turns out, she's the one who wrote that stupid goddamned poem about me.'

'Oh,' Darod said.

'Yeh,' Monique said. 'Name was Lan Dell. Wore a leather jacket and smoked this big tube of some kind of weed or something that stank up the whole lift.

'She says she's more comfortable in a club than an office, and so we end up in this bar. Filled with nothing but women, and this woman says they're my fan club.

'Fan club, in the name of Loki's pizzle! And so instead of being interviewed, I'm given this mike, and everybody's throwing questions at me.

'And the questions get real personal.

'And Dell starts stroking my knee, under the table.'

'What're you so upset by?' Montagna said. 'Can't be the first time someone as pretty as you got hit on by another woman.'

Monique looked perplexed.

'Yeh. 'Course you're right. Hell, I can even think of a couple of female officers in the Force who've been concerned about me sleeping alone. And I surely know how to handle men.

'I dunno. It can't be because we're in a strange place . . . I grew up all over.'

She thought about it for a bit.

'Maybe,' she said slowly, 'maybe it's because I felt, with that Dell woman, like I was in a zoo. Or a circus.'

'You are,' Darod said.

'I know, douche! Not that kind of circus. It was like everybody was waiting for something, for me to be the entertainment, and if I'd gone off with this Lan Dell that would've been some kind of victory for them.

'I dunno,' Lir said again, and lapsed into silence.

The circus was half-empty that night. Njangu made a few com calls, and found out there'd been a riot in the city, and transport was screwed up.

'Remember,' he asked Garvin, 'there were riots on Centrum when we were passing through, back when we were ree-cruits?'

'I do, and damned if I don't wish you hadn't reminded me.'

Froude came to Garvin the next day, with a stack of printouts.

'How long,' he asked, 'do you anticipate our being here?'

'Not long,' Garvin said. 'I've got a meeting tonight, and hopefully I can find a way to start feeding you the Centrum data we came here for.'

'Good,' Froude said. 'This world is not a healthy one, and I'd just as soon be gone.

'I happened to check the books, and things are not at all well.

'We take local currency, like we did back on Tiborg, and then convert it into Confederation credits. Failing that, we'll take interstellar credit transfers, right?'

'Of course,' Garvin said.

'The bookkeepers had a wad of the local money, and went to change it. No can do, the answer came back,' Froude said. 'They don't seem to have any credits . . . or, what they do have is being kept out of circulation.'

'By whom?'

'Some say the government. Some say this big industrial firm that's run by the Berta family.'

'Which I'm seeing tonight,' Garvin said.

'Maybe you ought to try to get the key to their vaults, then.'

'We aren't on this mission to make money,' Garvin said.

'I'm aware of that,' Froude said irritably. 'But I'm also aware we'd just as soon play nice, stable worlds.

'You want some other statistics? I did a little cheap research. Planetary employment is about thirty-five percent. A lot of people have flat given up looking for work and ride on the dole. The government doesn't seem to have any kind of restraining or any other plan, other than keeping its fingers crossed and hoping, one day, someday, the Confederation is going to reappear, buy all those parked starships, and whoopie do, it'll be pink clouds and happiness again.

'Not good,' Froude finished. 'As I said, let's get our business done here and get on our way.'

Garvin looked out the lim window as it climbed over a mountain. Below was a wide valley, with a large town in its center and factories spread out along the river.

He remembered the poem Njangu had quoted as they approached, said, 'Surely looks cold out there.'

'But it's nice and warm in here,' Kekri Katun said. She was absolutely perfect in a gray traveling suit and knee boots, although Garvin thought, purely for propriety's sake, she could have done up a couple of the blouse buttons.

'Landing in five minutes, sir,' the lim driver's voice said through the intercom.

'A question,' Garvin said into the mike. 'All these factories are part of Berta's holdings?'

'This valley, including the towns, and four other towns downriver that can't be seen in this haze,' the driver replied, 'are indeed *part* of the family's possessions.'

'It must be nice to be that rich,' Kekri said. 'I've always wanted to be rich. Then there's nothing to worry about, is there?'

'I wouldn't know,' Garvin said. 'All I know is whether you're rich or poor, it's nice to have money.'

He checked his appearance carefully. He hadn't thought, if Lady Berta was the muckety he'd been told, she would likely approve of his white-on-white-on-white ringmaster garb, and had chosen a conservative dark blue jacket, white shirt, and dark brown pants.

The lim braked, banked left.

Atop a low plateau, just where the town ended, a great mansion rose. It was ugly, a huge, seven-story rectangular box with a flat roof, no attempt being made with

architectural niceties. Atop the roof were various antennae and, Garvin was fairly sure, a standard electronics
suite for an antiaircraft missile site. Gardens spread
around it, all carefully designed and manicured.

The lim grounded in front of the mansion's steps, the
clamshell roof lifted, and the driver was out, offering
Kekri a hand.

The mansion's arched doors opened, and a woman who
could only be Lady Libnah Berta came out, unaccompan-
ied by any servants, to Garvin's surprise.

Berta was a big woman, big all over, easily two meters
tall. She was, Garvin guessed, in her eighties. Her face
was lined with the marks of power, and her lips easily
pursed in anger. Her hair was pure white, drawn back in
a bun, and she wore a long green skirt with red piping
and a matching long-sleeved jacket, a frothy white
blouse under it.

'Good evening, Gaffer Jaansma . . . and Miss Katun.'

She looked Kekri up and down once, then turned her
full attention to Garvin.

'Please be welcome to my home.'

'I'm grateful for the invitation.'

A wintry smile came, went on Berta's face.

'*Graav* Ganeel and I go back some years,' she said. 'In
fact, I remember . . . or claim to remember, at any rate,
dandling him on my knee when he was a toddler, while
I talked to his father, the king.

'When I remind him of that,' she went on, her smile
getting a touch broader, 'it seems to put him off his
stride a bit.'

She didn't need to add, and therefore easier to do business with.

'Come in,' she said. 'There's a chill in the air. I'll have
someone bring your bags in, and escort you to your

chambers. After you refresh yourselves, perhaps you'd join me in the library for a predinner drink.'

As they entered the huge house, Garvin noticed that somehow Kekri's blouse buttons had been done up.

The rooms they were shown into on the sixth floor were enormous, and rococo in their decoration.

'I feel like I've just dropped back in time,' Kekri said. 'Maybe a hundred years.'

'Maybe a thousand for all of me,' Garvin said.

The paintings on the walls were realistic, heroic, soldiers posing bravely in ancient suits, armored and space, there were horned animals at bay, wistful maidens watching their heroes go off to war, the colors starting to brown to match the fading archaic wallpaper. The chairs were soft, overpadded, with tassels at their ends. The tables were dark, highly polished wood, and the wall mirrors trimmed in gold.

The bed . . .

Kekri giggled.

'What did you tell them when you responded to the invitation?'

'I didn't tell them anything,' Garvin said truthfully. 'They said a companion, and I thought—'

'One bed? Shame on you, Gaffer Jaansma,' Kekri said. 'Bringing me out here in this howling wilderness, planning to take advantage of me, no doubt.'

'No, no. Honestly,' Garvin said, feeling about fifteen years old. 'Let me get ahold of that old fart who brought us up here, and see about getting you another room that—'

Kekri came up to Garvin, put her hands on his elbows.

'I really don't mind,' she said in that purr. 'I'm sure you're a man of high moral resolve. Certainly two people can share a common bed without anything happening. And if not . . .' She broke off, giggled. 'I guess we should be glad you didn't come here with Mr. Yoshitaro. I wonder if Lady Berta is *that* broadminded.'

Garvin began to step back.

'As long as we're here,' Kekri murmured, lifting her head, eyes closed, lips parted.

Jaansma would have been somewhat less than mortal if he hadn't kissed her. Her tongue went in his mouth, curled back and forth for a time.

When she slowly broke away, Garvin felt a little dizzy.

'Speaking of your friend,' Kekri said, 'I've got to be honest and say that he frankly scares me a lot. His eyes seem to look quite through you.'

'You want to know something even scarier?' Garvin said. 'If you told him that, he'd probably take it as a compliment.'

Kekri grimaced, sat on the bed, bounced.

'Changing the subject . . . Real feathers,' she said. 'That might be interesting.'

Garvin took a step toward her.

'No, no,' Kekri said. 'You take your bag, and go into that bathroom there and change. I don't think Lady Berta would like being kept waiting . . . at least not for very long.'

She giggled again.

'Besides, this will give you something to look forward to. Maybe.'

Garvin changed into ankle boots, slightly flared black slacks, a white shirt with black studs under a black monkey jacket.

Kekri came out of her bathroom wearing a sheath gown, with a jacket over it, both in sequined white.

'And aren't we both beautiful,' she said, holding out her arm.

He took it and they went out, down cavernous corridors, to the lift, down to the enormous hall that led to the library.

Inside there were holos, reels, shelves of ancient real books, maps of other worlds, portraits of stiff, dedicated-looking men and their noble wives, no doubt the lineage of the Bertas.

Libnah Berta greeted them, and a waiter took their drink orders. Kekri asked for pale wine, Garvin for a brandy with a glass of ice water that he planned to nurse forever, and Berta, without asking, got a tall glass full of multicolored liqueurs.

She asked them, as if she really cared, what they thought of Cayle, and was pleased they liked it so much.

Berta had two more of the spectacular drinks, Kekri another wine, and Garvin no more before they went in to dinner.

'I know it is considered rude to talk business over a meal,' Berta announced. 'But I have almost no other life, so forgive me.

'Also, I'm fascinated with various aspects of your most unusual profession.'

Her questions were penetrating, and it seemed she actually was interested in circus life – at least the financial aspects of it.

The meal was spectacular, in a very old-fashioned way – a consomme to begin, an assortment of grilled, breaded small fish, a roast in a rich, cream-looking sauce with sautéed vegetables, a mixed salad, and finally a dessert, flaming on the outside, frozen on the inside.

'I certainly hope you don't eat like this every night,' Kekri said. 'If you do, I want your fitness regime.'

'Of course I don't,' Berta said, with a laugh that sounded programmed. 'In fact, my advisors are generally unhappy with me for not eating at all when I'm working on a specific project.'

With each course came a different wine that Garvin barely tasted, and Kekri, to Jaansma's approval, took no more than a sip of. Berta drank heartily from each bottle and was completely unaffected.

Meal finished, she led the way back into the library, settled Garvin with another brandy, Kekri with a liqueur, and had another of her multicolored drinks.

'Now then,' she said as she settled back, 'why exactly, did you want *Graav* Ganeel to set up a meeting between us?'

Garvin thought of various subterfuges, decided on the semihonest one, explaining that his circus was heading toward Centrum, and would appreciate any help Berta Industries could provide about the various security devices they'd provided the Confederation around Centrum. He added, without giving details, that they already had charts, serial numbers, and descriptions of these devices and outposts.

Berta raised an imperious eyebrow.

'Well, I cannot say you're evasive, young man. But one thing you should know is that Berta Industries prides itself on its integrity. Once our services are contracted for, no one else has ever been given any details.'

'I can appreciate that,' Garvin said. 'But it's been ten years since you provided those devices, and at least five years since the Confederation has dropped out of contact with everyone, it seems.'

'True.'

'I'm not arrogant enough to say that a circus can do anything to restore what once was, but I'd like to try.'

'Frankly, I don't care much about your enterprises, Gaffer Jaansma. But there is this justification for my interest: Cayle is, perhaps not quite helpless, but certainly floundering without its Confederation business. We've not been able to establish new avenues of trade to compensate for the loss.

'Perhaps you've noticed the huge unemployment. I've tried to keep as many of my employees on as possible, but, of course, I'm not a charity.

'I'm afraid that the people out there, if they begin to lose faith in our government, may seek a more radical solution. Simple people will seek simple solutions.

'A man . . . or woman . . . who can offer easy answers would be very appealing.

'And, to be brutally honest with you, a good number of this system's magnates would support such a person, if for no other reason than they fear to lose what they have. And I could well be one of them, if there's a sufficiently large social disruption.

'No, I do not think your circus can do any good, could help us solve our problems, any more than the momentary relief of taking the people's minds away from their concerns.

'But something is always better than nothing.

'I shall think on this matter overnight, and give you my answer tomorrow.'

'Well hold me and kiss me where the sun don't shine,' Njangu muttered as he looked at the small case he'd found in Kekri's compartment. 'Either we're complete dunderbrains, or else this wasn't here the first time we searched her.'

'It wasn't here, boss,' one of the security techs said. 'I made thorough notes of the last time we went through her gear. The third thing we checked was in her cosmetics case, and I'm not blind enough to have missed that case.'

'A com of some sort,' Njangu mused. 'Run this up to your shop and disclose me its secrets.'

''Kay, sir,' a tech said.

'Be a little careful,' Yoshitaro added. 'Just in case there's something stupid inside like a suicide charge.'

'We could always keep with the idea that accidents happen,' Kekri said, kicking her shoes off.

'We could,' Garvin said, who suddenly decided he was going to seize the moment just for a change, and the hell with the consequences, for which thought he knew he'd unquestionably pay. 'Or I could light this candle . . . old-fashioned sort, that Berta here, plus the one on the other side of the bed.'

'You could do that,' Kekri said. 'And then what?'

'And then I cut the main lights like this, come over here, and kiss you.'

'And then what?'

'Then,' Garvin said, 'I take your jacket off, and slide your gown down to your waist like that. Then I kiss your neck, and some . . . other places a few times.

'Yes, you can be taking off my jacket, and unfastening my pants if you want.'

'Oh,' Kekri breathed. 'Yes.'

'Thank you. Now I'll find a way to kick these goddamned boots off, and push your gown down around your feet like this.

'Tsk. You're not wearing anything under it.'

'I don't like last-minute details to get in the way,' Kekri breathed.

'An excellent idea,' Garvin said, carrying her to the

bed. She lay, eyes half-closed, looking up at him as he took off his shirt.

'Now, if you'll lift your legs up so I can take hold of your ankles . . .'

Moments later, he ran out of words.

Garvin drank a cup of stimulant tea the cook had recommended, smiled politely at Berta across the table.

He thought of Njangu's advice: 'Screw her black-and-blue and get her singing our tune.' Not only was the bastard sexist, but he obviously thought too highly of somebody's capabilities. Not Katun's. Feeling very black-and-blue, he wondered if he'd be able to walk un-spraddle-legged on this inspection tour, put on his best face, and determined to tough it out.

He was a little disgusted to see Kekri, quite bouncy, making cheerful talk with Libnah Berta, and tried to find the energy to pour himself more tea.

The electronics security technician yawned and rubbed sleepy eyes.

'What we've got here, boss,' he told Njangu, 'is a neat little transceiver. In-system only, unless somebody is dogging us. And, so far, we haven't found anybody on our tail.

'The entire back is a light-sensitive charging system, not even needing UV light, which is fairly sexy. The set remains on at all times, so somebody . . . say a nice spy-ship . . . could enter whatever system we're in, activate the com with a set signal, then our spy can find out somebody's waiting to chat with her and take it from there. Naturally, it's got a record-and-blurt capability so she wouldn't hang herself out for too long.'

Njangu thought, poured himself another stim.

'I think,' he said, 'it would be very nice to put the com right back where we found it, except maybe, if there's room in the box, you can put a secondary circuit in that'll tip us if somebody rings Kekri up.'

'Already set up the circuitry, boss. Thought you might like something like that. Also piggybacked another circuit so we can static-up her transmission, and whoever's on the other end will have the devil's time making sense out of it.

'Now, all we need is what data she's after.'

Njangu grinned, drained his tea, touched his inside breast pocket where a copy of Kekri Katun's notes, kept in a simple substitution code, sat. Another copy, mostly broken, was with a crypto tech.

'Now that, my fine feathered friend, is what they call beyond your need to know.'

He rose.

'C'mon. Let's go down to the dukey and I'll buy breakfast. Garvin'll have some interesting things to listen to when he gets back.'

Berta's works ran on forever and a half kilometer. Garvin very quickly got tired of admiring huge extrusion machinery, engine-casting plants, lathes that could turn out something the size of a Nana-boat, programming divisions, and all the rest. He moved just a little awkwardly, not used to using his body to aim the pinhole camera in his lapel.

There were workmen about, but not many, and Garvin noticed most of them occupied their time polishing and maintaining, not building.

They ended up in a huge, stone building, very archaic in design, with webbed glass skylights, an open center, and row after row of terminals and operators along the walls. Outside were armed guards that Garvin rated as fairly alert.

'These are our archives,' Lady Berta said proudly. 'Going all the way back to the first tender the first Berta built . . . and used as a personal runabout.'

She came a little closer, lowered her voice.

'In these records is the information you asked me about, and it is as good a place as any to tell you I cannot permit you to access what you want.

'I'm sorry, but, as I have said before, there is a bond between Berta and its customers, a bond that's been unbroken for more than three hundred Earth-years.'

Garvin looked into her eyes, saw nothing but stern resolve, and knew better than to argue.

'Then,' he said, 'I suppose we'll just have to take our chances with whatever security devices remain around Centrum.'

'I am sorry,' Berta said, and just a bit of a smile came and went.

Now why, Garvin thought, and felt Njangu would be proud of him, *would she have taken the trouble to show me where the secrets are, and then tell me to bugger off? Let alone grin at me? Interesting I think I'll have to consider this.*

Ristori crawled carefully toward the bowl, where six Earth cats lapped milk. He inserted himself between two, started to take a drink, leapt back as a cat slapped him across the nose.

The children in the stands roared.

Again Ristori tried, again was batted away.

He got up, sat in thought for a while, then visibly brightened.

He got back down on his hands and knees, and suddenly he was moving like a cat, sinuously, slinking toward the bowl. The cats moved aside, evidently fooled, and Ristori began lapping milk like they did.

Damned glad, Garvin thought, watching from outside the ring as the applause began, *I changed my mind about Emton and his act.*

The cats were, surprisingly, one of the bigger hits. Garvin guessed it was because the cat wasn't an unknown pet, but no one in his right mind imagined they could ever be trained to do tricks.

Ristori got up and schlumpfed away, and five of the cats licked themselves twice, then rolled on their backs, paws in the air, and, seemingly without any direction from Emton, who lounged nearby, the sixth leapt on top of the lifted paws, and was bounced from cat to cat, a perfect tiny parody of the risley act in the second ring.

'Did we have fun with our Kekri?' Darod Montagna hissed, a smile on her face to fool the crowd.

'It was work,' Garvin tried.

'Of *course*,' Montagna said in utter disbelief. 'I hope you two made yourselves very happy. You can move her into your compartment if you want. I, certainly, won't be objecting.'

Garvin tried to think of something to say, managed a feeble 'but . . .' as Montagna stalked away.

The last thing he would do was move Kekri in with him. He certainly hadn't the energy, and Katun had shown no particular desire to press matters, although she'd been fairly affectionate on the flight back. It seemed obvious, Garvin thought with a bit of misery, not only had he failed to impress Katun, but he'd evidently blown what he did have with Montagna.

He'd barely had time to report his failure to Njangu, and learn Kekri was, indeed, a spy, before it was time for the evening show.

Sunk in self-pity, he almost missed the cats' scampering offstage, and the growl outside the tent of the big animals, waiting their cue.

Roustabouts muscled a huge cage down into position over the center ring, shut off its lifters, lashed it firmly in place.

Garvin snapped his whip three times.

'You can hear them, you can smell them, now they'll be coming in, fangs bared, claws ready. Watch your children, ladies and gentlemen, for these voracious, vicious beasts of the wild are barely under control.

'I myself wouldn't enter their cage on a challenge. Only their master, the impossibly brave Sir Douglas, dares that, and now, let's welcome him and his mankillers!'

Monique Lir wasn't paying much attention to the dancers on the stage of the Pendu club, either the clothed or the naked ones, listening to Darod Montagna snap out her anger.

'Are you sure you meant to cut everything off?'

'I'd like to have cut his futtering cock off,' Darod stormed. 'Preferably at the elbows.'

'Did you ever consider why the boss took that tits-and-ass wonder along with him?'

'Why . . . because he wanted to screw her! And . . . and because she's a lot prettier than I am!'

'Maybe on the first, so what on the second. That Mellusin woman he's involved with back on Cumbre might be a bit prettier than you as well. Did you maybe consider there was another reason?'

'Like what? What could there be?' Montagna demanded.

'Oh, say, maybe that somebody wanted Katun out of

town for the night. Maybe somebody wanted to search her dunnage.'

'*Giptel* doots!' Montagna snapped. 'How could you know that?'

'Because my . . . our, now again . . . compartment's on the same level as hers. And because I'm a very light sleeper. And because I saw Njangu, looking innocent, wandering around with a couple of his goons after people settled down for the night.'

'Oh,' Montagna said in a small voice.

'Now, if he *keeps* boffing her,' Monique said, 'all you can do is shrug, walk away, and forget about it. It wasn't as if you weren't warned.'

'No,' Darod said in a dull voice, and sipped her drink. 'Maybe I am being stupid. But it still doesn't set right.'

'No shiteedah,' Lir said. 'That's 'cause men, basically, blow *giptels*.'

'So what should I do . . . just hold in place?'

Monique, without answering her, looked up at the various male and female impedimenta being enthusiastically waved about by the dancers.

'I'll be glad when we lift off this frigging planet,' she muttered. 'The whole damned world smells of sperm. Sperm and cold, rusting iron.'

'Odd and odder,' Njangu mused. 'Hokay. Let's try one. Berta wants to go along with us . . . maybe . . . or maybe not even consciously. She wants order, law, and the rest of that bullshit people think is so goddamned important back in her life, and the only thing she can think of is the Confederation.

'She won't give us the data . . . but that doesn't mean it's sealed beyond recovery. 'Kay. I think me, and maybe a couple of friends, can help her conscience out.'

'Yeh,' Garvin said. 'I just wish somebody'd help mine.'

'Well,' Njangu said, 'it does look like you maybe weren't everything Katun dreams of . . . or maybe she was just curious, and that was part of her investigation, since the notes she took are all over the map.

'She might as well be some kind of ologist, doing a holo on circus folk. Go buy some flowers for Darod. Maybe that'll help, and she'll get over her piss-off, you betrayin' bastard, in an aeon or epoch or two.'

'Thanks,' Garvin muttered. 'So now you're going to make a run at making yourself into her honeytrap?'

'Not me, brother,' Njangu said. 'First there's Maev, who's one mean piece of work. Second, I'm hardly a superman, which maybe is what our Kekri is looking for. Third is, unlike some tall, blond sorts, who pose nobly in charges and circus rings, I know my limitations.'

'B . . . but . . . but you're the one who told me to do this,' Garvin sputtered.

'Ah well,' Njangu said. 'I've learned to move on from my triumphs. What I'm looking for right now, after examining your fuzzy, out-of-focus holos of the Berta plants, is a nice, reliable midget.'

TWELVE

'Thank you enormously for inviting me out,' Kekri Katun said.

'Thank *you* for coming with me,' Ben Dill said. 'It's nice, taking the prettiest woman in the ship out to help you buy maybe a painting or something with my ill-gotten wages.'

Kekri smiled wryly.

'I don't seem to get asked anywhere much. I feel like some kind of pariah, sometimes. Maybe because I'm from another world than the rest of you.'

'Aw balls,' Dill said rudely. 'Nobody's pariahing you,' he lied. 'We're from as many worlds as you can think of, so that doesn't matter. More likely, it's 'cause you're so pretty. Notice that a lot of the showgirls don't get taken anywhere? Don't think you're anything special in the way of a martyr.'

Kekri grinned, squeezed Dill's arm.

'Careful, lady,' he said. 'Don't go messin' with the pilot, even if he is the best in six systems and it is only a stinkin' lifter.'

'What're those weird-looking ships you usually fly?'

'The *aksai*,' Dill said. 'Built by the Musth . . . like Alikhan. They flew in combat . . .' and Ben suddenly remembered Njangu's warning, and his cover story, '. . . against some Confederation ships, just before the collapse.

'We know some people who know some people, and bought some of them.'

'You get along with the Musth?'

'Circus people get along with everyone,' Ben said.

Kekri seemed to feel a warning, for she found another topic.

'So what, exactly, am I supposed to do?'

'I prob'ly have the taste of a water buffalo as far as art goes,' Dill said. 'But my compartment looks pretty damn' bare. They told me about this art thing they do every weeks-end, along the river that runs through Pendu, and I thought maybe you could help me find something that isn't too atrocious.'

'A pilot,' Kekri mused. 'You want something with flying, or space in it?'

'Not a chance,' Ben said. 'I do it, and don't much want to look at it. Something abstract's more my line.'

Kekri looked at him with a bit of respect.

'So you have advanced taste in art, can lift a ton of weights, can fly *aksai*—'

'And just about anything else,' Ben said. 'No boasting.'

'And anything else,' Kekri said. 'What other talents do you have?'

'I'm a balding secret sex maniac, and modest as a sumbitch to boot.'

Kekri laughed, reached over, and patted him on the upper thigh.

''Kay, Mr. Modest. Isn't that a landing field down there?'

'Surely is, lady. Now watch this, and hang on to your stomach.'

Dill flipped the lifter on its side and dived straight down for the small field. He flared at the last minute and set it down, with never a scrape from its skids.

'And here we be,' he said. 'The river's right over there, so let's go see if there's anything worth buying.'

They climbed out, and an attendant approached, a bit wide-eyed at the woman and the monster of a man.

'Here,' Dill said, spinning a credit through the air. 'Don't let anybody put their initials on the pig, and keep it easy for me to get out!'

'Sir,' the attendant said, bowing repeatedly. 'Yes, sir! Would you like me to wash and polish it, as well?'

'Naah,' Dill said. 'It'd on'y get dusty all over again.'

As they walked away, he said, 'What'd I do wrong? Throw him the wrong coin or something? I thought he was gonna propose marriage.'

'One Confederation credit converts, somebody told me, if you can find a place to convert it,' Kekri said 'to about a week's wages in local currency.'

'Be damned! The hell with art,' Dill said. 'Let's go find us a temple and set up as money changers.'

The midget's name was Felip Mand'l, and he frequently referred to himself as 'Lucky Felip.'

'Of course Lucky Felip is delighted to help the circus, for doesn't my contract call for me to be "generally useful," besides my act? And I do know how to keep silent, and will admit I thought our troupe has some dark secrets, especially considering how we are now dressed, which is certainly not the norm for most troupes,' he said, a little adrenalined.

'But how did you come to pick Lucky Felip? There are over a dozen little people with Circus Jaansma.'

'I did a little asking about,' Njangu said. 'About people's pasts.'

'Ah! All that was a mistake,' Mand'l said. 'I was very young, and she was very pretty, and she swore those jewels had been taken from her by a jealous lover, and I was the only one who could climb up into the man's penthouse, and I *almost* got away with it.'

'Relax,' Njangu said. 'Back some time ago there were things I almost got away with, too.'

Mand'l looked at the other three in the back of the lifter. Like him and Njangu, Penwyth, Lir, and an electronics technician named Limodo wore black from head to toe, with roll-down watch caps on their heads, amplified light goggles on their foreheads, throat mikes in place. All wore small patrol packs.

'I, uh, notice that the four of you are carrying guns. Why was I not offered one?' Felip asked, trying to sound indignant.

'Do you know how to use a blaster?' Lir asked.

'Unfortunately, not. Not one of the talents I've been able to cultivate. But I am deadly with an old-timey projectile weapon, and can't think there's that much difference.'

'There is,' Monique said. 'We don't want you shooting yourself in the foot. Or me, either.'

'Ah,' the midget said, and subsided into his seat as the lifter low-flew into the mountains.

'Good farpadoodle,' Dill muttered, staring at a semi-active holo/painting almost as tall as he was. 'I didn't know there were that many shades of red, or that many ways of looking stupid waving a blaster about.'

'Sssh,' Kekri nudged. 'I think that's the artist over there.'

'Introduce me,' Ben said, 'and Mrs. Dill's favorite son'll pitch him right over that embankment into the river. He's too lousy to live.'

Artists, maybe two hundred, maybe more, had their works strung along a wide sidewalk, some leaning against the stone wall. On the other side was a three-meter drop to the gray, wintry river, with an occasional boat tied up along the wall.

'Come on,' Kekri said, tugging at his arm. 'We've barely begun.'

'Isn't there a bar somewhere? My taste seems connected to my taste buds, and maybe if I had a beer or six, some of this crap might look better.'

'Never buy art when you're blasted,' Kekri said. 'That's an old saying of my grandmother's.'

'Oh yeh? What'd she do to earn her keep to be so wise?'

'I think she ran a bordello.'

'By the Sun God's suppository, I better hang on to you,' Ben said. 'A whorehouse is just what I want to retire into.'

He snorted laughter.

'All right,' Kekri said. 'You're obviously in no frame of mind to look at any more art.'

'Especially not this shit. Why anybody thinks there's something mournful about a stupid painting of a stupid busted-up starship, its ribs showing through at sunset is way beyond me,' Dill said. 'Maybe I better stick to finger painting. My own.'

'That, I think, is one of their public houses,' Katun said, pointing.

'Awright! Now, we'll just wait for this convoy to float on past, and—'

The convoy was half a dozen heavy lifters, with

covered camion backs. The canvas came away, and men with guns piled out.

'Ohboy,' Dill said, grabbing Kekri's arm, and pulling her back toward the art booths. 'What the hell are we in the middle of?'

'Over there,' Kekri pointed, and ten or more lifters were crossing the river on a low bridge.

The men behind Dill started shooting at the second convoy, and men leapt from those lifters and returned fire. Heavy blasters atop the lifters slammed rounds at each other, and there were screams of fear, of pain.

Dill was flat on the pavement, half-atop Kekri, and the artist whose work he'd hated was beside him.

'What the hell is going on?'

The artist shook his head rapidly.

'Probably the anarchists are shooting each other up again. They can't agree as to the form of their organization.'

He screamed, flopped as bolts chattered along the walk, and through his back.

'This isn't safe,' Dill said, glanced around, then grabbed Kekri, who screeched in surprise. He ran backward, kicking over easels, cursing that he was unarmed, and someone saw him, fired, and missed.

Dill went over the embankment wall, and dropped into the river, going under, still with one hand firmly on Kekri's leg.

The two came up, Kekri sputtering.

'You better know how to swim,' Dill said.

'I do,' she said. 'Your little jumping act took me by surpnse.

''Kay,' Ben said. 'We'll go for that little boat over there, cut it loose, stay in the water on the far side, and let it take us downstream for a while.'

'Good,' Kekri said, starting to swim, then rolling on her back. 'You think fast.'

'A man my size has got to. Now shaddup and keep stroking.'

They swam hard for a few meters, then Dill spat water like a sounding whale.

'Shit,' Dill said. 'Anarchists fighting each other. What a *truly* screwed-up world this is.'

'Lucky Felip could dance the gavotte on this slab of steel,' Mand'l said into his mike as he went quickly up the webbed glass of Beta Industry Archives. 'I could do it on my hands.'

'Sharrup and bust us in,' Njangu answered.

Mand'l knelt, and there was a tiny flare as his torch lit. He took half-melted glass out with asbestos-gloved fingers, reached inside, found the catch, and opened the skylight.

'Enter voose,' he said.

'Toss the rope down first,' Limodo said. 'I'm no goddamned acrobat.'

Mand'l tied the rope off on something sturdy inside the archive building and threw it down to her. She went quickly up, hand over hand, and the other three followed.

Inside, they were on an iron platform, high above Berta's records.

They held for a moment in silence, scanning the dark inside of the building. All of the Legion troops held up circled thumbs and forefingers.

No watchmen. At least, none seen so far.

Njangu pointed down, and they crept down stairways to the main floor.

Limodo checked terminals, turned one on. For long

minutes she stared at the blue light, occasionally touching sensors. Finally, she nodded.

'I think I've got it,' and began her search, checking against a tiny screen she'd taken from her patrol pack with the serial numbers gotten on Tiborg.

An hour passed, then another as she wove her way into the bowels of the archives.

'At least there aren't any booby traps or firewalls,' she reported. 'Seems fairly straightforward.'

'FREEZE!' was Njangu's response, and they obeyed, seeing two men outside the main door, shining normal lights inside. No one moved, the men went away, and the search went on.

'And here we are,' Dill said, guiding the small boat in to a dock, jumping out with a painter, and tying the craft up.

'You impress me,' Kekri said.

Dill hopped back in the boat. It rocked and he caught himself against the roof of the tiny cabin.

'Then you might reward me, m'lady, with a kiss. Then we'll call for a liftout, let somebody come back for that damned lifter, and the hell with my artistic sensibilities ever again.'

Kekri lifted her lips to his, mouth opening. The kiss lasted, then got a little more intense. Her arms slid down from around his neck down his back, and then around and down his stomach.

Katun suddenly broke from the kiss.

'Ohm'gods!' she breathed.

'Uh . . . you knew I was a pretty big guy,' Dill said, slightly embarrassed. 'That includes—'

'Shut up,' Kekri ordered. 'Is that cabin unlocked?'

'Uh . . . yeh.'

'Then inside. Hurry!'

'Uh . . . 'kay.'

'Got it,' Limodo reported, attaching a small vampire recorder to the side of the terminal.

'Five, maybe ten minutes, and we'll have everything. Another five for me to clean up my tracks.'

Lucky Felip stirred from where he was hiding, just inside a lectern.

'You make things easy. I was expecting excitement.'

'Quiet,' Penwyth whispered into his com. He and Lir were on either side of the entrance, guns ready against intruders. 'It's bad luck to be confident.'

'Remember those jewels you went after,' Lir echoed. 'Almost ain't is.'

'Tails up, tails up,' Thanon and Phanon chanted, and the elephants obeyed, even the small Imp and Loti, linking trunks and tails, and the line swayed out of the tent as the lights came up.

'And that's all there is, ladies, gentlemen, children,' Garvin chanted. 'It's all out and over,' and the butchers swarmed the crowd.

'Don't forget your souvenir programs, a real memento of Circus Jaansma, something for you to keep for your memories until we come back this way again.'

'Early in the next frigging century,' Montagna muttered to herself. 'Or the one after that.'

She saw, in a front row seat, *Graav* Ganeel, staring after the elephants, face most wistful.

Big Bertha lifted two hours before dawn.

Monique Lir was on the bridge, looking down as the lights of Pendu vanished into the cloud cover.

'This frigging planet,' she observed to no one in particular, not knowing she was echoing Lady Libnah Berta, 'damned well needs the Confederation back. Or they're gonna end up marching in lockstep to some real fool and all end up dead or worse.'

THIRTEEN

N-space

'Probably most of you have an idea of what was going on,' Njangu told the Legion officers assembled on the bridge of *Big Bertha*, 'but here's the real skinny. I'll let Dr. Froude explain.'

'We've made some interesting progress so far,' Froude said. 'We now have . . . or think we have . . . a skeleton key of sorts to the Confederation, which hopefully will keep us from being killed by our own people or robots,' Froude said. 'From the nav points we're close to now, there's a six-jump sequence that will put us in the Capella system.

'However, I favor an eight-jump series, for one reason: This second set of navpoints, and I indicate them here on a greatly simplified chart holo, are "nearer" to the systems around Capella.

'I would like to nose around a bit, as close to Centrum as we dare, before committing ourselves.

'Comments? Questions? Additions?'

There were none, and so *Big Bertha* jumped again into N-space.

*

'This is most interestin',' Njangu observed as he checked several screens. 'This system, W-R-whocares, was supposedly empty. No listing on settlements, no listing on fortification, carried as UNOCCUPIED.

'Yet over on that world the detectors picked up a big chunk of metal.'

He keyed a mike.

'Ben, what do you have?' not bothering with formal call signs.

Silence for a moment, then:

'On my second orbit. What we've got is damned weird, Njangu. The detectors picked up what looks to me like a big goddamned fortress, modern, most of it underground. I'm transmitting pictures and realtime data for you to eyeball.

'But what's interesting is the thing's abandoned.'

'What do you mean?'

'I mean, my detectors pick up nothin' on no waves from nobody. Nothing on IR, nothing on radar, nothing on heat imaging, not even residue. On visual, there are hangar bays, nit and cleverly camouflaged, but the doors are hangin' open like the seat of my pants when I was poor day before yestidday,' Dill went on. 'I see what I think are weapons launchers, but with no missiles on the mounts. I've got me some scanners and some antennae. I chanced a low sweep, and nothin' went BINGO at me.

'It looks to me like people just got bored and up and left.'

'Could you bring *Big Bertha* in closer?' Froude asked the ship captain.

'Affirm,' Liskeard said, and the planet blurred, the screen showed the whorl of N-space, and then the planet filled the main screen.

'Sorry, Ben,' Njangu said. 'Forgot to tell you we were jumping in closer.'

'Oh, 'at's all right,' Dill said. 'I just saw you guys pull out on me, and now somebody's gonna have to clean up this here *aksai* cabin. This is not the place I want to grow old gracefully in all by myself.'

Froude was paying no attention to the chatter, but watching screens.

'I think Big Ben is maybe right,' he said. 'The Confederation . . . I'm assuming this was some kind of a secret base for something, since it looks like it's been there for a while, and who else but the Confederation would've spent who knows how many years building this . . . just up and left. Leaving the barn door wide-open.

'Very strange indeed.'

'Why,' Kekri said, 'did we spend so much time in that dead system today?'

'Damfino,' Ben lied. 'I was in the ready room playing with myself. Alikhan was the duty pilot.'

'Wasn't that weird to be just hanging out there without anything happening? Didn't Garvin give you some kind of clue?'

'Nawp,' Dill said. 'What's weird is that I've been out of my flight suit, wandering around nekkid and all, with a nicely worked up me in me hand, and I haven't leapt on you yet.'

'Wait a minute,' Kekri protested. 'We can't screw all the time! And we were talking . . .' and then she squealed, and for a time the conversation in their compartment was somewhat fragmented.

The next jump was through a dead system, with no surprises.

Sabyn/Sabyn I

The next jump was more interesting. There were supposedly three inhabited planets of the six in the system of Sabyn. They were listed as settled, with light manufacturing, mostly agriculture, no details on culture.

The *aksai* sweep reported life on all three worlds, no observable armament, no threats.

Garvin had *Big Bertha* brought out of N-space, and sent a 'cast for landing instructions.

There was no response to the first or the third com. Other coms were sent to the other worlds, with zed results.

Garvin, feeling his skin prickle a bit, put out all his combat ships, looking for trouble.

None materialized.

'All right,' he said. 'We'll do it the dumb way.'

As on Cayle, they snowballed the three populated worlds with 'casts, in-atmosphere fireworks. Again, nothing.

'Now, here is something.a bit out of the ordinary,' Alikhan sent from his *aksai* close to the first planet's surface. 'Transmitting pictures. What you are looking at is a landing field, but you will note it has been rather completely destroyed. The towers have been knocked down and the maintenance buildings bombed, as on Salamonsky. It would appear to me that the damage was done some time ago . . . a planetary year or more.

'However, the world is *not* abandoned. I sighted a small lifter, overflew it. It ducked away into a forest byway, and I lost it, not having my infrared pickup turned on at the time.'

The watch officer brought *Big Bertha* closer to the planet, and they waited some more.

'We were swept twice with radar from the planet's surface, but the band wasn't anything the computer said was used by target acquisition,' the electronics watch reported. 'Then nothing.'

Everyone looked at Garvin for his decision.

'Let's wiggle our fannies and see what happens,' he said. 'Put it down an that open patch of land near that torn-up field, and we'll set up canvas.'

'You are being a daredevil,' Njangu murmured.

'I'll want full air cover while we do,' Garvin said.

'Why're we putting the tents up, if I might ask?' Penwyth said.

'I can't think of any better way to signal that we're friendly.'

Their first customer was a tough-looking subteen farm boy, who walked up, listened, stone-faced to the spiel of one of the midway barkers to her solitary audience, waited until the chant broke for an instant, then demanded, 'Whatsit take to get in?'

'Only half a Confederate credit for the circus,' the barker said. 'Dunno what it'd be in your currency, but we're flexible, son, mighty flexible. The midway's free, but the attractions and the games require a small contribution.'

The boy nodded, went down the midway, looking curiously about.

Garvin was watching from the bridge of *Big Bertha*.

'Damned spooky to be the only flattie around,' he said, 'and you'll note everybody's working him, just for practice, no doubt.'

'Maybe you best slide on down and find out what's going on,' Njangu said.

'What, me, the ringmaster?'

'Yes, you, the ringmaster. Move out.'

Garvin obeyed.

The boy, in spite of his best efforts, couldn't help but goggle a little at the tall, white-clad blond man standing in front of him.

'Welcome to the circus,' Garvin said. 'My name's Garvin. Yours?'

'Jorma,' the boy said.

'Enjoying yourself?'

'Dunno yet.'

'Here,' Garvin said, taking a ticket from his pocket. 'Free admission to my circus. Better,' and he brought out more tickets, 'bring your whole family.'

'Don't need that many,' Jorma said. 'There ain't but me and Ma, and one baby sister left.'

'Left?'

'Since the damned Confederation come and gone.' Jorma spat on the ground.

Garvin recovered.

'What did the Confederation want? Don't mind my dumb questions, Jorma, but we're from way offworld, and haven't heard any news lately.'

'Bastards come every couple years,' Jorma said. 'Grab whatever's worth taking. Quick-butcher whatever cattle they can come on, freeze-dry our vegetables.' Jorma paused, and his face twisted, and he fought back, found control. 'They take anybody who wants to go with 'em.

'Sometimes people who don't. Like my sister,'

He scrubbed across his eyes with the back of his sleeve.

'That's not right,' Garvin said.

Jorma gave him a look of infinite scorn.

'And how're we supposed to fight back? No guns, and they've got rockets and ships.'

He pointed at the nearby field.

'They done that last time. Said they didn't want us messing around in space. Some peddler came through, said they shot up some of our cities pretty bad. I wouldn't know. Most of us live in little villages. Get in cities, you're a target. My dad went off, looking for work, and he never came back.'

'All of these raiders call themselves Confederation?'

'Yeh,' the boy said. 'And we got all these holos talkin' about how good the Confederation was for all of us. Lyin' sonsabitches!'

He caught himself.

'Sorry, mister. My ma says I'm not supposed to use language like that.'

'Doesn't bother me,' Garvin said. 'If I was in your shoes, I'd probably use worse myself.'

The boy smiled, very faintly.

'Maybe you're not a trap.'

'Trap?'

'Ma said the only ships that've come here in the last four years have been raiders. Before that, she said, there wasn't anybody for six, seven years.

'Before that, she swears there were *other* Confederation ships, but those were bringing things in, and not stealing everything we've got. All kinds of ships, not just warships, but transports, even liners. She said you could get on one, if you had credits, and it'd take you anywhere in the Universe.

'Anyway, Ma figured, when we heard your speakers in those weird-looking ships that you were just another way for us to get stolen.'

'Look,' Garvin said. 'If I wanted to steal you . . . or your mother . . . or your little sister, you think I'd go to the trouble of bringing in all those elephants?'

'Is that what they are? Like from Earth?'

'Maybe, a long time ago,' Garvin said. 'That herd goes through a ton of dried grass a day, maybe more. Plus they've got to have vitamins, and treats from the hydroponics area, or from our freeze-dried stocks.'

'Doesn't seem to make much sense just to grab me and my family,' Jorma agreed.

'Look,' Garvin said. 'I'll get a whole roll of tickets. You sell them for whatever you can get, keep half the credits.'

'Why me?'

'Because you were the first to show up, which means you've got some courage. Plus nobody'll get near any of us, 'til we've proved we're not the Confederation. Most likely, they'd take a shot, or wing us with a rock,' Garvin said.

'That's prob'ly true,' Jorma said.

Garvin took him over to a spieler's booth, took a roll of tickets about the size of the boy's chest, and gave it to him.

'You make money, we make money.'

Jorma nodded, considered, then, possibly afraid Garvin would renege, pelted back down the midway and disappeared into brush.

'I've got a tracer on him,' the speaker in Garvin's ear said. 'Want him tracked?'

'Yeh,' Garvin said. 'But nobody takes any action except by my permission. Period.'

That night there were ten people, including Jorma and his skeptical family. The next night, fifty.

Garvin kept the *aksai* and patrol boats in the air, constantly 'casting. Some of the cities had taken some damage from the air, but nothing was as shattered as Jorma's peddler had claimed.

The fourth night, there were three hundred people, some of whom had arrived by decrepit lifter or ground vehicles.

Clowns and butchers were augmented with Njangu's Intelligence analysts.

'The kid was telling the truth,' Njangu reported. 'Some folks who call themselves Confederation are milking this planet every year or so. But they're not dumb. They don't steal enough so people starve or can't keep the economy limping along.

'A lot of the people go with them willingly. But there's some . . . Jorma's sister, I'd guess . . . somebody gets the hots for and she's theirs.'

'Wonderful,' Garvin said. 'This'll be a nice reputation to live down. Wonder how many other worlds these phony Confeds loot?'

'Damfino,' Njangu said. 'But you want a really nasty thought? You ever think maybe this *is* the real Confederation?'

Garvin gnawed a lip, didn't answer.

'Another interesting bit of info,' Njangu went on. 'Nobody from whatever government exists has shown up to check out the circus.'

'That's damned unlikely.'

'Sure is,' Yoshitaro agreed. 'The only officials that've materialized are bureaucrats or village elders or whatever they call themselves. So this means the mucketies either are hiding in the bushes, scared shitless that we're somehow tied in with the kidnappers, or else they really don't have any government beyond the local yokels and the guys who keep the power and water running.

'That, I think, is impossible. Humans aren't that in love with anarchy.

'But it does give another fact. We've been prodding

gently, and nobody, and I mean nobody, down to little
kids, is willing to point to somebody and say, "Yeh he's
the prime minister's bootlicker" or such.'

'Nice tight discipline,' Garvin offered.

'Or fear, more likely.'

'Nobody ought to live that scared,' Garvin said.

'No shiteedah,' Njangu said. 'But there's a lot of us
who grow up like that.'

'Us?'

'Hell yeh,' Njangu said bitterly. 'Remember, I didn't
know there was anything other than run or get beat on,
big dog chews on little dog until I got shoved in the military.

'And ain't that a bastard,' he added. 'You gotta put on
a uniform to find out you've got anything called basic
rights? This goddamned cosmos sucks a big fat one.

'Maybe we ought to just go on back home and vege-
tate, since we've beat the butt of all the local baddies, and
let the frigging Universe go to hell in a handbasket.'

Garvin just looked at him, and Njangu forced a grin
and shrugged.

'Sorry. I've been pissy-headed lately. Oh yeh,' Njangu
said. 'Something else. People've been asking me how
much longer we're going to keep playing this world,
since we've found out what there is to be found out, and
nobody's got any money to make it worthwhile to hang
on, and counting the take in rutabagas is making Sopi
even balder.'

'Another four, five days,' Garvin said. 'I'm a soft heart,
but it's nice to see people come in all hangdog and walk
out smiling.'

'Yeh,' Njangu agreed. 'Nice. You ain't got a soft heart,
but a soft head.'

Mais

The next jump was to a nav point between systems, the one after that into the Mais system, with two settled planets, each with half a dozen moons, other worlds far out from the G-type sun listed as 'suitable for mineral exploitation.'

Preliminary reconnaissance by a pair of scoutships produced nothing, either positive or negative, other than both planets were still populated, and *Big Bertha* left hyperspace, the nav point, in the gap between inhabited and uninhabited planets.

She closed on the nearest world, and was neatly mousetrapped by two ships. *Jane's* listed them as 'Langnes-class light cruisers, currently second-line Confederation fleet service, moderately armed, extensive electronics suites, lightly armored, superior in maneuvering and reliability.'

Captain Liskeard looked at a blank screen, listened again to the unseen voice demanding they maintain present orbit and stand by for boarding, looked at Garvin for a response, got none.

'This is the Circus Ship *Big Bertha*,' he sent back. 'Intend planetfall on Mais II.'

'Make no attempt to land on any planet until you are clearanced,' the voice replied. 'And bring your two survey craft inboard, or they will be fired on.'

'Well, hmpty hmpty hmp,' Njangu said.

'Sir?' a tech moved a projection into Liskeard's view. It was of the closest planet and its moons, with various swirling readouts below each world.

'I think,' Liskeard said, 'they can hmpty hmp all they want. Look.' His finger reached out to a moon. through it, then touched another. 'Both of these moonlets are fortified. If the cruisers weren't dogging us, they could launch, and odds on the missiles would have enough sophistication to follow us back into N-space and go bang.'

'Mmmh,' Njangu said.

'Yeh,' Liskeard agreed. 'Especially since they didn't think they needed to bother to mention those fortifications. The bastards are cocky.' He looked worried. 'How are we going to handle this boarding?'

Garvin smiled wryly. 'That's one thing we won't have to worry about very much. There's never been a circus that isn't ready for the rozzers to do a shakedown day or night.'

'I just wonder what's going to come *after* the inspection,' Njangu said. 'Oh well.'

Garvin motioned the on-watch talker over, with her mike ready. 'Put out an all stations that we're being boarded, and no one is to offer any resistance without a signal.'

'Hide the women and the good towels,' Njangu added. 'Here comes trouble.'

One cruiser's lock opened, and a small boat shot out, arcing to intersect with *Big Bertha*'s yawning loading bay. The boat didn't enter, but mag-grapneled to the ship's skin, and suited, blaster-armed men floated out, and inside. Their suits were armored, and the helmets blank, with only a pickup instead of a viewport.

The boat unhooked and floated a few meters away from the lock, no doubt with weapons ready.

'Cycle the lock closed, sir?' the watch officer asked.

'Go ahead,' Garvin said. 'If they don't want us to proceed, they'll shoot you for a warning.'

But none of the weapons was lifted as the great lock

closed, air pumped back in, and the inner portal opened.
The half dozen suited men came into the main cargo
area.

Garvin walked forward, flanked by Njangu and
Penwyth.

'Welcome to *Big Bertha*,' he said. 'Inbound to Mais
Two.'

A voice came from a suit speaker:

'Your planet of origin?'

'Grimaldi.'

Silence, then:

'We have no listing for such a world. Your last planetfall?'

'Sabyn.'

'Purpose of visit there?'

'To make a credit, do some shows, have some fun,'
Garvin said. 'The same reason we want to land on Mais
Two.'

'Length of intended visit?'

'Perhaps two local weeks,' Garvin said. 'Less if we
don't draw a crowd.'

'Under the Confederation Act three-one-six-one, as
proper officials of the Confederation, we are authorized to
search your ship for illegal materials and contraband.'

'You're Confederation?' Garvin said, covering, thinking these bastards were the raiders, and maybe Njangu
had been right, worrying about what would happen after
the search.

'We are,' the voice said. 'Do you have any legal objections to our proposed search?'

'It wouldn't matter if we did,' Garvin said, 'since
you're the one holding the high cards and guns.'

The figure turned, spoke to the men behind her, and
they began to fan out.

'It might be better if I called certain of my men, and let them escort you around,' Garvin said, trying to sound amiable. '*Big Bertha*'s kind of complicated.'

The suited figure looked up, around.

'You could be right,' the voice said, sounding almost human. 'However, I don't think you should attempt any deception.'

'What you see is what there is,' Garvin said, and opened another channel. 'Dill, Montagna, Froude, Lir, report to the hold's main lock area immediately.' He went back to the general channel.

'If you and your men want to unsuit, it'll be a lot more comfortable.'

There was a pause, then the figure reached up, touched seals around its neck, and lifted the helmet clear. The figure became a woman, close-cropped brown hair, a not unattractive face that was very businesslike.

The other men and women did the same.

'We'll not unsuit completely,' she said. 'It's safer like that.'

'As you wish,' Garvin said. 'By the way, I'm Garvin Jaansma. Gaffer's my title, if you want one.'

'Commander Betna Israfel, Thirty-fourth Division Eighth Confederation Guard,' she said.

Garvin introduced Erik and Njangu, as the summoned men and women of the Legion arrived, then went off with the Mais.

'Would you care to visit our bridge?' he asked.

Israfel considered, then nodded.

'Surely. You don't appear to be anyone with anything to hide, I must say.'

'The only secrets we have are those of the midway, those of strange worlds and stranger games and magics,' Garvin intoned.

Israfel looked at him closely, decided Garvin was being humorous, granted him a smile. Garvin thought she didn't seem to have much of a sense of humor.

On the bridge, Israfel was offered refreshments, refused them, looked about the large room, its gleaming equipment and neatly dressed watch.

'You keep a very taut ship, sir,' she told Garvin.

'Thank you. My parents taught me any fool can be a pig,' Garvin said, hoping to be thought a trifle simplistic.

'I had to look up what a circus was, before I came aboard,' Israfel said. 'Are there many like you?'

'There were many circus ships, even convoys,' Garvin said. 'But that was before the Confederation, meaning no offense, vanished.'

'Frankly, for you, and us as well,' Israfel asked.

'But you're Confederation!'

'We are a detachment,' she said. 'Charged with providing security for the Mais system, no more. As far as what lies beyond the system . . . you know far more than we do, although that's something we of the garrison here don't like to broadcast, although you'd certainly find that out by yourself before long. It doesn't exactly increase the faith the locals have in us.'

Garvin chanced a comment, feeling a sudden warmth for these soldiers, no different than the Strike Force, even though they were far closer to the heart of the vanished Empire.

'In the Sabyn system, we were told they'd had raw materials and manufactured goods seized, on a regular basis, by ships claiming to be from the Confederation.'

'Yes,' Israfel said. 'Those pirates have tried three times to attack us. Each time, they've been driven off. But—' she broke off.

She didn't need to finish. Garvin could imagine trying to maintain a highly technological unit in a system without heavy manufacturing.

The Force had been lucky, even though cast to the frontiers, that Cumbre was as developed as it was.

'Do you have any idea where these self-styled Confederation troops are based from?'

Israfel shook her head, looked away, and Garvin realized he'd found out as much as he could from her.

But it was quite enough.

He regretted the week's commitment to playing Mais, because there didn't appear to be that much more to learn.

Mais/Mais II

Six days later, his opinion was confirmed. No one knew where these false Confederation units were from, only that they'd come three times, and been driven off, with fairly heavy casualties. The wounded and dead had been replaced by local recruits from Mais I and II, and a factory had been tooled up to replace the expended missiles. But the ships that had been lost were irreplaceable.

That was also why they'd only made one attempt to reach Centrum. The cruiser and its two destroyer escorts had simply vanished, and the Guard was reluctant to waste any more starships.

'Were we not required to keep the law in spirit as well as letter,' Commander Israfel told Penwyth, 'I'd surely like to commandeer those patrol boats and light survey ships you have.'

'It would take a while to learn to pilot an *aksai*,' Penwyth said truthfully. 'But we appreciate your honesty.'

Erik and Israfel had become a twosome, although
Penwyth swore that nothing more than light handhold-
ing was going on.

The circus was a raving success, and the Confederation
garrison had Garvin, Njangu, and other officers to dinner
twice. Garvin made a point of inviting Dill, not so much
to awe the soldiers as to his strength, but because he'd
bring Kekri along.

The younger male, and a couple of the female, officers
fell in love with her, to Garvin's amusement. But she
clung to Dill as she had ever since the ship had left Cayle
IV. He also brought along some of the showgirls and a
scattering of performers.

Garvin was mightily impressed with the detachment's
commander. She kept rigid discipline in the unit, and
never let on to anyone that she was the only authority
known. Rather, her orders were always signed FOR THE
CONFEDERATION, and her dealings with the civilians were
as if she was reporting daily to Centrum, with the stern
Parliament vetting her every decision.

Garvin almost took notes, thinking that one of these
years he might be in the same place himself, and need to
know how to handle matters. But after due consideration, he decided he didn't have the woman's basic moral
courage, and if he ever got stuck in a situation like this,
the first thing he'd do would be to tuck for the tall
timber.

One nice thing that happened to Garvin — Darod
Montagna had been closely watching the relationship, if
that was what it was, between Kekri Katun and Ben Dill.
One night she tapped at Garvin's compartment, asked if
he was interested in company. Mightily thrilled, he
invited her in, and she stayed the night. Garvin figured,
or hoped, anyway, he was forgiven for his indiscretion.

A bit cheered after the week on Mais that at least they weren't the only fools in the universe interested in keeping the Confederation alive, they made another jump.

This one was into Paradise.

Or so it appeared for a time.

FOURTEEN

Nelumbo/Nelumbo II

Nelumbo II was a beautiful planet, with small, mountained continents, mostly in the higher and lower temperate zones.

There was no inforrnation available whether or nor Nelumbo had been colonized, yet the first *aksai* in-system picked up radiation on the standard bands of a populated planet.

The recon sweep gave no reason for alarm, and so *Big Bertha* closed for a landing.

Garvin was beginning to enjoy the landing control dialogue: reporting presence of *Big Bertha*, then a few moments of rather stunned silence while someone found out what the blazes a circus ship might be. Then a frenzy.

They were given landing clearance, and, as usual, settled down on the outskirts of the planet's capital. This was a smallish city, built on the hills of a narrow peninsula, extending from a forested continent.

The promotional sweeps reported there didn't seem to be any slums in the city, only light industrial areas, and most of the housing looked palatial, great estates carefully built to give maximum privacy.

A crowd had assembled by the time Garvin ordered *Big Bertha*'s ramp dropped.

'Nice-lookin' folks,' Sopi Midt observed, rubbing his hands together in anticipation. 'Healthy sorts, look to be the type with credits.

'Heh,' he added, possibly inadvertently.

Midt was right – the people were nice-looking, of many colors, and well dressed. The lifters they arrived in were all of ten- to twenty-year-old Confederation design, and none was ramshackle.

Here and there Njangu spotted light blue uniformed men and women, but only a scattering.

Again, Garvin ordered the show out under canvas, and Fleam's roustabouts set to work.

By now, the troupe had fallen into its routine, the acts moving smoothly into the three rings, doing their acts, then off, and the performers helping other acts if they had time and no animals to feed.

Here they had their first real fright: a child, only three, wandered away from his mother. The hue and cry went out, and they finally found the boy. He'd managed to open the cage of Muldoon, the killer black leopard, and was sitting just inside, watching Muldoon watch him.

Sir Douglas went in before anyone had time to decide if Muldoon was being friendly, or if he was calculating how many mouthfuls the boy would provide.

Everyone involved got an enormous ass-chewing from Jaansma, and Njangu was ordered to put two of his security thugs on safety patrol, making sure nothing like that would ever, could ever, happen again.

But that was the only problem.

Sort of.

Njangu found out why Nelumbo wasn't in any of the data banks. Before the Collapse, it had been the chosen vacation home for the Confederation higher-ups, which was why the mansions, why the ecological sensitivity, why the carefully scattered population. Of course Confederation officials wouldn't particularly care to let the outside world know where their nearest and dearest could be found.

When the Confederation collapsed, it left more than two million vacationing men, women, and children abandoned on Nelumbo, plus the planet's necessary technicians and workers, and, of course, the families' blue-uniformed security teams.

Some of the people mourned their missing, but more began new lives. Women outnumbered the men about six to four.

'An easy damned life,' Garvin said. 'Not enough people to have screwed the world up, and lots of money so almost everything's automated.'

'Yeh,' Njangu said. 'Heaven itself.'

'What's the matter with that?' Garvin said. 'Isn't there someplace that's got to be perfect?'

'Probably,' Yoshitaro agreed. 'But I'll give you odds that we'll never be the bastards to run across it.'

The show went on for a week. Garvin made no signs of wanting to make the next jump toward Centrum, but spent his time in his office, working up new routines, or exploring the nearby city.

Njangu thought Garvin was maybe running some kind of investigation he wasn't ready to talk about, also thought Jaansma was being more than somewhat of a flake.

Garvin stood outside *Big Bertha*, listening to the rope caller as the crew guyed out the big tent, taking up the slack in the canvas:

'Speak your latin, speak it now.'

The ten men and women pulling on the rope chanted: 'Ah, heebie, hebby, hobby, hole, golong' once, then again in unison, then the crew moved to the next guy-line.

He smelled the evening air, and the wonderful scents from the pop-up buildings around the big tent: lion piss, manure, cooking steak from the dukey; other smells from the midway: corn popping, vehatna coming off the grill, real sawdust.

He dreamed of this life being all time, not a moment away from the fine art of killing people, seeing strange constellations overhead he couldn't identify. He thought of naming them as the circus roamed the galaxy – 'The Big Tent,' 'Horsedancer,' 'Strongman,' which brought him abruptly back to something resembling reality as the idea came of Ben Dill actually having stars named after him.

Fleam, boss canvas man, the unpromotable combat thug and knot expert, saw the first mote.

He was steering a small lifter, a gilly wagon loaded with freshly painted splashboards down the midway, and he moved aside for a young, but very well-dressed mother, her twin girls about twelve, and two of the blue-clad bodyguards.

For some unknown reason, he looked back, and saw one of the bodyguards slide his hand down into the waistband of one little girl's shorts caressingly. The girl's shoulders twitched, but she didn't pull away or say anything.

He gaped, then wider as the mother turned, obviously saw what the guard was doing, and quickly looked away.

Fleam, whose only soft spot might have been for little girls, felt his stomach roil, wondered if he should tell anybody about this, decided maybe it was none of his, or anybody else with the circus's business, then thought Njangu might find it interesting.

'Sometimes,' Garvin said, staring out at the lights over the ocean, 'sometimes, Njangu my friend, when we find a place like this, I really want to tell everybody to shove it.

'Sideways.'

'Which would accomplish what?' Njangu asked.

They sat, both a little drunk, on the balcony of a mansion they'd been invited to after a performance, a half-empty bottle of extraordinary brandy between them.

'Just going on,' Garvin said dreamily. 'We've got the circus going strong, and we could go until we die of old age, ducking baddies and playing places like this.'

'You don't think we'd hear from Froude, or Dill, or, God with a wooden leg forbid, Monique Lir?' Njangu asked. 'She's got a damned strong sense of duty and might want us to get our asses back in tune with the mission.'

Garvin muttered, drank brandy.

'Still,' he said. 'I remember, when we first joined up, the whole idea was to stick with the uniform bit until we got a good running shot at freedom and then the Confederation, the Force, and working for somebody else could pack their ass with salt and piddle up a rope.'

'Now we've got it, and what're we going to do?'

'Go on to Centrum and get our asses shot off, because we are gods-fearing patriotic morons,' Njangu said.

'Yeh. I suppose so,' Garvin said heavily. 'But still, be

thinking about living on a world like this . . . worlds like this.

'And how we could sweet-talk Lir into deserting.'

Darod saw the second sign. She was outside, after a show, cooling off, and saw a rather luxurious lim ground, and a pair of women start to get in, assisted by their blue-clad driver.

One said something to him, and Darod saw him frown. The second woman said something else. Darod couldn't tell what it was, but her voice was angry.

The driver backhanded the second woman, pushed both of them into the lim, slammed the door down. He started toward the driver's compartment, saw Montagna watching, and hard-eyed her.

Montagna, feeling the adrenaline rise, stepped toward him, automatically in a combat stance.

The driver hesitated, got in the lim, and took off.

Darod thought about what she'd seen, decided she'd tell it to Garvin. Garvin also found the behavior of the security man more than slightly odd, passed the word to Yoshitaro.

'We're certainly delighted to have you people visit us,' the man who'd introduced himself to Njangu as Chauda said. He was middle-aged, hard-faced, and wore light blue, but with golden emblems on his epaulettes. Njangu had spotted him as a top cop even before Chauda said he was the head of Nelumbo's security.

'Thank you,' Njangu said, wondering why he still felt a little nervous around a policeman, any policeman.

'It's a bit of a pity that you couldn't be persuaded to stay on for, oh, an E-year or thereabouts,' Chauda said.

'I think you'd get bored with us before then, and we'd be losing credits.'

'Maybe, or maybe not,' Chauda said. 'One problem we have here is a certain airlessness. You've given us fresh air.'

'People lived for a lot of centuries on just one world,' Yoshitaro said. 'They seemed to get along all right.'

'Did they? I remember reading about things like wars, riots, civil uprisings, and such,' Chauda said. 'But even so, that was in the days when they didn't know there was anything different.

'Show the flock a nice, new valley, let 'em feed and water in it, then tell them they can't go back there anymore . . .' Chauda shook his head. 'That might cause problems.'

'I still don't see how us staying a year would do any good, and, by the way, I haven't noticed space travel seeming to have cut down the amount of headbanging that goes on.'

'Well,' Chauda said, 'first, you've got a lot of talents in your circus that could train interested people to perform after you've gone on. For pay, I mean. Then, since you're experienced voyagers, we could possibly hire you to visit other worlds, and perhaps bring back other talents to keep us entertained.'

'Interesting idea,' Njangu said. 'I'll talk to the gaffer about it. If we were interested, what sort of officials would we be talking to? We've had some of your politicians come to the circus, but we haven't really made friends with them.'

'Don't worry about it,' Chauda said easily. 'I can handle everything on our end. There wouldn't be any problems.'

That, too, was reported to Garvin.

*

Emton's house cats were the great hit on Nelumbo They now had a whole new bag of tricks, from rolling balls while standing atop them, to doing a wire act (a meter above the ground, wearing specially sewn slippers), to letting birds land on their backs and preen.

Garvin had asked Emton about that one, and he said it'd only taken two or three brace of birds for the cats to learn what was and wasn't dinner.

The big cats had their own fans — there was always a knot of the security men around their cages, quietly admiring.

Sir Douglas complained quietly to Garvin that he really didn't like rozzers hanging about. 'Their faces gaffer, are too much like my cats when they feed.

'No, I insult my animals. There is greater intelligence on Muldoon's face when he eats than on theirs at any time at all.'

Alikhan saw the next sign. He was out with an *aksai* flying along the coast, when, about two kilometers ahead, he saw moving dots along the cliffs. For some reason, he climbed, and put a screen on them.

The dots were a dozen or so men, light chains around their waists. In front and behind were four blue-clad guards, carrying blasters.

He banked back to sea, cutting his drive, not wanting to be heard or seen.

This, too, was reported to Garvin.

'Perhaps,' Sunya Thanon said, most sadly, 'we have been fooling ourselves all these years, and there is no such place as Coando, and we, and our families before us, have created this lie so we do not give up hope, surrounded by evil and blood.'

'No,' Phraphas Phanon said, putting his arms around Thanon. 'It is out there. We just have to keep seeking.'

'Are you sure?'

'I am very sure,' Phanon said, hiding his own doubts.

Njangu walked up beside the man in coveralls, who had been busily running a small street sweeper, pretending not to notice Yoshitaro's obviously foreign clothes.

'Good evening, sir,' the man said tonelessly. 'Might I offer you some assistance if you've lost your way?'

'Matter of fact, you can. I'd like to have a chat with you, somewhere people in blue might not see.'

Njangu showed him a bill. The man pretended he didn't see it. Yoshitaro added a bill, then another, then a fourth.

'The fifth note got him,' Njangu said. 'I figured, go to the bottom rung with money, and you'll get somebody who won't mind talking. People at the top, people at the bottom have a lot in common – things are either so good or so bad they can afford a little honesty.

'This guy laid it out. He used to be a univee instructor. Then the collapse came, and things were a little rocky for a while. I'll write up a full report, but I thought you might want to know a little, right now, about your frigging Paradise.

'There were some riots, some people going crazy, and the security apparat took charge. This guy, Chauda, who's been chewing on my earlobe, seems to be the muckety.

'The deal was real simple, and never talked about. Things would be put back the way they were before the Confederation vanished, the wives and kiddies and such could pretend it was business as usual, and everything would be perfect.

'All they had to do was do whatever the boys in blue wanted. And I mean whatever.

'I guess Chauda's smooth enough so he doesn't let things get too far out of hand – if you're one of his goons, and want somebody, you can have them. But only for a while.

'The people go along with the program 'cause they know the exploitation . . . or at least the heel they're under at the moment . . . won't last forever, and the thugs like it, because they get variety with their villainy.

'Disagree, think maybe you'd just as soon somebody not grab your house or your wife or your son or daughter like Fleam saw, and they bust your ass down to streetsweeper or put you out in the forests, quote improving the parks end quote, or maybe there's other chain gangs that have other jobs that aren't as pretty.

'Or maybe they just take you out a few kilometers at sea, and invite you overboard for swimming lessons.'

Garvin slumped at his desk. 'Man, man. And things looked so nice here.'

'Don't they mostly everywhere?' Njangu said bitterly 'Nobody likes to look at the crapper direct and have to admit they're living in it.

'But sort of smooth over the surface so the turds don't float up too close, and maybe spraypaint things purple and use a deodorant . . .'

Yoshitaro let his voice trail off.

'So,' Garvin said, 'I guess the brightest thing is we fold our tents after the show tonight. I feel like a god-damned fool, and there's nothing but a worn patch in the greenery where we used to be, come sunrise.'

'You got a better idea?' Njangu asked. 'Sure as hell

there's no way we can change this damned world. Even if I heard any whisper of anybody out there in the bushes with a gun trying to change it, we don't have time to hang around to build some kind of revolutionary movement.

'Nope. We just vanish and hope that if there's ever a Confederation again, there'll be paybacks.'

FIFTEEN

N-space

'I've got something interesting, boss,' the electronics tech said to his superior.

'Go.'

'I was checking the monitors, to make sure we don't have any stray electronics leakage. And I found, just before we made this last jump, a bleat.

'I checked it out, and I can't trace it to any of our gear.'

'That's strange.'

'Stranger,' the technician went on. 'I ran a search all the way back, and found that damned bleat again, every time we made a jump after Cayle IV.

'We get it just as we jump, and also when we come out of N-space.

'I've spent most of two shifts trying to track it down, with zero-zed results.'

'I don't like this,' the officer said. 'I think I better make a report. And you put a bug on that frequency, and try to record the next transmission.'

'I've been thinking,' Maev Stiofan said.

'Yeh?' Njangu said cautiously.

'About when we get back.'

'Yeh?' Even more cautiously advanced.

'About all these screwed worlds we've been on . . . not to mention Cumbre and where we both came from. Howcum?'

'Uh . . . people are basically screwed-up?' Njangu offered.

'Sure . . . but that doesn't explain why . . . well, there used to be kinds of government that seemed to work. Or, anyway, that's what the disks say.'

'And of course, nobody'd ever lie to somebody as cute as you,' Njangu said.

'Come on!' Maev said. 'They can't lie like they were counting frigging cadence!'

''At's true.'

'So then comes this thing called the Confederation, and everybody sort of joins up, or gets joined up, and things hammer on for a thousand years or so.'

'More like so. A lot more so, in fact.'

'Then the Confederation gets invisible, and what we get are all these goat-screwed people, running amok in all directions, nobody seeming to have much of a government that works except maybe Grimaldi, and they don't seem to have much of anything, so that doesn't count.'

''Kay, I'm tracking,' Njangu said. 'But I don't see your point.'

'When we get back, assuming we survive Centrum and all,' Maev said patiently, 'then we grab all the guns and start trying to put things back together, right?'

'That's our hee-roic intent.'

'Maybe somebody ought to be looking at what kind of government comes back?'

'Not us,' Njangu said hastily. 'Soldiers make crappy governors. Everybody knows that.'

'But somebody's got to start thinking about what comes next,' Maev said stubbornly. 'Maybe by studying all the ways we've screwed ourselves might give somebody some ideas.'

'Like you?'

'Why not me?'

Njangu wanted to bleat out the reasons, then caught himself. Neither one of them had made any commitment beyond the moment, and had no claims on the other's future.

SIXTEEN

Mohi/Mohi II

Garvin glared at the battleship hanging not five kilometers distant on a *Jane's* screen. He tried to ignore the data scrolling past on how modern and heavily armed and state-of-the-Confederation it had been eight years ago, the most recent edition of *Jane's* the Legion had.

The battleship didn't get any smaller, nor did its two sisters flanking *Big Bertha*. Garvin might have convinced himself that the circus ship was huge, but these three warships dwarfed it, twice as long and half again as fat, but lethally curved instead of just obese.

They were well and truly trapped, four jumps from Centrum by these three ships and the swarm of accompanying escorts. Alikhan had entered this system, reported no ships within range of his detectors, and that four of the system's ten planets, as their data said, were still inhabited.

Big Bertha had left N-space, and, seconds later, the warships had jumped it. Either the circus had gotten careless, or these warships had sensors better than anything aboard *Big Bertha* and its smaller craft.

'I have a com on the Confederation standard watch freq, sir,' the watch radio officer reported.

'Plug it through,' Liskeard ordered.

'Unknown ship, unknown ship, this is the Confederation Protectorate Battlefleet Kin. Respond immediately or be destroyed.'

'This is the Circus Ship *Big Bertha*, inbound for Desman II, purpose, entertainment.'

'This is Kin,' the response came. 'Correct your records. The Desman system is now the Mohi system. You will be escorted to landing, and then you will be searched and determination will be made of your fate. Make no resistance, or—'

Njangu finished the phrase. 'Or you will be destroyed. Boss, I think we may have found the raiders.'

'Confederation Protectorate, eh?' Garvin said. 'Now I *really* wish we had a diplomat on board.'

Liskeard requested an orbital approach, for economic reasons, actually to give observers a chance to see as much of Mohi II as they could. The answer came back:

'Refused. Make direct approach to spaceport. Or you will be destroyed.'

'Varied in their approach to problems, aren't they?' Njangu asked.

'At least they don't seem to be taking us seriously,' Garvin said. 'They've only peeled off one battle-wagon and half a dozen escorts to get us safely to ground, deadly rep-tiles that we are.'

Njangu called the watch officer over: 'I want every eyeball on every scope we've got as we come in, to give me some idea of how deep the shit is gonna be, since we ain't gonna get the pleasure of peering about as we low'n'slow it down.'

The news was not good – Desman II, now Mohi lI, was a garrison world. Huge landing fields, most freshly built, dotted the landscape. Nearby were barracks complexes and factories.

'I suppose they're worried about trouble,' Dill said.

'Getting into, or out of?' Boursier asked.

Dill pointed to the screen showing the enormous battleship hovering above them as they made their final approach, didn't need to answer the question.

Lifters with chainguns in open mounts surrounded *Big Bertha* as its drive shut down, and troops doubled toward the ship, took positions around it.

'Damn, but we're dangerous,' Ben Dill said.

'Now all we have to do is convince 'em we're little pink pussycats.' Monique Lir said with a tight smile. 'Then, when they relax, we'll kill 'em all.'

Big Bertha was searched, very efficiently, in teams of five, taking more than a ship day and a half. As before, Garvin and his officers 'helped,' ensuring that no one found anything, at least anything important in the way of weaponry. These men and women of the Protectorate were realists, recognized the need for some weapons in these times, which simplified what had to be hidden.

One officer stopped, looking in some dismay at Alikhan, who was sprawled on a bulkhead, under which were some of the Legion's crew-served heavy weapons. She fingered her blaster.

'Is that creature dangerous? Should it not be caged?'

'It is of no real danger,' Garvin said. 'In so long as its handlers are careful.'

'If it were mine,' the officer said, 'I would have it penned up.'

Garvin smiled, and the search went on. Alikhan glowered after the party, ears cocked in mild anger.

'Handlers indeed,' he growled to himself. 'Little do these humans realize who is the handler and who the handled.'

The soldier peered around the bridge.

'Everything works,' he said.

'Of course everything works,' Froude said mildly. 'If it didn't, it would have no place.' Then what the man had said stopped him.

'When something breaks aboard one of your ships, what do you do?'

'We replace it, of course, with a new unit from the Confederation days.'

'But if you don't have a replacement?'

'Then we rely on other, redundant systems, and hope there are still sealed units in the warehouses back at our base to install when we return.'

'But you cannot fix what is broken?'

The soldier looked as if he thought he'd said too much, clamped his lips shut, went on.

Muldoon lay, very much at ease, in his cage, purring loudly.

The search team nervously admired his sleekness, passed on.

Muldoon stared after them, still purring. His claws were working rhythmically in and out of the matting on his cage's floor.

'We have found your ship to be free of forbidden materials and contraband,' the young officer welcomed. 'Remain in your ship until you are advised what stages we intend next for you.'

*

A half day later, the summons came: The commander of this circus ship, together with his high-ranking officers, and representatives of this so-called circus, were to present themselves to the *Kuril*'s presence on the next E-day. Transport would be provided.

Garvin picked his team carefully: he and Njangu of course; Alikhan, who could wear his combat harness carrying a Musth devourer-weapon and wasp grenades that wouldn't be recognized for what they were; Dr. Froude in his clown suit; Sir Douglas and a completely tame and unchained cheetah, Monique Lir, and Ben Dill for his ostentatious muscles and the hope he wouldn't have to use them.

Kekri Katun pouted to Ben that she hadn't been chosen. 'I would've thought Garvin would have taken at least one of the showgirls to, well, show off. And I certainly do that well, and tumble, and things like that.'

'Probably exactly why he didn't pick you,' Ben said. 'Supposing this *Kuril* took a fancy to you?'

'Oh. I guess . . .' Kekri's voice trailed off. 'Then what about Monique Lir? She's awful pretty.'

Ben thought of explaining just how lethal a package Monique was, thought better of it.

'Dunno,' he said. 'Which is why I ain't the gaffer.'

He still was having trouble calling Garvin anything other than 'boss' at best and 'giptel-brained asshole' or 'my rotten-crotch former gunner' at worst.

Froude looked about as the troupe shambled up the steps between rows of soldiers at rigid attention, blasters at the salute. Behind them were the military lifters that had brought them into this city from *Big Bertha*.

'I suppose this says everything about the Protectorate,' he whispered to Njangu.

'Maybe. But think good thoughts.'

The enormous building, stone, columned, in the style of an ancient temple, had been, according to an only half-obliterated sign: THE EISBERG CENTER OF MODERN ART.

'Wonder what they did with the paintings?' Ben Dill said.

'Probably used 'em for bumfodder,' Monique replied.

The officer leading them into the *Kuril*'s presence turned back and scowled. Evidently the troupe was not showing sufficient respect.

At least, Njangu thought, *Kuril* Jagasti looked like a proper dictator, just as Garvin looked the proper leader. After the late, unmourned Protector of Larix/Kura, Alena Redruth, who had resembled a medium-level bureaucrat rather than a ruler, he was ready for a goon who looked his part.

Jagasti was tall, lean, with a scarred neck and a beaked nose, his graying hair worn straight and long. He had the hard, predator's stare of an Earth eagle Njangu had seen in a holo. Or else he badly needed vision correction.

His throne was in the biggest room in the former museum, and was skillfully made of polished steel, weld beads deliberately not ground down, and dark leathers.

His entourage dripped weaponry from many eras, from contemporary blasters to ugly-looking fighting knives and close-combat tools.

Jagasti took his time looking over the troupe, then, without greeting them, asked their business. He looked puzzled at the reply.

'Entertainment? I am not sure I know what that is, other than seeing the destruction of a foe, the pain of an enemy, the delight in hearing his cities burn, his starships explode, his women scream, his warriors moan.'

Garvin nodded to Sir Douglas, who tossed a ball to his cheetah. Froude instantly started contesting the cat for the ball, mimicking the cheetah's motions.

Jagasti watched, stony-faced.

Garvin motioned to Ben Dill, who took a stance, and Monique Lir struck off from him, spun high in the air in a triple somersault, landed on her feet.

'Ah,' Jagasti grunted. 'You mean tricks.'

'I mean tricks such as the galaxy has never seen before,' Garvin said. 'With real Earth horses, elephants, fearsome beasts, strange aliens, men and women flying high above your head, games of chance and skill, clowns to make you helpless with—'

'Enough!' Jagasti snapped. 'I am not a prospective purchaser of your circus.'

Njangu was thinking that Jagasti might be the very model of a major waste-layer, but his navigation bridge might not be in that close a communication with his stardrive

A man, heavily bearded, stepped out of the throng.

'I am hardly superstitious, as you know, *Kuril*,' he said. 'Might not the arrival of these strangers be a sign, be something we can use to send around to our various troop encampments to lift their morale?'

'Their morale will be raised sufficiently by the sight of my brother lying dead in the dust,' Jagasti said, but he didn't sound that certain.

'A better idea,' another warrior said, a man in his forties, hard body just starting to paunch out. 'We should take what we will from these people, for surely they are not strong.

'Their men could become laborers, their beasts either

slaughtered if they prove dangerous or caged for our education, and their women . . .' He let his voice trail off, staring at Lir.

'That could be an option,' Jagasti agreed.

Garvin held back anger. 'I would think that anyone who claims to be the Protectorate of the Confederation would welcome innocent wanderers, especially those who have vowed, as we have, to do all in our power to bring the return of order and law.'

'The Confederation will return,' Jagasti agreed, 'as my late father swore.'

Interestingly, at the mention of Jagasti's father, everyone in the room bowed their heads for an instant. Garvin hastily followed suit, as did the others, except for Alikhan, who kept cold, reddening eyes locked on Jagasti.

'It will return,' Jagasti repeated. 'On my terms. My brother and I have sworn the same oath as my father, and were it not for certain . . . unforeseen developments of late, we would surely be making plans for our conquest of Centrum.'

Garvin glanced about to see if anyone preened at the word 'brother,' saw a thin, intense man, about ten years younger than Jagasti, purse his lips and nod hurriedly. Garvin noticed the man's eyes remained on his brother, his expression unreadable.

Njangu noted the look as well, filed it as possibly interesting.

'Of course this will happen,' the heavyset man said. 'No one doubts that, just as we don't doubt your traitor of a brother will be destroyed soon enough.

'But that doesn't answer the question of these intruders. We . . . all of us . . . believe that from power all else falls.

'I, for instance, am interested in this woman trickster. She, no doubt, with her muscles, could provide me with interesting evenings, and I don't doubt there are others like her in this so-called circus.'

He smiled unpleasantly, started toward Monique Lir.

Garvin stepped between them, and there was a blaster in the man's hand.

'Move aside,' the man ordered.

Garvin looked at the throne.

'Do you allow this mistreatment to your guests Jagasti?'

'I have not yet determined if you are my guests,' Jagasti answered. 'Or my prisoners. But I would suggest you obey Toba. He has a very short temper, and has killed more than his share.'

Garvin hesitated, then obeyed.

'My sympathies, sir,' he murmured.

Toba, grinning, came forward, reached out with his free hand to tweak one of Lir's nipples.

Flat-footed, Lir kicked, and the pistol spun up and out of Toba's grip. Before he could react, Lir's foot was back on the ground, and she spun, back-kicked with her other foot into Toba's face. He screeched in agony, staggered back, fell.

Lir was back in a stance as Toba sat up. He lifted a hand to his mouth, saw the gouting blood, spat teeth, sighed, and fell back, unconscious.

Alikhan's paw was on a wasp-grenade, ready to claw it into life and pitch it into Jagasti's lap, where the insect-like killers would come alive and deal the man a terrible death. Dill stepped wide, to give himself fighting room.

Njangu decided there didn't seem to be any other options other than running, wasn't up for it, and got ready to die.

To everyone in the troupe's surprise, Jagasti, after recovering from his astonishment, roared in laughter.

'Good! That was very good! Toba has always thought he could do anything he wished. I now rename him Gummy, and welcome you strangers as guests, for there is clearly more to you than is visible, and I suspect at least some of you of being warriors, not merely the despised servants we batten on.

'Perhaps your shows will, indeed, build the morale of my fighters.'

SEVENTEEN

'Uh, boss?'

'What's the problem, Ben?' Garvin asked.

'Kekri and I . . . actually, just Kekri . . . we need to have a talk with you.'

'Sure,' Garvin said.

'Private? And it'll take a while?'

'Come on in,' Garvin said, leading the two into his office. He noticed Kekri was carrying a small case.

'So what's the problem?' he said after the door closed.

'I'm . . . I'm a spy!' Kekri said, and burst into tears.

'Well I shall be dipped,' Njangu said. 'Full confession, she's an agent for—'

'Director Fan Bertl, back on Tiborg,' Garvin said. 'Just like you thought.'

'Hmm,' Njangu said. 'I'd been thinking about her, figuring we'd have to do cleanup before . . . how much longer before that thing Lir and Montagna planted wreaks havoc?'

'*You're* supposed to be the one keeping track of things like that. But I looked it up. About two E-months, which means two and a week here.'

'And she's given us everything she's got?'

'She's still being debriefed. But it looks like it.'

'What was she looking for?'

'Bertl didn't tell her . . . he just said report anything interesting, particularly about where these people are really coming from, and what their real intentions are. Guess he didn't trust her all the way, which is the only way to treat HUMINT.

'And there's an interesting little side note. She was supposed to transmit this diary when her little sender got a signal saying somebody was listening.

'Also, Bertl promised that she wasn't on a one-way trip. At a suitable moment, she'd be rescued. I don't know if Bertl was stroking her or not, but she surely believed someone would be there with a rope ladder.

'I don't like that at all,' Garvin went on. 'Especially since there's no way that I can figure out that Bertl could be tracking us.'

'*Damn*,' Njangu muttered. 'Wheels within cart-wheels. Would've been better if she didn't confess, so we could grab when that transmitter went off . . . if it ever did. Ben Dill went and did too good a job. What the hell good's an agent when she's all the way out of the chill?'

'That's another thing,' Garvin said. 'He's decided he's in love, and really hopes that neither of us set this whole thing up as any kind of a joke.'

'Oh.'

'He said he'd be really, really, really assed if we had.'

'I don't think I've ever seen Ben more than really, really, assed,' Njangu said thoughtfully.

'Me either,' Garvin said. 'Maybe we ought to send Kekri's whole file to the shredder? Especially the parts that might ah-hem have anything on your thoughts about me and Kekri.'

'I'll shred it twice,' Njangu said. 'Dill scares me snot-less.

'But let's keep that nifty little notebook/locator of hers handy. We still might need it someday.'

He sat shaking his head.

'*Damn*, but it's sour when a plan goes just the way it's supposed to, and you're still sucking wind.'

'Back to our device on Tiborg,' Garvin said. 'Did we screw up?'

Njangu began to say something, thought about it.

'You want a gut response . . . no. Goddamned politicians and their tradesy-ing power back and forth, and busting it off in people like you and me . . . good to see the whole damned lot of them in a thin spray on the walls.'

Garvin started to respond, but Njangu held up his hand.

'That's the gut feeling. But now that we're a bit away, and my head's out of me bung . . . maybe. A very large maybe, starting with the position that people who kill things and break people ought to stay the hell out of politics. Plus the idiots on Tiborg went and got themselves in this shitter, and they should be the ones to dig themselves out.

'We can't go around playing Saint John the Rescuer to everybody.'

'But isn't that what we're doing right now with this chasing about after the Confederation?'

'Goddamit, Garvin, don't confuse me any more than I can already confuse myself.

'In answer to your question . . . if I had it to do all over again, back on Delta, I don't think I would've done it. Or, rather, that I encouraged you to do it.'

'You think that way bad enough that we should think

about going back when we get free of these idiots, and turn off the machine?'

'That'll be a good trick in itself,' Njangu said. 'Naw. I don't think so. They were all a bunch of shitheels, and deserve a little maiming around the edges.

'Not to mention they'll sure as hell try to blow our ass up around our shoulder blades if we ever get within range of them again.

'Forget it,' he said. 'We've got enough problems and that'll sure as hell never rebound back on us, especially now that we've got Kekri and her little direction finder all neutralized.'

EIGHTEEN

'Thank you, ladies, for taking the time to listen to this parlari,' Njangu said. 'Does everyone have a drink or an inhaler?'

Ten of the circus showgirls, carefully selected by Yoshitaro for seeming lack of moral turpitude, were gathered in one of *Big Bertha*'s rec rooms.

'Perhaps you've noticed that the people we're among now are, shall we say, a little more direct than some of the other townies we've appeared before?'

'Damned straight,' one of the women said. 'I turned my back on two of the bastards last show, and they tried to rip my gown off for a laugh! Damned glad we're playing in the ship instead of under canvas.

'Direct hell,' she went on. 'Goons and rapists, if they think they can get away with it.'

'I think the technical term is "barbarians,"' another woman said.

Njangu scratched his chin, waited until the laughter stopped.

'What we want, what Gaffer Jaansma wants,' he said, 'is to play a few dates here and there in this system, then proceed on our course toward Centrum.

'The Protectorate isn't keen on that idea.'

'Why not?' a woman asked.

'Because, I suspect, they've got designs on whatever remains of the Confederation themselves.'

'And we're a threat?'

Njangu held out his hands.

'It seems so.'

'Idiots!' another woman snapped.

'Quite possibly,' Njangu said. 'Which is where my proposal stands. I'm looking for volunteers who wouldn't mind making friends with some of these Protectorate sorts.'

'You mean, officers, high-ranking types?'

'I certainly don't think your average deck ape might be able to talk about things we might be interested in hearing.'

One of the women, a Delot Eibar, whom Njangu had pegged as somewhat quicker than others, looked at him skeptically. 'You mean pillow talk.'

'Not necessarily,' Yoshitaro said carefully, feeling the tiny bit he had of what he guessed other people called 'morality' squirm. 'Just . . . talk.'

'But not *not* necessarily, either,' Eibar said.

Njangu didn't answer.

'What other kinds of spying are you doing?'

Njangu smiled blandly.

'Oh. I get it. If one of us goes and falls in love instead of the other way around, she won't have any pillow talk of her own?'

'You are a clever woman,' Yoshitaro said.

'Maybe,' Eibar said. 'If . . . if I go for a proposition like that, it would have to be my choice. I don't want to get rammed into the sack with some thug who hasn't taken a bath in a year or so.'

'Agreed,' Njangu said.

'Now, since this is way outside being "generally useful," might I ask what this bit of cherry pie will pay?'

'If any of you agree, you can double your contract price,' Njangu said.

There was a murmur from the showgirls. Njangu got up.

'Talk about it with each other. I promise no risk and if anything seems a little shaky, we'll have you wired, with security backing you, and we'll break anything up that looks like it's getting troublesome.'

'Security,' a girl murmured. 'Like that Ben Dill?'

'I'm sorry,' Njangu said. 'Ben's a big man, but he's no more than that.'

'Yeh,' Eibar said skeptically. 'Yeh, sure. Not that it matters, since Kekri Katun's got his chastity belt keys.

'At any rate,' she went on, 'I think I understand what you're looking for very, very well.'

'And *I* think,' Njangu said, 'that scares me a little.'

Monique Lir swayed, looked seductive, and beckoned to the sad-faced Froude. He looked down from his perch, swayed, flailed his hands, recovered his balance.

Again, Monique beckoned, and this time, Froude saw a balance pole, which just happened to have a midget at each end. He picked it up, seemingly not noticing the little people, and stepped out onto the wire toward Lir.

He dipped, almost fell, the midgets flailed with him, and the audience bayed amusement.

Monique, as secure on her wire as if she were bolted on, looked down at the packed stands. It was what used to be called a sawdust crowd, she knew, with all the stands full and people sitting on the deck. It'd been that way for seven shows, and she didn't like it any better now than before.

There was nobody in the crowd except men and women, all in uniform. No children, no old people, no civilians at all, not even government officials, since Jagasti believed anyone connected with the Protectorate should be part of the military.

Froude overbalanced, and fell, still holding on to the balance pole. But somehow he didn't come off the wire, but spun through a full circle, still holding the pole and little people, and was back on top again, to thundering applause. Froude looked a bit shaken – this gag, heavy on antigravity devices, even though there was a *ra'felan* catcher hanging overhead, was a little new. This was only the third time they'd done it since Froude had the idea and rehearsed it endlessly, a meter off the deck into a trampoline.

Lir wondered how they'd get through these bastards and on about their business toward Centrum. This circus stuff was interesting, but the thrill was starting to fade.

She really wanted to put her uniform back on, assemble the troops, and go out and beat the butts of some of the yoinks she'd endured over the past months.

Lir was more than willing to start with the morons below who called themselves the Protectorate.

Njangu, Dalet Eibar, and Bayanti, Jagasti's younger brother, sat in a closed skybox, watching the caracoles of the circus below them. Bayanti, Yoshitaro was pleased to note, kept flicking looks at Eibar when he thought Njangu wasn't looking.

'You actually have a life like this?' Bayanti asked. 'Just traveling about, doing these shows?'

'It's what we've chosen,' Njangu said.

'We like . . . excitement,' Dalet put in suggestively.

'These are dangerous times for wanderers without support,' Bayanti said.

'Which,' Dalet added, 'is why we like to get along with everyone.' She smiled.

Njangu thought that was about enough, so he triggered a sensor on his belt com. It buzzed, and he answered the false summons to the bridge. He apologized to Bayanti, asked Dalet if she'd mind escorting him about and show him whatever he wanted, left.

He left it to Eibar to explain that she and Njangu weren't companying each other, that she had no one special and, in fact, hoped she'd meet someone to show her about this fascinating system the circus had landed on.

He also made a note to adjust Dalet's contract.

'You were a soldier, once, I think,' Phraphas Phanon asked Alikhan.

The Musth considered, decided there was no harm in speaking the truth. 'I was.'

'We would like to hire you to teach us something,' Phanon said, and Thanon nodded eagerly.

'If I know something of worth, you have but to ask,' Alikhan said. 'It will help pass the time. I am bored being stared at by these short-haired idiots and thought a horrible monster.'

'We want you to teach us how to use weapons.'

Alikhan's head darted back and forth, lifted his paws in surprise.

'Why do you wish to learn such?' he asked.

'These are troubled times,' Phanon said. 'We feel vulnerable, needing to be able to protect our gray friends.'

'That is not hard to understand,' Alikhan agreed. 'But why have you come to me?'

'First,' Thanon said, 'you are the one we have decided

most clearly was, perhaps even is, a soldier, although there are those such as Mr. Yoshitaro or Mr. Dill we suspect of having once had such a trade.'

'I didn't know that,' Alikhan said. 'I thought Ben Dill was too fat to be a soldier.' He was proud of himself for making a human joke, couldn't wait to tell this to Dill.

'You see? We are not sure.'

'The problem will be,' Alikhan said, 'the actual firing of the weapons. I assume you do not mean to learn the tools I carry with me on occasion, since I have but two sets of them with me, and they would be very difficult for a human to use.

'I doubt if these Protectors would be impressed should we take some of the ship's blasters outside and start banging away at targets.'

'We thought of that. Could you not teach us the working of these weapons, how to load, aim, fire them, and then, at a better time, perhaps we could shoot for real?'

Alikhan thought.

'Yes. Yes, I could do that. And, in return, I would ask a favor?'

'Whatever we have is yours.'

'I would like you to introduce me to one of your elephants and perhaps, if he learns I am no threat, to give me a ride?'

Njangu sent out agents, some openly to what remained of the planet's libraries, some more covertly. A bit at a time, cautiously, skeptically, he was building a history of this Protectorate. All data were, of course, categorized in the aeons-old classification:

A: A participant in the reported events.
B: A witness.
C: Accurate source.
D: Not dependable.

To this was added the evaluation of the information:

1. Information verified through two additional B-
    or C-level sources.
2. Information probably accurate, but no high-
    level verification.
3. Information not verified, but fairly logical.
4. Rumor.

Muldoon leapt out from his perch on an elephant stand toward the waiting lion, who boomed a roar at him. The leopard tucked, and the lion caught him on his paws, bounced him to a tiger, who risleyed him on to the next, waiting cat, almost throwing him into Sir Douglas, who cracked his whip menacingly, then back to the lion and to rest.

The crowd was silent in awe for an instant, then boomed approval.

Muldoon yawned complacently at the recognition, licked his paw.

'Very damned good,' Garvin said. 'I like the way that everybody's looking at everybody else's act—'

'You mean stealing,' Sir Douglas grinned.

'I never use words like that. Congratulations. You make it look dangerous.'

'Around me, there is never danger,' Sir Douglas said loftily. Garvin grinned, went back to Ring #1 as the cats were cleared out of the center cage.

'I'll not tell the gaffer your fingers were crossed

when you said that about no danger,' Darod Montagna said.

'I thank you,' Sir Douglas said.

'Maev, if you'll take the door,' Njangu said.

She nodded and, pistol half-hidden, stepped out of the small conference room, buried in the middle of *Big Bertha*'s command module.

Inside were the ranking members of the Legion, plus Doctors Froude and Ristori.

'What we're going to get here,' Garvin said, 'is a short history lesson on who these Protectorate sorts seem to be, which may help us figure out what to do next.

'Since Dr. Froude is probably the best of us at syncretic thinking, I've asked him to do the lecture, which is based on almost all of Froude's, Njangu's, and his staff's digging and delving. Doctor?'

Froude leaned back in his chair and started talking.

About twenty E-years earlier, the Confederation had begun hiring entire population groups, those considered warrior-types, for security, and keeping them as integral units, rather than relying on the more conventional military like the Navy or the Legions.

No one in the audience had heard of this practice having been done before, nor did anyone have any idea why something this primitive and dangerous was begun.

'I wish,' Garvin said, 'that we had a few of the old soldiers with us. Maybe *Caud* Williams or Rao knew of such units, and why the Confederation chose such a step.'

'I'll make a guess,' Yoshitaro said. 'They got paid in loot and worked cheaper.'

There was a murmur of laughter.

'I wasn't being funny,' Njangu said, and the laughter stopped.

'Monique,' Garvin went on, 'you're the closest thing to an old soldier around. Did you ever hear of anything like this?'

'No,' Monique said, then stopped, thinking. 'Wait a sec. Before I joined up, when I was an opera dancer, somebody said something once about being damned glad that the local soldiers were regulars, since she was getting tired of chasing off shag artists.

'I don't remember her saying any more.'

'Interesting,' Froude said, and went on.

'These people now calling themselves the Protectorate had been moved closer and closer to Centrum evidently as problems on the homeworld worsened.

'Then the Confederation fell out of contact with everyone, including these charmers.

'The father of these three brothers who now are running things got the interesting idea that he was strong enough to take Capella and Centrum and then dictate what should come next.

'The Confederation should dissolve Parliament after "electing" a strong leader to put things back together, allowing no systems to declare independence, and to destroy any worlds attacking Confederation members.

'He seems to have been a very cautious man, for his first steps were away from Centrum, taking control of other systems like Sabyn, turning systems like Mais into puppets, and so on. We are sure they control at least twenty systems now, maybe more.

'The way the Protectorate operates is to skim only the cream from these systems, leaving enough for the worlds to keep functioning, not hurting them badly enough to tempt them to revolt, and, evidently, instantly coming down with an iron heel on anyone who dissents. I've heard of at least two worlds that didn't listen to reason and got the nuclear treatment.

'I haven't been able to find out just how long Jagasti's father thought it would be before the Protectorate was ready to make a hard move on Centrum although I did get a couple of hints that recon units were sent out, never to return. They were probably destroyed by whatever war fleets the Confederation still has operational, backed by the mechanical security devices around Centrum.'

'Things were going well,' he continued. 'And then the old man had the lack of grace to die. A surfeit of eels or some such. I couldn't tell, through the holos' purple hosannas at the funeral.

'I don't think any of his sons did the usual junior tyrant act, and slipped a shot of radioactive bilgewater in the old bastard's nightcap, or piss poison in the porches of his ears.

'Regardless, he's dead, and so Jagasti, who has a reputation of being a most noble warrior, although what real war he's fought doesn't get mentioned, takes over as *Kuril*.

'He has nowhere near the ability of his father at keeping all of these thugs somewhat under control, and so the number two son, who evidently fancies himself a Greater Leader, stomped off, with his supporters, and now holds two systems, Degasten and Khon, and keeps saying that he's the rightful *Kuril*.'

'What about the third son?' Garvin asked. 'He was at the circus the other night.'

'I'm developing certain areas of interest with him,' Njangu said, trying to sound pompous. 'Bayanti is ambitious, but it doesn't seem, so far, that he's thinking about striking out on his own.

'However, I'm thinking of ways of encouraging his ambition.'

'That's a very fast precis of this Protectorate,' Froude said. 'I've got far more details for anyone interested.'

'The question now is what do we do? It doesn't seem that the Protectorate, for their own paranoiac reasons, will encourage or even allow us to make the next four jumps to Centrum.'

'I get the idea,' Njangu put in, 'that we're increasingly well thought of by Jagasti and crew. Which is good in one way, but makes it very hard for us to tiptoe out the back door without Jagasti getting a lethal – for us – case of the pouts.'

'What we need,' Garvin said thoughtfully, 'is a way to put some shit in the game, without us getting brownish in the process.'

The people in the room looked at each other.

No one's expression suggested she or he had the slightest idea.

Njangu's lips were moving up Maev's inner thigh when he sat bolt upright.

'I'll be a sunnuvabitch!'

'You damned sure are if you don't go back to what you're doing,' Maev managed, with a sharp intake of breath.

But Yoshitaro paid no mind, was sitting up, and touching com buttons.

'This,' Garvin's voice came, 'had better be goddamned important, Njangu. There is a time and a place for everything, especially for using this number.' He appeared to be breathing hard.

'Boss,' Njangu said proudly, 'I have a scheme.'

NINETEEN

'I propose,' Njangu said, 'to make the situation worse.'

'For whom?' Froude asked, amused. Garvin yawned sleepily, said nothing. The three were gathered in Garvin's cabin office, waiting for a stim.

'Certainly not for us,' Yoshitaro said. 'At least, I hope not.

'Look at what we've got. Three brothers, barbarians, two of 'em at least not getting along. They're plotting on grabbing all the gold, but, like their father, don't appear quite ready to make the big jump and go after Centrum. I'd guess if this Gegen, who's floated over to Degasten with everyone he can subvert, wouldn't mind at all if Big Brother Jagasti happens to trip and fall on his saber.'

'Your points are undebateable,' Froude said.

'Therefore, I propose to throw some shit in the game, as they used to say,' Njangu said.

'What species of doots?' Garvin broke off as a mess attendant came in with a tray, then, after he'd left, waited for an answer.

'Suspicion will lie on every hand. And foot,' Njangu said. 'I'm going to convince these three yahoos they're about to get assassinated.'

'Good,' Garvin said. 'Who's going to be the head of the plot?'

'Why, me, of course.'

'For all three?'

'Can I juggle, or what?' Njangu said, slurping caff.

Jagasti's idea of fine sport was equipping lifters with probes, and hanging a cloth of a given color from one of them. The others . . . ten to a side, two men to a lifter . . . tried to take the cloth away or protect the flag-carrier until he reached a goal.

As far as Njangu could tell, there weren't any especial rules, except all lifters should withdraw to their end of the field while an ambulance rescued the survivors of a crash.

At least blasters didn't seem to be permitted.

'Interesting sport, *Kuril*,' Yoshitaro said.

'Yes! It is the sport of men. Real men! Supposedly we first played it, riding animals, back on our homeworlds. But now it is much faster,' Jagasti said.

'And kills even more of our best fighters,' Bayanti said.

'Life is just a waiting for death,' Jagasti said impatiently. 'Men get weak, become like women, unless they test themselves.'

Bayanti was about to say something when two lifters soared high, then dived on the flag-bearer. The first slammed into the flag-carrier, sending it spinning, the flag carried away by the slight breeze. The second lifter speared it, and, at full drive, jinked right, then left, then through the goal.

Jagasti was on his feet, bellowing praise, promising rewards to the scorers and the screen.

Bayanti looked at Njangu strangely, then away.

Jagasti returned to his seat, a metal vee with canvas strung across the metal.

'You, Bayanti,' he said. 'Go praise those pilots, and give them . . . give them permission to join my First Imperials. This alien has said he wants to discuss something with me that is private.'

'And your brother isn't entitled to hear that?'

'I shall decide that,' Jagasti said. 'Later.'

Bayanti got up, then stamped from the prefab enclosure.

'Brothers!' Jagasti said, shaking his head. 'Do you have any, Yoshitaro?'

'I wasn't that lucky,' Njangu said.

'No, you are the lucky one,' Jagasti said. 'It must be wonderful, growing up, not having to watch your back or to be able to run without someone trying to trip you.

'Then, when you have finally seen clear to the goal, to have one of your own blood call you a fool, say you are not entitled to what you've won, and declare himself your enemy.

'You are young yet, and do not know what it is to have your own flesh a traitor, betraying what he knows is right.'

Njangu waited.

'Never mind that,' Jagasti said. 'My problems are my problems. Tell me why you wished to see me in secret.'

'I want,' Njangu said carefully, 'to make your problems mine.'

'What does that mean?'

'As you've no doubt figured out, Circus Jaansma is a bit more than it appears.'

'I knew it! I knew it!' Jagasti exulted. 'No one but a fool goes about in bloody times such as these doing no more than swinging through the air and hoping to be rewarded for it.

'Tell me. What else do you do?'

'It depends,' Njangu said. 'Sometimes we do no more than we offer at first. But sometimes, when we deal with the right kind of people, and the reward is great, we provide certain services.'

'You are still being vague.'

'I'll be specific, then,' Njangu said. 'For a fee, which we'll negotiate in advance, I think we can rid you of your brother, Gegen, and leave the way clear for you to continue your conquest of Centrum.'

Njangu thought Jagasti's eyes glowed yellow, like those of Muldoon the leopard before he tried to rip someone's face off.

'This is a *long* damned shot,' Darod Montagna complained. 'Plus this is one shitty platform to shoot from.'

Montagna lay behind a rather skeletal weapon, a still-experimental sniper rifle. It looked like something a child had built from a construction set, all struts and bolts. Rather than use a conventional blaster bolt, the weapon fired an old-fashioned solid projectile.

The caliber was shockingly large – almost 18mm. The projectile was shielded from gravity and winds with a miniscule antigravity dropper in its nose that would keep the round on a flat trajectory for as far as six kilometers.

The magazine held three rounds, the bullet weighing about 170 grams, and traveling at just under 2,000 m/sec. Above the action was an ugly stabilized sight, giving a variable magnification of from 2x to over 200X.

It was deliberately weighted, for stability and to reduce recoil, to over eighteen kilos, and, of course not being shoulder-fireable, had a shocked, rear-pointing bipod up front and an equally angled monopod at the rear. It still would have kicked the marksman's shoulder into next week without two heavy springs in the stock against the action's rear, giving it almost ten centimeters of recoil, like an ancient cannon. Not that the piece could ever be considered fun to fire.

Montagna was right about the firing platform's stability – she lay on the deck of a lifter hovering at about two-thousand meters, the weapon sticking out its lowered rear ramp.

'Stop sniveling, Nimrod,' Lir said as she ratcheted rounds half as long as her forearm into the rifle's box magazine. 'And you're supposed to miss the bastard, remember?'

'Yeh,' Montagna said, squirming. 'But I gotta get at least close enough to make him think he's a target, right?'

Montagna wore a very tight shooter's jacket, and the rifle sling with an autornatic tensioner ran from the weapon over her back, down between her legs, and back up to the gun's stock. She couldn't have wiggled if she'd tried.

The lifter swayed in the breeze, and Lir muttered 'Stop that,' to the autopilot, trying to keep the lifter dead stable, using three points – the nose of *Big Bertha*, a dozen kilometers away, barely visible, Mohi II's second moon overhead, and a distant mountain.

Montagna sighed, peered through her sight at the mansion, five kilometers distant, its stone façade glittering in the rising sun. She found the steps, swept over the waiting lim, moved up to the main entrance. She ran it up to full magnification, decided this was the best it was going to get, backed the wheel down a turn.

Lir had a pair of stabilized glasses on the mansion's entrance as well.

They waited. Montagna felt the dawn breeze, brisk in her nostrils.

'The driver just popped to,' Lir warned. 'He's got to be on the way.'

Montagna saw the door of the mansion come open, breathed in . . . out . . . held it . . . touched the first of the very old-fashioned set triggers. A heavy breath on the second trigger would set the rifle off.

A man . . . clearly Bayanti . . . came into sight, talking animatedly to someone.

Montagna touched the trigger, and the rifle, in spite of its flash/sound suppressor at its muzzle, slammed the Last Trump.

Montagna, ignoring her mind saying, *You flinched, you dumb-ass bitch*, forced the behemoth back on target, waiting to see what happened while the bullet went on its way. By the time she had her sights back, the huge bullet had made a decent-size hole in the stonework about a meter above Bayanti's head, and he was flattened on the stairs, his companion bravely lying atop him, shielding him from another shot from the assassin.

'I think you signified,' Lir said.

'Guess so,' Darod said, unstrapping herself, and rubbing her shoulder. 'Damn, but this sumbitch kicks.'

'Decent shot,' Lir said. 'Now let's go home and see how much of Njangu's shit this stirred up.'

It was considerable.

Jagasti summoned Njangu within the day.

'Someone,' he said icily, 'tried to kill my young brother this morning.'

Njangu pretended surprise.

'That was all the commotion this morning. We were turned back from the city twice.'

'You were lucky you were not fired on,' Jagasti said. 'My men were in shock, and most trigger-happy. Now, you are officially given the commission to take care of my brother Gegen, as you said you could do.'

'I said I could try to do.'

'You *will* do it,' Jagasti said. 'I do not respect failure, particularly when someone not familiar to me volunteers for a task, then does not succeed.

'You can have any resources you need, any amount of credits.

'Now go, accomplish your mission!'

Degasten/Ogdal

Njangu wished they'd had room in *Big Bertha* to conceal a small destroyer, or, better, one of the Musth *velv*. But covert operations is exactly like hiking – there's never room enough in the pack for everything that might be needed. So they took a Nana boat, and had one of the Protectorate's battleships transport it two of the three jumps to the Degasten system, where Gegen and his dissidents headquartered.

Njangu took four with him: Ben Dill as pilot, Monique Lir; Alikhan because an alien with big ears might be useful, and Danfin Froude as his 'handler.'

Ogdai was Degasten's most settled world, and Dill set an open orbit toward the planet as soon as they came out of N-space, after leaving a small object just beyond the nav point.

Unsurprisingly, they'd only been in normal space a ship-hour or two before a pair of heavy cruisers dropped on them, ordered them to stand by for boarding, and performed the usual search. As usual, they missed various items Njangu had well hidden about the ship. He was starting to realize Garvin was right when he said a professional smuggler always stole the march on customs.

Njangu declared his intent as 'forward man for a circus.' Their ship was escorted to a distant, barren field, and he was told to stand by.

Four officials of increasing rank came, were told of Circus Jaansma and its desire to play Ogdai and Degasten's other worlds, and here was an example of their artists, looked startled when Njangu said the circus was currently appearing on Mohi II. The last, and highest-ranking, was also told that Yoshitaro wished an audience, if that was what it was called, with *Kuril* Gegen.

The officer looked at Njangu haughtily. 'The *Kuril* hardly needs to be involved in deciding whether to allow a group of entertainers to appear in our system.'

'Of course not,' Njangu agreed. 'But he could be interested in something involving his brother.'

'Jagasti? What? You can tell me. I report to *Kuril* Gegen myself.'

Njangu smiled, didn't answer. The officer stared at him for a while, then left.

Two days later, the summons came: Njangu to be ready at dawn the next day, alone.

'I don't suppose,' he asked Maev, 'if there's any way I can put a secret gun up my wahoonie or something.'

'You can shove a frigging howitzer up there for having this idea of yours that surely sounds like you're gonna end up at the bottom of somebody's dungeon,' Dill said. 'But no. There's never been a weapon made that wouldn't show up on at least a density detector. If you feel murderous, bite him to death.'

'Mmmh,' Njangu said, and at dawn was pacing back and forth outside the Nana boat's lock.

A rather bulky lifter settled down, with two destroyers floating overhead, and Njangu was ushered aboard and told, unceremoniously, to strip. He pretended indignation, actually felt none, and was escorted into a room by two obvious medical types, and told to wait.

I just hope, he thought, *they aren't into laxatives and vomitoriums. Never can tell when these damned barbarians run out of peep-bo machinery in the walls and start using the good ol' soapy water.*

But evidently the machines still worked, for Yoshitaro was told to get dressed, and his treatment became noticeably less chilly. But Njangu wasn't given access to a compartment with a screen or porthole.

They landed after about two hours estimated flight time, and Yoshitaro was ushered out and greeted by four men in uniform-like gray, and a smiling young man who introduced himself as *Maj* Kars. Njangu noticed the smile never touched the man's eyes, but then he'd been accused of having the same chill look himself.

'Forgive the care,' Kars said, 'but it seemed worthwhile, since you said you had something about the *Kuril*'s brother to discuss, and we hardly consider Jagasti someone to take casually.'

'No,' Njangu said. 'He certainly is not.'

The landing platform was atop a huge stone fortress that must have been a thousand years old, standing above a large city. The fortification might have been a monument until recently, but had been brought up to contemporary requirements, with little consideration for niceties such as architecture or historical importance. Stone gun turrets had been cut off flat, and various antennae mounted on steel decks. Domes had been rebuilt so missile launchers protruded through them. Here and there along the walls and roofs blisters with chainguns sat like boils, and on the once-gardened grounds were entrenchments and pillboxes.

Kars motioned Njangu to an open door, and the six went into an elevator, which dropped precipitately for quite a long time. Yoshitaro guessed they must've been a hundred feet or more underground before his stomach returned and the elevator stopped, and he was taken down a long corridor.

There were no guards in the corridor, which impressed Njangu that perhaps Gegen kept his security where it was most important — very close at hand.

Kars opened a double door, bowed, and Njangu entered the presence of *Kuril* Gegen of Degasten and Kohn, as he would no doubt style himself.

This Gegen was also a model of a modern barbarian: He was not that tall, but very solidly built, a man who'd seriously lifted weights for a time, but, now in his thirties, had gotten a bit lazy. He had a neatly combed, short beard and close-cropped hair, just beginning to gray.

Unlike Jagasti, he'd learned the virtue of simplicity, and wore plain gray, with a Sam Browne belt with holstered pistol, knife, and pouch. The only concession he made to barbaric excess was the Squad Support Weapon leaning against his chair — the Confederation-issue blaster, this one configured with a long barrel, laser sight, and bipod.

Njangu noted something interesting, and added it to his datafile: there were clear plastic walls between the door and *Kuril* Gegen, no doubt blaster- and grenade-and bulletproof. A very careful man.

Kars made a quiveringly correct salute, and Njangu touched his forehead with a respectful civilian knuckle.

'I understand you have arrived here with two

requests,' Gegen said without preamble, in a nice bar-barically growly voice.

'You are correct, *Kuril*.'

'Do you actually think my brother will give you leave for your . . . circus, it is, correct? . . . to come here and perform?'

'Possibly yes, possibly no.'

'And what, exactly, did you wish to see me, personally, about Jagasti?'

'About the possibility of his no longer being your enemy.'

Gegen snorted. 'Ask the solar wind to stop blowing. Ask men to stop lusting after what their neighbor has. Ask entropy to reverse itself.'

'I didn't say anything about *asking* Jagasti,' Njangu said.

'Perhaps I misunderstood what you meant by circus,' Gegen said. 'I looked it up in the encyclopedia, and there was no suggestion of your group having might enough to sway Jagasti in anything.'

'All that it takes to sway any man is a tiny bit of steel, correctly applied,' Njangu said. 'Which your brother well realizes, for he's commissioned me to remove you.'

Kars hissed, reached for his gun. Njangu ignored him. Gegen motioned, and Kars froze.

'So you thought you could come to me and get a higher price for Jagasti's death?' Gegen sounded amused.

'Exactly,' Njangu said, giving Gegen his best see my steel teeth and realize what a killer I am look.

'He bought your approach without requiring any proof of ability?'

'Why not?' Njangu said. 'He has nothing to lose. I fail, I fail, and his vaults remain full. If I succeed . . .' Njangu held out his hands.

'You mean you asked for no payment in front?'

'I did not.'

'Hmmp. You are confident.'

'No, sir. Just competent.'

Gegen smiled briefly.

'How would you go about such a task?'

Njangu shook his head.

'One of the people in our circus is a magician. He told me once he showed how his tricks were done, after a show, and the people were terribly disillusioned and disappointed.'

'What would you require of me?' Gegen said. 'I cannot believe that you would sell out my brother without any credits changing hands.'

'I am confident in the quality of my work,' Njangu said.

'I must think on this.' Gegen frowned.

'While you do,' Njangu said, 'perhaps you would give permission for the handful of troupers I brought with me to show their abilities to however many of your upper echelon you wish.'

'No,' Gegen said. 'I trust you not, Yoshitaro. So I'll hardly play the fool and give your associates a chance to decimate my staff.

'But you may perform if you will. My *junior* officers will be quite amused, I think.'

Njangu made a hasty readjustment to his plan, decided it'd still work, got up, bowed.

'You are careful, indeed, *Kuril*.'

'That,' Gegen said, 'is how I survived growing up with a monster for an elder brother.'

The show wasn't much, but the small crowd, less than half a hundred, seemed to enjoy it. Njangu decided the

most likely crowd on this first night would come from
Gegen's bodyguard and headquarters, since those closest
to the throne normally scarf up the first goodies.

His plan, therefore, might indeed work.

At least it would put some shit in the system.

Dill did his strongman act, then Monique used him as
a sawhorse and thrower for tumbling and acrobatics.
Froude brought the dreaded Alikhan from his cage, and
had him do some basic tricks.

The soldiers eyed the monster warily, and the Musth
did his best to appear completely crazed.

Froude bashed him back into his cage, and used
Njangu as a straight man for some card tricks and simple
magic.

Evidently prestidigitators weren't common with these
people, for the officers were utterly enthralled.

The four aliens, less, of course, the monster, were in
sight the entire evening.

Alikhan went out the back of his cage, using the
hinged secret door, took a small parcel from its hiding
place near the Nana boat's emergency lock, barely
crowded through that lock into the open air. The parcel's
timer had already been set, and it was mag-clipped to
one of the patrol ships that'd brought Gegen's officers.

The show ended, to roars of approval, and the soldiers
dispersed.

The timer on the parcel had ticked down fifteen minutes . . .

An hour and three-quarters later, the first timer
clicked, and the magnetic timer shut off. The parcel
tumbled down through the air, into a dense forest, not far
from Gegen's great fortress.

'It is working,' Alikhan reported from a control panel
on the Nana boat. It was indeed, the pieces of the parcel

breaking away, and thin metal legs unfolding. At the top of the tripod was a long tube which glowed, and started emitting various radiations on various wave bands.

'Our package is on its way,' Dill said, noting a flashing readout on his heads up display.

Just beyond the nav point the boat had used to enter the Degasten system, the first package Njangu had left came alive. It was a Shrike missile, given an auxiliary fuel tank, set to home initially on the drive of the Nana boat.

'Now, let's get our target rearranged,' Njangu said. 'Makes me nervous that sucker's homing on my roof.'

Froude tapped fingernails against his teeth. 'Let us see . . . assuming our homer came off the Protectorate boat when it should . . . that would put it down about here,' he said, looking at a screen. 'Gegen's headquarters are over here . . . so I'll target the Shrike . . . here. Close enough to wake the cooks up early.'

'Less talk, more setting,' Monique urged. 'I'm with Njangu, and don't appreciate incoming.'

'A touch . . . a slide . . . another touch . . . and there you have it, m'lady,' Froude bowed. 'It should wander in-atmosphere in a bit.'

The Shrike did, searing past the atmospheric patrol craft at near lightspeed, a searing comet in Ogdai's upper atmosphere, then a smashing explosion not three kilometers from Gegen's castle.

At that speed, the missile, even with its small explosive charge, made quite a large, radioactive crater. It woke up the cooks and everyone else around Gegen.

The device on the tripod a couple of kilometers away flashed, then fell over. The destruct charge on the laser sight 'unfortunately' didn't completely destroy the device, and its power supply was more than enough to be found by searchers just after dawn, enough to explain

that some monster had used the device to guide the
Shrike in on its target, but without clues as to who operated the device.

Njangu Yoshitaro stirred in his sleep, perhaps feeling
the explosion through the kilometers of rock, and the
boat's hull, then, smiling, returning to his dream of
money.

'Might I ask, *Kuril*, what has made up your mind so
firmly to hire me?' Njangu asked.

'No,' Gegen said. 'And if I had not had your ship
watched continuously, I might think what I know to be
impossible.

'Let us just say you've proven your point, and that my
brother is accelerating his plans for my destruction.

'I bid you carry the war home to him, and, when you
have succeeded, you can name your fee.

'Within reason, of course.'

Njangu and company, still gloating gently at the success
of their phony laser-guided missile attack, were picked
up, as arranged, by Jagasti's waiting battleship for the
jumps back to Mohi II.

Jagasti's lim, with two battleships overhead, lowered
toward the desecrated museum. As it passed below a
thousand meters, a sensor clicked, and the left half of the
lim blew off.

The explosion pinwheeled guards into the air. Jagasti
grabbed his seat cushion, jumped clear of the tumbling
wreckage, had time to pull the straps on and activate the
dropper.

The antigravity mechanism clicked on, and slowed his
fall, so his only injury was a broken ankle, making a bad

landing on one of the statues he'd had ripped out of the museum.

'Somebody did what?' Njangu asked.

'Went after Jagasti's lim with a bomb,' Garvin said. Dunno how they missed him.'

'Son of a bitch,' Njangu said slowly.

I assume that wasn't one of your fiendish thingies, given the sincerity of your response,' Jaansma said.

There's more than me putting shit in the game,' Yoshitaro said, then, still reverently:

'Son of a bitch!'

TWENTY

Tiborg/Tiborg Alpha Delta

The Civic Palace was packed. In minutes, according to custom, as the year changed, the Constitutionalists would hand over power to Dorn Fili and his Social Democrats.

Fen Bertl sat with the other Directors above the central podium, looking about beatifically.

Things would change a bit now, with the new regime, but they would essentially remain the same, and Tiborg would be run as it always had been: carefully, economically, reasonably, with power remaining in the hands of those who deserved it.

Thank the God he didn't believe in, Bertl thought, the flurry of trouble with Fili's ambition, that damned circus, and the Constitutionalists' intransigence had ended long before the citizens went to the polls and voted as they'd been taught.

He looked down, at the podium packed with the elite of both parties and the outgoing Premier, then at the floor, at the party workers, happily working themselves up. As soon as Fili shook hands with his opponent, and uttered the time-honored words of 'I succeed you, sir,' they'd go into a mild frenzy and snake-dance around the stadium until dawn, chanting the slogans that, tomorrow morning, would be dust like the campaign itself, and Tiborg would go on as it had for another six years.

Bertl took a moment to consider old business, particularly that circus, now long gone. He thought of his spy, that woman, whatever her name was.

He thought, ruefully, that held possibly overreacted with everyone else, first with the locator to follow them to the Capella system, if that was indeed their destination, and then adding . . . Kekri, that was her name.

It would be just as well, he decided, to drop the whole matter, abandon the tracker probes they'd been sending out every time they were notified the circus made another jump, and not waste credits or energy launching more.

There didn't seem to be much point in dispatching any expedition after the circus ship.

Capella and Centrum could wait for another few years, and they could mount their own expedition if it seemed necessary.

As for the spy . . . Bertl smiled. It was unlikely she'd come to harm, either remaining with the circus or wherever they decided to abandon her, if she was exposed. She was certainly a survivor type. And if they decided to take extreme measures . . .

No. It didn't matter.

The band built to a crescendo.

The Constitutionalist Premier stood, smiling, and the smile looked almost real, waiting for Dorn Fili.

Fili, flanked by Sam'l Brek, his aide, came up the podium steps. Bertl frowned. Brek should not, no matter how important he was to Fili, be sharing this spotlight.

He could get his rewards, like the rest of the SD, in tomorrow's clear daylight.

The Premier turned, holding out his hand.

Fili took it.

They waited for a moment, eyes on the cesium clock high overhead.

'I succeed—'

Lir and Montagna's bomb went off at that moment, just as it'd been set to do. A hundred kilos of Telex had been carefully fitted under the podium, formed to look like one of the supports, and color-matched by the two women.

A shaped charge, it blew straight up, and Fili, Brek, and the outgoing Premier became no more than a reddish haze, as did almost all of the parties' hierarchies.

Stonework fragmented, shotgunning up and out, decimating the Directors and then the faithful below.

Bertl was sent tumbling backward, body cushioned by other Directors behind him, crashing through chairs, but landing on his back.

Deafened by the blast, in shock, he pulled himself up to a sitting position, not realizing his right arm was broken in two places, looked in horror at the smiling head of another Director in his lap, pulsing gore.

He knew, he knew who'd done this, who had to have done this, and the hell with forgiveness, the hell with forgetting about those aliens.

Before anything else, Fen Bertl, in the end as human as anyone, now wanted revenge. For himself, for his party, for his fellow Directors, for Tiborg itself!

TWENTY-ONE

Mohl/Mohl II

Njangu Yoshitara was going quietly nuts, especially since he realized he'd caused his own insanity.

Kuril Jagasti had been hounding him near daily since his return from Degasten, almost an E-month earlier. When would he make his move against Gegen? What would it be? He had promised much, and so far had delivered nothing.

Jagasti was right.

Njangu thought at first he'd accomplished a deal with the phony missile attack on Gegen. But all that it seemed to have done, Jagasti's handful of agents on Degasten reported, was drive Gegen into the depths of his fortress, where he did nothing, as far as external events indicated.

Njangu wondered if Gegen had more than one string to his bow, and had been responsible for the sabotage on Jagasti's lim.

Without hinting anything to Njangu?

That would make him a really subtle sort of barbarian, having two sets of killers in the field.

The other likely candidate for the sabotage had to be

Jagasti's little brother, Bayanti. And what would have set him off? The phony long-distance shooter, making him believe it was Jagasti behind the trigger men?'

But there seemed to be nothing amiss with Bayanti's relationship with Jagasti. At least he said and showed nothing to Delot Eibar, who was definitely earning her bonus.

Besides, what would Jagasti's death get him? Bayanti didn't seem to have much interest in Jagasti's constant military maneuvers and evolutions, or, at any rate, said nothing publicly.

Njangu didn't discard little brother entirely, but thought him not a likely candidate for this completely unknown Master Schemer.

A local lad? Or lass? Somebody who'd decided enough of tyranny, now was the time to make a stand? But the scarce populace Njangu encountered were completely terrorized and worn down, and so he discarded that option.

What made matters a little worse was Jagasti's habit of weekly banquets, like any decent techno-savage, at which he would praise the few who pleased him, and castigate the failures. Those, of course, included Njangu, and it didn't help that Jagasti couldn't be specific about Njangu's failures, but merely rail on at him for being an ignorant, boastful alien, whose only talent appeared to be fripperies and con games.

A couple of Jagasti's goons thought that meant Jagasti was calling Njangu a womanish sort, and decided to lie in wait for him after a banquet.

Yoshitaro handily demolished both of them, not bothering to pull any punches, and, when questioned, shortly admitted to Jagasti he'd killed both of them, and why couldn't the *Kuril* control his own court?

But that got little accomplished, except to raise the general hostility level.

Meantime, the circus continued performing for the soldiery, even more popular than before.

Especially popular was the tiny Jia Yin Fong, whose mother had made a small Protectorate uniform for her. She cannonballed around the top of the tent, from her parents' teeterboard to *ra'felan* high above to Lir. swinging from a trapeze, giggling happily. The soldiers thought she was their mascot.

Njangu gloomed over maps of Gegen's fortress. Dammit, Angara should have let them take a nuke along . . . assuming he had some stashed somewhere in a secret armory. Maybe he could put a force atop Gegen's fortress, slide the nuke into an elevator, send it down, and . . .

Gegen's quarters were probably shielded.

And besides, he didn't have a nuke in *Big Bertha*.

Njangu thought maybe the late Confederation wasn't quite as dumb as he'd thought.

He checked military holidays, thinking that Gegen might come out to review his troops, and he could get Montagna and her hellshooter in range.

But Jagasti's younger brother seemed content to sit far underground and wait.

For what, Njangu knew: the assassination of his brother, Jagasti.

Njangu considered that briefly. It would be fairly easy to smuggle some sort of gun in and give Jagasti a third eye. And then what? He wasn't about to mount a suicide mission.

A bomb suggested itself, but after the incident with the lim, Jagasti had all rooms swept twice before he entered them.

The worst of it was all of these complications were caused by Njangu Yoshitaro being a terribly, terribly clever intelligence operative.

Garvin couldn't decide whether to worry or think the whole mess funny. He compromised by keeping the Legion members ready for any eventuality, and spent many hours plotting with Yoshitaro, trying to figure a way to the next stage.

It came of itself.

Maev, who'd taken to going to the banquets with Njangu more out of pity than thinking he needed body-guarding or because she'd developed a taste for the overcooked game animals Jagasti served, automatically cased the situation as they went up the aisle to their assigned table. Jagasti's table ran across the large hall, once the museum cafeteria, and long tables ran down the room at ninety degrees from it.

'Back door's not locked,' she whispered to Njangu as she'd been trained. 'Stairs look open, only one guard. There's an exit behind Jagasti, as always, but guarded.'

Njangu nodded, not needing to reply. He was wondering what, if anything, he could do to get out from under the inevitable harassment.

He sat down, and the room filled. He winked at Delot Eibar as she entered with Bayanti, sat at the head table.

Jagasti, flanked by four guards, came in almost last, as was his custom.

He took his place at the head of the table, unbuckled his combat harness, and hung it from his chair. Then he poured a glass of ice water and drained it.

He banged it down, and picked up a pitcher of the very light, almost nonalcoholic wine he favored, filled another glass. So far, very much according to custom.

'I greet you, guests, friends, and warriors,' he called.

Again by custom everyone at the table filled glasses from their own pitchers, held them ready.

'To the Protectorate, and to the Confederation we all serve, and to the oath that we shall restore it soon! '

He drank, and so did everyone else.

Next, he would set the glass down, call out introductions of people who hadn't been there before, sit down, and wait for the first course.

Instead, Jagasti lowered his glass, and coughed. At first it was experimentally, then harder and harder.

The glass spun from his fingers, shattered, unnoticed, on the floor.

Njangu noted Jagasti was turning several interesting shades of purple.

His mouth flapped open, shut as his eyes bulged.

Both hands reached for his throat, and he spun, fell into the table, knocking it skidding away.

In an instant, Bayanti was kneeling over his brother. He picked him up in his arms, moaning, 'Oh, brother. Speak to me. Speak to me. Don't die. Please don't die.'

Jagasti made a disgusting noise like he was trying to vomit, convulsed, was still.

The hall was frozen.

Bayanti let his brother's body down, stood, and, from nowhere, a gun was in his hand.

'Guards!' he shouted. 'To me!'

Doors banged open and gray-uniformed soldiers ran toward him, blasters ready. The doors were secured, and a grim-faced line of men stood between Bayanti and the banquet guests.

'Murder,' Bayanti breathed. 'Foul murder. Poison! Someone in the kitchen is an assassin. You! *Maj!* Take a detail to the kitchen, and arrest everyone! Hold them in close arrest, ready for transport for interrogation!'

The officer saluted, and ordered men off. In seconds, from the kitchen, Njangu heard screams, shouts of fear.

'My brother . . . my brother is dead,' Bayanti said brokenly. 'Now it is . . . now it must be . . . my task to carry on his duty. I shall try to fulfill his mission though I am hardly worthy of standing in his boots.

'Yes, Jagasti. I promise, and everyone here promises, we shall restore the Confederation.

'And we shall not wait, we shall not delay, there shall be no more war games or sporting bouts that kill the best of us, but we shall move at once.

'I declare Operation Jagasti. First, my brother will be cremated, as he wished, and his ashes held, to be scattered over Centrum when we seize it.

'But first we must destroy the traitor Gegen, the one who ordered this vile murder.

'I order, within the week, all my armed forces ready to begin an attack on Gegen.

'He shall die for his fratricide, and any of his men who dare stand with him shall do the same.

'Now, I bid all of you, from soldier to statesman, yes . . .' and his eyes caught Njangu's '. . . even those who think they can give no more than a moment's laughter to ease the way of our warriors, now is the time.

'The battle is at hand.

'This is the beginning of the final war to bring back the Confederation, and I can only wish my dear brother Jagasti could be here to cheer and witness it!'

On the way out Maev leaned close to Njangu and lifted her eyebrow.

'Not bad,' he said judiciously. 'He could have used a little old-fashioned glycerin on his cheeks to make it perfect. Now, as soon as he has the body burned and all the

cooks shot after somebody confesses, there'll be nothing
to hold back Bayanti the Magnificent!'

A soldier heard the last part, missed the sarcasm, and
nodded in approval, rubbing his red eyes, his tear-stained
face.

'I suppose,' Yoshitaro said, 'this was *one* way to get
matters up and running.

'I just don't think it's a very good one, and liable to
get us all body-sacked.'

TWENTY-TWO

Bayanti, in the days that followed, put shame to the idea that younger brothers always follow in their elders' shadows. Dalet Eibar found time on her hands to report his doings, for Bayanti was in constant motion, from Protectorate world to world, fleet headquarters to shipping companies.

He had not been speaking emptily when he said everyone would be part of this battle. Training battalions were pronounced ready for battle as they stood and fed into the battle roster. Merchant ships were given hasty armaments, often no more than a pair of missiles magclipped to the ship's hull and a simple computer and launch mechanism hung somewhere on the bridge.

To those who worried about losses in the invasion of Degasten costing them dear when they moved against Centrum, his answer was brief:

'The replacements, though they don't know it, now serve with Gegen. After we destroy my brother, his men and women will be given one chance to redeem themselves for their treason.'

Garvin was mildly surprised when Bayanti summoned him, to give him his orders for the invasion.

'I chose to do this personally,' he explained, 'because you are aliens, and know little of our struggles.

'Also, to be personal,' and he colored slightly, looking at Dalet Eibar, who sat primly beside him, 'since your circus brought this woman to me, who appears to have luck with her, I feel I owe you a debt.'

'No, *Kuril*,' Garvin said. 'You owe me nothing.' Except to let *Big Bertha* go on her way, and he couldn't quite figure a way to put the request, and then it was too late.

'But I do, and so I will give you an opportunity to serve me, and to be present for my triumph, at which time you and your crew will be rewarded.

'I propose to keep you and your ship in our rear echelon during the landing on Degasten. When a landing zone has been cleared and is secure, we shall send for you.

'I envision your men, women, and animals being of great use in helping our wounded recover their morale before returning to battle, as part of our Retraining Force.'

There was nothing to do but bow, offer profuse thanks, and not look at Eibar, who was trying not to laugh.

There were fifty troops, under the command of a *Tain* Kaidu, assigned to *Big Bertha*. Kaidu, who looked to be a fairly competent soldier, if not a hardened warrior, explained that the soldiers were to ensure there was no hint of mutiny while the circus was with the military. 'I know civilians, for some unknown reason, fear and hate serving under us. Think of me, Gaffer Jaansma, as your strong right arm.'

Garvin looked at him carefully, saw no trace of irony.

'Now what?' he asked Njangu.

'Now we deploy our people, to make very close friends

with these guards, and wait for the time being right to haul ass away from these lunatics.

'Speaking of very close friends' — he sighed — 'and of battlefield conversions, at least we won't have to worry about rescuing our Dalet. I got a message, through the means I set up before we chased her into Bayanti's bedroom.

'I saved and printed it.'

He passed a slip of paper across. All it read was:

He may be a son of a bitch but right now he's my son of a bitch.

'Oh, grand,' Garvin said sarcastically. 'No worries about rescuing her now, and of course it'd never cross my mind that Eibar might really, really fall in love and start singing to Bayanti about everything, starting with us and what we're after.'

''Course not,' Njangu said. 'That would be a good example of befouling one's own nest, also known as crappin' on the old mess plate, wouldn't it?'

But he held up crossed fingers.

'Twenty-seven seconds to lift, sir,' the watch officer told Liskeard.

'Got it . . . somebody want to gimme a ship count of all those zoomies out there?' Liskeard asked.

It was just dusk, and the horizon was lit with ships taking off.

Garvin lost track at eighty-two.

Tain Kaidu, beside him, was starry-eyed, watching the might of the Protectorate move against Degasten.

'Ten seconds to takeoff,' the bridge talker said.

Liskeard poised his hand over the sensor.

'Counting . . . four . . . three . . . two . . . one . . . lift!'

Big Bertha shuddered, came free of the ground, hovered tentatively, decided to keep on climbing.

'And so, the bountiful battlefleets of the proud Protectorate coolly climbed toward space, their glorious goal the degenerate dissolutes of the ghastly Gegen,' Garvin said.

Liskeard snorted.

'Poetry' Kaidu breathed. 'Real poetry. Damn but I'm glad I lived to see this day.'

N-space

'When,' Kekri Katun asked Ben Dill, 'will we take them?'

'Pardon?'

'Don't play innocent, Benjamin! Remember, I'm the spy that found out everything!'

'Not quite,' Ben said. 'There are secrets within secrets.'

'Like what?'

'Like when we take them,' Ben said. 'Besides, nobody told me, either. Probably when they least expect it.'

'How superbly analytical,' Kekri said sarcastically. 'I'm going to the gym. The least I can do is be in some kind of shape when we start hitting people.'

'We?'

'Who else do I have to side with now that I've snitched off my employer?'

'Strong point,' Dill said. 'But can't we get in some kind of shape right here?'

'Doing what?'

Ben whispered in her ear, bit it, and Kekri yelped.

'Later!'

'Later I might not have the steam for something that exotic,' Dill muttered.

'Then that'll be your tough luck, won't it, mister?'

'I have decided,' *Tain* Kaidu said, 'to require the circus to turn in all firearms. We shall hold them safe until needed.'

'Not sure if that's a good idea,' Njangu said. 'Although, of course, we'll cheerfully obey. But you've got to remember that most of the firearms . . . the handful that we do have . . . are required in the event any of the animals break free.'

'If that happens,' Kaidu said, 'my soldiers will be able to respond within seconds.'

'Morning, gentlemen,' Dr. Froude said cheerfully as he, Fleam, and two other men wearing coveralls carried toolboxes and piping into the long bay as signed to the Protectorate's security detachment.

'Whazzat you're doing?' a noncom grumbled.

'You've got more people in here than the present conditioner can cycle,' Froude said. 'We're running an extra line.'

'Well . . . that's damned thoughtful,' the warrant said.

'Thought the smell was your feet,' a soldier called to his mate, and the workmen set to.

By the end of the ship-day, the new line ran down both sides of the compartment, out, and down the corridor and into another, smaller compartment. There it was linked to a small pump, entirely separate from the ship's air-conditioning system.

Two dozen weapons were turned in to the Protectorates. Four of them were archaic, hand-worked projectile weapons, two were blank-only show weapons and the rest were blasters Njangu said were normally handed out when *Big Bertha* made a landing on an unknown world.

Of course, many more, and the crew-served SSWs, were still hidden about the ship in search-proof hideys.

Kaidu, who said he was a reasonable man, told Njangu he had no interest, of course, in the missiles in the *aksai* or Nana boats.

'Just trying to keep myself and my men safe,' he said.

'Couldn't agree with you more,' Yoshitaro said heartily.

'I do not understand this about guns,' Sunya Thanon said to Ben Dill. 'I asked Alikhan, and he said an explanation might be more logical coming from a human, since all Musth are always armed.'

'Ask,' Ben said, who knew the two elephant handlers were trying to learn to be soldiers and had laughted his ass off watching Alikhan learning to ride an elephant.

'These Protectorate men who took our guns,' Thanon said, 'now have power over us, is that not correct?'

'Correct.'

'Then, is it not true that, in an equal society, all men ought to have guns, to keep from being downtrodden?'

'Uh . . .' Ben hesitated, remembering great heaps of people he knew were incompetent to have any weapon beyond a basic rock. 'Sort of. Maybe.'

'So then,' Phraphas Phanon said, 'anyone who tries to not permit you to have a gun is a budding tyrant, and should be killed.'

'That's taking things a bit too far,' Ben said. 'Like, maybe several light-years. Tell you what. I'm just a common, ordinary weightlifter. Whyn't you ask somebody intelligent, like Dr. Froude?'

'Good,' Thanon said brightly. 'We shall do just that.'

But Froude didn't have a good answer to the question either.

Felip Mand'l curled around the overhead duct, watch in hand, as the four Protectorates went by. They didn't look up, and if they had, wouldn't have thought to find a little person above them.

After they were out of sight, he made a note of the time, went down a doubled-knotted cord to the deck, and off to report to Maev Stiofan, who had the security watch.

The soldier held out a bit of fruit to Loti, the smaller of the two baby elephants. Loti, a polite sort, curled her trunk up as she'd been trained, came forward, daintily plucked the morsel, and swallowed it.

A second later she squealed in pain and then rage as the pepper-packed fruit went down her throat.

The soldier roared laughter as the elephant stumbled back toward her mother, moaning.

Still laughing, he turned, and met the eyes of Sunya Thanon.

His laughter died, and his slung blaster slipped off his shoulder.

But Thanon did nothing more than look at him.

The soldier backed down the corridor to a port went through it hastily.

'The question is,' Danfin Froude said to Njangu, 'is what you plan on putting down the pipeline for our guests.'

'Dunno,' Njangu said, evading Froude's eyes. 'Something that'll take 'em out quick.'

'Logic would suggest a lethal gas,' Froude prodded. 'That will prevent future problems.'

'Yeh,' Njangu said. 'And everybody in the circus including half the Legion people aboard, will think that I'm a murderous bastard.'

'Indeed,' Froude agreed. 'First, I can reassure you most of them already have that opinion, and, secondly, a sleep gas is a deal harder to synthesize than something that does a nice, clean job of killing.'

'I dunno,' Njangu said again.

'*Do* think about it,' Froude said, smiling gently.

'You know,' Sunya Thanon whispered to Phraphas Phanon, 'I have had a terrible thought.'

'Kiss me and it will go away.'

Thanon obeyed. 'But it is still here.'

'Then tell me about it.'

'Perhaps this Coando that we seek . . . the land where elephant and man are equal and friends . . . really does not exist.'

'I know it does,' Phraphas said firmly. 'Just as I know we shall find it.'

'Perhaps we are living in it,' Thanon said. 'Living in it here and now, on this *Big Bertha* ship and with the circus, not knowing our luck.'

Do not think that, my love.'

'All right,' Sunya said doubtfully. 'At least I shall try not to.'

'I've decided,' Garvin announced, 'this whole operation has become entirely too much of an adventure.'

'Is 'oo ready to go home and hide under the bed?' Darod teased.

'Uh, no,' Garvin said, as Jasith came to mind. 'Not quite yet.'

'What you've got, troop, is low morale.'

'You think so?' Garvin asked.

'Yup,' Darod said, sliding out of her nightgown. 'All you need is to get your little lights screwed out, and you'll be perfectly 'kay.'

'Couldn't hurt,' Garvin agreed.

Emton, looking for one of his cats, hoping the little idiot hadn't wandered into this big-cat caging area, rounded a corner and froze in horror.

Tia, the missing cat, was crouched across a corridor from the leopard cage. One leopard, Emton thought that evil black bastard Muldoon, was lying very close to the bars.

Tia got up, and pranced close to the bars, and Muldoon swiped at her.

'Tia! Come here!' Emton almost shouted.

The black kitten looked at her supposed owner, made a sound like 'prrt,' danced toward Muldoon, and avoided another strike.

Emton darted forward and grabbed Tia.

'You are stupid, truly stupid,' he scolded. 'Big cats, wild cats absolutely hate little cats! What do you want, to be that monster's dinner? Thin-sliced kitten?'

Tia looked up at Emton and started purring.

'I think you might be able to use this,' Ristori told Garvin, handing him a key.

'What is it?'

'The key to the contraband arms cabinet you gave *Tain* Kaidu.'

'How'd you get your hands on it?'

'A simple plunge, with one hand, four straight phalanges to hook, and it was mine. That, by the way, is a copy. I returned the original to the *Tain*, and he never noticed.

'I thought, thought, thought those guns might be useful in the coming days.'

'Well,' Njangu told Maev, 'I think we're as ready as we're going to be.

'Now all we need is a little external distraction for our guards.

'A good healthy space battle would do just fine.'

TWENTY-THREE

Degasten/Ogdai

The old theory, before Man went into space, was that someone in a spaceship or satellite had an innate advantage over his planet-bound enemy. This was the 'gravity well' belief – the fighter on the ground would have to overcome gravity to get his missiles or ships on an equal plane for combat.

The basis was from ancient wars, where the man on the clifftop or castle rampart could happily cock a snook and drop heavy things on the attacker below.

In fact, it didn't work out that way in space, since the 'gravity well' proponents didn't bother to consider that any ship bombarding an object on the ground would be in a predictable orbit. All the defender had to do was launch a flock of missiles into the orbit of that ship or satellite overhead, and matters would take their course.

Sometimes, the old saw was true, just as sometimes the belief that 'the bombers will always get through' was correct.

But not often, and certainly not for Bayanti's attack on Gegen's stronghold of Ogdai.

The fleet held about three AUs off Ogdai, and the elite first wave attacked.

Their intent was to take geosynchronous orbits and bombard Gegen's forces from space, especially his stronghold. Other ships were to orbit the world, taking targets of opportunity or assigned targets from Bayanti's Command and Control craft.

When everything was sufficiently pulverized, the troopships would land.

Of course, neither of the 'Protectorates' worried about the original inhabitants of Ogdai, although no nuclear devices were used, since Bayanti wanted to occupy turf that wasn't gently glowing.

Gegen, not being stupid, had laid careful defensive plans — several species of unmanned satellites, down to the completely antique kinetic variety, were positioned in various orbits around Ogdai, plus bases on all three of the planet's moons.

A swarm of patrol ships launched as soon as Bayanti's fleet entered the Degasten system, plus Gegen already had about half his fleet offplanet.

Gegen waited until Bayanti's first wave was committed, and his computers could analyze their tracks. Then he struck. Well-emplaced missiles shot up from the planetary surface, and the waiting satellites were activated and went after their targets.

Inner space was a horror of explosions, ships exploding, tearing apart, going out of control and pinwheeling down into gravity's claws. Just out-atmosphere was a snarling dogfight of fighters, all control lost as they went after targets or tried to evade contact.

Half a planetary day later, and the remnants of Bayanti's first wave reeled back toward the fleet.

Gegen's ships dived back for their bases to rearm and wait.

Bayanti raged on the bridge of his flagship, threatened commanders with relief, with being shot, accusing them of cowardice and treason.

'Now?' Garvin murmured into Froude's ear. They were on the bridge of *Big Bertha*. *Tain* Kaidu watched the biggest screen worriedly, two of his soldiers behind him.

Lounging near the rear of the bridge were Lir, Njangu, Maev, and Ben Dill.

'Let's give it time to develop a little more confusion,' Froude said.

Bayanti feinted with his second wave, drawing Gegen's forces offplanet. Then, escorted by three battleship squadrons, he sent in his attack transports. Ships slammed in, ramps dropped, and troops on foot and in Aerial Combat Vehicles got the hell away from the landing zone as ground-to-ground missiles hurtled in.

Next, the units should have formed up for the attack.

Instead, they just sat there, in tight defensive perimeters. Possibly their high commander had been killed and no one took charge, possibly that officer froze in place.

Bayanti's troops were getting hammered, slaughtered as they sat, while Bayanti fumed again on his bridge.

He fought for control, found it, studied his main tac screen, trying to figure what to do next.

It took a while – describing the battle from afar suggests there was coherency, analyzable movement, instead of swirling madness.

Bayanti made a decision, ordered all frequencies to all of his ships opened, and ordered all combat ships of any configuration to attack, repeat attack.

They were to swarm Ogdai, taking any target they could.

Most of Bayanti's warriors obeyed, and armed transports, light escorts, dived in-atmosphere, headed for the ground.

Gegen's antiaircraft systems broomed them from the skies, but there were more behind them.

Gegen's fortress was a mask of flame, the land around it fire and the shatter of crashed ships. But it seemed completely unharmed, its defenders still fighting hard.

'Now?' Garvin muttered again.

'I think so,' Froude said.

Garvin snapped his fingers.

Tain Kaidu had an instant to turn, to see Njangu on his feet, two steps and in the air, feet together, lashing out.

His neck snapped, and he chicken-flopped to the deck.

One of his bodyguards had a pistol out, and Maev shot him. The other unslung his blaster, just as Lir's knife buried itself in his throat.

'Now, goddammit, why no fun for Ben Dill?' Ben asked plaintively.

'Shaddup,' Garvin ordered. 'Liskeard, get us out of here!'

The ship captain obeyed.

Just before the main screen blanked as *Big Bertha* jumped into hyperspace, Garvin saw a dot that was in fact, a battleship, dive vertically into Gegen's fortress, at the center of the swarm.

'Shit!' Dill said, having seen the dive. 'Wonder what happened? Wonder if they got Gegen?'

'Dunno,' Garvin said, motioning to a talker, as the crazy blur of N-space surrounded them. 'Don't care. Got other stuff to worry about.'

TWENTY-FOUR

N-space

None of the dozen soldiers in their bay heard the quiet hissing begin. There should have been more off shift in the compartment, but the invasion wasn't a calming influence.

The gas was nonlethal. Later, Njangu was accused of getting softhearted or -headed, particularly by Ben Dill and Alikhan, especially considering, as Froude had suggested, how much simpler a killing gas like hydrogen cyanide was to manufacture.

Yoshitaro protested, vainly, that he wasn't getting sentimental, but was worried about the rather improvised piping springing a leak and killing people he cared about. 'Although for somebody like you two, I'll cheerfully make an exception,' he muttered.

Only one soldier heard the noise before she was overcome. After a few minutes, a suited member of the Legion checked the compartment, nodded in satisfaction, and left the sprawled bodies for a cleanup detail.

Two soldiers trotted down a corridor, blasters ready. They didn't look up, didn't see Lucky Felip crouched behind a pressuring unit overhead. Aiming carefully with the small-caliber projectile weapon his father's father had carried against the pranks of the biggers, he shot both of them in the head, then sneered at the memory of Lir's caution in not arming him, back on Cayle IV.

He jumped down onto one corpse, went looking for other targets.

The arms locker was open, and Running Bear was busily handing out weapons. He noticed, without much surprise, that more of the waiting people were from the circus than the Legion.

Seven Protectorates swept through one corridor in the animal caging. They whirled, hearing a growling, saw two bears charging them, huge-clawed paws sweeping the deck.

They fired . . . but the bolts smashed into the creatures without effect. Then the bears were among them, slashing, tearing with their fangs.

The sole survivor ran hard, put his back to a wall, and fired again.

The creature coming at him, blood dripping from its mouth, was unhurt.

The soldier went mad, spun his blaster and shoved the muzzle into his mouth, pulled the trigger.

Meters away, the robot bear's operator saw and threw up over her control panel.

Now the 'Peace March' boomed through the ship, and the troupers went looking for weapons.

A soldier was backing down a corridor, blaster ready, his mate in front of him.

He didn't hear a hatch slide open. Then a soft voice said:

'Remember me?'

He spun, saw Sunya Thanon, a handler's billhook in his hand. The hook slashed in, took him in the eye and smashed him to the ground. Thanon twisted the hook free, drove it deep into the man's throat.

'And how does *that* taste?' he asked.

The man's partner had his gun up as Phraphas Phanon shot him through the open hatch.

'I do not feel bad,' Thanon said. 'That was for all the cruelties we have taken.'

Phraphas Phanon shook his head.

'That is not good, that is not the Way. But I do understand.'

Somehow the horses' enclosure had been sprung, and animals galloped in panic back and forth across the huge show area.

Rudy Kweik and his wives were among them, trying to bring them under control.

A soldier saw a shot, fired at Kweik. He missed, but the bolt sent splinters up from the metal deck into Kweik's legs. He shouted, went down.

The soldier took aim to finish the man.

High overhead, in the rear of the control blister, Darod Montagna shot once, and the man spun back fell dead.

She grinned humorlessly, looked for other targets.

Half a dozen Protectorates were crouched behind an improvised barricade. They heard growling, snarling, and saw Alikhan, flanked by Ben Dill.

One fired, and the two Legionnaires ducked for cover.

An overhead hatch opened, and Monique Lir dropped down onto the deck, Squad Support Weapon firing.

The soldiers tried to return fire, were too late.

One came into the open, and Alikhan dropped him with his acid-pistol, burning a head-size hole in his chest.

Ben Dill looked for a target, saw nothing but bodies.

'Aw, goddammit!' he growled. 'You went and did it to me again!'

Erik Penwyth shot two soldiers down, thought they were both dead, trotted forward.

One rolled to his side, fired, and the round seared along Erik's side. He shouted in pain, went down, hand reflexively pulling a grenade from his weapons harness, thumbing it into life, and rolling it against the soldier.

The man reached for the grenade, didn't make it as it went off, tearing him almost in half.

'Medic,' Penwyth moaned. 'Goddamnit, medic!'

The soldier ran hard down the corridor, away from the nightmare that had killed three of his fellows, a man with his face and chest painted in black-and-white stripes, stripped to the waist, wearing only a leather diaper and leggings. The horror had shot down two of the soldier's companions with a pistol, hurled a small ax into the middle of the third's face.

The soldier had fled, hoping to find the exit from this ship, from these alien people.

Something moved ahead of him, something small and black. He fired, missed, and the animal darted around a corner.

He ran on behind it, away from that monster behind him.

The soldier saw the animal again, no bigger than his arm, running hard, close to a cage. He had his blaster ready to club it down when a black, clawed foreleg flashed out, caught his uniform, pulled him against the barred cage.

An instant later, Muldoon's hind leg tore at his neck, and blood gouted.

Tia came back around a corner, saw the body, and began purring loudly. An echoing purr came from Muldoon as he curled up, lifted his hind leg, and began cleaning it.

A soldier crouched in the center ring, behind a clown cart, trying to get a shot at Darod, high above.

He didn't see the *ra'felan's* tentacle until it had him around the waist. He tried to turn, to shoot at the octopod, then the *ra'felan* smashed him against a bulkhead.

The *ra'felan* considered whether it bothered him to have killed, decided not, swung back up into the top of the hold, looking for another soldier.

The shouts echoed down the corridors, louder than the booming 'Peace March.'

'Rube!'

'Hey, Rube!'

The circus troupe, some with blasters, some with improvised weapons, combed their ship for the soldiers.

Two circus people were wounded, five died, but all of their panicked guards died.

'All right,' Garvin said. 'That's that. Dump the ones we gassed into a lifeboat and kick it out into normal space.

'Damned if I care where it ends up.'

'Your orders, sir?' Liskeard asked.

'Make the first jump for Centrum,' Garvin said, thinking that was probably as close to a historic statement as he'd ever make.

'Right,' Liskeard said, then stopped. 'Sir, could we hold for a second? I've got to check with my electronics people.'

Garvin frowned, losing the historical moment.

'Go ahead.'

Liskeard touched sensors, and a mike swung down. He spoke into it, listened, then nodded.

'Sorry I didn't report this before, sir. But our electronics people have picked up a stray transmission.'

'From where?' Garvin asked.

'From us. They've tried to track it down, but sans results.'

Garvin blinked.

'Going where?'

'We don't know that, either. But it happens as we jump, then again when we come out of hyperspace.'

'I want to see that report,' Garvin said. 'Right away. And hold on the jump.'

He waved the nearest talker over.

'Get Yoshitaro, Doctors Ristori and Froude to the bridge. Immediately.'

'If it weren't highly unlikely,' Froude said, 'I'd suspect that someone put a bug on us back on Cayle IV.'

'Somebody did plant a device,' Njangu said, and told them about the transmitter Kekri Katun had. 'But I checked its recorder, and there's been no transmission to or from her at all. Although I've got to remind you, Garvin, that she was told by Bertl, that Director she was hired by, that she would be picked up at the proper time. Maybe he wasn't lying.'

'Most interesting, interesting,' Ristori said. 'Might I make a suggestion?'

'Of course.'

'Let's make the assumption that we are, somehow bugged. Would it not be possible to delay this jump closer to Centrum, and, instead, jump to some dead system where we can sweep the ship until we find whatever it is that's leaking, bleeding, transmitting?'

Garvin thought, saw Njangu nodding reflexively.

'Better safe,' he decided, 'than dead meat.'

TWENTY-FIVE

Unknown World

Erik Penwyth stared morosely at the screen as *Big Bertha* settled for a landing.

'All green and nice, lots of water, and no population?'

'If there is,' Garvin said, 'they're keeping well under cover, and don't use any known frequency.'

'Yeh,' Penwyth said. 'A no-doubt-goddamned Eden.'

'Sure,' Njangu said. 'Since this whole system doesn't seem to have a name, why not? This'll be Eden IV, 'kay.'

'Prob'ly monsters under every leaf,' Erik said.

'Now, just 'cause this is the first time you went and got your plow shot off, don't get cranky,' Njangu said. 'Just to make you happy, we'll call the system Eden, and this planet Lonrod after your honey. Howzat sound?'

Penwyth considered. 'Fine, I s'pose, assuming that Karo and I are going to be together for all eternity.' He thought for a moment. 'After due consideration, whyn't you go back to Scheme A, and go with Eden IV?'

No monsters appeared under any leaf, and so Garvin approved of letting the animals out for exercise and air, which was almost precisely E-normal, and anyone who wanted out for exercise, assuming they were armed and stayed within sight of the ship.

Meanwhile, he put every woman and man with any electronics experience looking for the source of that beep. The problem was that no one knew what triggered it, so there didn't appear to be any way of setting it off, short of making another jump.

Techs used signal projectors that broadcast up and down the spectrum of frequencies, but without result.

Njangu triggered Kekri Katun's transmitter twice, but that produced nothing, either.

His mood grew sourer as the hours passed, and then they'd been onplanet for four local days.

Nothing.

Like his charges, Emton was an early riser, and, again like them, once dawn was properly greeted, he went back to bed.

He led his six yawning cats through the animal area Tia ducking a mock-lunge from Muldoon as she passed his cage, to the gangway. He'd taught one of the cats to rear onto her two legs and bring a paw up in mock-salute for the watch, who, grinning, returned it.

The troupe went down the gangplank, into the dewy grass, just as the sun's rim came above the horizon.

The cats were taken out to 'stale,' Emton's wonderfully archaic word.

Tia finished her business, tried to start a fight with another cat, was batted sharply twice.

She bounded through the grass, looking for trouble, finding none, and came to one of the ship's monstrous fins.

As she'd done for three days, she sniffed at the metal, found where it not only didn't smell right, but had exactly the right pliability.

Purring loudly, she began sharpening her claws, slowly at first, then, as they dug in, faster.

Emton came on her then.

'Ohmigawd . . . ohmigawd . . . Tia get away from there! You're ruining our ship!'

Tia gave it another pull, just to remind Emton of who was in control, allowed herself to be picked up, and thumped on the flank with Emton's forefinger in punishment.

'Oh my God,' Emton said, staring at the bare plas, and the narrow rip where things, unknown things, strange-looking electronic unknown things, showed through. 'I'd better tell somebody. Oh my God.'

'Well smack my ass and call me Sally,' Garvin said in some astonishment. There was a crowd around *Big Bertha*'s fin.

'I'm sorry, sir. Tia didn't mean—'

Garvin became aware of Emton and the throng.

'Mister Emton,' he said formally, 'I think you may have done us the greatest service of any trouper, and you can, if the technicians are correct, count on a very, very large bonus when we jump for home.'

Emton blinked in bewilderment. Garvin motioned to Njangu.

'Clear 'em out, if you would.'

'Big rog, Gaffer.' Njangu called his security people, ordered them to get rid of the gawkers.

'That's what I think it is, isn't it?' Garvin asked an electronics officer.

'Cats *shouldn't* be able to scratch through the skins of starships, sir.'

'Careful, mister. Sooner or later you'll be putting the uniform back on, and wiseasseries will be remembered.'

'Sorry, sir.' The officer knelt, ran his finger around the tear. 'See how it protrudes from the ship's skin just slightly? I'd guess maybe a mag-couple, maybe some kind of ultra-glue was used to stick it on.'

'So somebody snuck up on us,' Garvin mused. 'Tied this can to our tail, and we've been banging away ever since.'

Garvin took Froude and Ristori aside.

'You think that's what we've been looking for?'

'Might well be,' Ristori said.

'So how would it get word back?'

'Possibly some kind of device like my Ohnce-Bohnce buoys,' Froude said, 'Or, another way that would work is for some sort of missile to be linked to the sender.

'Assuming Cayle IV as its origin, which is logical, when we jumped from there, the first missile was launched. It went into N-space after us, homed on that second signal, which makes it a pretty sophisticated piece of electronics right there, then jumped back out in whatever normal space we'd emerged in.

'Possibly another missile would then be launched to join it, and that one would leapfrog the first and jump with us when we left the next system. Or else the second missile would replace the first, but that would require the first's fuel and drive to be constantly in danger of being depleted.

'Each missile, probe, whatever they chose to call it, would signal back to its mate, then that in turn would 'cast a signal until it eventually reached this Bertl.

'Very sophisticated, beyond my Ohnce-Bohnce so much so that I would doubt the system is original with Cayle IV. Probably provided by the Confederation, or maybe one of the science worlds.

'In any event, it's something I plan to steal once we get back to Cumbre.'

Njangu had come up and heard most of Froude's theorizing.

'So there'll be another probe jumping into this system in a time?'

'Precisely. Which will leave us the thrilling task of finding it, a metal toothpick, in a star system,' Froude said. 'That could take a while.'

'Like forever,' Ristori agreed.

'Or maybe not a probe,' Njangu said. 'Maybe a couple of battleships.'

'Why?' Froude said.

'Let's just say a certain date . . . and a certain event . . . back on Cayle IV, have passed,' Njangu said.

'Oh crud,' Garvin said, remembering the bomb.

'I'd be expecting the worst . . . or else nothing, assuming we got the right people,' Njangu said. 'But I don't think it'd hurt to put out the Nana boats on the edge of atmosphere, with sensors all a-twinkle.

'Chaka and his flight suits need some exercise, anyway.'

'Good idea,' Garvin said. 'Now, let's dissect this pimple and see what we've got, in reality.

'Make sure the techs work carefully.

'The bastards might have booby-trapped it, to discourage curiosity.'

It was dusk, near the end of the first dogwatch, and Erik Penwyth was looking forward to his relief. His side hurt, still not healed, and he was hungry.

The troupers were all inside, most still in the mess tent, and the trampled field around *Big Bertha* was empty.

Penwyth caught a flicker out of the corner of his eye. Reflexively, in case this world did turn out to have fangs, he stepped back inside the lock. He picked up a pair of stabilized binocs, looked out again.

On the edge of the field, where low trees rose, were two figures. He had time enough to see that they were dark-skinned, very hairy, almost fur-bearing, and stood half-erect. He caught a flicker of something at one's neck – a bit of mineral on a thong?

Then they were gone.

Penwyth considered the name he'd given the system, the world, grinned wryly.

Perhaps.

Or perhaps not.

Five days later, one of the Nana boats reported something.

Or, rather, three somethings.

Not probes, but former Confederation battle cruisers.

Garvin ordered the boats to lie doggo out-atmosphere and wait for orders.

A few minutes later, Kekri's transceiver blurped into life. Njangu was all ready for that.

Several messages were already encoded – not quite the cipher built into the machine, but something just a bit off. The static machine also would confuse the issue. Plus the data being transmitted from Kekri's transceiver to the battle cruisers was the engineering specifications for *Big Bertha*'s primary drive, in excruciating detail.

That would slow the code technicians aboard the cruisers down for a while.

''Kay,' Garvin reported to his war council. 'Since this is the first time they've wanted data from this transceiver, plus something else that happened recently on Cayle IV, it's pretty obvious this is where the hand gets played out.'

He smiled grimly.

'I'm very damned tired of being kicked around and running.'

The three *aksai*, with Dill, Boursier, and Alikhan prone in the flight pods, floated out of *Big Bertha*'s cargo area, then slowly climbed, through drizzle and heavy clouds, toward space.

They didn't do their usual zooming because the secret armories on *Big Bertha* had been opened, and two ship-killing Goddard missiles, six meters long, 60cm in diameter, hung on the mounts set up back on D-Cumbre, under each wing of the *aksai*.

Liskeard hoped the watch aboard the three cruisers might be a little lazy, and, as long as the locator showed the circus ship hadn't moved, they might not be over-eager on their radars. That was another reason for the *aksai* to lift at far less than full drive – the cruisers' proximity sets might be set to shrill if anything closed on them at too high a speed.

The warships hung in a geosynchronous orbit over *Big Bertha*, halfway between Eden IV and its single moon.

The *aksai* cleared atmosphere, held their orbit until Eden was between them and the cruisers, went to full drive for deep space.

Close to Eden's moon, they braked and reset their drives, to come back in a high-speed looping orbit directly at the ships.

Ben Dill watched them close on one of his screens.

'No challenge, no nothing, just sitting quackers, aw, poor babies,' he said, then, into his mike, 'Dill One . . . beginning attack pattern.'

Two mike clicks came from the other *aksai* indicating his 'cast had been received.

He was no more than a thousand kilometers from the

cruisers when he activated the Goddard targeting systems. Minutes later, both beeped. Target acquired. He set both for the nearest cruiser.

'Dill One . . . closing,' he 'cast. 'On the high ship, targeted. Launch One . . . launch Two . . . breaking off.'

'Alikhan . . . on the center ship. One is gone . . . two.'

'Boursier, on the last scrap pile. One fired . . . the second's gone.'

There was no sign of alarm or alert from the cruisers as the six missiles homed. All impacted, and there was nothing but three perfectly circular balls of flaming gas in space.

'*Big Bertha*, this is Mrs. Dill's favorite son. Coming home, with the broomstick tied to the mast . . . we've got a clean sweep here.'

''Kay,' Garvin said. 'Now, if there's no more dicking around to be done, let's go on to Centrum.'

'Takeoff within thirty seconds,' Liskeard said.

The locator, and Kekri's transceiver, had been left behind, just in case they held any surprises.

The circus ship lifted away, vanished.

Two days later, the two primates Erik Penwyth had seen found the courage to approach these strange objects.

The one wearing a bit of mica on a string of gut chanced touching the transceiver.

It beeped at her.

She yelped, and, followed by her mate, ran for the trees, never again to come near this cursed place.

TWENTY-SIX

Unknown System

The bridge was crowded as Njangu and Garvin slid in, finding a place away from the command console.

N-space still swirled about them.

Njangu saw a communications officer sniff the air. He could have told the man what the smell was – the stink of fear, waiting to see what would happen when *Big Bertha* entered this booby-trapped system, but didn't. The virgin would figure it out in a few moments all by himself.

Garvin caught Liskeard's eye, nodded a go-ahead.

'You have the security data from Cayle?' Liskeard asked an officer sitting in front of a screen.

'Affirm. Up and running.'

Liskeard tapped a talker.

'All stations, battle ready,' he ordered. 'All compartments seal, report integrity.'

Liskeard listened to the clatter of returns, and an officer said:

'All compartments sealed, sir.'

'Stand by to exit hyperspace ... on my signal ... now!'

Screens unblurred, and *Big Bertha* was in normal space, hanging not far from a ringed planet.

'Receiving signal on watch frequency . . . N . . . N . . . N . . . origin one of two moons at two-A main screen.'

'Respond with R . . . R . . . R . . .'

'Receiving signal . . . C-nine-eight-A-R-two.'

'Wait . . . wait . . . send challenge response of four-five-I-X-two-two.'

'Signal sent . . . waiting . . . waiting . . . response of C . . . C . . . C . . .'

'That's clearance.'

There was a moment of relaxation.

'Stand by for next jump,' Liskeard ordered. 'Twenty seconds . . .'

'I have activity from planetary surface.'

'ID it!'

'Ships . . . several ships . . . taking off . . . correction. Missiles.'

'Ship targeted.'

'Activate ECM.'

'Activated, sir. Trying to acquire control.'

'Twelve seconds to hyperspace.'

'Missiles will be in range in . . . thirty seconds. I have ten bogies homing. Correction. Four missiles jumped into N-space . . . no proximity report . . . six missiles remaining in normal space . . . proximity twenty-four seconds.'

'Six seconds to hyperspace.'

'Four missiles exited N-space . . . homing . . . homing . . .'

'Two missiles taken over . . . three . . . three diverted . . .'

'Three seconds to hyperspace.'

'Single missile homing . . . seconds . . .'

'Jump!'

The world went swirly.

'Now, if that goddamned missile has lost us . . .'

Silence for some seconds.

'We lost it.'

'Whew.'

'Where the hell did that missile launch come from and why?' Liskeard demanded. 'I thought we had all their security codes.'

'I thought so, too,' Garvin said

'Maybe a system bought from another supplier?'

'Maybe . . . or maybe those goddamned missiles got a little rusty around the ears and got independent?'

'One more jump, and then Centrum.'

'Let's get through that one more first.'

'Silence on the bridge except for business!'

Njangu noticed the smell was stronger.

Unknown System

The screen showed a tight cluster of planets close to the sun, a scatter of ice giants on the fringes. The nav point had brought them out in a band of asteroids.

Eyes scanned screens, then, in a jumble:

'I have metallic objects homing on us!'

'Indicated asteroid has made a launch . . . count of twenty-seven missiles . . .'

'I have inbound ships from inner worlds . . . guesstimate robot interceptors . . .'

'Unknown objects homing on ship . . . ID as possible kinetic satellites . . . count thirty-five . . .'

'Metallic objects probably active mines . . . send countersignal three-four-Q-Q-Q-three . . .'

'Roger three-four-Q-Q-Q-three . . .'

Missile diversion send six-six-seven-eight-nine-nine-zero.'

'Sending six-six-seven-eight-nine-nine-zero.'

'Interceptors disappeared into N-space.'

'Interceptor code single word WAVEN.'

'Roger WAVEN, waiting for reappearance . . .'

'Mines have aborted, countersignal worked.'

'Inbound missiles self-destructed.'

'Interceptors returned to real space, sending WAVEN . . . WAVEN . . . no effect . . .'

'ECM attempt to lock on interceptors . . . no apparent effect.'

'Countermissiles stand by for launch, on command,' Liskeard ordered.

'Interceptors returned to N-space, sent signal of RAFET, I say again, RAFET.'

'RAFET approved acknowledgment of challenge response. They've gone back home.'

'Anything else out there trying to eat us alive?'

Silence, then a storm of negatives.

'Seven minutes to next launch,' Liskeard said. 'Don't relax.'

Capella

'Stand by for reentry,' Liskeard ordered. 'If they've got anything that'll come after us, let's try to get a jump on 'em. That last was a little bit close for me.

'Four . . . two . . . we're out!'

They entered a system with a medium main sequence sun, five planets within habitable range, one too close in, three farther out.

'Capella,' somebody breathed. Garvin thought it might be him.

'Anything?'

A string of negatives.

'There's got to be *something* out there standing guard,' Liskeard said.

'Maybe they're saving their surprises for when we're on the ground,' Njangu said.

His throat was very dry.

TWENTY-SEVEN

Capella/Centrum

Njangu's worries didn't last long.

As they closed on Centrum, the com officer made the standard arrival notice/request for landing instructions on one of the watch frequencies.

It was as if he provided a reveille call.

A slow reveille call, for it was on the third repetition that Centrum Control snorted awake and informed *Big Bertha* to take a parking orbit, and stand by for clearancing.

Froude shuddered a little.

'Clearancing, eh? Well, whatever happened, we can assume the teachers of Common were the first to go under.'

'I think,' Njangu said to Garvin, 'you and I had best get flashed up.'

They dressed in their conservative best, but could have taken their time, because it was three ship-hours before the watch frequency came alive, advising the ship *Bag Berna* to stand by for boarding and inspection.

The ship approaching them was identified by their *Jane's* fiche as unknown, which Njangu assumed meant built less than eight years ago, when their latest copy of *Jane's* had been sent off to the far frontiers.

'Destroyer class, it appears,' Liskeard said. 'Zoom me in closer if you can.'

A tech brought up a screen with a realtime visual, zoomed in until the destroyer appeared no more than half a kilometer distant.

'Interesting,' Liskeard went on. 'It's spent a lot of time in-atmosphere . . . not hangared . . . look at the corrosion on the outer hull. Not drydocked in a while. Not very shipshape, my friends.'

He watched the ship's approach. The destroyer killed its secondary drive and braked into a parallel orbit two thousand meters away from *Big Bertha*. Mag-couples shot out. One missed, the other clanged against *Big Bertha*'s hull, and winches brought the two ships closer.

'Sloppy piloting,' Liskeard assessed. 'I would have horsewhipped myself for something that ground-pounder.'

Space-suited figures swam across emptiness, into *Big Bertha*'s main lock, were cycled into the main hold.

There were a dozen of them, and, already waiting, were Garvin, Njangu, Monique Lir in spangles, Froude, not in his clown outfit, Alikhan, and Ben Dill in a muscle outfit, very picturesque and harmless.

The Confederation men and women didn't wait for anything like an atmosphere check, but evidently assumed since most of their greeters looked human, they must breathe something close to E-normal.

Helmets were doffed. A man, not much more than a boy, looked around. 'Sheesh, what a goddamned big ship,' he said, audibly.

Monique Lir started to frown at this indiscipline, hid her reaction.

A long-haired woman stepped forward.

'I'm *Haut* Fenfer, of the *Thermidor.* Welcome to the People's Confederation.'

Garvin noted the change in the name.

'And I'm Garvin Jaansma of Circus Jaansma. These are my staff members.'

'Your homeworld?'

Garvin decided to answer carefully, and make no mention of Cumbre.

'Garibaldi.'

'I'm not familiar with that system,' Fenfer said, and somebody in the ranks snickered

'Your purpose in entering the Confederation?'

'To entertain the people of Centrum and this system's other worlds,' Garvin said.

Fenfer hesitated. 'You'll have to bear with me a bit . . . you're the first ship I've ever cleared.'

Njangu kept his poker face firmly in place.

'Did you, uh, have any problems approaching Capella?' she asked.

'None,' Garvin said.

Fenfer looked perplexed.

'That's good. Uh, do you have any contraband aboard?'

'This is the first time we've visited Capella,' Garvin said. 'What is contraband?'

Fenfer took a list from a pouch, began reading:

'Weapons-grade fissionable devices . . . subversive propaganda . . . narcotics not permitted by the Confederation . . .' The list went on. At its end, Garvin shook his head solemnly.

'None of the above. Except for dangerous animals which are part of our show, and are always properly caged and watched.'

'You're sure?'

'I'm sure.'

'I guess the animals won't be a problem,' Fenfer said. 'Would you object to an inspection?'

'Of course not. My staff will be happy to escort your people around.'

Fenfer turned to her team.

'Very well. You have your instructions.'

'Assuming there are no problems,' Fenfer said, 'I have orders to escort you, Gaffer Jaansma, as commander of this ship, to *Dant* Romolo, on our fleet's flagship.'

'I would be honored,' Garvin said. 'Shall we get the inspection out of the way? I don't want to keep *Dant* Romolo waiting.'

Fenfer passed Monique Lir, gave her a meaningless smile.

Lir responded in kind, didn't wrinkle her nose.

Either Fenfer's suit needed decontamination, or else the woman could use a bath.

Fenfer's ship, the *Thermidor*, wasn't that clean either, Garvin thought. The bulkheads and decks had been mopped and swept, but here and there he spotted patches given a lick and a promise.

Similarly, the crew members were sloppily dressed, some wearing bits of civilian clothes with their uniforms.

They didn't have what the military called, in a word Njangu always hated, 'smartness.'

Yoshitaro never gave a damn whether a trooper had her/his nose spit-shined, but knew a well-trained grunt moved with a certain snap, had an easy familiarity with his/her duties.

Not the women and men of the *Thermidor*.

They behaved, Njangu decided, like sailors who were

two weeks or less short of discharge and simply didn't give much of a tinker's damn.

Garvin thought it a bit odd that the *Thermidor*'s Commanding Officer didn't bother to come down from the bridge to the compartment he and Njangu were held in, close to the airlock, out of curiosity if no more.

He chanced asking their guard, a friendly-faced *Dec* who'd told them he was one of the ship's quartermasters. As part of the 'search' team, he'd been infinitely curious about the circus and how it operated, and said, wistfully, that he hoped he'd get ground leave before they left.

Garvin scribbled out an Annie Oakley, said he hoped to see him there and he'd personally give him a tour of the midway, clown alley, and the tops.

He chanced asking why the quartermaster's CO hadn't come down and introduced himself.

The quartermaster looked up at the wall speaker which Garvin thought interesting in itself, then said, in a low voice:

'He doesn't know what to think about you yet.'

'Why doesn't he come down and get some input to make up his mind?' Njangu asked.

'No, no,' the man said. 'He hasn't been *told* what he thinks yet.'

He refused to elaborate who would be the one who'd dictate opinion, and was relieved when the speaker beeped and announced they'd be closing on the *Corsica* in zero-seven minutes.

The *Corsica* was huge, a battleship more than two kilometers long, bristling with missile stations and chainguns for secondary armament.

It was also very smart, indeed, overheads, bulkheads, decks gleaming, uniforms spotless, their wearers moving with snap and panache, saluting officers with a greeting and a slogan that must have been changed regularly.

This one was 'train hard, fight easy,' one of the oldest and most deceptively false saws in the book. More realistic, Njangu thought, would be 'train hard, fight hard; train easy, fight harder.'

Njangu thought the ship and its crew were perhaps a little *too* nit and tiddy.

An aide, who didn't introduce himself, ushered them through an outer office with busy yeomen into *Dant* Lae Romolo's cabin, which was rather sparse with computer projections hung haphazardly here and there on the walls. The only holo was that of a rather severe woman.

From Cumbre on, Garvin had the rather romantic dream that all this sneaking and subterfuge would end with him being able to stand at attention in front of a high-ranking Confederation officer, salute him, and report as he should:

'*Caud* Garvin Jaansma, Commanding Second Infantry Regiment, First Brigade, Strike Force Angara from the Cumbre system, reporting in to the Confederation, sir.'

But now he thought better of the idea.

Dan Romolo was a fairly small man, with a round face, thinning hair he clearly didn't have the vanity to have revitalized, and the beginnings of middle-age spread.

This did not mean Romolo was, in any way amiable-looking or soft. His face was prematurely lined, comfortable with command, and his cold eyes stared hard.

Njangu was reminded of the late dictator Redruth, and didn't like the hint at all.

'Welcome to the People's Confederation, and its capital system,' Romolo said, and there was a slight, possibly sarcastic, emphasis on 'People's.'

'Your homeworld is Grimaldi.'

'Yes, sir,' Garvin said.

'My star charts show that as a barely colonized world,' Romolo said.

Garvin was surprised.

'It's been settled for at least four hundred years, sir, as a base for traveling circuses like mine.'

'Don't be surprised,' Romolo said. 'During the course of . . . shall we say, change, in the Confederation, many records were either destroyed by accident or mislaid and have yet to be recovered.'

'Change, sir?' Garvin said. 'All we know . . . all the worlds we come from or landed on . . . is that the Confederation has fallen out of contact with its systems.'

'Also, none of the military units we encountered have been in contact with Centrum,' Njangu chanced. 'Sir . . . what happened?'

He heard honest plaintiveness in his voice.

Romolo took a careful breath.

'The Confederation Parliament went through a sea change, very rapidly, after a long period of stress, a few years ago.

'The new members of Parliament have been forced to spend all their time rebuilding the homeworlds bringing order, and unfortunately haven't been able to provide the Confederation with leadership or security.

'It's truly unfortunate, and all of us hope the situation corrects itself within the next few years.'

Garvin knew he should have kept his mouth shut but couldn't. This was, after all, the culmination of everything.

'Sir . . . what we've just gone through, getting here which was always my dream . . . well, it's pretty close to pure chaos out there. We *need* the Confederation.'

Romolo's lips thinned, and he nodded sharply.

'I'm not surprised. Let me ask you something . . . I believe you prefer the title of Gaffer . . . did you have any difficulties in reaching Capella?'

'We had to evade some people who called themselves the Confederation Protectorate a few jumps back,' Garvin said. 'And some of the worlds we attempted to perform on weren't that friendly.'

'But nothing else?'

'Not really, sir,' Garvin said. 'What, specifically, did you have in mind?'

Romolo was silent, thinking

'That's interesting. Very interesting. I think it might be valuable for us to examine your logbooks.'

'With our pleasure, sir.'

'That can be done later,' Romolo said. 'I'm sure you'd like to make planetfall as soon as possible.'

'It's been a long series of jumps, sir,' Garvin said.

'I'll happily give you a release to land where the People's Parliament allows, with my recommendation that you be permitted to perform as desired and given the full freedom of Centrum. You'll be assigned a pilot within the ship-day to ensure you make proper landing.'

'Thank you, sir. I hope you'll find the time to be our guest.'

'Unlikely,' Romolo said. 'I find that my duties here, away from the comforts of Centrum, take up all of my time.'

He didn't sound like he was sorry about that.

'A circus,' he said, pretending sociability. 'I remember, as a boy, my mother taking me to a circus. That was in the old days, when there *were* things like circuses, and entertainment that wasn't always supposed to be good for you.

'There were monsters and animals and people doing amazing things. Amazing.'

Then he dropped the effort, came back to the present.

'Very well. That's all.'

'Sir?' Njangu asked.

'Would it be possible for me to inquire as to whether anything is known about one of the Frontier Worlds? I had a brother . . . I hope I still have him . . . serving with the Confederation forces . . .' Njangu tried to sound worried.

'My writers in the compartment outside have access to all Confederation records,' Romolo said, a bit impatiently, too big a man to worry about small things like brothers. 'You're welcome to ask one of them before you transship.'

Garvin tried to keep from saluting, from doing a smart about-face, from looking like a military sort, and they went out.

'What was the name of this world again?' the yeoman asked.

'Cumbre,' Njangu said. 'D-Cumbre. All the worlds of the Cumbre system had letter-names, my brother said.' He spelled Cumbre carefully.

The woman tapped sensors, shook her head.

'Nothing at all on Confederation Main Records or our star charts. What about the name of the unit, although it's unlikely there'd be anything under that listing.'

'Uh, the last note I had from him said it was, uh Strike Force Swift Lance. Its commander was named Williams.'

Again, sensors were touched.

'I'm sorry. Perhaps you've got the unit name wrong, in which case you should check with Confederation Military Records once you're on Centrum.'

*

'Son of a bitch,' Garvin said, as *Big Bertha*'s lock cycled, and they pulled their helmets off.

'Son of a bitch indeed,' Njangu said

'I think we need a drink.'

'Several. And get Froude and Ristori's asses for chasers and consultation.'

'I'm making some very interesting, very tentative theories,' Froude said. 'You, Jabish?'

'I wouldn't use interesting so much as astounding, preposterous, absurd,' Ristori said. 'Perhaps I should pour this fine engine-room juice back in the snifter.'

'Uh-uh,' Njangu said. 'I want you to keep up with us, and what you're coming up with can't be any weirder than what Garvin and I are probably thinking.'

'Then talk to us, Gaffer Jaansma,' Froude said. 'You're the CO, so we'll let you be the first to dangle it out there.'

''Kay,' Garvin said. 'This stress Romolo talked about. I'd guess that must've been the riots we heard about when we passed through Centrum as recruits.'

'Maybe,' Njangu allowed. 'Or maybe the stress was worse. Like uprising, maybe. Or riots that never stopped.'

Froude looked at Ristori, and both nodded tentative agreement.

'So when things fell apart, they really fell apart. I don't have any idea what this frigging People's Confederation is, or this People's Parliament,' Njangu went on. 'But this thing about records being lost lets me get very, very weird on what might've happened.

'Maybe,' he went on, carefully not looking at the other three, 'in this period of stress somebody blew up the Military Records Division.'

'That's reaching,' Ristori said.

'Besides,' Garvin said, 'there's always backups.'

'Yeh,' Njangu agreed. 'And lemme stretch some more. Not only were the central records blown all to hooey, which I can see a mob doing who's been shot up a few times by folks in uniform, but maybe the backups are either on other worlds or some of those sets of records nobody seems to have located.

'Shitfire, if they could lose any reference to Cumbre—'

'*And* have Grimaldi's records a few hundred years out-of-date,' Garvin interrupted.

'Why the hell couldn't they forget about a few thousand grunts called Strike Force Swift Lance?' Njangu finished.

'Not enough,' Froude said, although Ristori, stroking his chin, was shaking his head in disagreement. 'Why haven't they sent anybody out to start touching bases?'

'I'll give you the easy answer,' Njangu said. 'And the hard possibility.

'The easy one is that if everything turned to shit on Centrum, everybody with any kind of authority was busy trying to keep his own ass behind the firing squad instead of in front.

'Think about it, Danfin. Everybody we know who comes from one of the Confederation worlds who got interested in politics has said they'd been sort of ignored for a long time before the bottom fell out. For some worlds it was five years, for some twenty, some even longer.'

'True,' Froude said. 'I can remember trying to communicate with colleagues in other systems who'd done interesting papers, and never being able to make contact.'

'As can I,' Ristori said. 'Even before I went on the

road. It was a constant complaint at the conventions I used to attend, before terminal boredom struck, that whole segments of the Confederation were being lost and valuable, long-term sociological studies would never be available.'

Njangu nodded smugly.

'Let me tell you a little story. As soon as I finish what's in my glass, take the decanter away from Jaansma, then get some more of that chilled tea for a chaser.'

Njangu did as he'd promised, drank deeply, then returned to his chair, slouched back in it.

'When I was very, very small,' he said, 'there was this group of tearaways a street or so over. I was far too young to join them, which was a good thing because they ended up getting nailed by the cops, given condit, and that was the end of that.

'Anyway, they were real dumb-birds, 'cause they were stealing from people around them, which of course guaranteed somebody would eventually snitch them off, which is what happened.

'Now, I lived in a shit-poor part of the world, and nobody could afford proper security devices, but they sure as hell didn't want to come home from work or a hard day's thieving and find their flats stripped barebones.

'So they started putting in iron bars. Over the windows, over the doors.

''Course, you can cut through iron fairly easy, but that takes time and work, and thieves don't fancy either.

'The point of the story is there was this one man, wife had left him with two kids, down two buildings. A fire started one night in his apartment, and he had all his ironwork neatly bolted in and locked.

'I guess he couldn't find the keys to the locks in time.'

'The man burned?'

'To a crisp,' Njangu said. 'And the kids.'

Garvin got it first.

'All those damned security devices we had to beep and burp and code our way through are like the iron bars?'

'Just that,' Njangu said. 'The goddamned Confederation went and built itself a fortress, and then forgot how to get out of it.

'That's why Romolo . . . and the boarding officer from that destroyer . . . were so curious about any difficulties we might have had coming into the Capella system, and why he wants to look at the logbooks, which I'll be falsifying as soon as tomorrow's hangover goes away.'

'That's . . . well, not impossible,' Froude said. 'And I'll accept the codes were destroyed. But wouldn't they push their way through, very carefully?'

'Why? They had troubles here at home. And as for people from the outside . . . how many ships do you think it takes to vanish . . . blown all to hell by those frigging robots . . . before people quit trying?'

Garvin followed Njangu's lead, and poured himself a drink.

'I suspect,' he said slowly, 'if that's the explanation, or even just part of it, Centrum is going to be very goddamned interesting.'

'Not to mention borderline lethal,' Yoshitaro said.

TWENTY-EIGHT

The guide pilot was a wizened woman named Chokio with very wise eyes. Liskeard told her that *Big Bertha* wasn't the strongest ship for gravitational stress, a complete lie, so he'd appreciate it if she'd approve a nice, quiet lowering approach that'd take them a while to reach ground.

'Cert'nly, Cap'n,' she said. 'Besides, gives you a good chance to have a look at Centrum. Y' been here before?'

'No,' Liskeard said truthfully. Garvin came on the bridge, heard her question, shook his head untruthfully, figuring a flash visit as a bare-ass recruit in the rear rank wouldn't count for much.

'Give you a chance at th' glory what were Rome. See how things can get totally screwed . . .' and she caught herself. 'Sorry. Meant how things can change in not ver' long.'

As they closed on the planet, she grinned, and told Liskeard to open up a screen and gave an aim point.

It showed long ranks of starships, drifting aimlessly in orbit, loosely linked together with kilometer-long cables.

''At's th' Confederation Fleet . . . that which didn't get caught on the ground and tore up when things . . . changed, or was out Beyond, and never come back. Or left a'terward and never come back.'

'What was it like when . . . well, the way you put it, things changed?' Garvin asked.

'It was shit-ugly for anyone wearin' a uniform, didn't seem to matter if you were a soldier or a postman,' Chokio said. 'I was very damned glad to be on th' moon as a girl operatin' a pushmepullme yard tug. Friends of mine on groundside said it got definitely nasty out.

'Not that it wasn't warranted,' she said hastily. 'Damned Confederation bureaucrats and their thugs'd been pushin' folks around for too long. The people had enough, and so they started lashin' out in all directions.

'Sometimes they got the right direction, sometimes . . .' She shrugged and pretended to consult a screen as *Big Bertha* entered atmosphere.

'Almost wish this ship of yours was like some of the oldies,' Chokio said. 'Thin-skinned enough so you could hear air whip, and have lousy enough heat exchangers so it'd redden up. That was back when there was romance in space travel.

'Brought one of those back to Centrum not long ago,' she said. 'It was some kind of old survey ship, and I guess they thought it'd have Confederation records or something.

'Never heard anything more about it.'

Big Bertha made a first orbit, shallowly descending as it went. Every viewscreen, every port was crowded, and as they got lower, it was easy to see the 'changes.'

Centrum was . . . had been . . . a carefully planned world, with huge islands of apartments near buildings that had to be governmental for their gray ugliness. In between stretched lakes and green belts.

In a closed compartment, Njangu and his Intel people

were correlating what they saw with the map of Centrum they'd bought from Kuprin Freron, back on Tiborg Alpha Delta.

'See th' parks?' Chokio said. 'Kinda shabbied up, aren't they? They were built not just for runnin' and playin', of course. Intended to cycle off CO_2, so folks could keep breathin'.

'When people got done rippin' and tearin', and realized th' heat wasn't on, some of th' fools decided to get in th' parks with saws, and *really* get back to th' land.

'The Cits . . . citizens . . . wouldn't listen to anybody telling 'em about oxygen regeneration, thought anybody who did were bigbrains, prob'ly part of the Old Order, and thought they'd make good targets.

'Finally, had to give orders to the People's Militia made it a capital offense to cut down a tree.

'Not that anybody ever *considered* telling any Cit she didn't have the right to breed 'til we all have to breathe in alternate beats. Nawp, anything scientific was part of the old way of thinkin'.'

She shook her head, said, almost under her breath 'People always seem hell-bent on makin' themselves into the worst damn' fools they can, don't they?'

Liskeard didn't answer, and *Big Bertha* closed on the ground, flying over a huge, burned-out ruin.

'That was Riot Troops' headquarters. Barracks, holding cells, landing platform on top. It went up like a torch, the first day of the rising. Heard there weren't any of 'em got through that night, which was at least one of the good things the change brought, and I think I'm talkin' a bit much.

'Got orders to bring you down at Mainport. I guess th' powers that be this week might want to see themselves a circus. Hell, I'm curious myself.

'Just hope the Mobiles approve of circuses, so everything goes smooth.'

'What are the Mobiles?' Garvin asked.

'Th' Mobilization Party. They're the cuttin' edge or at least they tell everybody they are, and seem to believe it, of th' change right now. They . . . and their leader . . . make sure everything's headed in the right direction.'

'Who's leading them?' Garvin asked. 'Might be a good idea to stay on his side.'

'Things, they say, are changin',' Chokio said. 'But then, they always are. A year or so ago, I would've mentioned the Freedom Party and Abia Cornovil, who's always interested in things new. Now, it's the Mobility. Next year . . .' she shrugged. 'Who th' hell knows.

'Anyway, The Mobiles' current leader's a Fove Gadu.

'Gadu's one of those folks who knows better'n you what's best for you, and doesn't mind cuttin' a few throats or givin' a few lethal injections to those who disagree.'

Abia Comovil was a big man, middle-aged, naturally muscled, going a bit to pot, who dressed simply and wore his straight hair almost to his shoulders. If this were another planet than Centrum, Njangu would have thought him an ex-farmer. He found later that Cornovil had been a statistician, but the shovel and hoe must not have been too distant in his genealogy, for he was the one who'd taken charge of keeping the parks as intact as possible.

Strangely, he'd had a bad complexion as a boy, which he never had repaired, on a planet that would have had the best cosmetic medicos.

His voice was as burly as his presence, and his booming laugh could be heard throughout the ship.

Cornovil had insisted on seeing everything and meeting everyone, and was fascinated with every detail, from how horses handled N-space to how Sir Douglas cycled the pungent cat shit.

He appeared no more than a cheerful peasant, and both Yoshitaro and Froude had to keep reminding themselves that this man had ridden the crest of what appeared to be roiling anarchy for almost a generation, and had to be a great deal more than he appeared.

Cornovil insisted on having a drink with Garvin and his staff. Jaansma, rather maliciously, served him their own triply distilled engine-room swill.

He purpled a little, but kept from choking.

'Great gods,' he said. 'No wonder you're so eager to get out of space. Does this crap improve with age?'

'Yours or its?' Froude asked. 'I've almost gotten to liking it.'

'I'll send over some brandy imported from Second World,' Cornovil promised. 'If you people propose to keep the Mobiles entertained, you can't be poisoning yourselves.'

'A question,' Froude said. 'Someone implied that this Mobilization Party has a great deal of power. Just how does the People's Confederation work, politically?'

'Quite frankly,' Cornovil said, 'we're still working things out, just as we've yet to be able to redeem the promise the Confederation made to other systems to provide peace and open trade.

'We have a Parliament of One Thousand, which supposedly is elected by the people. Anyone can run in the yearly race, at which one-third of the seats are at stake, and a simple majority qualifies you for admission. But in fact, there are a dozen parties. Since the Mobiles are now the strongest, you'd be advised to support their views if you wish a chance at election. My own, the Freedom League, is at least holding it's own. Others . . .' he shrugged, 'come up, go back down, sometimes after being found out as secret supporters of the Old Confederation.'

'How are the votes managed?' Njangu asked, and Cornovil looked at him warily.

'That's a pretty sophisticated question for somebody as young as you are,' Cornovil said. 'Does a circus require a political expert?'

'It's hard, visiting a dozen worlds a year, and wishing to keep on the good side of everyone,' Froude said to get Njangu off the hook, '*not* to have an interest in politics.'

'Ah,' Cornovil said. 'The votes are . . . handled, as you put it, somewhat carelessly. In the last three elections, in fact, there've been a number of accusations of fraud.' He shrugged. 'Unfortunately, the accusations were all against the Mobilization Party, which, being the most active and militant at the moment, responded strongly.

'*Very* strongly.'

Njangu felt it wise not to inquire further, especially when Cornovil looked at him coldly, and Yoshitaro saw, once more, that slight gleam he'd seen before in the eyes of powerful men who'd gotten that power without any regard for honesty or legality.

But, three days later, two barrels of brandy arrived, as promised.

A man weanng a black sash, which made him an officer of the People's Militia, arrived, and informed Garvin that the circus was given permission to occupy the Central Stadium, both for quarters and performing, and he was ready to escort them there.

'I don't like this at all,' Garvin told Njangu.

'Me either,' Yoshitaro agreed 'This whole damned place feels shaky, and I'd surely like to stick close to the ship.

'You see any way we can get away with it?'

'Nope.'

'Then let's line up the troops and parade on in. But let's give everybody who's in the know a gun. And we'll keep *Big Bertha* ready to lift and at standby. Plus we can maybe pray a little, if you remember any good gods' names.'

The circus, elephants, cats, horses, clowns, little people, acrobats streamed toward the Central Stadium. The sidewalks on either side of them were packed.

But Garvin couldn't make a call. On some blocks the people were silent, staring, almost hostile. On others, they cheered wildly.

He decided he'd have to play things as they came.

He didn't find much comfort knowing the 'possum bellies,' the storage compartments under the lifters, were packed with weaponry.

The route had been hastily papered with flyers for Circus Jaansma. Garvin noted, with considerable amusement, that all of the flyers on one building had been posted upside down.

That had to have been done by an I&R sort, who'd also learned more than a bit about circus lore – the upside posters were traditionally put up for Home Sweet Home, the season's last play before they made for winter quarters.

Cumbre.

Garvin wondered if they'd make it.

They reached the Central Stadium. The best that could be said about the building was that it was huge big enough for three or four circuses.

Fleam, the boss canvas man, was running around the

arena, muttering, trying to determine where he'd put everything and everyone, trailing harried roustabouts in his wake.

Others explored the upper stories, found rooms for all.

The building smelled of decay, abandonment, and everyone, animals, people, felt uneasy.

But there was no other choice.

'I shall certainly try to appear for your opening show tonight,' Fove Gadu said to Garvin and his staff.

If Abia Cornovil had a slight megalomaniacal gleam to his eye, Gadu broadcast it. He was thin, hair disheveled, and he'd missed a patch here and there when he'd depiled last. His clothes were indifferently clean and it seemed as if he might not have bathed in the last day or so.

'I understand Abia Cornovil visited you,' Gadu said, pretending to be casual. 'What was your impression?'

'Why, he seemed quite in charge of things,' Garvin said. 'He wasn't really here long enough for me, at least, to make any stronger opinion.'

'I see,' Gadu said. 'He made no mention of how he saw what place you might have here on Centrum, then?'

'None, other than he wanted to see our performance, and was most interested in touring our facilities.'

'Oh? Any comments?'

'None other than admiring.'

Gadu changed the subject, asked many questions about *Big Bertha*'s passage to Centrum. It was obvious he knew well about Capella's self-imposed blockade. Finally, he seemed satisfied, quirked his lips in what he might have imagined to be a smile, and left.

'Whoo,' Garvin said. 'Cornovil gave me the chills; this bastard made my dick fall off.'

'Mine just shriveled up and wrapped around my back-bone,' Njangu said. 'What about you, Monique?'

'He reminded me of a couple of sorts I ran across over the years,' Lir said. 'Fortunately, both of 'em are dead now.'

'By whose hand?'

Lir smiled, didn't answer.

Darod Montagna did a backflip off her horse as she came out the Back Way, landed easily on her feet.

Rudy Kweik, leg wounds still healing, limped toward her.

'Well?' he asked.

'Well what?' Darod said.

'What's your call on the townies? I can't get close enough to be sure.'

Darod shivered, not from any cold, hugged herself.

'I can't make them out,' she said slowly. 'One section'll be cheering like bandits, the others look at you like they want to put a bomb in your shorts.'

'I don't like this,' Kweik said. 'Sopi Midt says the midway's doing spotty business. Gambling booths do all right, but nobody's interested in the games of chance that pay off in stuffed animals.'

'Maybe the gazoonies have figured out how fixed everything is,' Darod suggested, realizing how easily she'd started using circus jargon.

Kweik snorted.

'A gilly figure out a gaff? They know nanty, or they wouldn't be gillies, now would they?'

'That's one way to figure it,' Montagna said.

'The only way I figure it is that we'll be damned lucky to make the run for home without a serious clem,' Kweik said. 'You might want to make sure you take care of yourself.'

'I always do,' Montagna said.

'Not with that whopping great boomer you saved my life with,' Kweik said. He dug into a pocket of his baggy pants, took out a small pistol.

'Here. Midt's found a source for them. Twenty credits. They shoot projectiles, which makes me wonder if they come out of some museum. Tuck this away. A present for someone who might make a good horse rider in thirty or forty years.'

'Where, exactly, am I supposed to stash this little toy?' Montagna said, grinning and doing a pirouette. Her costume didn't have room enough to hide a penknife.

'Find a place, Darod,' Kweik said. 'I know, feel in my bones, this clem coming on. And it won't be one fought with sticks and stones.'

TWENTY-NINE

The war council on the nearly deserted *Big Bertha* was particularly grim, and included two new members: Chaka and Liskeard. Not sure why they were invited, they held to the back of the small group: Garvin, Njangu, Lir, Froude, and Ristori.

Garvin looked very tired.

"Kay. Let's make this quick. We've got another show tomorrow, and I'd just as soon nobody wonders where we are.

'We came out here almost a year ago looking for what happened to the Confederation, and hoping it was something simple we could help bandage up, and it would be back to something resembling business as before.

'And what a can of frigging worms we unsealed.'

He nodded to Njangu, who took the floor.

'Probably we should've assumed there wasn't just one easy frigging problem with the Confederation. The first thing, which we knew going in, was that big chunks of the Confederation had been allowed to slip out of contact over the last twenty or more years.

'Troops were getting bounced back and forth and in and out, like our Legion, and those Protectorate fellows we just left cutting each others' nuts off out.

'I wouldn't guess there was much control on these units by the Confederation, to point out the obvious.

'So the Confederation, really, had to have been falling apart for a long time, a lot longer than anybody was willing to admit.'

Froude and Ristori nodded unhappily.

'When Garvin and I were passed through seven years or so ago, there were already riots going on.

'Those, I guess, got worse and worse, and what happened was a general system collapse, ending up with this wonderful People's Confederation.'

Froude stood.

'A little elaboration here, if I might. I've done some wandering about, trying to find any scholars that didn't get themselves shortened by a head during the collapse, or who aren't hiding deep in some hole somewhere.

'I found some bits and pieces. The initial fighting seems to have been spontaneous. Nobody knows for sure, but I'd guess an average riot got out of hand . . . or was successful, depending on your point of view.

'The Riot Troops, who were supposed to keep order, got massacred.

'A period of general anarchy came next. A lot of Confederation records, and their keepers, went under during this time, including the main Military Records Division and General Staff system.

'Then some people got together with a common cause – probably grabbing power for themselves – and enough others fell in behind for them to declare themselves a government.

'Then something interesting happened. That party, once it got power, got conservative and drew a line saying that's enough of a revolution for us.

'But it wasn't enough for the people who'd been the

original rioters. Another party got formed, to the left of the first, and they started screaming that the first party was nothing but Confederation lackeys, and it was time for their heads to roll.

'They *were* rolled, and that second party was on top, and said, enough of a revolution.

'But the people of the streets . . . they don't even seem to have a label . . . didn't have the power, and so here came a third gathering. They took out the second group, and were in charge for a while.

'That group, by the way, was the Freedom party, which Abia Cornovil, who most of you met, is the head of.

'Again, no satisfaction for the people on the bottom. They got involved with this Fove Gadu, who'd formed the Mobilization Party.

'It's interesting that it was formed to push for the People's Confederation to reach out for their old holdings, out to the stars.

'Some expeditions were sent out, found out their own booby traps backfired on them, since nobody had the records on how to defuse them, or couldn't find them if they did, and so the Mobilization Party looked for a new cause.

'It appears as if they're now grabbing for the center ring, and we arrived just a little short of what may be another coup.'

He sat down heavily.

'That's about that,' Garvin said. 'So now the questions:

'Do we have a good idea of what happened?'

He got nods, agreement.

'Enough so we can think about ending this recon mission, which has got to be the longest in history?'

Again, agreement.

'So we can . . . if we can . . . scurry on out of here for home, report to *Dant* Angara, and let him try to decide what the Strike Force is going to do next.

'Because, at least from my perspective, next is going to take some serious figuring and is way the hell beyond me at this point.'

'The first question,' Lir said, 'is how do we break contact and get off Centrum?'

'I don't know.'

'Let's say we can,' Chaka said. 'We still have that Romolo and his battleship sitting off Centrum, and he'd probably object to us just fading off stage right.

'I don't see us having enough *baraka* to take him on, let alone winning.'

'The luck of Allah might not be required,' Liskeard said. 'I've got an idea that should shorten the odds with him. But I've got zero-burp about how the hell we rescue the circus and lift without all kinds of alarms going off.'

'Nor do I,' Garvin said. 'Again, events sort of dictated what we'd have to do when we landed here, and we weren't given many choices.'

'We might have no other option,' Ristori said, 'than to accept some losses in changing the order of things.'

'*Soldiers* take losses,' Froude said, trying to keep anger out of his voice. 'Most of the people over in that stadium are civilians.'

Ristori didn't answer, but held out his hands helplessly.

'We've got damned near every small arm aboard over at the stadium already,' Lir said. 'I just don't see any way to get the troupe back here . . . not even filtering people through a few at a time.'

'And I know damned well,' Njangu added glumly 'none of the animal folks will even think about abandoning their creatures, which doesn't make being sneaky any easier.'

'Which leaves us stuck between the lid and the bottom of the shitter,' Garvin said. 'The bad guys have the first move. All of them.

"Kay. Now that we're all depressed, back to your posts, and we wait until we get an opening.'

'There's one slight thing that Chaka and I can do that might help when the balloon goes up,' Liskeard said.

'Which is?'

'Which starts with giving that dictator-in-the-making *Dant* Romolo exactly what he said he wanted.'

THIRTY

Four men hung in emptiness. Between them hung two Shadow antimissile missiles, with their bases inside a curved box and a Goddard shipkiller, with an unsightly bulge over its guidance area. A welding pencil flared, went out, flared again.

'That's that,' the technician said, putting the pencil back in his belt pouch.

'And that,' Chaka said, 'is unquestionably the ugliest jury-rig I've ever seen, let alone had a hand in building.'

'Don't be so modest,' Liskeard said. 'I think it's just plain gorgeous. Especially if it happens to work, which I doubt.

'Now, let's get our asses back to the scow and continue the mission, like they say. We're only halfway through.'

Their suit jets spurted white, and they moved back toward the Nana boat floating thirty meters away.

About three kilometers away floated the mothballed remains of the Confederation fleet.

Dant Romolo received them personally on the bridge of the *Corsica*, rather eagerly accepted the package they'd brought.

'Is there anything else in your records that might be of use to me?' he asked.

'No offense, sir,' Chaka said. 'But not exactly knowing what you want from our logs, it'd be hard saying. But you've got all the data our instruments normally assemble and record.'

'Good,' Romolo said. 'I'm sure it'll be of use to me . . . and to the People's Confederation.'

Again there was that peculiar, half-mocking emphasis on the word 'People's.'

Chaka nodded, trying not to salute, and left the Corsica.

'Now we'll see if all your forgeries keep him happy,' he said.

'They'll keep him quiet for a while,' Liskeard said. 'I hope.

'Meantime, we've got bigger worries. I got a canned 'cast bounced from *Big Bertha* an hour ago.

'That Gadu character they were telling us about has stood up in their Congress or Parliament or whatever the hell they call it, and has named Abia Cornovil a traitor to the People's Confederation, and said he's betraying them to foreign influences.

'Since we're the only foreigners to show up lately, it looks like the shit is starting to come down.

'There's another speech . . . a major address, according to what the 'cast said . . . that'll be made tomorrow.

'I think we better get on home so we're right in the middle of the X-ring.'

THIRTY-ONE

Garvin thought that forever after he'd associate politicians, and their rhetoric, with the rotting smell of the
Central Stadium.

A holo was set up in the middle of the stadium's green
room, which was packed, about half troupers, the other
half Forcewomen and -men.

Fove Gadu's image stood in the middle of a chamber
with wooden paneling, and old-fashioned desks and
chairs. But any dignity ended there. Gadu was raving,
and Garvin swore he could see spittle fly:

'. . . this beast, this betrayer, the man who once was
the best of us all, this traitor Abia Cornovil, now corrupted and betraying the People's Confederacy with these
outlanders!

'My colleagues and I doubted our senses when we first
had evidence of this betrayal, which would put all of the
Capella system in the hands of foreign enemies, desperate
animals and aliens who would shatter the centuries-old
faith the people of the Confederation have had!

'But the evidence was irrefutable, and with great
sorrow, yet determination, last night an emergency
plenum of this Parliament ordered Abia Cornovil's
immediate arrest, and for him to be brought before us,

and, through us, all Centrum and its worlds, to be judged!

'Unfortunately, Abia Cornovil had made plans for his escape. In attempting to stop him, his lifter was brought down, and he died in the crash!

'So should all of Centrum's enemies perish!

'But our task is not yet over. For in the heart of Centrum these outsiders still linger, doing who knows what damage, who knows what damage has already been done in their insidious—'

'Screw this,' Lir said, slapping the off switch.

'Yeh,' Garvin said, getting to his feet.

'You heard what the bastard said.

'They'll be coming for us.

'Let's not disappoint them.'

THIRTY-TWO

It only took a couple of hours for the Mobiles to show up. While they were waiting, the troupers blocked all the exits they could find, although Garvin wasn't sure they'd caught them all, and Forcemen took up fighting positions.

Garvin and Njangu watched as the approach streets to the stadium slowly filled solid, the throng rolling slowly toward the stadium and the empty midway booths in front of it, chanting various slogans as they came.

Garvin keyed the stadium's PA system, which included outside speakers, on:

'Attention! This building will be defended if any attempts to enter are made. Do not approach, on danger of bodily harm or worse! Again, do not approach!'

The crowds hesitated. Garvin started to give another warning, and, from somewhere in a building down the street, what appeared to be four blasters fired in near unison, and the speakers scrawked into silence.

'Not bad shooting for basic rioters,' Njangu observed.

'Not bad at all,' Garvin agreed. 'How much you want to bet there's some Pipple's Militia posted out there?'

'Hah. I've got better intentions than to die broke in a riot,' Yoshitaro said.

*

Aboard *Big Bertha*, armorers swore as they unbolted missile pods from the three *aksai* and hoisted chaingun pods in their place.

'Leave a couple of Shrike tubes on each bird,' their warrant advised. 'These Centrum people might have a patrol ship around for the potting.'

On the bridge, Liskeard looked again at a projection of the stadium, and also cursed. The people there would have to make their own escape. The closest landing point was at least five blocks from the stadium in a tiny park he thought might be big enough for his ship to land in. Anything closer . . . he went over the ground centimeter by centimeter.

There *was* a razed building less than a block distant but its ruins were reaching claws, and he dared not chance landing on top of them.

'Maroon all of us here,' he muttered. 'Hopeless. Frigging hopeless.'

But he kept looking at the holo of that building.

Three volleys slammed into the stadium from gunmen in the front ranks of the Mobiles, sheltering behind the ruined midway. Darod Montagna had smashed a window, and set her sniper rifle up on a table, back far enough so there would be no reflection from her sights.

She saw someone with a blaster, and shot the gunman . . . no, she thought, it was a woman . . . down, looked for another target.

'You know,' Ben Dill said thoughtfully to Kekri Katun, 'there's always a chance that Ben isn't going to be able to save the day.

'Particularly stuck in this goddamned cement mausoleum instead of boomin' around in my *aksai*.'

'Don't get gloomy on me,' Katun said. She had a blaster cradled in her arms.

'I'm not,' Ben said, 'Just bein' realistic. And . . . and, well, I want to know, in case anything happens, that I, well, I sort of love you.'

'Sort of?'

'Sorry. I love you.'

Katun smiled at him.

'And I love *you*.'

Ben leaned over and kissed her, then looked startled.

'You know, I can't remember anybody ever saying that to me? Not lately, anyway.'

Kekri whispered in his ear, and Dill's eyes were wide.

'And I can't remember anybody, *ever*, telling me they wanted me to do *that* to them.'

'Stick around, big boy,' Katun said. 'There's *lots* of things you've never done.'

'Maybe that's the best incentive I ever heard for not getting killed.'

Njangu and Maev were going downstairs toward the central floor when the speakers came alive again, and 'Peace March' boomed through the stadium.

'I think,' Yoshitaro said, 'I could learn to hate that frigging song.'

Jabish Ristori lay on his stomach, aiming a blaster through a kicked-out floor window.

Danfin Froude sat next to him, back against the wall, wishing that they'd moved faster and gotten a blaster apiece.

Two stories below, the Mobiles seethed and shouted, crashing through the midway booths. Rocks sailed toward the stadium, and an occasional blaster bolt or old-fashioned bullet whined off the cement.

'There,' Froude said, pointing. 'That man right there, at the corner of the building. He's got some sort of weapon. Kill him.'

Ristori nodded nervously, found the man in his sights, and put his finger on the trigger.

'Well?' Froude said.

Ristori was shaking uncontrollably.

Froude thought of saying something about Ristori's abstract bloodthirstiness, but kept silent. He pushed his friend away from the window and took the blaster from him.

He took careful aim, touched the trigger.

The round spanged off the building just above the gunman, who dived for cover.

'At least I got him worried,' the scientist muttered.

Blaster fire chattered through the glass doors of the stadium, and the two Forcemen behind the tripod-mounted Squad Support Weapon spun away, lay moaning.

Felip Mand'l ran to the gun, squatted behind it. He'd been watching the gunners as they carefully fired single rounds at named targets.

'I think I've got it,' he muttered to himself, sighted at a line of people, and let half a belt of caseless ammunition go. Bodies pinwheeled, there were screams, and people were running in panic.

'I *like* this,' he said, and then there were two troupers beside him, both clowns in full makeup, with boxes of ammunition.

Lucky Felip found another knot of people trying to hide behind the midway's shooting gallery, sprayed the area with the rest of the belt.

A clown slammed a new belt into the gun, its barrel smoking hot.

'Hold down your shooting,' he told Mand'l. 'Don't want to burn out a barrel.'

Lucky Felip grinned at him, nodded acknowledgment.

'The hell with pistols,' he shouted. 'I *love* this!' and more blaster bolts arced into the crowd outside.

'Screw all you buggers! In the ear and in the ass!'

The two men pushed at the door again, then again. It refused to yield.

A very big man with a very big hammer pushed his way to them, ordered them to stand back.

His hammer smashed again and again, and the door went down.

Whooping rage and excitement, the Mobiles were inside the stadium.

Njangu heard the shouts, knew what they meant, and shouted orders to Forcemen around him to spread out, get down, and not get taken from the rear.

Garvin, in his upper-floor observation room, also heard.

'Come,' Alikhan said calmly. 'There is work for us below.'

The two grabbed their weapons and clattered downstairs toward the stadium's main arena.

A *ra'felan* tried to pull himself higher in the rigging as he saw gunmen spill into the arena. One man saw the movement, crouched, aimed.

Monique Lir, curled around the kingpost, blew him in half, grinned, found another man, killed him, and methodically continued her slaughter.

*

Sopi Midt scuttled from the circus's pay tent across the arena floor, a large red box under his arm.

He saw the woman with a pistol.

'No!' he shouted. 'I'll share . . . don't . . . you can't . . .'

The woman, having no idea what Midt was screaming about, shot him in the chest, then again as he writhed in blood.

The box hit the floor, smashed open, and credits spilled out.

The woman dropped her pistol, scooped up money, and Lir killed her from above. Three others tried for the treasure, and Lir lobbed a grenade down.

After that, the circus's cashbox was left completely alone, bills and coins spread across the arena floor amid sprawled bodies.

'Come on, Ticonderoga,' Emton coached. 'Come on with the rest of us so we can find a place to hide, where we won't get hurt.'

Ticonderoga, crouched under *Raf* Aterton's podium, lashed his tail, looked in another direction, pretending not to hear.

The other five animals were already huddled in a large, wheeled carrier.

'Come on, you horrible animal,' Emton pleaded. He heard a noise, looked up, and saw two grinning Mobiles coming toward him, one with a club, the other with some sort of hook on a pole.

'Oh, go away you silly creatures,' he said, pulling one of the small pocket pistols the late Sopi Midt had procured from an inner pocket. He pointed the pistol at the men, squinched his eyes closed, pulled the trigger twice.

He heard a scream, and a thud. Emton opened his

eyes, saw one man laying motionless, the other writhing, clutching his stomach.

Emton got up, went to the wounded man, put the pistol to the man's head and, again with closed eyes, pulled the trigger.

By the time he got back to the podium, Ticonderoga was in the carrier, with the others.

Rudi Kweik's horses were surging against the ropes keeping them in the big room used for a cage. One gelding slammed into the rope netting, and it tore away, and the horses ran for freedom.

Kweik and his wives, shouting, waving their arms, were almost trampled.

A gunman saw Kweik hobbling into the arena after his *vrai*, shot him.

Jil Mahim saw Kweik go down, dropped the gunman, then darted out, grabbed Kweik by the neck of his voluminous shirt, dragged him back into an entryway where Fleam crouched, weapon ready.

'If any of the bastards get close . . . tie a knot in their tails,' she said.

Fleam actually smiled. 'They won't even get close.'

She opened her aid pouch, tore Kweik's shirt open, winced as she saw the hole in his chest, close to his heart.

Shaking her head, she felt his back, found an exit wound. It wasn't a lung shot, she thought hopefully.

Kweik opened his eyes, smiled at her peacefully, then his body contorted, and he was dead.

Mahim pulled his shirt back in order, glanced at Kweik's wives as they began wailing, put them out of her mind as she scuttled along the wall toward another casualty.

*

A dozen men froze as Alikhan came out of a passage, a devourer-weapon in one upper paw, a wasp-grenade in his other. He shot two men, thumbed the wasp-grenade, and tossed it into the midst of the Mobiles.

They screamed as the grenade went off, and the pseudo-insects hummed out of the shattered box, stinging as they went.

Alikhan shot two more, and the others panicked, seeing the huge bullets strike, and then the maggotlike creatures inside spill out, expand, and begin eating.

None of them made it back down the passage to the stairs they'd come up.

Running Bear, sensibly clad in a coverall, ran at the head of fifteen troupers into the rear of the Mobiles.

He shot a woman with a bloodstained butcher knife, then realized he was shouting aloud.

To his eternal shame, it wasn't one of his people's half-remembered war cries, but the circus cry of 'Hey, Rube.'

Maev ran into the bear handlers' position, saw the two robots standing immobile, their handlers sprawled in death.

'Son of a bitch,' she said, pulled one body out of the way, put a helmet on as she got behind the controls.

'I think I almost remember this,' she muttered, and Li'l Doni came alive.

She steered him out of the position, toward a cluster of Mobiles bent over a couple of bodies.

One man turned, saw the shambling creature, and screamed. A woman shot the robot, saw her round impact, then Doni's claws ripped her throat away.

The Mobiles ran in all directions.

A few made it to safety.

'Now, let's go looking for somebody else to mess with,' Maev muttered and, out on the arena floor, Li'l Doni shambled about at her bidding.

'The question is going to be,' Sir Douglas said in a reasonable voice to Njangu, 'whether we can put the pussies back where they belong, afterward.'

'Yeh,' Njangu agreed, keeping his blaster ready again remembering Garvin's story, long ago on a burning rooftop, about why he'd joined the military, after setting a circus's cats on a crowd during a big clem.

'Well, nothing ventured,' Sir Douglas sighed, and began opening the doors of the lifter-mounted cages.

The animals hesitated, and Sir Douglas went to the rear of the cages, began firing his blank pistol into the air.

'Come on,' he said. 'Help me.'

Njangu obeyed, clanging his blaster barrel along the bars.

The cats reluctantly surged out of their cages and went down the passageway toward the arena floor.

'I'd suggest,' Sir Douglas said, 'you get in here for a few minutes, where it's safe.'

Njangu thought that a very good idea.

The cats, angry, scared, came into the arena crouched, tails lashing.

Mobiles saw them, moaned in fear.

Possibly if they'd charged the cats, they might have frightened them back down the passage. Instead, people made one of two very fatal choices: they either stood frozen in fear or they ran, both perfectly familiar behavior of animals' prey.

Roaring, bounding, the beasts pounced, killing, killing again, and bloodlust built.

A few of the Mobiles had the courage to shoot at the

cats, but only one hit, searing a bolt down one lion's side. A moment later, a smashing paw tore his head off.

The Mobiles were in full flight, back toward the side entrance they'd broken through.

'I guess,' Sir Douglas said reluctantly, 'we'd best go and tuck our friends back where they belong.'

'I have one . . . three . . . five launches,' an electronics officer reported. 'Maybe more. Patrol ships of some sort. Medium-size.'

Liskeard stood in the center of his bridge, considering his options.

There were none.

He waved to a talker.

'Is Boursier ready to launch?'

The talker asked.

'Sir, Boursier One is ready.'

'Launch!' Liskeard ordered. 'Try to give any close support you can at the stadium, and take out any of those patrol ships that get in your way.'

The *aksai* in the hold dropped from its mag-couples wobbled on its antigravs toward the open lock, was out into the open air.

Liskeard took a deep breath, made a decision.

'Close the lock and stand by to lift.'

The stairwell to the exit was packed with pushing Mobiles, trying to get out of this arena of horror.

Njangu appeared at a landing above. He held a sack in one hand.

'Hey!' he shouted.

A few heard him through the din, looked up.

Njangu thumbed one of the grenades in the bag to life, dropped the bag in the center of the throng below.

He ducked back out the door he'd come in through, deciding he didn't want to see what happened in four . . . no, three seconds.

The Mobiles boiled out into the street, just as Jacqueline Boursier, swearing madly, fought the *aksai* never intended for low speed close air support, down the avenue toward the stadium.

She saw people running, starting to shoot at her, gawping in horror, and she toggled a sensor.

Her chaingun churned 35mm collapsed-uranium bullets in a six-thousand-round stream into the street below, red tracers, red death.

She lifted into an Immelmann at the end of the avenue, came back, trying not to notice the buildings just a couple of meters below, very close to her wingtips.

Garvin was in a room, trying to help Knox keep the showgirls from complete hysteria when his belt com buzzed.

'Gaffer . . . this is *Big Bertha*. Stand by for pickup.'

Garvin forgot about the women, ran hard for the main entrance.

Big Bertha, bigger than the stadium, bigger than any building in the city, banked overhead, then its nose lifted.

'He can't do that,' Danfin Froude said.

'But he is,' Ristori said.

He was. Liskeard backed *Big Bertha* on secondary drive toward the sort of vacant lot. Its landing fins, then the ship's bulk itself, smashed down on the ruined building.

Smoke-blackened facing fell away, then the building's steel framing bent, broke, and *Big Bertha* was safely down, even if canted at a bit of an angle.

Some of the Mobiles chanced shooting at the transport, but a hidden port opened, and a pair of chainguns yammered, smashing buildings open as if they were cardboard.

'That's a good kitten,' Sir Douglas soothed, as a tiger and two lions, growling, went past him back in the cages.

'Nice kitties,' Njangu said nervously. A lioness bounded down the passageway, and into the cage.

'That's all but one,' Sir Douglas said.

'And here he comes,' Njangu said.

Muldoon, dark stains on his black coat, prowled down the passageway. He paused, eyed Njangu thoughtfully, licked bloodied jaws, went inside.

'All right,' Sir Douglas said. 'Now, let's get these cages in the air.'

He banged the cage door shut, and Njangu started breathing again.

The stadium PA crackled on.

'*Big Bertha* is here! Everybody to the main exit for loading! Don't hurry, don't panic,' Garvin's voice said. 'We've got plenty of time, and nobody will get left.'

Jiang Fong, his wife and child, the other acrobats trailing, were the first to reach *Big Bertha*, trotting up the ramp and through the lock.

'Names . . . quickly,' Erik Penwyth called.

Fong answered, and Penwyth made check marks on a list.

Next came the horses, trotting together, Darod Montagna and Kweik's widows behind them, chivvying them up the ramp, back toward their safe houses.

Darod turned back, unslinging her blaster.

'You're supposed to stay aboard, once you make it,' the officer told her.

'I'm still not through doing paybacks,' Montagna snarled, and went back across to the stadium.

'Tails up! Tails up!' Sunya Thanon and Phraphas Phanon were chanting and, obediently, the elephants, in a long line, streamed out the main entrance toward the steps, following Sir Douglas's cat cages.

One brushed against the ticket booth, collapsing it.

Thanon and Phanon darted to the front, their blasters ready.

Thanon saw a man with a rifle, shot at him, missed. The man fired back, and Thanon screamed, went to his knees.

Phanon was beside him. Thanon stared at him, not recognizing Phanon for a moment.

'I wish,' he tried. 'I wish . . .'

He coughed blood.

'Perhaps I am now going to Coando,' he said. 'I will wait for you there.'

Phanon's eyes were blurred as he heard his lover die.

He looked up, saw a bottle spewing fire spin toward him, smash down, and explode. The flames took him, and he screamed, tore at himself as his flesh blackened, fell across Thanon's body.

The elephants were milling, Imp screaming, close enough to the molotov to have gotten burned.

Two women with improvised spears ran toward the bulls. The spear was yanked away from the first by one raging bull, and the beast's rolled trunk shot out, smashing her skull.

The second tried to run, was taken, lifted, and hurled, almost casually, against a building.

Alikhan ran out of the stadium, eyes red in rage, a devourer-weapon in each paw, firing, and then there were no attackers left alive to shoot.

'Tails up! Tails up!' he called, and the elephants swayed back and forth, hesitating, then remembered the command, even if it came from an unfamiliar voice.

Obediently, once more in line, the elephants followed Alikhan, Imp and Loti close at his side, across the street and up the ramp into the starship.

Alikhan led the elephants back to their area, wished he had time to soothe and feed them, knew better.

He found a lift, went to the top of the starship, found Dill buckling himself into an *aksai* Kekri Katun trying to help.

'Come on, partner,' Dill said. 'I want some blood.'

'I alssso,' Alikhan hissed, normally perfect Common lost a bit in his rage as he opened the canopy of his own ship. 'In bucketsss and barrelsss.'

In a holo studio halfway across the city, Fove Gadu was in mid-'cast:

'Oh no, we of the Mobilization Party have found Abia Cornovil was not the only one corrupted by the aliens. We have a list of over a hundred men and women, high-rankers all, who've leagued themselves with these monsters.

'Even now, as our fearless men and women are bringing down these offworlders, we have squads of the People's Militia out, tracking down these traitors, to bring them to People's Justice . . .'

Aboard *Big Bertha*, a com officer motioned to Liskeard. On an inset screen was the image of Gadu, pounding his fist on a podium.

'Sir, I've got a perfect fix on him.'

'You're sure it's not an echo antenna?'

'Very sure. I've got all three of that station's antennae plotted, and this ain't none of them.'

Liskeard smiled, motioned to a talker.

'Come, ladies,' Knox said as he chiwied the showgirls toward *Big Bertha*, weaving through enginerewing lifters waiting to go up the ramp. 'Don't panic, don't smear your makeup, and I guarantee I'll have the Gaffer issue a bonus for this whole day's silliness.'

One of the women shrieked as two *aksai* floated out of the starship, not a meter overhead, then climbed for altitude.

Darod Montagna gunned down three Mobiles crouched safely – they thought – in an entranceway then jerked sideways as rounds pinged off the sidewalk around her.

She rolled to her feet, dived for a solid-looking, only half-destroyed midway booth. The sniper's bolts slammed in around her.

'Pinned down, by all the hells,' she growled. 'What a goddamned amateur thing to do.'

She heard a roar, and went even flatter as a strange-looking patrol ship, not twenty meters overhead flashed past, cannon winking along its stub wings.

Gunfire chattered close, and she rolled over, blaster ready, as Garvin dived in beside her.

'Hey,' she said.

'Hey,' he managed. 'What're you doing out here?'

'The same thing you are,' Montagna said. 'Being pinned down. You're about a hell of a rescuer.'

'I'm sorry,' Garvin said. 'I saw you getting your ass in a jamb and thought I could help. I'm short a Zhukov . . . all I've got is me at the moment.

'Normally, enough. But now . . .'

The patrol ship came back by, but this time Boursier's *aksai* was on its tail. Someone on the ground put a burst through the *aksai*'s fuselage.

Boursier's ship fought for altitude, juddering, almost stalled, went inverted, corrected, managed to brake and floated back inside *Big Bertha*.

'Hope to hell whoever's pushing that boat got that patrol ship,' Darod said.

'Hadda be Jacqueline . . . and no, she didn't,' Garvin said. 'Here the bastard comes again, and I think we're his only goddamned target!'

'Go pick on somebody your own size, you bully!' Darod shouted.

Obediently the patrol ship lifted, and began an attack pass on *Big Bertha*.

A weapons officer aboard *Big Bertha* toggled two Shrikes, and they flashed out, struck the patrol craft and blew it into fragments.

Flame and fragments clattered down around Garvin and Darod.

'Come on, you buttbreath Buddha,' Montagna shouted. 'No goddamned friendly-fire casualties allowed here!'

Garvin saw movement to his front, fired, and the movement stopped.

'Forget about incoming friendly rounds,' he said. 'There's enough folks out there on the ground trying to get us killed.'

Five Centrum patrol ships drove toward the distant bulk of *Big Bertha*. None of them saw the two *aksai* and the pair of Nana boats until the first two patrol ships blew up.

The surviving three banked away, two holding wing-mate discipline, the third going for the deck and full speed.

'Come on, come on,' Ben Dill crooned, seeing one patrol ship dance in his sights. A Shrike beeped at him, and he let it go, switched his aim to the second patrol ship.

It suddenly rolled, went for the deck, Dill's *aksai* after it. He noted detachedly the first patrol ship bursting into flames, a ball of flame rolling down a wide avenue, flames spreading in its wake.

The second ship was weaving back and forth. Dill found it in his sights, fired without the Shrike telling it was ready.

The missile went off about ten meters from the patrol ship. The Centrum craft rolled and, still at full speed, crashed, tumbling, through a high-rise government-looking building.

Dill banked away, went for altitude, waited until his breathing slowed a little bit, keyed his mike.

'Uh . . . Alikhan One, this is Dill One. Need any help?'

'Alikhan . . . this is an elusive one. I think I might use some . . . no. He just flew into my missile.

'Do you see anything else to shoot at?'

Ben scanned his screen.

'Not really. Guess we go orbit Big Momma and strafe a little.'

'I think I shall look for groups of people,' Alikhan responded, 'and perhaps lighten my ammunition load when I do.'

*

Gunfire blasted above Garvin's and Darod's heads, and four Forcemen, Njangu at their head, doubled toward them, found shelter, waited.

No return fire came.

'I guess we went and killed the last brave Mobile,' Njangu said.

'Now, if you two are through screwing around out here, would you like to dust yourselves off and get your asses back to where they should be?'

Garvin gingerly picked himself up, helped Darod to her feet.

'Yeh,' he said. 'But I gotta tell you, young Yoshitaro, you've got the shittiest rescuer's patter I've ever heard.'

'If you don't like it,' Njangu said, 'feel free to go to my competition.'

'. . . the moment of victory can be only moments away,' Gadu went on. 'I have instructed my friends to be sure and take prisoners, hopefully the leaders of this evil cabal, so they may testify at the trial of our traitorous—'

He broke off, staring through the soundproof window at a very black, very ugly Nana class patrol ship hovering no more than fifty meters away.

Chaka triggered his chaingun, and the rounds tore the studio – and Fove Gadu – into shreds.

'I don't know if that contributed to peace in our time,' he said into his mike, 'but it sure as hell made *me* feel a lot better.'

The band came out of the stadium proudly, still blasting the 'Peace March.' Halfway across the avenue, Aterton shouted a number, and they changed into the 'Confederation Anthem.'

A bit of shrapnel spanged off the concrete, took a timpanist in the leg. His drum, held up by a dropper, bounced away down the street, booming each time it hit.

The band cascaded up the ramp, through the lock, and was aboard.

Just behind them, the two *aksai* floated into the ship.

'Is everyone accounted for?' Garvin asked.

'Checked and checked twice,' Erik Penwyth said. 'Everybody's aboard, including all of our casualties.'

'We're sure,' Njangu said, sounded weary. 'I made two checks through that frigging stadium myself before I decided you needed some rescuing.'

Garvin lifted his com.

"Kay. Take us upstairs.'

'I have four ships closing,' an electronics officer reported as *Big Bertha* lifted through the stratosphere. 'ETA . . . guesstimate . . . four-three. Distance, maybe two parsecs.'

'Can you make any of them?'

'Again, a guess, sir. But I'd try three destroyers escorting a very large ship. Probably the *Corsica*.'

Liskeard turned to a weapons officer.

'How close is he to the baby we planted out by the mothballs?'

'Oh . . . one-five. Closing fast.'

'At one-zero, launch the Goddard.'

'Understood one-zero, sir.'

The bridge was very silent except for the routine mumble of the watch talkers.

The weapons officer was staring into a radar screen.

'One-one . . . one-zero . . . on its way.'

Half a system away, the modified Goddard stirred into life.

The *Corsica*, its three escorting ships in a vee in front of the battleship, drove at full power toward Centrum.

Dant Lae Romolo stared in some disbelief at the screens showing the chaos on the planet.

'*Damned* civilians,' he said to himself. 'They should never have allowed this situation to worsen!'

He scanned the huge bridge. Everything was as it should be, calm, proper. He saw, on a main screen, the symbols of the mothballed fleet 'below' him thought there would soon be reason to activate and man them.

'Sir,' an electronics officer reported, 'we have an unknown ship leaving Centrum.'

'No doubt that's the invading circus ship,' Romolo said. 'There should be no problem intercepting it before it tries for hyperspace.'

The incoming Goddard was barely big enough to show up on-screen, an ignored dot until an electronics officer looked at a proximity screen.

'Sir,' he said calmly to the officer of the deck, 'I have an unknown object . . . coming in very fast . . . closing on us.'

The OOD blinked.

'What is it?'

'No identification, sir.'

The man hesitated, then: 'ECM, can you acquire it?'

The woman tried, shook her head.

'Negative, sir. It's small . . . probably a missile . . . seems to be remote guided, but I can't grab the frequency.'

'All compartments . . . seal ship.'

'Sealing ship, sir.'

Alarms screamed through the *Corsica*.

'All stations, report integrity.'

A talker began reporting.

'Weapons, take out that incoming,' Romolo said. His voice was calm, unworried.

'Yessir . . . acquiring . . . acquiring . . . Launch one! Launch two!'

Two missiles spat from the *Corsica*'s tubes, while officers screamed at the escorts to wake up and do something.

The tricked-out Goddard 'saw' the counterlaunch, and its controller aboard *Big Bertha* launched the two Shadows.

The four missiles intersected and exploded.

'Hit! Hit! . . . That's a negative . . . missile still closing . . . Intersect in five . . . four . . .'

'Counterlaunch, dammit!'

'Counterlaunching . . . waiting for target to—'

The Goddard slammed into the *Corsica*'s engine area, and flame balled for an instant, was taken by vacuum.

Romolo was pitched headfirst over a console, landed sprawled across another as sirens screamed and alarms bonged.

He picked himself up, tried for broken bones, hoped that alien ship who'd so comfortably fooled them all had done as much damage on Centrum as he hoped.

Hoped and needed.

''Kay,' Garvin said. 'That's that.

'Captain Liskeard, would you like to take us on home?'

THIRTY-THREE

Cumbre/D-Cumbre

'And how long has this been going on?' Garvin Jaansma said, staring at the holo of the rather handsome young man, listening to his words and wincing at the cliché.

'Five . . . maybe six months,' Jasith Mellusin said her voice shaking, afraid of Garvin's utter calm. 'You were gone a *long* time. Over a year, you know.'

'I know,' Garvin said, thinking of Darod Montagna and then Kekri Katun. 'Who is he?'

'One of my vice presidents,' Jasith said. 'We used to play together . . . when we were kids. I guess he was sort of my childhood sweetie. Please don't be mad at me.'

'I'm not mad at anyone,' Garvin said.

He felt very tired. All he wanted to do was leave this mansion, and go, by himself, without even Darod, to some island without any people, where all he'd have to do is sleep and eat.

'I'll send somebody to pick up my stuff,' he said, going to the door.

'Garvin,' Jasith said. 'Will we still be able to be—'

The door clicked closed before her last words.

Garvin went swiftly down the huge steps, remembering this wasn't the first time he'd left this mansion. But this time, he realized, his heart didn't seem to be as broken.

He got in his lifter, started the drive, thought about their return.

Operation HOMEFALL was a success. *Big Bertha* had been given a hero's welcome, everyone aboard made a citizen of Cumbre. Some . . . a lot more than he would have thought . . . took advantage of the offer, and decided to put together a circus to work Cumbre, and other systems when it became possible. Among them was Fleam, who decided he'd finally found a career with ropes and canvas, and used his unexpected bonus to buy out of the Force.

Liskeard had been offered full redemption by *Dant* Angara, which he wasn't sure he wanted, and, while considering his options, had taken those troupers who wanted to go back to Grimaldi, all comfortably rich with their pay and surprise bonuses from Mellusin Mining.

As for Njangu . . . he and Maev had quietly separated, Maev having bought her way out of the Force and announcing plans to return to school.

Njangu had, quite strangely, told Garvin he was going fishing, for pity's sake, in some tiny village over on the coast. He'd invited Jaansma to join him, saying, equally mysteriously, that 'Deira probably had a friend or six to spare, if she's not married, and I bet that wouldn't make much difference if she is.'

Garvin shrugged.

Maybe . . . or maybe not.

That solitary island sounded better and better.

He realized how much he'd changed, aged even, which was pretty melodramatic thinking for somebody not yet thirty. He'd walked into the military's trap, and now it appeared it had snapped closed on him.

He had no idea whether or not he liked the change.

Garvin looked up, through the lifter's canopy, at the night sky and the stars.

Beyond them, drawing him more strongly than anything he'd ever known, though, was the scattered jigsaw puzzle of the Confederation.

Chris Bunch is the author of the Sten Series, the Dragonmaster Series, the Seer King Series and many other acclaimed SF and fantasy novels. A notable journalist and bestselling writer for many years, he died in 2005.

Find out more about Chris Bunch and other Orbit authors by registering for the free monthly newsletter at www.orbitbooks.net

THE VATTA'S WAR SERIES

Elizabeth Moon

An explosive military SF adventure

Kylara Vatta was a military cadet destined for great things, until an act of kindness incurred the Academy's wrath and ended her career. Instead of the expected disgrace, her trader family gave her captaincy of a small ship, to sell for scrap. But in typical flagrant disregard of orders, she saw the opportunity to make a profit and save the ship.

Several upgrades later, she is determined to retain her independence in the cut-throat world of interplanetary trading. But a complex political situation becomes increasingly dangerous, and she becomes far more involved with the military than she had planned in her new career.

She must keep her wits, and trade on every bit of her hard-won experience, or she – and her family – could lose everything.

For high-octane action read:

TRADING IN DANGER
MOVING TARGET
ENGAGING THE ENEMY
COMMAND DECISION

THE STAR RISK SERIES

Chris Bunch

If you've got the cash, they'll take the risk

STAR RISK

M'chel Riss spent years of her life in the Alliance Marines, only to be assigned to a desolate outpost. Then she came to the attention of Star Risk, Ltd. A mercenary outfit struggling for recognition, Star Risk has the required ragtag bunch of misfits. But why do they take on such a multitude of insane missions, with so many odds stacked against them? Money, fame, glory . . . but mostly the money.

THE SCOUNDREL WORLDS

Skyball is popular, challenging, and violent. In other words, the greatest sport in the universe – and the mercenary team of Star Risk, Ltd. has been hired to keep it galaxy-friendly. Two opposing worlds are neck and neck, and lately the game's been a real killer . . .

THE DOUBLECROSS PROGRAM

The Star Risk, Ltd. team find themselves in the middle of a strange assignment: a staged bank robbery that involves putting the money back. But the job takes an even stranger turn when they get caught up in a full-fledged war over an addictive new consumer product.

THE DOG FROM HELL

While escorting a group of privileged and wild girls from a finishing school on Earth to one of the luxury worlds, the Star Risk Ltd. team crosses paths with the much feared Cerebus Systems – and they have just put Star Risk, Ltd. at the top of their enemies list.